The Design and

Implementation

of Programs in

FORTRAN 77

Hans Lee
Paul Munsell

Michigan State University

PRENTICE HALL Englewood Cliffs, New Jersey 07632

Library of Congress Cataloging-in-Publication Data
Lee, Hans.
    The design and implementation of programs in FORTRAN 77/Hans
Lee, Paul Munsell.
        p. cm.
    Includes bibliographical references.
    ISBN 0-13-199993-1
    1. FORTRAN 77 (Computer program language) I. Munsell, Paul.
    II. Title.
    QA76. 73.F25L42   1990   89-26661
    005.262--dc20   CIP

Editorial/production supervision: George Calmenson
Cover design: Lundgren Graphics, Ltd.
Manufacturing buyer: Margaret Rizzi

©1990 by Prentice-Hall, Inc.
A Division of Simon & Schuster
Englewood Cliffs, New Jersey 07632

LIMITS OF LIABILITY AND DISCLAIMER OF WARRANTY;
The authors and publisher of this book have used their best efforts in preparing this book and software. These efforts include the development, research, and testing of the theories and programs to determine their effectiveness. The authors and publisher make no warranty of any kind, expressed or implied, with regard to these programs or the documentation contained in this book. The authors and publisher shall not be liable in any event for incidental or consequential damages in connection with, or arising out of, the furnishing, performance, or use of these programs.

Printed in the United States of America
10 9 8 7 6 5 4 3 2 1

ISBN   0-13-199993-1

Prentice-Hall International (UK) Limited, *London*
Prentice-Hall of Australia Pty. Limited, *Sydney*
Prentice-Hall Canada, Inc., *Toronto*
Prentice-Hall Hispanoamericana, S.A., *Mexico*
Prentice-Hall of India Private Limited, *New Delhi*
Prentice-Hall of Japan, Inc., *Tokyo*
Simon & Schuster Asia Pte. Ltd., *Singapore*
Editora Prentice-Hall do Brasil, Ltda., *Rio de Janeiro*

Contents

Preface

If you want to learn something about programming that will be maximally relevant in the real world of engineering and science and if, in the process, you want to understand what you are doing and why, then this book is what you are looking for. We would like to believe that we could use the subtitle "A Thinker's Guide to Programming" or, just as well, "Commonsense Programming." If we have described you well so far, here are some additional characteristics that probably also fit: You like solving problems and want to learn additional ways to do so. You want to know about programming but you want sufficient hands-on, practical experience to be comfortable with your understanding. Furthermore, you do not want to spend all your time memorizing the syntax and grammar of a programming language but do want to know why you are doing something before beginning to do it. You like to be creative, but you are also interested in developing skills that will be acceptable to those who will be involved with your programming. You like to learn from explanations and rules, but you also like to have examples so that you may learn indirectly and by imitation. You like to learn concepts, definitions, and fundamental ideas in context with adequate explanation. We will describe these characteristics as we proceed, but we trust that you find yourself described reasonably well.

What is our overall strategy for leading you toward these goals? We believe in placing the whole process in the real-world context of programming as it is practiced in business, engineering, government, and scientific enterprises. Using such a setting as a backdrop, we attempt to engage you in doing what you will then have to do: analyze problems in ways so that they become solvable. We feel that it is not easy to do this without also knowing about the common constructions found in programming languages and, at the same time, knowing something about a specific language. Consequently, we describe the common language constructions and also immediately begin to introduce FORTRAN 77, a user-level language widely used in engineering and science. *But the basic core of this textbook is the process of developing a design of a solution to a problem.* Such a design will best meet your actual needs: accurate solution of the problem; readability by a wide assortment of people who may or may not have training in programming ease of implementation in a user-level computer language; and ease of modification.

There are various commonsense reasons for our approach that you may not have ever considered, in addition to those already mentioned. First, the amount of software (already written computer programs) available is increasing. Second, there is an increasing amount of research on automating code generation. With these changes, there will be a decrease in the demand for professional coders but an increase in demand for those who can design new systems. Thus, these changes led us to the realization that more elementary training in what was once called programming should be spent on the problem-solving and on the design phases rather than on the coding phase. Second, the problems to be solved in the future may change, but the general strategies of problem solution are likely to remain useful. Third, the fundamentals of how a computer does arithmetic will continue to be of great importance to users in engineering and science and justifies the observation that the difficulties of computer methods for numeric computation — and the difficulties associated with program verification — will be of increasing concern to engineers and scientists. Consequently, we stress the problem-solving and design phases of developing computer programs. Further, we have included some material to aid you in your understanding of how a computer does arithmetic and how this can sometimes lead to plausible-appearing, but meaningless, computer output.

We have assumed that you, the student using this textbook, will be a freshman preparing for a major in some field of engineering or science and that you will have completed at least a first course in calculus. We have assumed that as you study this text you will have 2 hours a week in a computer laboratory staffed by a teaching assistant and that you will also have an additional 2 hours a week of computer access.

Although this text is designed for use in a semester, it may be used in a quarter term by adjusting the programming exercises and computer access appropriately. This textbook stresses the (1) **design** of programs that are (2) well **structured** using a (3) **top-down** approach with (4) **step-wise refinement.** In addition, we stress (5) **defensive programming** and the elements of (6) **good programming style.** These six components of good programming practice describe what we believe to be important for a beginning student to learn. This textbook is designed to assist you in understanding each of these components and in acquiring the skills required to develop and write good programs. Unlike most other texts in programming, we have devoted a substantial proportion of the material to the development of your skills in the design of programs. We have used a style of writing that is more like nonmathematical texts, especially by the use of a more informal style with a somewhat higher redundancy rate than is common either in mathematical or computer science textbooks. We have included a coding manual and a guide to the preparation of designs. Each of these is presented as an appendix. In our courses, students refer to these as they work on a given exercise. Use of the appendices saves time and programming frustration and assists in the natural learning of good programming practices.

Our text is based on our convictions and on our trying to accommodate some important curriculum considerations. These include the following: (1) The major hurdles in learning to program occur *before* the coding phase. (2) There are, in fact, three major hurdles. The first is to understand the problem. The second is to find a solution to the problem. The third is to design a program to solve the problem. However, the coding phase itself is not a major hurdle, as long as the three major hurdles have been successfully negotiated. (3) The key to succeeding in the design of a program is a concise, precise, and logically clear design. Further, the design should be "closer" to the client's program request than to the code. Here, we are speaking cognitively. In addition, one objective of an introductory course should be to teach the skills associated with creating a design. (4) We feel that an iconic system for stating designs is much superior to the currently popular use of pseudocode. Most pseudocode languages are, in fact, similar to the Pascal programming language. In any case, the use of pseudocode imposes an additional burden on the student because it is asking the student to learn a language that is as complex and as difficult to master as a programming language before he or she may learn a programming language. Although pseudocode may be satisfactory for a professional programmer who already knows Pascal or a Pascal-like language, we have rejected its use for a beginning programming student. Our design system is based on the iconic system known as the Nassi-Schneiderman (1973) iteration graphs, or structured designs. We have modifed their notation so that it may be prepared using a computer word-processing system. (5) The FORTRAN language itself can be partitioned into three fairly distinct levels: beginning, intermediate, and advanced. (6) Some FORTRAN constructions should be considered archaic and therefore should not be used. (7) A first course in programming should consider only the beginning level of the FORTRAN language. (8) The depth of treatment of mathematical topics must be limited to accommodate the level of mathematical preparation of the students. (9) The curriculum requirements of many fields in engineering and in science require that the first programming course be taken in the freshman year. This further restricts the range of topics and the possible exercises that may be used in the first programming course. (10) Finally, the curriculum demands of several fields preclude a second course in programming. This places further demands on the introductory programming course. *This text is the result of our integration of the goals of teaching the six components of the art of programming with the ten points stating our convictions and giving some curriculum considerations.* We have attempted to limit our consideration and use of FORTRAN to those features meeting the specifications designated by the document *American National Standard Programming Language FORTRAN, ANSI X3.9–1978*, which is designated FORTRAN 77.

Acknowledgements

We would like to express our appreciation for the very fine radio programming made available through National Public Broadcasting and Michigan State University's FM Station, WKAR. Many hours of keyboarding this text were sustained by broadcasts of recorded music, the "Metropolitan Opera" (sponsored by

Texaco, Inc.), the "New York Philharmonic," and "A Prairie Home Companion." We present Garrison Keillor a copy of this book in support of our request to be authorized for "raw bits" and to thank him for sharing his Saturday evenings with us. To Garrison Keillor we say, 'Tusen takk.'

I, Hans, would like to thank Ed Carter, who so willingly gave his time to listening and who shared his insights on common sense, learning, and teaching. I also wish to express here my special debt to Trina for the unrestrained emotional support and the undemanding love she has given me and my family over the last few years.

We wish to acknowledge the emotional and intellectual support given to us over the years as the ideas and the text emerged. We thank Jeff Livesay for urging us to continue the foot-stomping preaching-reaching-teaching mission for developing students' skills in structured programming. We thank the CPS 300 teaching assistants who so often redirected our thinking and who had to interpret our ideas to the students in the course. These teaching assistants included Carol L. Hofmann, Chris Johnson, Mark Misovich, Mike Misovich, and Jim Taylor. Carol Hofmann and Mike Misovich also contributed immensely by checking designs, implementing the designs in FORTRAN, and proofreading. We also acknowledge the contributions of Henry Ballard and Barbara Karcher, each of whom also taught the second course in programming, CPS 300. We wish to thank the students in our courses, CPS 120 and CPS 300, who by their struggles so often showed us the need for an even better method to teach the design and implementation of programs in FORTRAN.

We wish to thank the following reviewers of this text: Michael G. Gonzales, Gwynedd-Mercy College, Gwynedd Valley, PA; Richard Albright, University of Delaware; and Ida Flynn, University of Pittsburgh.

We immensely appreciate the various contributions of Chuck Severance, who first encouraged us to use the RNF typesetting facility on the CDC CYBER computer and then supported our retrieval of this manuscript and its conversion to file format acceptable to another word processor.

We wish to thank the various members of the faculty and staff of the Department of Computer Science of Michigan State University who assisted us in so many ways. We must single out Jim Burnett for special mention. Jim taught FORTRAN to hundreds of students over the years. Jim was always friendly and had a cheerful smile for everyone. Unfortunately, he died in a tragic airplane accident. We will miss him and his contributions to our department.

We wish to thank the following for their continued emotional support and for their attempts to teach us some common sense: Gil Apps, Tom Badgley, Rudy Key, and Dick Williams.

We greatly appreciate the support of our families and apologize for the strains caused by the production of this text. Each of us has a special debt to our children. We hope that each of them may have a meaningful and personally satisfying life.

1

Overview

1.1 OBJECTIVES OF THE AUTHORS

We have developed this text to aid you in learning to design programs, to translate designs into FORTRAN 77, a computer language widely used in engineering and science, and to remove errors from the FORTRAN version of your program. We have made a number of assumptions. We assume that you are probably either a second- or third-term freshman or a sophomore in engineering or in science; that you have completed the first course in the calculus; that you are interested in increasing your skills in problem solving using some abstract thinking; that you are using an interactive or a remote-job-entry system to enter your standard FORTRAN 77 code into the computer; and that you are able to type well enough to enter your code into the computer without undue strain and frustration. Further, we assume that the most frequently encountered programming task in almost all fields in engineering and science is obtaining a numeric solution for a mathematical equation.

1.2 STUDENT PERFORMANCE OBJECTIVES

By the time you have completed your study of this chapter, you should be able to distinguish the *design* of a program from the *implementation* of the design in standard FORTRAN 77; you should be able to explain why it is desirable to strive to write programs using only the standard FORTRAN 77 constructs; and, finally, you should be able to state what your own objectives are in completing this text.

1.3 FLOW-OF-CONTROL AND VARIETIES OF
CONTROL STRUCTURES

Before we can talk about design or code, we must introduce the basic logical principles that are fundamental to the process of computation. Although these principles
will be reflected both in the design and in the code, we introduce them in the context
of the flow-of-control of the execution of a program. The **flow-of-control** of the
execution of a program is the sequence in which the instructions are executed by the
computer. Most languages designed for numeric processing of data in engineering
and science applications follow a simple sequential execution, unless specified otherwise in the program. That is, unless the programmer includes statements designed
to specify some alternative sequence of execution, each statement is executed in the
order in which it appears, from the top of the program to the bottom of the program,
as listed on the output device.

To specify flow-of-control in a program, three types of **control structures** are
used. The following control structures are sufficient for writing programs in engineering and science:

(1) A sequence
(2) A selection
(3) A repetition

A **sequence** consists of a series of statements, each one of which is executed in
the order in which it appears. A **selection** is sometimes called a *conditional, decision,* or *if.* A selection frequently includes testing whether some condition specified
by the programmer is true; if and only if the condition is true, some other statement
or set of statements is executed. A **repetition** consists of a sequence of statements
that are repeatedly executed either for a specified number of times or until a specified condition is reached. Thus, each of the following would be implemented using a
repetition: (1) Repeatedly execute these statements ten times; (2) Repeatedly execute
these statements while some specified condition *remains true;* (3) Repeatedly execute these statements until a specifed condition *becomes true.*

A programmer transforms an unintelligent computer into an enormously pow-
erful electronic instrument for the extension of the human mind by combining these
three categories of structures and by tailoring them to the specific program. We want
to assure you that you will find this small set of control structures sufficient for the
design and implementation of programs. To illustrate how these control structures
are reflected in the design and in the code of a program, we will present a client's
program request, a design for a program to meet the program request, and, finally,
the FORTRAN code for the design. The program will contain at least one example
of each of the three enumerated control structures: (1) a sequence, (2) a selection,
and (3) a repetition. These illustrate all the fundamental control structures you will
ever need to implement any program. Naturally, though, there are many refine-
ments you will still need to know. The example we have chosen is designed to
give you confidence in our claim that these control structures are sufficient to do the

task. Also, the example is designed to create a broad and subsequently useful reference point.

1.4 A PROGRAM REQUEST

Suppose that an experienced programmer had been requested to prepare a program to convert a list of temperatures, each followed by a *C* to indicate a temperature measured on the Celsius scale or an *F* to indicate a temperature measured on the Fahrenheit scale, to the corresponding temperature on the other scale.

The formula to convert a temperature, *t*, from degrees Fahrenheit to degrees Celsius, *given in algebraic notation*, is:

$$\frac{5}{9}(t - 32)$$

The formula to convert a temperature, *t*, from degrees Celsius to degrees Fahrenheit, *given in algebraic notation*, is:

$$\frac{9}{5}t + 32$$

Even in such a simple problem, an experienced programmer may ask the client to clarify a few details before proceeding but will soon produce a design, such as the one presented here in Figures 1.1, 1.2, and 1.3. The meaning of the special dia-

---

preamble for PROGRAM TEMPCV

ABSTRACT:	TEMPCV converts temperatures, measured either on Fahrenheit or Celsius scale, to the corresponding value on the other scale.
INPUT:	a temperature and the scale (given as letter C or F)
OUTPUT:	echo of the input and the value of the converted temperature
DESIGN HISTORY:	H. Lee, 1MAR82
CODING HISTORY:	none
REFERENCE:	Lee, Hans and Paul Munsell. The Design and Implementation of Algorithms in FORTRAN 77. (Preliminary edition) 1982.

ID DICTONARY:

ID	TYPE	MEANING	USE
CTF	NA	Celsius To Fahrenheit	subroutine name (1 argument)
FTC	NA	Fahrenheit To Celsius	subroutine name (1 argument)
SCALE	character of length 1	SCALE	variable
TEMP	real	TEMPerature	variable

Figure 1.1   The Design of TEMPCV   *(continues)*

flow-of-control for PROGRAM TEMPCV

preamble goes here

specifications go here

WHILE there are data

> output: prompt for the value of the temperature to be converted
>
> input: the value of the temperature
>
> output: prompt for the value of the scale on which the temperature was was measured
>
> input: the value of the scale
>
> output: echo the values given as input for temperature and scale
>
> IF   scale is 'C'
>
> | THEN | ELSE |
> |---|---|
> | call SUBROUTINE CTF | IF   scale is 'F' |
> | | **THEN** — call SUBROUTINE FTC / **ELSE** — output error message |

output 'normal program termination'

STOP

END of PROGRAM TEMPCV

Figure 1.1   (continued)

grams employed in the design will be explained in subsequent chapters. Here all you need to know is that the design is intended to be read from the top to the bottom.

A **design** is a diagrammatic representation of the essential components of the control structures and other computations required to obtain the numeric solution of

preamble for SUBROUTINE CTF

ABSTRACT:	CTF(TEMP) converts a temperature supplied as the argument from degrees Celsius to degrees Fahrenheit
INPUT:	none
OUTPUT:	the temperature in degrees Fahrenheit
DESIGN HISTORY:	H. Lee, 1MAR82
CODING HISTORY:	none
REFERENCE:	Lee, Hans and Paul Munsell. The Design and Implementation of Algorithms in FORTRAN 77. (Preliminary edition) 1982.

ID DICTIONARY:

ID	TYPE	MEANING	USE
RESULT	real	RESULT	variable
TEMP	real	TEMPerature	argument

flow-of-control for SUBROUTINE CTF(TEMP)

preamble goes here

specifications go here

RESULT = (9.0/5.0) ∗ TEMP + 32.0

output RESULT with label

RETURN

END of SUBROUTINE CTF

Figure 1.2   The Design of CTF

an equation by the use of a computer. We present these designs in terms of the control structures, sequence, selection, and repetition. This enables us to make the design simpler than the eventual code so that the design, in fact, becomes useful in the initial phase of the development of a program.

The drawn lines are important parts of the designs we present. The words we use are also significant. These aspects are part of the "technical" language associated with the design process. We urge you to examine these features carefully as we present them. The symbols or icons we use in the designs are based on the work of others (Nassi and Schneiderman, 1973.)

Figure 1.1 presents the design of the main program. As you can see in Figure 1.1, the design begins with some information about the program, identifying preamble for SUBROUTINE FTC

ABSTRACT: FTC(TEMP) converts a temperature suppled as the argument
             from degrees Fahrenheit to degrees Celsius

INPUT: none

OUTPUT: the temperature in degrees Celsius

DESIGN HISTORY: H. Lee, 1MAR82

CODING HISTORY: none

REFERENCE: Lee, Hans and Paul Munsell. The Design and Implementation
             of Algorithms in FORTRAN 77. (Preliminary edition) 1982.

ID DICTIONARY:

ID	TYPE	MEANING	USE
RESULT	real	RESULT	variable
TEMP	real	TEMPerature	argument

flow-of-control for SUBROUTINE FTC(TEMP)

preamble goes here

specifications go here

RESULT = (5.0/9.0)* (TEMP − 32.0)

RETURN

END of SUBROUTINE FTC

Figure 1.3   The Design of FTC

the program, listing the "identifiers," or the names of variables, and explaining how
the names are used. Figure 1.2 is the design for a subprogram called CTF, which
converts a temperature given in degrees Celsius to the corresponding temperature in
degrees Fahrenheit. Figure 1.3 is the design for a subprogram called FTC, which
performs the Fahrenheit-to-Celsius conversion. You should note that all three designs have a similar structure — an opening descriptive section containing material
that helps a human reader to understand what is to come; an intermediate section
containing a sketch of the program; and a closing section containing the END statement, which indicates the end of the design of that particular design unit.

A common error in designing a program to do these conversions is to mix up
the two different cases, employing the correct formula but at the wrong time. Be
sure to compare the equations given given earlier for performing the conversions
with the designs for the two subprograms. In this design you would want to ask
yourself, Is the correct equation used to convert from Fahrenheit to Celsius? Also, Is
the correct equation used to convert from Celsius to Fahrenheit?

Our experience leads us to assert that once you have a good design worked out, you will find it easy and straightforward to write the code (whether it be in FORTRAN or some other computer language.) Of the two tasks, producing a design and writing the code, it is, in fact, the design task that is the harder skill to acquire. It is for this reason that we stress the design process. If you invest some effort in the design process, in the long run you will save an enormous amount of time, greatly reduce frustration, and produce better programs, confident that they are correct and that they will be easy to maintain.

A copy of the FORTRAN code produced by the programmer to implement the design is given here in Figures 1.4, 1.5, and 1.6. Do not attempt to understand the technical details of these figures now. Merely read them from top to bottom.

```
      PROGRAM TEMPCV
C
C
C ABSTRACT: TEMPCV CONVERTS TEMPERATURES, MEASURED EITHER ON
C           THE FAHRENHEIT OR CELSIUS SCALE, TO THE
C           OTHER SCALE.
C
C INPUT:    A TEMPERATURE AND THE SCALE (GIVEN AS LETTER C OR F)
C
C OUTPUT:   ECHO OF THE INPUT AND THE VALUE OF THE CONVERTED
C           TEMPERATURE
C
C DESIGN HISTORY:
C           H. LEE, 1MAR82
C
C REFERENCE:
C           LEE, HANS AND PAUL MUNSELL. THE DESIGN AND
C           IMPLEMENTATION OF ALGORITHMS IN FORTRAN 77.
C           (PRELIMINARY EDITION.) 1982.
C
C
C ID DICTIONARY:
C
C ID        TYPE            MEANING         USE
C
C CTF       NA              CELSIUS TO      SUBROUTINE NAME
C                           FAHRENHEIT      (1 ARGUMENT)
C
C FTC       NA              FAHRENHEIT      SUBROUTINE NAME
C                           TO CELSIUS      (1 ARGUMENT)
C
C SCALE     CHARACTER       SCALE           VARIABLE
C
C
C TEMP      REAL            TEMPERATURE     VARIABLE
C
```

Figure 1.4   FORTRAN Version of SUBROUTINE TEMPCV

```
C
C
C
C SPECIFICATIONS
C
      CHARACTER SCALE*1
      REAL TEMP
C
C                                      BEGIN EXECUTION
C
      PRINT *, ' '
      PRINT *, 'PROGRAM TEMPCV CONVERTS TEMPERATURES FROM '
      PRINT *, 'ONE SCALE, EITHER CELSIUS OR FAHRENHEIT, TO'
      PRINT *, 'THE CORRESPONDING TEMPERATURE ON THE OTHER SCALE.'
      PRINT *, 'TO QUIT, PRESS RETURN WHEN THE PROGRAM PROMPTS'
      PRINT *, 'FOR THE NEXT TEMPERATURE TO BE CONVERTED.'
      PRINT *, ' '
C
C   WHILE
1     CONTINUE
        PRINT *, ' '
        PRINT *, 'GIVE A TEMPERATURE, ENTERED WITH A DECIMAL POINT.'
        READ (*,*, END=2) TEMP
        PRINT *, 'GIVE THE SCALE, EITHER BY ENTERING'
        PRINT *, ' ''C'' IF THE TEMPERATURE JUST ENTERED WAS IN CELSIUS'
        PRINT *, 'OR BY ENTERING'
        PRINT *, ' ''F'' IF THE TEMPERATURE JUST ENTERED WAS IN '
        PRINT *, 'FAHRENHEIT.'
        PRINT *, 'THE SURROUNDING SINGLE QUOTE IS REQUIRED.'
        READ (*,*, END=2) SCALE
C
C
        PRINT *, 'A TEMPERATURE OF ', TEMP, 'MEASURED ON THE ', SCALE
        PRINT *, 'SCALE WAS ENTERED.'
        IF (SCALE .EQ. 'C') THEN
          CALL CTF(TEMP)
        ELSE IF (SCALE .EQ. 'F') THEN
          CALL FTC(TEMP)
        ELSE
          PRINT *, 'A SINGLE LETTER, EITHER C OR F IS EXPECTED.'
          PRINT *, 'THE LETTER RECEIVED WAS THE LETTER ', SCALE
          PRINT *, 'IF NO LETTER APPEARS AFTER THE WORD LETTER '
          PRINT *, 'IN THE ABOVE LINE, DEPRESS RETURN WITHOUT '
          PRINT *, 'DEPRESSING THE SPACE BAR BEFORE DEPRESSING '
          PRINT *, 'THE RETURN. THIS WILL TERMINATE THE PROGRAM.'
        ENDIF
      GO TO 1
C
C   ENDWHILE
C
```

(continues)

Figure 1.4 (continued)

```
2      PRINT *, 'AN END OF FILE WAS DETECTED ON THE LAST READ.'
       PRINT *, 'THE PROGRAM IS DESIGNED TO QUIT EXECUTION WHEN '
       PRINT *, 'AN END OF FILE IS DETECTED.'
       PRINT *, ' '
       PRINT *, 'NORMAL PROGRAM TERMINATION'
       STOP
       END
```

Figure 1.4   (continued)

```
       SUBROUTINE CTF(TEMP)
C
C
C ABSTRACT: CTF(TEMP) CONVERTS A TEMPERATURE SUPPLIED AS
C           THE ARGUMENT FROM DEGREES CELSIUS TO DEGREES
C           FAHRENHEIT
C
C INPUT:    NONE
C
C OUTPUT:   THE TEMPERATURE IN DEGREES FAHRENHEIT
C
C DESIGN HISTORY:
C           H. LEE, 1MAR82
C
C REFERENCE:
C            LEE, HANS AND PAUL MUNSELL. THE DESIGN AND
C            IMPLEMENTATION OF ALGORITHMS IN FORTRAN 77.
C
C
C ID DICTIONARY
C
C ID         TYPE            MEANING            USE
C
C RESULT     REAL            RESULT             VARIABLE, LOCAL
C
C TEMP       REAL            TEMPERATURE        VARIABLE, ONLY
C                                               ARGUMENT
C
C
C SPECIFICATIONS
C
       REAL RESULT, TEMP
C
C                                       BEGIN EXECUTION
C
       RESULT = (9.0/5.0) * TEMP + 32.0
       PRINT *, 'THE CORRESPONDING TEMPERATURE IN FAHRENHEIT IS ', RESULT
       RETURN
       END
```

Figure 1.5   FORTRAN Version of SUBROUTINE CTF

```
      SUBROUTINE FTC(TEMP)
C
C
C ABSTRACT: FTC(TEMP) CONVERTS A TEMPERATURE SUPPLIED AS THE
C           ARGUMENT FROM DEGREES FAHRENHEIT TO DEGREES CELSIUS
C
C INPUT:    NONE
C
C OUTPUT:   THE TEMPERATURE IN DEGREES CELSIUS
C
C DESIGN HISTORY:
C           H. LEE, 1MAR82
C REFERENCE:
C           LEE, HANS AND PAUL MUNSELL. THE DESIGN AND
C           IMPLEMENTATION OF ALGORITHMS IN FORTRAN 77.
C
C
C ID DICTIONARY:
C
C ID        TYPE            MEANING          USE
C
C RESULT    REAL            RESULT           VARIABLE, LOCAL
C
C TEMP      REAL            TEMPERATURE      VARIABLE, ONLY
C                                            ARGUMENT
C
C
C SPECIFICATIONS
C
      REAL RESULT, TEMP
C
C                                    BEGIN EXECUTION
C
      RESULT = (5.0/9.0) * (TEMP - 32.0)
      PRINT *, 'THE CORRESPONDING TEMPERATURE IN CELSIUS IS ', RESULT
      RETURN
      END
```

Figure 1.6   FORTRAN Version of SUBROUTINE FTC

The standard FORTRAN 77 implementation of the design of the main program is listed in Figure 1.4. Similarly the standard FORTRAN 77 implementation of the design of the CTF subprogram is listed in Figure 1.5, and the standard FORTRAN 77 implementation of the FTC subprogram is listed in Figure 1.6. You have noticed that the design is presented in three pieces, the main program and two subprograms; likewise, the FORTRAN code is presented in three pieces, each corresponding to a piece of the design. This illustrates a fundamental strategy for the successful programming: break the task down into relatively independent pieces. (This is referred to as divide and conquer!)

You will profit by reading both the design and the program before you start reading the next section. In examining the design (Figures 1.1, 1.2, and 1.3) and the FORTRAN 77 code (Figures 1.4, 1.5, and 1.6) you should try to see what relationships exist between the structure of the design and the structure of the FORTRAN 77 code. Under no circumstances, however, should you worry about being able to produce either a design or code yet. These skills will be developed later.

Finally, we have included a copy of a possible interactive session with program TEMPCV (Figure 1.7). We suggest that now, before going on to read the next section, you study these figures. In fact, because we consider the task of guessing and then verifying your guess to be a critical technique in language acquisition, we state this as an exercise.

```
PROGRAM TEMPCV CONVERTS TEMPERATURES FROM
ONE SCALE, EITHER CELSIUS OR FAHRENHEIT, TO
THE CORRESPONDING TEMPERATURE ON THE OTHER SCALE.
TO QUIT, PRESS RETURN WHEN THE PROGRAM PROMPTS
FOR THE NEXT TEMPERATURE TO BE CONVERTED.

GIVE A TEMPERATURE, ENTERED WITH A DECIMAL POINT.
*100.0
 GIVE THE SCALE, EITHER BY ENTERING
 'C' IF THE TEMPERATURE JUST ENTERED WAS IN CELSIUS
 OR BY ENTERING
 'F' IF THE TEMPERATURE JUST ENTERED WAS IN
 FAHRENHEIT.
THE SURROUNDING SINGLE QUOTE IS REQUIRED.
*'C'
A TEMPERATURE OF 100.MEASURED ON THE C
 SCALE WAS ENTERED.
THE CORRESPONDING TEMPERATURE IN FAHRENHEIT IS 212.

GIVE A TEMPERATURE, ENTERED WITH A DECIMAL POINT.
*212.0
 GIVE THE SCALE, EITHER BY ENTERING
 'C' IF THE TEMPERATURE JUST ENTERED WAS IN CELSIUS
 OR BY ENTERING
 'F' IF THE TEMPERATURE JUST ENTERED WAS IN
 FAHRENHEIT.
THE SURROUNDING SINGLE QUOTE IS REQUIRED.
*'F'
A TEMPERATURE OF 212.MEASURED ON THE F
 SCALE WAS ENTERED.
THE CORRESPONDING TEMPERATURE IN CELSIUS IS 100.
```

(continues)

Figure 1.7 An Interactive Session with PROGRAM TEMPCV

```
GIVE A TEMPERATURE, ENTERED WITH A DECIMAL POINT.
*0.0
 GIVE THE SCALE, EITHER BY ENTERING
 'C' IF THE TEMPERATURE JUST ENTERED WAS IN CELSIUS
 OR BY ENTERING
'F' IF THE TEMPERATURE JUST ENTERED WAS IN
 FAHRENHEIT.
THE SURROUNDING SINGLE QUOTE IS REQUIRED.
*'C'
A TEMPERATURE OF 0.MEASURED ON THE C
 SCALE WAS ENTERED.
THE CORRESPONDING TEMPERATURE IN FAHRENHEIT IS 32.
GIVE A TEMPERATURE, ENTERED WITH A DECIMAL POINT.
*

AN END OF FILE WAS DETECTED ON THE LAST READ.
THE PROGRAM IS DESIGNED TO QUIT EXECUTION WHEN
AN END OF FILE IS DETECTED.
```

Figure 1.7   (continued)

EXERCISE

In the FORTRAN program, indicate which sections of the FORTRAN code illustrate sequence, which sections illustrate selection, and which sections illustrate repetition. (*Hint:* You will want to compare the FORTRAN code with the record of the interactive session to do this.)

1.5 STANDARD FORTRAN 77

FORTRAN 77 is the name of a computer language originally designed for the statement of algebraic formulas, especially those using matrices, in a form suitable for submission to a computer. The original FORTRAN was developed by the International Business Machines Corporation in the early 1950s. The original FORTRAN is now thought of as the first version of FORTRAN, but the Roman numeral I has never been used in its name. A later version, called FORTRAN II, was widely used. Although a FORTRAN III was in fact used within the IBM Corporation, it was never released. However, FORTRAN IV was commercially released and widely used. The newest version is designated as standard FORTRAN 77 by many computer vendors, although Control Data Corporation refers to it as FORTRAN V.

Incidentally, **FORTRAN** is an acronym for FORmula TRANslator. The formulas being translated are algebraic formulas. Hence, the language is especially designed for obtaining the numeric solution to algebraic equations or systems of equations that commonly arise in engineering and science. FORTRAN obviously is popular for such applications because it has been designed for them, and it has been used and refined over a number of years. However, it is also widely employed today because over the many years of usage, a number of procedures, complete programs, or programming systems (sometimes called *packages*) have been written in FORTRAN. Thus, many people in chemistry, engineering, and physics use programming systems originally written in FORTRAN. There also are several FORTRAN systems available for social sciences that produce cross-tabulations of data and perform various statistical tests.

What makes FORTRAN 77 *standard* FORTRAN 77? The answer is quite simple. A committee produced a document that specifies the standard. *American National Standard Programming Language FORTRAN* is the full title of the document. It is published by American National Standards Institute, Inc., and is further identified by their publication number as ANSI X3.9-1978. This document defines two versions; one is called *Full Language* and the other is called *Subset Language*. Incidentally, ANSI FORTRAN is somewhat carelessly used to identify standard FORTRAN 77 by some vendors. Most likely, in current texts (published since 1978) ANSI FORTRAN refers to the Full-Language version of standard FORTRAN 77 unless otherwise specified. *American National Standard Programming Language FORTRAN* is written primarily for professional implementers of FORTRAN. Sometimes it is used as a reference by experienced FORTRAN programmers.

In our text, we do not introduce all features of FORTRAN, as some of them are not necessary or appropriate for a beginning programmer, are inappropriate for problems to be executed on large computers, or are archaic. Nonetheless, we do stress the use only of standard features of the language.

We feel that standard FORTRAN 77 should be taught to college engineering and science students because it is the language most likely to be encountered in jobs in these fields and because a large set of programming systems written in FORTRAN already exists. We stress the use of only the standard version because programs should be written so that they will work on different computers. If you use nonstandard features, you could easily find yourself (or your client) spending a lot of time and effort reprogramming to get your program to work correctly on another system. Do yourself a favor and use only standard features.

1.6 EXERCISES

Although Chapter 1 was designed primarily to provide an overview of the design of a program, there are a number of possible exercises from which you could select one to carry out. As we do not recommend that you attempt to create an entirely new design at this time, you are necessarily limited to modifying the design for the temperature conversion presented in this chapter. Thus, you would copy most of our design. A very few sections would have to be changed. But we urge you to prepare a complete design, in pencil, on *unlined paper,* writing on only one side of each sheet.

In engineering and science there often is a need to convert from one unit to another, such as miles to kilometers or kilometers to miles, just as we created a design to convert temperatures measured in degrees Fahrenheit to degrees Celsius or from degrees Celsius to degrees Fahrenheit. Tables containing the necessary information are frequently included in various engineering and science texts, usually under the heading *conversion factors*. Consequently, we will give only a few here. Many exercises can be constructed from conversion factors. Merely modify our temperature-conversion program to perform some other scale conversion. Be sure to change the output messages, the comments within the program, and, of course, the variable name(s). Construct the design to convert from one scale to another in either direction. Here are a few conversion factors:

To convert from	To	Multiply by
Liters	U.S. liquid gallons	0.2642
U.S. liquid gallons	Liters	3.785
Kilometers	Statute miles	0.6214
Statute miles	Kilometers	1.609
Degrees (angle)	Radians	0.01745
Radians	Degrees (angle)	57.296

2

A Series of FORTRAN Programs

2.1 INTRODUCTION

Our method for introducing FORTRAN coding will be to present a series of short FORTRAN programs with accompanying commentary. Each program serves as a review of previous ones, and each new program introduces one or more additional features of the language. To get started, let us suppose that you want to do the simplest thing possible that gives some response when the program is executed so that you can verify that the program worked. The simplest thing you can do is to print out a message. A program to do this is presented here as PROGRAM ONE.

```
      PROGRAM ONE
C PROGRAM ONE MERELY OUTPUTS A MESSAGE
C SO THAT I CAN VERIFY THAT I CAN
C USE THE FORTRAN SYSTEM
C
C PROGRAMMED BY H. LEE, 1MAR82
C
      PRINT *, 'PROGRAM ONE'
      PRINT *, 'YIPPIE! I MADE IT.'
C
      STOP
      END
```

2.2 PROGRAM ONE

There are several things about this program about which we should comment. First of all, FORTRAN was developed when input to the computer was by punched cards that contained 80 columns. But, as cards are being used less and less frequently, we will speak of lines instead of cards. (One line is equivalent to one card.) The designers of the FORTRAN language decided to put some restrictions on how the columns were to be used. First of all, columns 73 through 80 were not to be read by the FORTRAN language translator. Thus, these columns cannot contain any part of a FORTRAN statement. They do, however, remain available for recording sequence numbers and other desired identification. Second, columns 1 through 5 were reserved for statement labels. These will be explained when statement labels are needed. However, if the letter *C* appears in column 1, that line is considered to be a comment for people to read. The remaining contents of such lines are completely ignored by the FORTRAN translator. These comments, however, are very important, as they help us to remember what we wrote the program for, what it is to do, and how to use it. We also insert lines into our program containing a C in column 1, (but otherwise blank) to leave blank lines, thereby improving the legibility of the program itself. Except on a comment line, column 6 is reserved exclusively for indicating that the given line is a continuation line. This will be explained when this feature is needed. Columns 7 through 72 are available for the main part of a FORTRAN statement. When a program is listed on paper, each line on the screen corresponds to one line in the printed listing.

An editor is used to enter a FORTRAN program on an interactive, or remote-job-entry, system. As different computer systems have different editors, we cannot explain how your editor works, although it may automatically place your entries in the correct columns. However, you as a student learning to read program listings should have a knowledge of FORTRAN's use of specific columns for specific purposes. To summarize, you need to know which columns are reserved for what purpose because this information gives you additional clues about the interpretation of each FORTRAN statement.

PROGRAM ONE is a single program unit, and such a program unit is called a **main program.** From the standpoint of style, the first program unit should be a main program. Normally, the main program unit begins with the word *PROGRAM* and is followed by a name that the programmer creates.

Programmer-created names are called **symbolic names.** In the case of the line PROGRAM ONE, the word *ONE* is the symbolic name of the program. All symbolic names in FORTRAN must begin with a letter. Optionally, this letter may be followed by up to five additional letters or digits or mixtures of letters and digits. Thus, A, A1, XYZ123, RAT3S, and ANSWER are all acceptable names. However, 8A and BIGNUMBER are not acceptable as names because the first begins with a digit and the second contains more than six letters. The program unit ends with the word END, consisting of the three letters E, N, and D, without any following punctuation.

All program units must contain END as the very last statement of the unit. Each and every program unit terminates with the word END, and there is exactly one END in each program unit. This FORTRAN statement is an indicator to the FORTRAN system that there are no more FORTRAN statements to be translated from this program unit.

In the listing of PROGRAM ONE, the first line is the word PROGRAM followed by the word ONE. The word PROGRAM is recognized by the FORTRAN system as an indicator of the beginning of a program unit and is recognized by the FORTRAN system as a specific word of the language. Words such as PROGRAM, END, PRINT, and STOP are called **keywords.** These words have specific meanings, which you must learn. *You should never use these keywords except as defined.* The word PROGRAM is followed by the symbolic name ONE, which is the name chosen by the programmer for this main program. Notice that ONE does follow the rules for creating names; namely, it begins with a letter and is optionally followed by up to five additional letters or digits. The end of this main program is indicated by the line containing END.

Between the line PROGRAM ONE and the line END are the FORTRAN statements, which constitute the remaining portion of the main program. Immediately after the line containing PROGRAM ONE are several lines that begin with a C. As a matter of style, each program unit should include some opening comments that describe the program unit and state both the name of the programmer and the date on which it was verified as apparently working correctly. The lines that begin with a C but are otherwise blank are inserted to improve legibility. As a matter of style, these practices should be observed in all programs so that it is comparatively easy for you or other programmers to understand the program logic.

A **line printer** is an output device designed to print on paper. A **terminal** has a screen upon which output may be displayed. The **PRINT** statement is a FORTRAN command to print something on the output device. This usually means to print the output on paper *or* to display the output on the screen of a terminal. What is to be printed is listed after the comma. In the case of PROGRAM ONE, we would expect to see the following on the output device:

```
PROGRAM ONE
```

The apostrophe marks in the statement

```
PRINT *, 'PROGRAM ONE'
```

indicate a command to print the literal characters PROGRAM ONE. Notice that the apostrophe, a single stroke, appears at both ends of the message to be printed. Be sure to distinguish the key for the single stroke, ', from the key for the double stroke, ", on your keyboard. Also notice that the apostrophes themselves do not appear as part of the output. The PRINT statement we have used here is a simplified version in which the asterisk and comma are required.

Recall that we said that the END statement is a keyword that is always required at the end of each program unit. The END statement in FORTRAN is somewhat like the phrase *The End* presented at the end of a motion picture. In the motion picture The End informs the viewer that the story is complete. In FORTRAN, the END statement is an indication to the FORTRAN system that this unit of the program is complete and ready to be translated. Consequently, when the FORTRAN system encounters the END statement, it translates the FORTRAN within that unit into a language the computer can understand. This translated version of the program is stored in the computer memory.

For the time being, we will assume that the FORTRAN system translates a program into machine language. The FORTRAN translator, or **compiler**, as it is more frequently called, does this in a very special manner. It compiles each unit of a FORTRAN program *independently* of every other unit. Thus, it compiles each unit by itself, unit by unit, in the order in which the units appear. This continues until all units of a job have been compiled. After all units of a job have been compiled, the system starts executing the machine-language version of the program. The FORTRAN **STOP** statement indicates where execution of the machine language program is to stop. If the STOP statement is not included in a FORTRAN job, then execution will terminate when execution encounters the machine-language equivalent of the END statement of the PROGRAM unit. Execution may also terminate if the program exhausts the data it is reading or if some error condition is encountered.

2.3 PROGRAM TWO

We now turn to PROGRAM TWO, which is designed to extend the previous program so that we can input a numeric value and output the same value, thereby demonstrating to ourselves that we know how to input and output a numeric value as a variable.

```
      PROGRAM TWO
C
C
C PROGRAM TWO STARTS TO TEST HOW TO INPUT A NUMBER
C WITH A FRACTIONAL PART.
C
C PROGRAMMED BY H. LEE, 1MAR82
C
C SPECIFICATIONS
C
      REAL TEMP
C
C                               EXECUTION:
      PRINT *, 'PROGRAM TWO'
      PRINT *, ' '
      PRINT *, 'PROGRAMMED BY H. LEE, 1MAR82'
      PRINT *, ' '
C
C                               PROMPT FOR INPUT
      PRINT *, 'GIVE TEMPERATURE AS A NUMBER WITH'
      PRINT *, 'AN EMBEDDED DECIMAL POINT'
      PRINT *, ' '
      READ *, TEMP
      PRINT *, 'TEMPERATURE = ', TEMP
C
      STOP
      END
```

Our goal is to move toward a program that will solve one of the simplest types of equations that you may encounter in your courses. We selected the task of making temperature conversions. Consequently, we want to work with numbers that have fractional parts. In computers, these are recorded as digits with a decimal point. We use (and highly recommend that you use) *embedded* decimal points; that is, we recommend a digit on both sides of the decimal point.

FORTRAN distinguishes numbers that may have fractional parts or exponents, which are called **REALs,** from numbers that cannot have fractional parts or exponents, which are called **INTEGERs.** There are other possibilities: complex numbers (numbers with imaginary parts) and characters (letters of the alphabet, punctuation marks, and the blank space). To make these distinctions, we speak of the *type* of the variable. Thus, we may speak of type REAL, type INTEGER, type COMPLEX, or type CHARACTER, or we may ask questions such as, What is the type of TEMP? At the top of each program unit, the programmer indicates the type of all variables to be used in that program unit by using the appropriate FORTRAN statement, such as REAL, followed by a list of the variable names that are to be of type REAL. REAL TEMP is a FORTRAN *type specification*. To specify is to give information to the FORTRAN system by the use of a FORTRAN statement designed for this purpose. Thus, REAL TEMP *specifies* the variable, TEMP, to be the symbolic name of a REAL variable. In a type specification, the name of each variable is separated from the following name by a comma. As you may see in the example, REAL TEMP, no comma appears between REAL and the name of the first variable. The names should be listed in alphabetical order to assist other people in reading the program. FORTRAN requires that *all specifications must occur before the first executable statement* in each unit of the program. Specification statements contain information used by the compiler. (As it were, specification statements are "used up" by the compiler and "disappear" before execution begins.) An executable statement commands the computer to carry out some action during the execution phase. In PROGRAM TWO, the first executable statement is the first PRINT statement.

Because integers are numbers without fractional parts, they are entered as digits without any decimal points. However, because reals may have a fractional part, they are entered with a decimal point. Further, so that the decimal point is noticed, we recommend that a real number should be entered with an embedded decimal point, even if it is necessary to include a nonsignificant zero. Thus, we would enter 0.1 or 1.0. Negative numbers are indicated by a minus sign immediately before the first digit. An optional plus sign may appear before the first digit of a positive number. *Commas are not permitted in integers or in reals*.

The following are acceptable as real numbers:

$$0.0 \quad 0.1 \quad +0.3 \quad -0.00001 \quad -17893.003 \quad +256.0$$

The following are all acceptable integers:

$$0 \quad 1984 \quad +2691 \quad -94627$$

In many computer languages, numbers with fractional parts are represented internally by a complicated system that we will not discuss here. However, just as the fraction one-third cannot be represented exactly by the decimal value 0.33333, no matter how many 3s are used, many numbers with fractional parts may not have an exact representation in their internally represented form.

We recommend the style features included in PROGRAM TWO. We use the comment SPECIFICATION: to indicate where the specifications begin; we use the comment EXECUTION: to indicate where execution begins; and, other than the required C in column 1 to indicate comments, we leave columns 2 through 39 blank in order to enhance the readability of programs. Be sure to notice that there is a C in column 1 of many of the lines, indicating that these lines are comments. Recall that such comment lines are completely ignored by the FORTRAN translator. Thus, the words SPECIFICATION and EXECUTION, as well as the other words on the lines beginning with a C in column 1, are neither keywords nor symbolic names; they merely are for human readers.

The simplified version of the READ statement,

```
READ *, TEMP
```

begins with the keyword READ, which is a command to input something. The asterisk and the comma are required parts of the syntax. The comma separates the first portion of the command from the list of variables to be read. Here the list consists of only one item, TEMP, a symbolic name for a variable. When this program is compiled, the system assigns a **location** in computer memory to hold the value of the variable TEMP when it is read, i.e., when, during execution, the READ *, TEMP is encountered. Programmers usually use the term **storing** to mean that a value is placed in a location in the computer memory.

After we read the value, the value remains available to use unless we change it. In PROGRAM TWO we merely output the value of TEMP. This is done by using the statement

```
PRINT *, 'TEMPERATURE = ', TEMP
```

which is a command to output two things given in the list, namely, the string of literal characters, TEMPERATURE = , and the value of TEMP. The value of TEMP is printed, not the word TEMP. Closely examine this print statement again. It commands the computer to output two things. The first thing is the character constant

```
TEMPERATURE =
```

whereas the second thing is the value of TEMP. The apostrophes are not part of the output; they serve to **delimit** the character constant. A **character constant** consists of a pair of apostrophes surrounding one or more characters. Thus, at the very least, a character constant in a PRINT statement must require three consecutive columns: an apostrophe, a character, an apostrophe. The character may be a blank. Notice that the second item, TEMP, is not surrounded by apostrophes. Thus, TEMP in this context does not denote a character constant. Consequently, we would *not* expect to see the following as the output:

```
TEMPERATURE = TEMP
```

Instead we would expect to see a number after the = sign. To see this, we execute the program. Figure 2.1 is a copy of our interaction with the executing program.

```
PROGRAM TWO

PROGRAMMED BY H. LEE, 1MAR82

GIVE TEMPERATURE AS A NUMBER WITH
AN EMBEDDED DECIMAL POINT

*212.0
TEMPERATURE = 212.
    STOP
```

Figure 2.1   Interactive Execution of Program TWO

In this figure we see the various messages resulting from the PRINT statements. Notice that the

```
PRINT *, ' '
```

statement prints a blank line. Everything up to the line beginning with the asterisk is a result of the PRINT statements.

The examples we have used have been executed using an interactive system. In such a system, a user's program can request input from the keyboard. When computing in FORTRAN using an interactive system, the FORTRAN READ statement is used to request input from the user who is sitting at the keyboard. When an interactive system is waiting for input from the keyboard, everything just halts. Except in the rather unlikely case that the user knows in advance for what input the computer is waiting, the user may not be able to continue the execution of the program. Consequently, interactive systems have a mechanism that permits a programmer to instruct the system to display a prompt character on the screen. (Exactly what character is the prompt character may vary from system to system.) A **prompt character** thereby alerts the user that the computer is waiting for the user to enter a response from the keyboard before continuing. An interactive system can be made to display a prompt character on the screen whenever an executing program requests input from the keyboard.

Good programming practice requires that all programs be written assuming that some nonprogrammer will eventually be the user of the program. Consequently, good programming practice includes the requirement that the programmer display on the screen some message before the prompt is made. This message is to explain exactly which information is wanted from the user and, frequently, also to explain the format required.

In a noninteractive system, both the entire program and the data are copied into memory before the execution begins. The user then does not "interact" with the program during its execution. Hence, when using card input or remote-job-entry, prompting is not done.

The asterisk serves as the the **prompt character** used by our operating system. The purpose of a prompt character is to remind the human sitting at a terminal or at the computer that the program is waiting for input from the keyboard. The prompt character has not been standardized, and some systems may use some other character. Following the asterisk in Figure 2.1 is the number 212.0, which is the value of the temperature that we entered from the keyboard when we saw the prompt, that is, the asterisk. Then, the line

```
TEMPERATURE = 212.
```

in the listing of the interactive session is the result of the execution of the statement

```
PRINT *, 'TEMPERATURE = ', TEMP
```

and the appearance of the word

```
STOP
```

is the result of the execution of the STOP statement in the program.

2.4 PROGRAM THREE

PROGRAM THREE consists of two program units. As we have mentioned, the first program unit must be a main program. The first END indicates the termination of the main program. Immediately after the first END is the keyword SUBROUTINE, which indicates the beginning of the next program unit and identifies this unit as a subroutine. The subroutine terminates with the second END.

```
      PROGRAM THREE
C
C PROGRAM THREE USES A SUBROUTINE
C TO CONVERT A TEMPERATURE FROM
C FAHRENHEIT TO CELSIUS.
C
C PROGRAMMED BY H. LEE, 1MAR82
C
C SPECIFICATIONS
C
      REAL TEMP
C
C                              EXECUTION:
C
      PRINT *, 'PROGRAM THREE'
      PRINT *, ' '
      PRINT *, 'PROGRAMMED BY H. LEE, 1MAR82'
      PRINT *, 'THIS PROGRAM CONVERTS A TEMPERATURE'
      PRINT *, 'GIVEN ON FAHRENHEIT SCALE TO THE'
      PRINT *, 'CORRESPONDING VALUE ON THE CELSIUS SCALE'
      PRINT *, ' '
C                              PROMPT:
      PRINT *, 'GIVE THE TEMPERATURE WITH AN EMBEDDED DECIMAL POINT'
      PRINT *, ' '
      READ *, TEMP
      CALL CONVRT (TEMP)
```

(continues)

```
      PRINT *, ' '
      PRINT *, 'NORMAL PROGRAM TERMINATION '
      STOP
      END
      SUBROUTINE CONVRT (TEMP)
C
C SUBROUTINE CONVRT CONVERTS FROM FAHRENHEIT TO CELSIUS
C
C PROGRAMMED BY H. LEE, 1MAR82
C
C SPECIFICATIONS
      REAL RESULT, TEMP
C
C                                  EXECUTION:
C
      RESULT = (5.0/9.0)*(TEMP - 32.0)
      PRINT *, 'A TEMPERATURE OF ', TEMP
      PRINT *, 'GIVEN IN FAHRENHEIT, CORRESPONDS TO'
      PRINT *, 'A TEMPERATURE OF ', RESULT
      PRINT *, 'MEASURED ON THE CELSIUS SCALE.'
C
      RETURN
      END
```

Within the main program, the new FORTRAN statement

```
      CALL CONVRT (TEMP)
```

is introduced. This statement is a subroutine call, that is, the command used to invoke the subroutine with the name CONVRT and to pass one argument, with the name of TEMP, into the subroutine. Incidentally, the word *argument* is from the use of the word in mathematics in the phrase "the argument of the function...."

All subroutine calls have the same form. Each begins with the keyword CALL, followed by the name of the subroutine, followed by a list of the names of the variables to be made available for use in computation within the subroutine. In FORTRAN a **list** simply consists of a sequence of the names of the variables separated by commas. The parentheses surrounding the list of variables that are to be passed as arguments to the subroutine are required. Arguments in FORTRAN are two-way communication devices. Consequently, in FORTRAN the argument list is a mechanism whereby (1) values of variables may be made available to the computations within the subroutine and (2) values computed with a subroutine may be made available to the calling program unit. Thus, as the argument list is used to pass values between program units, some programmers speak of passing values by the argument list.

If you have sensed that we have been talking as if the computations within a subroutine are relatively independent of the computations in the program unit that calls the subroutine, you are correct. In fact, the strategy of making little programs that are independent of one another but yet can be linked together in a limited sense led the designers of FORTRAN to make it possible to have subroutines in

FORTRAN. This property of the independence of subprograms greatly simplifies the task of solving large problems. It simplifies the task in two important aspects: (1) It permits a programmer to "divide and conquer," that is, to break a complicated problem up into small pieces that may be solved separately; and (2), it permits a very large programming task to be assigned to two or more different programmers, who can work on the program at the same time without having to know about the details of the subprograms other programmers are developing. All that the different programmers need to know is which variables are used in the argument list for what purposes and, only in general terms, what the subprogram does.

PROGRAM THREE may be thought of almost as two separate programs; one (the main program) inputs a temperature and calls another program (the subroutine) to compute the value of this on the Celsius scale. Thus, in this admittedly casual description, the CALL statement in the main program is a command to go somewhere else (the place to which it is to go is specified by the name after the keyword CALL) and do something. Further, when the "something" is done in the subroutine, the system resumes where it left off in the calling program using the new value. In PROGRAM THREE, the calling program is the main program, THREE; the called program is the subroutine, CONVRT; the call occurs in the main program; and the execution returns to the

```
PRINT *, ' '
```

statement. Thus, the CALL statement is a command to jump out, do something, and return. The location of the call statement determines the point at which the execution jumps to the subroutine. Execution returns to the first executable statement after the CALL statement.

In SUBROUTINE CONVRT two variables are used, RESULT and TEMP. Both are specified to be of type REAL, meaning that they will be used to represent numerical values that may have fractional parts. Also notice that TEMP is specified to be REAL *within the subroutine as well as in the calling program*. **THIS IS IMPORTANT!** Any subroutine is independent of any other program unit with which it is used, except for what the programmer specifies should be available to other units. (Here, the argument list is employed to communicate values. There is another method to communicate values between units available in FORTRAN that will be illustrated later.) But in FORTRAN the fact that TEMP was specified to be REAL in the main program is *not* communicated to the subroutine. The *only information* that is communicated is the location in memory where the stored value (the value of the variable) is to be found. The computer cannot determine the type of any value stored in memory by examining the contents of the memory location. Hence, TEMP must be specified to be REAL in *both* places. In the subroutine, CONVRT, examine the statement

```
RESULT = (5.0/9.0) * (TEMP - 32.0)
```

which is an example of an arithmetic assignment statement. An **arithmetic assignment statement** is a command to execute the arithmetic computations on the right of the *replacement operator* and assign the resulting value to the variable name given on the left-hand side of the replacement operator. The character = is the replacement operator. In English, we should read the statement we are considering as

> The current value of the type REAL variable, RESULT, is to be assigned (i.e., is to be replaced by) the value of the quotient of five divided by nine multiplied by the current value of TEMP less thirty-two.

Thus, what you may think of as an equal sign is, in FORTRAN, called a replacement operator. We urge you to speak of the replacement operator or think of the phrase replacement operator whenever you see the = sign in FORTRAN. The significance of this is discussed again later.

The last new construction in the subroutine is the word

RETURN

which merely indicates that at this point in the program the system should return to the calling program by executing the first executable statement following the call statement that led to the jump into the subroutine.

Again, be sure that you notice the difference between a RETURN statement and an END statement. Recall that there are two distinct phases in the processing of your program by the FORTRAN system. The first phase is the translation of the program from the form you have given (that is, from FORTRAN code,) into another form the computer can execute. This translation is called compiling. The second phase consists of the execution of the compiled version. Thus, the END statement is an indication to the FORTRAN compiler that this statement (i.e., the END) is the last statement of this program unit to be compiled. On the other hand, a RETURN statement becomes a command to return to the calling program when the execution reaches the point where the RETURN statement occurred. Figure 2.2 shows interactive execution of PROGRAM THREE.

```
PROGRAM THREE

PROGRAMMED BY H. LEE, 1MAR82
THIS PROGRAM CONVERTS A TEMPERATURE
GIVEN ON FAHRENHEIT SCALE TO THE
CORRESPONDING VALUE ON THE CELSIUS SCALE

GIVE THE TEMPERATURE WITH AN EMBEDDED DECIMAL POINT

*212.0
A TEMPERATURE OF 212.
GIVEN IN FAHRENHEIT, CORRESPONDS TO
A TEMPERATURE OF 100.
MEASURED ON THE CELSIUS SCALE.

NORMAL PROGRAM TERMINATION
    STOP
```

Figure 2.2 Interactive Execution of Program THREE

2.5 PROGRAM FOUR

Suppose that we try to make our program more realistic simply by adding the capability of processing more than one temperature when we execute the program. First though, recall that if we had more than one temperature to convert using PROGRAM THREE, we would have to execute PROGRAM THREE repeatedly. This is inconvenient, as we have to enter a number of commands to get the program to execute. Further, the program must be both compiled and executed for each value to be converted. Also, it is more costly, as there is some cost associated with the compilation of the program. Therefore, we seek a mechanism whereby we can repeatedly read a new temperature and, for each, execute the CALL of the subroutine to do the conversions. If we were to do this using only the information we have so far, we might try to design a program that would input the first temperature, convert it, output the result, then input the second temperature, convert it, then output it, and so on. This is the method used in PROGRAM FOUR to carry out exactly three conversions. But surely there must be a better way. And, there is!

```
      PROGRAM FOUR
C
C PROGRAM FOUR USES A SUBROUTINE
C TO CONVERT A TEMPERATURE FROM
C FAHRENHEIT TO CELSIUS.
C
C PROGRAMMED BY H. LEE, 1MAR82
C
C SPECIFICATIONS
C
      REAL TEMP
C
C                              EXECUTION:
C
      PRINT *, 'PROGRAM FOUR'
      PRINT *, ' '
      PRINT *, 'PROGRAMMED BY H. LEE, 1MAR82'
      PRINT *, 'THIS PROGRAM CONVERTS A TEMPERATURE'
      PRINT *, 'GIVEN ON FAHRENHEIT SCALE TO THE'
      PRINT *, 'CORRESPONDING VALUE ON THE CELSIUS SCALE'
      PRINT *, ' '
C                              PROMPT:
C                                 1ST CONVERSION:
      PRINT *, 'GIVE THE TEMPERATURE WITH AN EMBEDDED DECIMAL POINT'
      PRINT *, ' '
      READ *, TEMP
      CALL CONVRT (TEMP)
      PRINT *, ' '
C                                 2ND CONVERSION:
      PRINT *, 'GIVE THE TEMPERATURE WITH AN EMBEDDED DECIMAL POINT'
```

```
         PRINT *, ' '
         READ *, TEMP
         CALL CONVRT (TEMP)
         PRINT *, ' '
C                                              3RD CONVERSION:
         PRINT *, 'GIVE THE TEMPERATURE WITH AN EMBEDDED DECIMAL POINT'
         PRINT *, ' '
         READ *, TEMP
         CALL CONVRT (TEMP)
         PRINT *, ' '
         PRINT *, 'NORMAL PROGRAM TERMINATION '
         STOP
         END
         SUBROUTINE CONVRT (TEMP)
C
C SUBROUTINE CONVRT CONVERTS FROM FAHRENHEIT TO CELSIUS
C
C PROGRAMMED BY H. LEE, 1MAR82
C
C SPECIFICATIONS
         REAL RESULT, TEMP
C
C                                     EXECUTION:
C
         RESULT = (5.0/9.0)*(TEMP - 32.0)
         PRINT *, 'A TEMPERATURE OF ', TEMP
         PRINT *, 'GIVEN IN FAHRENHEIT, CORRESPONDS TO'
         PRINT *, 'A TEMPERATURE OF ', RESULT
         PRINT *, 'MEASURED ON THE CELSIUS SCALE.'
C
         RETURN
         END
```

However, before we describe a better approach to processing a number of temperatures using just one execution of the program, let us point out some poor features of PROGRAM FOUR. Obviously, it is designed to perform exactly three conversions. There might be just one, or two, or more than three temperatures to convert at different times when the conversions are wanted. So, having the program designed to perform *exactly* three conversions is too inflexible and restrictive. Even if one were to retain the strategy of introducing a number of calls to the subroutine, the conversion of a different number of values requires that the program itself be modified each time there is a different number of values to be accommodated. This is cumbersome and frequently leads to errors. Further, it means that anyone using the program would have to be able to modify the program as well. For these reasons, the strategy represented by PROGRAM FOUR for repeating computations is rejected. Figure 2.3 shows interactive execution of PROGRAM FOUR.

```
PROGRAM FOUR

PROGRAMMED BY H. LEE, 1MAR82
THIS PROGRAM CONVERTS A TEMPERATURE
GIVEN ON FAHRENHEIT SCALE TO THE
CORRESPONDING VALUE ON THE CELSIUS SCALE

GIVE THE TEMPERATURE WITH AN EMBEDDED DECIMAL POINT

*212.0
 A TEMPERATURE OF 212.
 GIVEN IN FAHRENHEIT, CORRESPONDS TO
 A TEMPERATURE OF 100.
 MEASURED ON THE CELSIUS SCALE.

GIVE THE TEMPERATURE WITH AN EMBEDDED DECIMAL POINT

*32.0
 A TEMPERATURE OF 32.
 GIVEN IN FAHRENHEIT, CORRESPONDS TO
 A TEMPERATURE OF 0,
 MEASURED ON THE CELSIUS SCALE.

GIVE THE TEMPERATURE WITH AN EMBEDDED DECIMAL POINT

*-16.0
 A TEMPERATURE OF -16.
 GIVEN IN FAHRENHEIT, CORRESPONDS TO
 A TEMPERATURE OF -26.66666666667
 MEASURED ON THE CELSIUS SCALE.

NORMAL PROGRAM TERMINATION
     STOP
```

Figure 2.3   Interactive Execution of Program FOUR

2.6 PROGRAM FIVE

We urge you to study PROGRAM FIVE and to see whether you can interpret its distinguishing features. You may be unable to understand some of the new constructions, but these will be explained next. But do try to guess what the program does before you read the explanations.

```
    PROGRAM FIVE
C
C PROGRAM FIVE USES A SUBROUTINE
C TO CONVERT A TEMPERATURE FROM
C FAHRENHEIT TO CELSIUS.
```

```
C
C THIS VERSION USES A REPETITION CONTROL STRUCTURE.
C
C
C PROGRAMMED BY H. LEE, 1MAR82
C
C SPECIFICATIONS
C
      REAL TEMP
C
C                                       EXECUTION:
C
      PRINT *, 'PROGRAM FIVE'
      PRINT *, ' '
      PRINT *, 'PROGRAMMED BY H. LEE, 1MAR82'
      PRINT *, 'THIS PROGRAM CONVERTS A TEMPERATURE'
      PRINT *, 'GIVEN ON FAHRENHEIT SCALE TO THE'
      PRINT *, 'CORRESPONDING VALUE ON THE CELSIUS SCALE'
C
C     WHILE
1       CONTINUE
        PRINT *, ' '
C                                   PROMPT:
        PRINT *, 'GIVE THE TEMPERATURE WITH AN EMBEDDED DECIMAL POINT'
        PRINT *, ' '
        READ (*,*,END=2) TEMP
        CALL CONVRT (TEMP)
        PRINT *, ' '
        GO TO 1
C     ENDWHILE
C
2       CONTINUE
      PRINT *, 'AN END OF FILE WAS DETECTED ON THE LAST READ'
      PRINT *, 'THE PROGRAM IS DESIGNED TO QUIT EXECUTION'
      PRINT *, 'WHEN AN END OF FILE IS DETECTED.'
C
      PRINT *, 'NORMAL PROGRAM TERMINATION '
      STOP
      END
      SUBROUTINE CONVRT (TEMP)
C
C SUBROUTINE CONVRT CONVERTS FROM FAHRENHEIT TO CELSIUS
C
C PROGRAMMED BY H. LEE, 1MAR82
C
C SPECIFICATIONS
      REAL RESULT, TEMP
C
```

(continues)

```
C                                     EXECUTION:
C
      RESULT = (5.0/9.0)*(TEMP - 32.0)
      PRINT *, 'A TEMPERATURE OF ', TEMP
      PRINT *, 'GIVEN IN FAHRENHEIT, CORRESPONDS TO'
      PRINT *, 'A TEMPERATURE OF ', RESULT
      PRINT *, 'MEASURED ON THE CELSIUS SCALE.'
C
      RETURN
      END
```

As the need to repeat computations on different data sets is a frequently recurring one, computing languages include constructions to enable the programmer to do this easily. These constructions are methods for creating repetitions. The method we illustrate shortly with PROGRAM FIVE is a method for specifying an indefinite number of repetitions. We want to be able to instruct the computer by the use of FORTRAN to execute a set of instructions repeatedly *while there is a temperature to be converted*. The construction then is called a *while* loop. That is, it is a method of saying, While there are data to be processed, repeat these instructions. Standard FORTRAN does not include a while statement. However, it is quite common and easy for a FORTRAN programmer to construct a while loop. We have done so in PROGRAM FIVE, where the while loop is indicated by the comment WHILE, which precedes the first statement of the loop, and by the comment ENDWHILE, which follows the last statement of the loop.

The essential elements of the WHILE loop are:

```
      1       CONTINUE

              READ (*,*,END=2) TEMP

              GO TO 1

      2       CONTINUE
```

These four standard FORTRAN statements are those we use to implement a while construction to input an unspecified number of items up to an end-of-file. In a computer system, data are usually thought of as appearing in a file. A **file** is something like a labeled folder in a filing cabinet. The computing system includes a special computer-detectable signal, called an **end-of-file,** which is used to indicate that there are no more data in a file.

Before we may continue our explanation of this while loop, we must introduce some of the FORTRAN constructions that permit the programmer to specify the flow-of-control in the program. (The phrase *flow-of-control* is the commonly used expression equivalent to the phrase *flow-of-execution*. Either phrase is used to refer to the order in which statements are executed.)

Several FORTRAN statements permit the programmer to transfer to a statement label. A **statement label** is a sequence of one or more digits in columns 1 through 5. At least one digit of a statement label must be nonzero. For example, in

PROGRAM FIVE the

```
                         GO TO 1
```

statement is a standard FORTRAN statement, which, when executed, transfers the flow-of-control to the statement bearing the digit 1 as its statement label. Thus, in our example here, when the execution reaches the GO TO 1 statement, the next statement to be executed is the statement labeled with the digit 1. In this example, the statement labeled 1 is the 1 CONTINUE statement. Consequently, when executed, the GO TO 1 statement transfers control to the 1 CONTINUE statement. A statement label may be used with most executable FORTRAN statements. However, we use—and urge you to use—a stylistic convention in which the flow-of-control is transferred to a CONTINUE statement whenever the statement directing the transfer is a GO TO statement.

The **CONTINUE statement** merely serves as a means for providing a line upon which a statement label may be written if you do not choose to use some other FORTRAN statement. Although the CONTINUE statement is considered to be an executable statement, when execution takes place, the effect is as if execution flows over the statement without doing anything. Then, when the flow-of-execution reaches the CONTINUE statement, the first statement immediately following the CONTINUE statement is executed. The CONTINUE statement merely serves as a means to provide a statement label. The digit 1 in column 1 is the statement label.

The READ statement we have used is a simplified version of the READ statement. The asterisks may be regarded as part of the required syntax of this version of the statement.

The READ statement

```
              READ (*,*,END=2) TEMP
```

is the FORTRAN standard READ statement containing the optional command to transfer the execution of the program to the statement label given after the END= sequence. Here, we have used 2 as our statement label. Thus, this READ statement is a command to input a value to be assigned to the variable TEMP; but, if an end-of-file is encountered, execution is transferred to the statement

```
              2       CONTINUE
```

which is followed by the statement

```
       PRINT *, 'AN END OF FILE WAS DETECTED ON THE LAST READ'
```

This statement prints a message informing the user that an end-of-file was encountered. The construction END = 2 may be thought of as another mechanism available to the programmer to specify the flow-of-control. It operates just like a GO TO statement. Thus, you may think of the END = 2 statement as meaning

> When an attempt is made to read a datum but no datum is found, GO TO 2 and continue execution at that point.

(The word *datum* is the singular form of the word *data*.) But the END= construction can appear only in a READ statement, and it may not appear in other contexts. We strongly recommend that you use the END= construction in all READ statements.

Before you continue studying this text, we urge you to spend a few minutes trying to sketch what you would expect to see on the output device. We state this as an exercise.

EXERCISE

Write the sequence of statements that you would anticipate would be observed as output as a result of executing PROGRAM FIVE when the user entered, in the following order, the values 32.0, 212.0, -17.0, +212.0,-199.9 followed by an end-of-file.

2.7 PROGRAM SIX

In the sample programs we have introduced, we have illustrated various constructions that we want to combine into a general program to perform temperature conversion. But before we may create a satisfactory general temperature conversion program, we need to explain one more FORTRAN feature. We have assumed (or were told by our client, who asked us to design the program) that the general program to perform temperature conversion is to be able to convert either from Celsius to Fahrenheit *or* from Fahrenheit to Celsius. Thus, we have the need to be able to indicate whether a temperature given as input is measured on the Celsius or on the Fahrenheit scale. The temperatures are given as real values, that is, as numbers that may have a fractional part. But a number representing a temperature does not contain the information about which scale is being used. So, we want to use a mechanism to indicate the scale being used. For this purpose, we have chosen to use the letter *C* to indicate Celsius and the letter *F* to indicate Fahrenheit. To do this using FORTRAN we must use a variable of type CHARACTER. This usage appears in PROGRAM SIX. We again call to your attention the property of "type." You should remember that we stated that there are various properties associated with variables. *A variable has a programmer created symbolic name; a variable is assigned to a memory location; a variable has some type associated with it, such as INTEGER REAL, or CHARACTER; and a variable either has some value stored in the memory location or is undefined (as to value.)* We wish to use a variable of type CHARACTER, meaning that we want to be able to use a character (here, a letter of the alphabet) as the value of the variable. For variables of type CHARACTER, FORTRAN requires that the programmer declare the variable name to be of type CHARACTER.

```
      PROGRAM SIX
C
C PROGRAM SIX IS TO TEST OUT MY UNDERSTANDING
C OF TYPE CHARACTER.
C
C PROGRAMMED BY H. LEE, 1MAR82
```

```
C
C SPECIFICATIONS
C
      CHARACTER SCALE*1
C
C                                            EXECUTION:
C
      PRINT *, ' '
      PRINT *, 'PROGRAM SIX. A TEST OF TYPE CHARACTER.'
      PRINT *, 'PROGRAMMED BY H. LEE, 1MAR82'
      PRINT *, ' '
C                                            PROMPT:
C
      PRINT *, 'GIVE A SINGLE LETTER SURROUNDED BY'
      PRINT *, 'APOSTROPHES'
      READ *, SCALE
      PRINT *, 'THE LETTER READ INTO SCALE WAS ', SCALE
      PRINT *, 'NORMAL PROGRAM TERMINATION'
      STOP
      END
```

In PROGRAM SIX we have chosen to use SCALE as the variable name. We specify SCALE to be type CHARACTER by the statement

CHARACTER SCALE*1

which also supplies the information to the complier that space for only one character need be reserved for the variable SCALE. Thus, the keyword **CHARACTER** specifies the following list of one or more variables to be of type CHARACTER. This list consists of the variable name, followed by the asterisk, followed by the length (that is, the maximum number of characters to be assigned to the variable as the value of that variable). Like all lists, if there is more than one element in the list, consecutive list items are separated by commas.

When a user enters a character value, that value must have an apostrophe on each side. These apostrophes are called *delimiters*. When one or more blanks appear either alone or with other characters surrounded by apostrophes, the blanks are significant. That is, 'A' is used to enter a character value, A, and the fact that it is of length 1, but ' A ' is used to enter the character value A and the fact that it is of the length three, i.e., a blank, an A, and a blank. The FORTRAN system would have required that the variable to be used to store ' A ' be specified to be type CHARACTER of length 3 or greater. Consequently, we could not use PROGRAM SIX to input ' C ', nor could we use it to input any of the following: 'CELSIUS', ' C', 'C ', ' C '. Each of the listed character values is greater than length one, as blanks are legitimate character values.

Remember. Within a pair of apostrophes *blanks are significant characters* and therefore must be included in the character count.

Figure 2.4 shows interaction of PROGRAM SIX.

```
PROGRAM SIX. A TEST OF TYPE CHARACTER.
PROGRAMMED BY H. LEE, 1MAR82

GIVE A SINGLE LETTER SURROUNDED BY
APOSTROPHES
*'f'
THE LETTER READ INTO SCALE WAS F
NORMAL PROGRAM TERMINATION
     STOP
```

Figure 2.4 Interactive Execution of Program SIX

2.8 A STUDY RECOMMENDATION

In this chapter, we have talked about FORTRAN coding. Before you go on the next chapter, in which we discuss the designing of programs, we highly recommend that you reread this chapter on coding. However, to make this rereading worthwhile, you should avoid thinking of this material for at least 2 days before you reread it!

2.9 EXERCISES

1. Following is a list of items, one item per line. We claim that no item below may be used as a symbolic name in FORTRAN. For each item, explain why it is unacceptable as a symbolic name. (*Hint:* Many students find the defect in the last item quite difficult to detect, but a FORTRAN system would object to it.)

   CONSULTANT
   MAGICNUMBER
   3RDTRY
   3736
   3.1316
   0THER

2. Explain why each of the following items should not be used as a symbolic name in FOR-TRAN. Again, there is one item per line.

   END
   PROGRAM
   STOP

3. In the following list, where there is one item per line, each item would be incorrect if it were to be used as a numeric value. Explain what is incorrect in the syntax for each.

   + -212.03
   763,923.791
   $12.95
    12
   33%
   2.14x(10)+3
   12.20.06
   30/7/84

4. Each of the following lines has at least one syntax error if it were to be included as code in a FORTRAN program. Carefully identify and explain each error.

```
TEMPERATURE = TEMP
INTEGER, A, B, I
PROGRAM 4TH
INPUT (*,*,END =5) T
GO TO START
REAL X, Y,
'TEMP' = 3133.79
PRINT *, ''
PROGRAM ONE
PRINT *, " SAMPLE OUTPUT FOR CLEAR READING "
```

5. Here are a few FORTRAN statements. Reorder them to form a correct program. You may want to omit one or two statements. You may want to correct a syntax error in one or two. But you are not to add entirely new statements. (Do not be misled by the fact that the program may look odd; the task is merely to revise it so that it is syntactically correct and so that it will execute.)

```
C       INTEGER INDEX, NUMBER, ROW
C       PROGRAM ORDER
C       PROGRAMMED BY JO JO
C
7       CONTINUE
        END
        PRINT 'The MAGIC NUMBER IS ', 'NUMBER'
        READ (*,*,END = 7) 'NUMBER'
        STOP
```

3

The Design of Programs

3.1 INTRODUCTION

After learning a few FORTRAN statements, reading several programs, and writing a few programs, beginning students are often presented with a more demanding programming exercise only to find that they are at a loss when it comes to writing the program. If we were to ask such a student what the problem is, the student might be able to say, "I don't know. But I feel that I know how to write each FORTRAN statement separately, but I can't link them together to write a whole program." In our experience, the problem is not that students do not know enough FORTRAN but rather that they lack experience in the design of programs. Consequently, at this point we introduce the intellectual tools and the building blocks used to design programs rather than introducing additional FORTRAN constructions.

3.2 THE PROGRAMMING SETTING

We have found that students can understand the programming task much better if we describe the task as if it were occurring in a large programming firm. In such a setting, the client, who probably knows little about programming or computers, presents an original statement to the systems analyst, who converts the program request into a design. Then he or she gives the design to the coder. The coder converts the design to FORTRAN code, i.e., to FORTRAN statements. The coder also tests the FORTRAN program and makes necessary corrections. It should be noted that the coder does not meet with the client directly. The coder consults only with the systems analyst. Further, at least in this firm, all interactions between client and systems analyst, as well as those between systems analyst and coder, are written.

36

3.3 THE COMPONENTS OF THE PROBLEM-SOLVING TASK

The design of programs has much in common with other forms of problem solving. In particular, almost any discussion of problem solving points out that the first step in problem solving is to define the problem. We, too, stress the importance of this as the first step. Although company policy in our hypothetical firm requires a written program request from the client, the systems analyst is trained to assume that the client's request is an incomplete and probably misleading statement of the problem. That is, by training and from experience, a systems analyst assumes that the first task is to define the problem. (By the way, the systems analyst is not taking an unrealistic viewpoint. After all, the client is probably not a systems analyst, nor is it likely that the client is a coder.) The program request is a written request prepared by the client. Prior to the first face-to-face exchange with the client, the systems analyst studies the request and prepares a list of clarifying questions. Then, in a meeting with the client, these are discussed. The systems analyst analyzes the program request in terms of input, transformation, and output. That is, the systems analyst thinks about the programming task as one in which certain outputs are requested. Then the systems analyst identifies the needed inputs and transformations required on these inputs to produce the requested outputs. After clarifying any questions that arise, the systems analyst produces a revised program request along with the cost-time estimates for the client's approval. If the revised program request is approved by the client, the systems analyst creates a design.

A **design** is a written description of the program in the form of a diagram, which can be given to a coder for translation into FORTRAN statements. Thus, a design represents an intermediate step in the programming process. It comes between the first step, defining the problem, and the third step, coding. In this position in the programming process, a design should be decidedly less technical than the computer code to be generated, yet precise enough so that coding from the design is a straightforward task for a coder experienced in FORTRAN. At the same time, the design must be more detailed and more organized than the revised client's request.

The design is given to the coder, who converts the design to FORTRAN statements. The coder also tests the program and makes any necessary corrections. When it is apparently working correctly, it is given to the systems analyst, who verifies that the program is a correct interpretation of the design and that it has been fully tested. Then the systems analyst makes the program available to the client.

Thus, the computer problem-solving process is composed of the following steps:

(1) Defining the problem
(2) Designing a solution
(3) Coding the design
(4) Designing test data
(5) Testing the code using the test data
(6) Verifying that the code is a correct interpretation of the client's request

Actually, we are somewhat oversimplifying the problem-solving process, since in real life a systems analyst might have to consider two, three, or even more possible solutions in Step 2, including making partial or complete designs, before finally deciding that one solution was more complete, more efficient, more accurate, and so on. For Step 1 the programming team might have to go through several false starts before the client's real problem is fully clarified. In other words, programming in part is an art, as there are several correct ways to solve the same problem. However, to simplify the process, we try to avoid presenting many alternatives at this time. Now, let us turn to the job of the systems analyst after the problem is fully specified. Anticipating somewhat the material to come, we can say at the broadest level of analysis that the design of a solution can take the general form of selecting which of the three possible control structures should be used for each step of the solution.

3.4 DESIGN ALTERNATIVES: THE FLOW-OF-CONTROL

To proceed to the design step the systems analyst must know what alternatives are available. As we have already mentioned, there are three major options available: sequence, selection, and repetition. Although sequence, selection, and repetition are the three different kinds of logical structures a programmer may use to specify both the sequence of steps to be done and the decisions to be made in the program, they are usually referred to simply as the **control structures.** We usually refer to them as part of a more complete system, presented here as Figure 3.1, which is a tree diagram of the control structures.

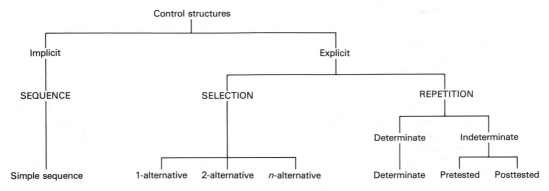

Figure 3.1 Tree Diagram of the Control Structures

Figure 3.1 shows that the diagram starts at the top. We are then immediately confronted by two branches, one labeled *implicit* and the other *explicit*. The order in which the computer carries out the instructions is implied by the order of the instructions. Hence, this is called *implicit ordering*. But to be very useful, a computer system must include some provision for the programmer to specify some ordering other than this sequential, uninterrupted top-to-bottom ordering. Indeed, such provisions are available. As these alternatives necessitate an explicit statement of the ordering, the other branch of the tree is labeled *explicit*. Each branch below the explicit node thus contains a control structure in which the programmer specifies an ordering that is other than the implied simple sequential ordering.

The terminating tips of the tree diagram of the control structures are called *terminal nodes*. As you see in Figure 3.1, there are seven terminal nodes. Under the sequence branch, there is only one terminal node. Under the selection branch, there are three terminal nodes. Likewise, under the repetition branch there are three terminal nodes.

3.4.1 The Sequence Alternative

The sequence alternative has only one terminal node, which we call **sequence.** Some authors call this terminal node simple sequence, but we see no need to add the qualifier.

3.4.2 The Selection Alternatives

The selection branch provides the analyst with the mechanisms for selecting what is to be done next. The basis of the selection is a test created by the analyst. To do this, the analyst creates a test by writing an expression that can be either true or false. Such an expression is called a **logical expression.** For example, a programmer may write a logical expression to determine whether the value of one variable is less than the value of another variable. Other possible relationships between two numeric quantities include any of the following: less than or equal, equal, not equal, greater than, and, finally, greater than or equal. Logical expressions constructed by using these **relational operators** may be called **relational expressions.** When such an expression is inserted into a selection, it is frequently called a **test**.

In the one-alternative situation, the test controls one set of instructions. If and only if the test condition is true, the set of intructions is carried out. If the test condition is false, the set of instructions under the control of the one-alternative structure is not carried out. (The set of instructions could be just one instruction.)

The two-alternative structure is frequently used in almost all programming application areas. This terminal node is called the two-alternative node because there are two alternatives available. This means that two different sequences of instructions could be used at this point. That is, depending upon the outcome of the logical test, either one sequence of instructions or another set of instructions—*but not both*—would be used. If the test condition is true, one set of instructions is used. If the test condition is false, the other set of instructions is used. (Again, the set of instructions might consist of just one instruction per set.)

It is common for many authors and designers to nest two-alternative selections within two-alternative selections. Although we ourselves followed this practice for some time, we concluded that it is preferable to use the general *n*-alternative selection, as described next. The *n*-alternative selection is preferable, we believe, because it is logically much clearer. Also, both the one-alternative selection and the two-alternative selection are special cases of the more general *n*-alternative selection.

The purpose of the *n*-alternative selection is to permit the programmer to select one alternative from a list of *n* alternatives. As we present this structure, there are

$n - 1$ tests. Following each test is a set of one or more instructions. Following the $n - 1$ sets of instructions is the nth set of instructions. That is, there are n sets of alternatives, and each set of alternatives, except the last set, begins with a test. But there is no test preceding the last set of instructions.

As always in structured programming, the flow-of-control enters the structure at the top. In this structure, this implies that the first test is evaluated. If the first test is true, the first set of instructions is executed, and then execution flows to the first statement after the n-alternative selection. If the first test is false, the first set of instructions is not executed, and execution flows to the evaluation of the second test. If the second test is true, the second set of instructions is executed, and the execution flows to the first statement after the n-alternative selection. If the second test is found to be false, the second set of instructions is not executed, and execution flows to the next section of the structure. This pattern of evaluation continues until either a test is found to be true or until all $n - 1$ tests have been found to be false. If all $n - 1$ tests are found to be false, the set of instructions comprising the last, or nth alternative is executed. After the nth alternative has been executed, the flow-of-control passes to the first statement after the n-alternative selection. Thus, when all $n - 1$ alternatives have been found to be false, the nth set of instructions is always executed. Consequently, the nth set of instructions is used to process any case not covered by the tests. This "all other cases" is useful for processing an error condition, as presented in a later chapter.

3.4.3 The Repetition Alternatives

The last branch in the diagram of the control structures contains structures that permit repetitions. A repetition is often called a *loop*. A repetition permits the programmer to specify that a series of instructions is to be repeated with a new set of data. The repetition branch is shown with two subbranches. The left subbranch is labeled **determinate**, meaning that the number of repetitions is determined prior to entering the loop itself. In a determinate repetition the number of repetitions remains fixed throughout the execution of the instructions within the loop *and may not be changed as a result of computations within the loop*. The other branch is labeled **indeterminate**, meaning that the number of times the loop is to be repeated is not determined prior to entering the loop. As the number of repetitions is not determined prior to entering the loop, the loop itself must contain a way to determine when the repeating is to terminate. (A loop that does not quit repeating is called an **infinite loop,** a common programming mistake inadvertently created when there is an error in stating when the repetitions are to terminate. It is to be hoped that the system will have a built-in safety valve that will terminate your job if you accidentally create an infinite loop. This is one reason the system has a limit on the number of seconds your job may be computing or a limit on your overall job cost.)

The indeterminate repetition has two subbranches. One is designated the **pretested** branch, whereas the other is designated the **posttested** branch. The test is the device used to terminate the looping process. As you might imagine, the designations of these two as pre- or posttested implies that the language permits the programmer to have the test at the top or at the bottom of the loop.

3.4.3.1 The pretested indeterminate repetition.   The loop known as the **pretested indeterminate repetition** has a test at the top of the loop. The test is in the form of a logical expression (i.e., an expression that can be either true or false.) If and only if the expression is true, the loop is executed once. Then the test is made again. If and only if the expression is still true, the loop is executed again, and the test is again performed. At any time the test is made (including the very first time), if the expression is false, the instructions within the loop are not executed, and the flow-of-control passes to the first statement after the loop. In other words, the pretested indeterminate loop is equivalent to the command:

Execute the instructions below *while* the test is true.

Caution.   Notice that (1) the test is made only at the top of the loop; (2) the test is made *only* when the flow-of-control flows into the test expression at the top of the loop; and (3) the test is performed exactly once each time for each execution of the loop.

In our experience, this caution is necessary because beginning students sometimes conclude that the execution of the loop ceases whenever instructions within the loop appear to cause the test (the logical expression) to be false. This conclusion is incorrect because the test that controls the execution of the while loop is not evaluated except when execution flows into the while loop. It is only when the test is evaluated that a flow-of-control decision is made.

3.4.3.2 The posttested indeterminate repetition.   The posttested indeterminate repetition is less frequently used than the pretested structure just described. In the **posttested indeterminate repetition,** the test is at the bottom of the loop. Thus, the instructions inside the loop are always executed at least once. The flow-of-control enters as always at the top of the structure. Thus, it enters the body of the loop that contains the instructions to be executed. These instructions are executed, then the test at the bottom of the loop is evaluated. If the test is false, execution returns to the top of the loop. If the test is true, the execution goes on to the next structure after the loop. That is, the flow-of-control leaves the loop. Thus, this posttested indeterminate repetition is characterized by the English command:

Repeat the above instructions *until* the test is found to be true.

Notice that the test is made only at the bottom of the loop and that the test expression is evaluated only when the flow-of-control enters this bottom statement in the loop.

3.5 DESIGN DIAGRAMS AND MODULES

In this text the design of a program will be constructed entirely from the set of seven control structures just discussed. A unique design diagram is used to represent each of the seven control structures. The diagrams used in this text are based on work of Nassi and Schneiderman (1973). The complete design is a rectangle, composed of other smaller rectangles. The implication is that they are to be read, rectangle by rectangle, from the topmost rectangle to the bottommost rectangle, without skipping any rectangle in the descent from the top to the bottom. Each rectangle must be finished before the next rectangle is entered. We call these rectangles *modules*.

A **module** is a very small sequence of consecutive statements that has the following characteristics:

(1) A module computes only one thing (when speaking conceptually about the function of a module).

(2) The only entrance to a module is at the top of the module.

(3) The only exit from a module is at the bottom of the module.

(4) There is one exception. When an error is detected, execution may terminate within the module.

A design consists of two major sections. The first major section is called the *preamble*. The preamble consists of information for aiding the human reader of the design. You saw a design in Chapter 1. There you may verify that our design for the program that performs the temperature conversions, TEMPCV, has a preamble containing the following parts: an abstract, a list of the input, a list of the output, a design history, a list of any reference(s), and an identifier dictionary. The latter lists each of the identifiers used in the design, the type of each variable, the meaning or expansion to a length longer than the number of characters used of the identifier name, and the use of the identifier. Notice that the list of identifiers is given alphabetically.

The second major section of a design consists of the *flow-of-control specifications*. This section is presented as a series of design diagrams. Notice that the horizontal and vertical lines are a significant part of the design. Also, when a design is prepared for reproduction, the entire design may not fit on a single page. In general, a design that does not fit on one single page may be split so that the preamble appears on one page and the flow-of-control appears on another page. Beginning students will probably encounter only designs that can be presented on one or two pages, as just described.

3.6 THE DESIGN DIAGRAMS

We present the set of all seven design diagrams in Figure 3.2. The words within them and the lines as they appear in the various diagrams are significant. In each one, the flow-of-control enters at the top of any diagram and exits at the bottom. In the creation of a design, these diagrams are used as the *only* available building blocks. No other means for specifying the flow-of-control is permitted. Each diagram is different from any other. The diagram for sequence is merely a rectangle. The diagrams for selection are fairly similar to each other in their broad aspects but differ from each other in the repetition diagrams. Each of the repetition diagrams contains what resembles an "L." The rectangle within the L is called the *body*. One or more structures may be inserted into the body. Obviously, all the repetition diagrams share the distinctive appearance of the L.

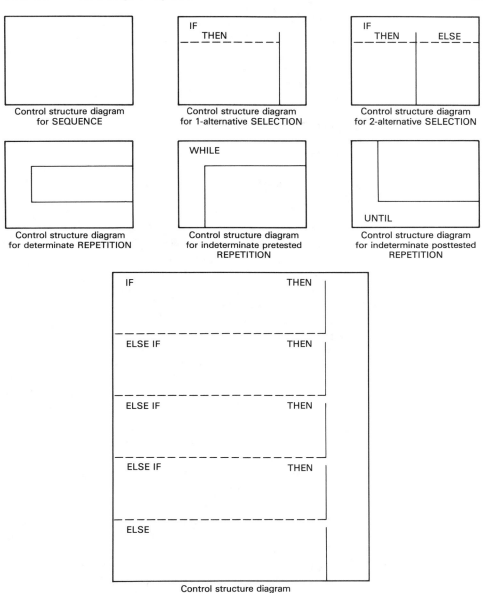

Figure 3.2 Design Diagrams

These diagrams are uniquely associated with each of the terminal nodes of the tree diagram of the control structures. Thus, each diagram represents one of the possible structures you may use in creating the overall design. If a programmer utilizes only these seven control structures, the programmer is employing a style of programming called *structured programming*. Although the phrase structured programming takes its name from the fact that only these seven structures are used, the phrase almost always implies as well that each structure is a short module. To stress this fact, we characterize the programming methodology we are describing as *modular structured programming*.

3.7 DESIGN AND IMPLEMENTATION

In the design phase we read the client's request for a program (which all too often is far from complete and, in fact, may not describe what the client really wants). We then jot down our interpretation of the various things that are requested. Then we think about how to obtain these items. We may make notes to ourselves. During this part of the thinking, the material that comes to mind may not be neat or logical. Normally, we do not think in a nice, simple sequential fashion. Ideas may come and go in almost any order. Thus, we may start with trying to figure out what is to be printed as the answer, then jump to what is needed as input, then jump back to the middle of the computations, and so on. Not only is this usual, but we believe that it is natural. It may well be an efficient way for us to solve problems. Further, we suspect that in the initial stages of considering a problem, it is not very helpful to try to think about a problem in any other way. In particular, we suspect that it is quite disfunctional to try to force ourselves to be organized in the initial stages of thinking about a problem. But notice that we qualified this statement by stating "in the initial stages of thinking" about the problem. We did not say that the entire process of design will be unordered, cluttered, disorganized, or messy. But we have encountered a few students who seem to try to force themselves to think in the rigid patterns they imagine the computer uses — i.e., they try to think like a computer. As this tactic frequently produces feelings of frustration, we discourage it.

Although we firmly believe in being disciplined about the design and implementation of programs, we feel that the organization comes in a later stage than the initial thinking stage. We imagine that the way we solve problems is to proceed through several stages. In doing this, we may return to earlier stages and start all over using a different approach. We may record our ideas on paper. As we delve deeper into the problem, we start organizing these ideas, leading to the preparation of yet another draft of our notes. Eventually, we prepare a final paper, or in the case of a design of a computer program, a formal diagram. This formal diagram is highly organized, and the principle of organization of the formal diagram is similar to the organization of the sequence of statements that will be the implementation of the program.

To summarize, a *design* is a written description of the program in the form of a diagram, which can be given to a coder for translation into FORTRAN statements. As an intermediate step, the design should be decidedly less technical than the computer code, yet precise enough so that coding from the design is a straightforward (although time-consuming) task for a coder experienced in FORTRAN. If the design were not simpler than the FORTRAN program and at the same time more organized and more detailed than the client's original job request, there would be no point in producing the design. Incidentally, we might think of the task of converting a design into code as a task that could be done by the computer itself. Thus, we might imagine that a design diagram would be direct input to an optical reader of a computer system. In fact, there is some research in computer science addressed to a related approach — the construction of a computer-based editing system to be used by a systems analyst to create a design. Then, the computer would code the design directly from the design produced within the computer system.

3.8 INPUT-TRANSFORMATION-OUTPUT ANALYSIS

It is very easy even for experienced programmers to lose sight of the "big picture" in the rush to finish a high-priority project on time. In the most fundamental sense, to design is to organize the computations required to take input, to transform input into some desired output, and to print the resulting output. A careful analysis of what is wanted, that is, what output the client wants, is the beginning point. Then the designer must identify both the input required to produce this output and the transformations required to convert the input to the desired output. We highly recommend that throughout the entire process of programming, you as programmer continually return to this topmost level of analysis. As a caution, though, we want to remind you that the end product is a program ordered as three consecutive steps: input, transformation, and output; however, the implied order in the end product of input first, transformation second, and output third is not valid as a guide to the ordering of the steps of program development. In program development at the topmost level, we most often begin with a statement of the desired output. We then must ascertain what transformations are required to produce this output and also what input is required. Frequently, in discussions with a client, a programmer will come to the realization that the client has not thought through the problem very well.

Also, the process of developing an understanding of the problem to be solved at this topmost level of input-transformation-output is markedly nonlinear. As we gain further insights into a problem, we have to jump around, modify, add, or abandon previous analyses, and so on. Although we stress an organized approach to program design and implementation, we also feel that the student programmer should not attempt to curtail the nonlinear aspects of the problem-solving process. In the early stages of problem solving, and especially at this topmost level, in which you are attempting to gain an understanding of the problem as a whole, this jumping around in a nonlinear manner is to be expected. To attempt to carry out the task in a linear, nicely organized manner will probably lead to frustration and tension. Moreover, it is quite probable that it will not help solve the problem! But the eventual goal is to see the problem as a sequential process in which first is given some input that the computer then transforms to the final product, output. We recommend carrying out an input-transformation-output analysis of the client's programming request as the first step in thinking about the programming task. We also recommend thinking about the design and the program as an input-transformation-output process.

3.9 EXERCISES

1. In an essay examination in a course using this text, the instructor asked the students to define a module. She received the following two answers. She awarded 15 points out of a possible of 15 points for the first answer, but only 5 points for the second answer. Explain why.

   Answer A:
   A module computes only one thing. It has one entrance and it is at the top. It has only one exit and it is at the bottom.
   Answer B:
   A module computes only one thing. It has one entrance at the top. It has one exit at the bottom.

2. Describe the circumstances under which the following two design segments would effectively behave identically with respect to the execution of instruction one, instruction two, and instruction three. Assume that instruction one in one design segment is the same as instruction one in the other, and so on.

| instruction one |
| instruction two |
| instruction three |
| WHILE (testone) |
| instruction one |
| instruction two |
| instruction three |

| instruction one |
| instruction two |
| instruction three |
| UNTIL   (testtwo) |

3. Describe the circumstances under which the following two design segments would effectively behave identically with respect to the execution of instruction one, instruction two, and instruction three. Assume that instruction one in one design segment is the same as instruction one in the other, and so on.

```
IF (testone)
    THEN
------------------------------------------------------------------------
instruction one
instruction two
instruction three
```

```
        instruction one
        instruction two
        instruction three
UNTIL   (testtwo)
```

4. Under what circumstances would the following two design segments behave identically with respect to the execution of instruction one, instruction two, and instruction three?

```
instruction one
instruction two
instruction three
```

```
        instruction one
        instruction two
        instruction three
UNTIL   (testone)
```

5. Draw the design diagram that performs as follows:

Step 1. Execute the initial statements in this structure.
Step 2. Evaluate the test expression that appears in the bottom portion of this structure.
Step 3. If the test expression is true, exit from this structure. If it is false, again do all the instructions within this structure, starting at the top of this structure.

6. Draw the design diagram that performs as follows:

Step 1. Evaluate the expression that appears in the top portion of this structure to determine how many times the instructions contained within the structure are to be repeated.
Step 2. Repeat the instructions the number of times obtained in Step 1 and then exit from the structure.

7. Draw the design diagram that performs as follows:

Step 1. Evaluate the test expression in the top portion of this structure.
Step 2. If and only if the test expression is true, execute the remaining instructions within the structure and then exit from the bottom of the structure. If the test expression is false, immediately exit from the bottom of the structure, thereby omitting the execution of the instructions within the structure.

8. Draw the design diagram that performs as follows:

Step 1. Evaluate the test expression in the top portion of this structure.
Step 2. If the test expression is true, one set of instructions is executed and then execution exits from the structure. If the test expression is false, a different set of instructions is executed and then execution exits from the structure. Both sets of instructions are contained within this structure.

9. Draw the design diagram that performs as follows:
The entire structure consists of n sets of instructions. Each of the first $n - 1$ sets of instructions begins with a test expression. Execution begins by evaluating the first (i.e., the topmost) test expression. If and only if this test expression is true, the first set of instructions is executed; then the remaining $n - 1$ sets of instructions are skipped, with flow-of-control entering the first statement after this structure. If the first test expression evaluated to false, the first set of instructions is skipped and the second (from the top) test expression is evaluated. If the second test expression is true, the remaining instructions within the second set are executed, the other sets are skipped, and flow-of-control enters the first statement after this structure. If the second test evaluated to false, the remaining instructions within the second set are skipped, and the third test expression is evaluated. If all $n - 1$ tests are false, the last set of instructions is executed, and the flow-of-control leaves the structure.

4

Input and Output with Format Statements

4.1 INTRODUCTION

There have been only a few data items in the programs you have seen so far. However, in many situations the program must be designed to read a very large number of data items. Further, the data may have been obtained from some other source. This may imply that the data are already in a computer-readable form. Such data would be called a data file. But there is a problem: The data are already in computer-readable format. Thus, they may not be prepared so that the programmer can use the very convenient form

```
READ(*,*, END=2) iolist
```

which depends upon the data having been written with one or more blanks as separators and which also depends upon the data being on the file INPUT. More control of the input/output process is needed and is indeed supplied by FORTRAN. The purpose of this chapter is to describe those FORTRAN constructs that may be used by the programmer in order to specify more of the details of the desired input/output.

4.2 REPRESENTATION

A computer must translate numbers given in decimal notation (base 10) and characters (A through Z, ., $, *, and so on) into a form it uses. This implies that eventually, before execution, everything must be mapped onto a series of 1s and 0s, since the computer 'understands' only these sequences of 1s and 0s.

You might find it helpful to keep in mind the following: At the time the computer reads the program and the data, the computer does not know what it is reading.

49

Thus, it reads everything as if it were all characters. It is only after the program has been translated that the information the computer needs to interpret the data is available. The data are said to be **represented** in the computer. There is an exact representation for all integers, but only some reals have exact representations. The algorithm used to represent integers is quite different from the algorithm used to represent reals. This means that the representation of $+1$ as an integer is quite different from the representation of $+1.0$ as a real. The algorithms used to carry out the translation from base 10 (decimal) numbers to the base 2 (binary) representation vary from computer to computer, so we do not describe them here. However, you should be aware of the fact that in most computers, the memory locations in which the represented values are stored *do not contain any associated information about the type of the value being represented*. Not only can a computer not determine the type of numeric value stored in memory, it is also unable to distinguish between character data, instructions, and numeric data. In other words, if a programmer were to see the contents of a location in memory printed as a series of 1s and 0s he or she would not be able to determine what is being represented by the series of 1s and 0s.

4.3 MACHINE-LANGUAGE INSTRUCTIONS

On most computers, when all the addends are integers, one set of instructions is used to perform the addition operations, but when some of the addends are real, different machine-language instructions are used. The type specification provides the information required by the compiler to generate the proper addition instructions.

4.4 COMPONENT FORTRAN CONSTRUCTIONS FOR FORMATTED INPUT

To supply the information that the computer must have to interpret data correctly, FORTRAN includes an OPEN statement, a FORMAT statement, and several input/ output statements. The OPEN statement specifies a file name and the unit assigned to the file. The FORMAT statement supplies a detailed description of the desired material to be treated as input or to be given as output. The input/output statements include a list of the variables that are to be transmitted. This *iolist* used in input/output statements is extremely critical because the FORTRAN system also uses the *iolist* to drive the transmission process. The dual usage of the *iolist* is a subtle notion that will become clearer when examples are considered. Here it is sufficient to state that the program inputs or outputs the elements of the *iolist* by referring to an associated FORMAT statement to make necessary interpretations of the types of the variables being transmitted. Thus, the *iolist* interacts with the FORMAT statement to accomplish the transmission. The result of using a READ statement utilizing a FORMAT statement depends upon the exact layout of the data. The fact that the *iolists* associated with the READ statement, the FORMAT statement, and the data are interdependent sometimes causes conceptual problems for programmers trying to use formatted input/output.

The statements utilized to create formatted input/output are used by the language processor to determine the values. If an input statement is used, the *iolist* specifies where in memory the values are to be stored; that is, the variable names in the list designate the memory locations in which the values being read are to be stored. If an output statement is used, the *iolist* specifies where in the memory the values to be transmitted to the output device are to be found; that is, the variable names in the list designate the memory locations in which the values are to be found. The FORMAT statements used with input statements must supply the information as to where each datum begins and where it ends. The FORMAT statements used with output statements must specify how many columns on the output device are to be used for each datum. Thus, the input/output statements, with their associated format statements, specify which rows and columns are to be interpreted as belonging to which variables.

It may be helpful to think of a grid. For example, many computer screens are able to display 80 columns and 24 rows. For such a screen, we may imagine that there are faint grid lines that divide the screen into 80 × 24, or 1920, small boxes. *Each small box may contain either exactly one symbol or one blank.* Notice that we said *one symbol.* A number is usually composed of several symbols. Thus, 3.1416 is composed of six symbols and would require six boxes in the grid for display. Similarly, -32.0 is composed of five symbols and would require five boxes in the grid for display.

Some of the conceptual difficulty beginning programmers have with input using format statements is the natural tendency to see and to speak of 3.1416, for instance, as a number. That is, we automatically group consecutive digits and think of them as a whole. A computer does not have this capability. In this example, it must be told which set of consecutive columns is to be treated as a single number and also what variable name is to be used for this number. Before we continue with the detailed discussion of the input, FORMAT, and output statements, we will consider the OPEN statement, which makes available to the computer system information as to where data are to be found or where they are to be written.

4.4.1 The OPEN Statement

The OPEN statement is usually written in the form

```
OPEN(UNIT=u,FILE=fin)
```

where *u* stands for the unit number of the file to be opened and *fin* is a character expression whose value is the name of the file to be opened. The first character in *fin* must be an apostrophe; this is followed by a letter, optionally followed by one to five letters or digits, followed by an apostrophe in our system, but there may be some variation in other systems. There are additional parameters that may be incorporated in the OPEN statement, but they are not frequently used by the beginning programmer. One exception is the parameter BLANK = , which is used with the value NULL to specify the interpretation of blanks in numeric fields when read under format control. The unit number is an integer number that is also used as the number of the unit in the input/output statement. Thus, the number in modern computing systems is merely the means of specifying which input/output device is to be used. The operating systems of different computers specify different conventions and restrictions on the range of unit numbers allowed. Usually, these numbers are only nominal numbers; that is, they are merely used as the names of the device, just as the number on a football player's jersey is used to identify the player. The following are examples of the OPEN statement:

```
OPEN(UNIT=12,FILE='MEN')
OPEN(UNIT=15,FILE='MYFILE')
OPEN(UNIT=27,FILE='DATA1')
OPEN(UNIT=38,FILE='DATA2')
OPEN(UNIT=19,FILE='WOMEN')
```

As a stylistic convention, we will open file INPUT on unit 5 and open file OUTPUT on unit 6. We will use the BLANK=NULL parameter on unit 5 and the optional UNIT= form for both files. Thus, we will use

```
OPEN(UNIT=5,FILE='INPUT',BLANK='NULL')
OPEN(UNIT=6,FILE='OUTPUT')
```

for our examples. The exact meaning of the files 'INPUT' and 'OUTPUT' depends upon your computer system and how you are using it. When we use these file names, INPUT refers to the keyboard of our terminal and OUTPUT refers to the screen of our terminal. Once used in an OPEN statement, file names such as INPUT and OUTPUT should not be used as names in other contexts or to designate other files. The other file names used in the examples (MEN, MYFILE, DATA1, DATA2, and WOMEN) were names we created for other files. The use of such additional files is not considered in this text.

    Important.   Always keep an INPUT file separate from an OUTPUT file. On most systems, you will find that the system will not permit you to output on the INPUT file. Nor will you be able to input from the OUTPUT file. However, the system may not prevent you from trying to do both input and output operations on the same file if it is not the system INPUT or the system OUTPUT file. Sometimes a beginning programmer may attempt to write on a file and then read from that same file from the same program. This should not be done!

4.4.2 The READ Statement

The READ statement you have seen,

```
READ(*,*, END=2) iolist
```

is a command to store the values found in the file that had been opened with the unit number specified by the first parameter. The first parameter, in this case the first * in the READ statement, is the unit number — i.e., the number of the unit that contains the data to be read. The asterisk itself may be looked upon both as a placeholder and as an indicator to the system to use the system-defined unit for input.

The second parameter, here containing the second *, is the statement number of the FORMAT statement to be used in transferring the data. When the asterisk is used in this position, the system uses a predefined procedure, which expects blanks to separate each data element.

The third parameter contains the statement label of the statement to which the execution should be transferred if an end-of-file is encountered while attempting to read. You may recall that an end-of-file encounter indicates that the computer has attempted to read more data than are actually present. The *iolist* is a list of the symbolic names. These serve both as the names of the variables and as the names of the locations in memory in which the values of these variables are to be stored.

The following are examples of the READ statement (but they too become fully meaningful only in the context of a full program, which includes the OPEN and FORMAT statements necessarily used with the READ statement):

```
READ(7, 701, END=991) NAME, AGE, SEX, HEIGHT, WEIGHT

READ(7, 713, END=993) METAL, ATWT, TEMP

READ(7, 775, END=935) NAME, STREET, CITY, STATE, ZIP
```

4.4.3 The FORMAT Statement

The standard form of the FORMAT statement is

statement label FORMAT (format specification list)

where the F of FORMAT begins in column 7 or beyond and the closing parenthesis occurs before column 73 (if the FORMAT statement is not continued on subsequent lines). As usual, the statement label is a number appearing in columns 1 through 5 of the line. The format specification list is a list (i.e., elements separated by commas) of edit descriptors. The **edit descriptors** specify how the external data are to be converted to the internal representation. We present here several of the possible edit descriptors available in FORTRAN. These are given in Table 4.1.

TABLE 4.1   FORTRAN EDIT DESCRIPTORS

Form	Usage
Iw	Integers
Fw.d	Reals (floating-point representation)
Gw.d	Reals (an alternative edit specification for floating point representation)
Aw	Characters
BN	(Sets blank significance property to null)
BZ	(Sets blank significance property to zero)
nX	(Skip)
/	(Go to the next line)

The notation used in the edit descriptors may be interpreted as follows: The lowercase w is used to stand for width. Thus, if the datum requires three columns, the width used is 3. If the datum is to be converted to floating-point representation (i.e., type real) then w specifies the total number of columns for the entire number, its decimal point, and any sign. Usually, w is referred to as the field width. That is, a **field** is the total number of columns required to contain the *largest* number of columns needed for the number (one column for each digit, one column for the sign, and one column for the decimal point if the number is real.)

On input, the value of w specifies the field width for the largest possible value that could appear in the *input*. On output, the value of w specifies the field width for the largest possible value that could appear in the *output*. Obivously, to determine an appropriate value for w, a programmer must know the range of possible values for the associated variable.

The integer edit specification, Iw, is the most straightforward. It merely specifies that the number appearing in the w columns is to be converted to an integer representation. Thus, if we let b denote a blank, bbb3 would be interpreted as the positive integer 3 if an I4 edit specification were used. Values from integer 0 through 9999 could be read by the edit specification. If age of humans were to be used as an integer variable in a program, a field width of 2 might be used, thereby permitting integer values from 0 through 99 to be read. If the programmer wanted to be able to record values greater than 99 but less than 1000, then a field width of 3 would be required. In all cases, if $+$ or $-$ signs appear in the data, one additional column is required for the sign.

To save columns in large data files, it has become customary to enter real data without entering the decimal point. This necessitates that the edit descriptor for reals specifies where the decimal point is to go. This is done by the value of d in the edit descriptor. For a floating-point descriptor, the value of w must be large enough to include the number of columns specified by d. (Thus, in the Fw.d edit descriptor, the value of w must be at least 2 plus the value of d to account for both the decimal point and for a possible sign.) *Note:* If a decimal point has been entered in the data, then that decimal point specifies the fractional part and any value of d given in the edit specification is ignored. Consequently, unless you have to prepare a large file of real-valued data, we recommend that you always include the decimal point in real numbers.

On input, the Gw.d edit descriptor works just like the Fw.d edit descriptor. However, on output, it may produce values that the Fw.d edit descriptor is unable to represent. Since a beginning programmer will not likely enounter such values and since the Gw.d edit descriptor appears only in the full-language version of standard FORTRAN, we do not use it.

The input of numbers under format control using the I or F edit descriptors requires some care. Consider the following situation: you enter a single digit, say 3, followed by a carriage return. What value do you expect to be read if you are using an I3 edit descriptor? The answer depends on other attributes of your program or your FORTRAN system. If you are reading from a unit that was opened with the OPEN statement we gave, the system will interpret the number as 3. However, if you did not use our OPEN statement, the number might be interpreted as 300. This depends upon how nonleading blanks are interpreted in a field read by the execution of the I3 edit specification. If the I3 edit specification appeared in a format statement along with a BN edit specification preceding it, the I3 and all subsequent *I* and *F* specifications in that format statement would read values interpreting nonleading blanks as null. The OPEN statement we used included the parameter BLANK= NULL, which determined that nonleading blanks in numeric fields read by the execution of an *I* or a *F* edit specification are to be interpreted as null. (We do not recommend use of the alternative value, BLANK=ZERO. BZ is the edit specification that produces the situation in which blanks may be interpreted as zeros.)

The nX edit descriptor is used to skip *n* columns. This is frequently necessary, as the data as received from some source may include unwanted data—i.e., data that are to be ignored by the program you are writing. The nX edit specification is used in output to skip *n* columns.

In all cases, *w* must be a nonzero, unsigned, integer constant. Also, *d* must be an unsigned integer constant. Finally, *n* must be either a nonzero, unsigned, integer constant or omitted if only one additional column is to be skipped.

4.4.4 Data

Last, but not least, is the data component. We shall consider the data to be on a line, one symbol per column. To talk about the data any further necessitates the introduction of the concept of a field. A **field** is set of adjacent columns that are thought of as a whole. There is no indicator in the data itself where fields begin and end when using FORMATTED input/output. For example, consider the line

```
1984CDC3.1416IBM123456789.123456789.123456789
```

where the first digit appears in column 1 of a line of data. If we were to ask you to guess what fields are present, you might guess that 1984 is a field, 4 columns wide, that contains the year. Also, you might guess that CDC is a field, 3 columns wide, containing the name of a computer manufacturing corporation; that 3.1416 is a field, 6 columns wide, containing the value of the constant PI; and that IBM is another field, 3 columns wide, containing the name of a computer manufacturing corporation. But then it seems impossible to guess what the rest of the line might be. Although these might be good guesses, there is nothing present in the information we have so far supplied that may be used to confirm them.

Data are frequently written without spaces between fields. Although this practice of writing the data without spaces or other indicators of the beginning and the ending of a field makes the result difficult for us to read, it is of no concern to the computer system. The practice of writing data in this compact form arose when punched cards were used in preparing data for the computer. A punched card had only 80 columns in which to record data. Hence, to save space, blanks were not used to separate data items. Consequently, it was necessary for the designers of FORTRAN to include language constructs that permitted the reading of data from such cards. The FORTRAN constructs had to include a means to specify the type of the data — whether they were to be treated as character, integer, or real. It also had to specify how many columns constituted each data field. In addition, there was another space-saving mechanism used with real variables; namely, the omission of the decimal point. For real variables the constructs had to be able to specify where the decimal point was to be. Of course, in addition to describing the nature of the data, the constructs also had to be able to specify the locations in memory into which these data items were to be stored. The specification of the locations was done by having the read statement include a list of the variables. More precisely, the read statement included a list of the symbolic names of variables used in the program. The details of specifying the type of the conversion to be used (whether character, integer, or real) are assigned to the FORMAT statement.

Caution.   It is easy for students to wonder about the necessity to specify the type of conversion wanted in the FORMAT statement when the FORTRAN program already contains type declarations for the variables. The problem arises because by the time the FORTRAN compiler has translated your FORTRAN program into (ultimately) machine language, the compiler no longer has that original type information available. The computer system is not able to detect the occurrence of a mismatch between the declared type and the type conversion specification implied by the choice of edit descriptor. Such a mismatch will produce incorrect results but no notification that an error has been made. *The programmer is responsible for making the type of conversion correspond to the type of the variable.*

4.5 AN EXAMPLE

A program containing the type specifications

```
CHARACTER ADDRESS*29, CITY*15, NAME*29, STATE*2
INTEGER    SSN, YEAR, ZIP
REAL       HOURS, PAYRT, TAXRT
```

and containing the FORTRAN statements

```
      OPEN(UNIT=5,FILE='INPUT',BLANK='NULL')
      READ(5, 501, END=901) NAME, ADDRESS, CITY, STATE, ZIP,
    1 SSN, PAYRT, TAXRT, YEAR, HOURS
  501 FORMAT (A29, A29, / A15, A2, 1x, I5 / I9, F6.3, F3.3, I4, F4.2)
```

when given the following three lines of data:

```
Ms. C. M. Jones               2355 Prospect Street
Okemos       MI 48864
331299889 175631211982412533344455566677788899000
```

would make the assignment of values to variables as given in Table 4.2

TABLE 4.2 ASSIGNMENT OF VALUES TO THE VARIABLES

Symbolic Name of the Variable	Assigned Value
NAME	Ms. C. M. Jones
ADDRESS	2355 Prospect Street
CITY	Okemos
STATE	MI
ZIP	48864
SSN	331299889
PAYRT	17.563
TAXRT	0.121
YEAR	1982
HOURS	41.25

4.6 A FEW ADDITIONAL EXAMPLES

The following specification and OPEN statements are assumed to be in the program unit containing the READ statements used in the examples:

```
OPEN(UNIT=5,FILE='INPUT',BLANK='NULL')
CHARACTER DATE*7, NAME*10, ZEBRA*30
INTEGER   COL, I, INDEX, N
REAL      A, B, C, RN
```

Further, assume that the first character of each data line appears in column 1 of that line. Finally, assume that if there is a blank in a data line between any two characters, there is exactly one blank between the two characters. Finally, assume that 901 is a statement number referring to an output statement that would write a message indicating that an end-of-file was encountered.

The data line

```
1A 1984IS COMING XYZ
```

read by

```
      READ (5, 510, END=901) A, NAME

  510 FORMAT (2X, F5.0, A10)
```

would assign to A the real value

```
                 1984.0
```

and to NAME the character string

```
              IS COMING
```

The rest of the data line would be ignored.

It should be noted that as NAME has been specified to consist of 10 characters, the 10 characters that are stored in the memory location reserved for NAME are

> ISbCOMINGb

where *b* indicates a blank character.

If the same data line were read by

> READ (5, 511, END=901) A, NAME
>
> 511 FORMAT (3X, F4.2, 3X, A8)

then the result would be to assign to A the real value

> 19.84

and to NAME the character string

> COMING X

The rest of the line would be ignored. Again, it should be noted that

> COMINGbXbb

where *b* represents a blank, is actually stored in the memory location reserved for NAME. This is so because the 3X, F4.2, and 3X portion of the FORMAT statement consumes 10 columns. Then, the A8 edit specification reads the next 8 columns, storing the result *left justified* in the location for NAME. As NAME had been specified to provide a maximum length of 10, there are two columns not assigned a value from the execution of the A8 edit specification. These two columns, which are the rightmost columns in NAME, are each assigned the blank character. These columns are said to be **blank filled.** It is common to speak of the A edit specification as a command to *left justify and blank fill*.

If the following two consecutive lines of data,

> 1234567890 JONES AND COMPANY
> 2234567890 CRANE AND COMPANY

were read by the two consecutive statements

> READ (5, 521, END=901) A, NAME
>
> READ (5, 521, END=901) A, NAME

using the format

> 521   FORMAT (F1.0, 8X, A10)

both lines would be read, but the second read would store the information into the same memory locations that were used to store the information read by the first read. (Hence, we may say that *reading is destructive,* meaning that whenever a datum is stored in a memory location, it replaces whatever was previously there and this replacement destroys the previous contents.) After both reads were executed, A would have the real value

$$2.0$$

and NAME would contain the character string

```
O CRANE AN
```

The other material on the lines would have been lost.

If the data line

```
12345678901234567890123456789OABCDEFGHIJKLMNOPQRSTUVWXYZ
```

were read using

```
READ (5, 531, END=901) A, B, C, NAME, ZEBRA

531 FORMAT (F10.5, F10.5, F10.5, A1, A2)
```

we would expect that A, B, and C each would be assigned the real value

$$12345.67890$$

and that NAME would have been assigned the character string

```
Abbbbbbbbb
```

whereas ZEBRA would have been assigned the character string

```
BCbbbbbbbbbbbbbbbbbbbbbbbbbbbbbb
```

which consists of the characters BC followed by 28 blanks. The remaining material on the line would be lost.

Because it is quite common to have a number of values to be read with the same edit specification, the FORTRAN language has incorporated a repeat factor in the edit specification system. Thus, a programmer may write 3F10.5 in place of F10.5, F10.5, F10.5 in a FORMAT statement. Consequently, the preceding FORMAT statement could have been written as follows:

```
531 FORMAT (3F10.5, A1, A2)
```

The result would have been the same as described before. Notice, however, that we cannot combine the A1 with the A2 edit specification, since A1 specifies 1 character and A2 specifies 2 characters.

4.7 FORMATTED OUTPUT

In place of the admittedly convenient PRINT statement, a programmer may specify the exact layout wanted for any output by the use of the WRITE statement. The form of the WRITE statement is

```
WRITE (unit, fmt) iolist
```

where *unit* is the unit number specified in an open statement and *fmt* is the format statement label of the FORMAT statement to be used.

Important.   You should use a unit number to designate an output file that has not been used to designate an input file. Thus, a beginning programmer should NEVER attempt to read and to write on the same file.

The use of the FORMAT statement with a WRITE statement is quite similar to the use of a FORMAT statement with a READ statement. There are, however, two marked differences. When the programmer WRITEs, he or she may include character strings in the FORMAT statement. Also, when the programmer WRITEs, he or she *always* should specify the vertical spacing (i.e., specify on which line the output line is to appear.) Later in this chapter we describe how to specify the vertical spacing.

4.7.1 Character Strings in FORMATs for Output

A programmer may include character strings in a FORMAT statement that is to be used with a WRITE statement. This is done merely by including the character string, enclosed by an apostrophe at each end, in the FORMAT edit specifications. Obviously, the string is inserted in the list of edit specifications at the place it is to appear in the output. A format may express only character string edit specifications if the programmer so desires.

4.7.2 Vertical Spacing and Carriage Controls

When a programmer directs output to the printer, FORTRAN strips off the first character of any line it writes. It does not print this initial character, and it uses the initial character to control the vertical spacing of the output. The system uses the values blank, zero, and one with the standard meanings as follows:

A blank moves to the next line before writing.

A zero inserts a blank line and then moves to the next line before writing.

A one moves to the top of the next page before writing.

It is very desirable to have some method whereby the programmer is always conscious of the distinction between READing and WRITEing with respect to the systems using the first character in the material to be written as a carriage control. Consequently, we urge that the programmer always explicitly use one of these carriage-control edit specifications in each FORMAT statement to be used with a WRITE statement. Therefore, we recommend the use of the carriage controls as specified in Table 4.3 as the first edit specification in each FORMAT statement to be used with a WRITE statement.

TABLE 4.3   CARRIAGE-CONTROL EDIT SPECIFICATIONS

Edit Specification	Meaning
' '	Space vertically to next line before writing
'0'	Space vertically two lines before writing
'1'	Space to top of page (or screen) before writing

Note: The first edit specification is a blank.

4.7.2.1 Examples of writing.   The commands

```
WRITE (6, 601)

601 FORMAT ('1', 20X, 'PROGRAM TESTER FOR PHONES')
```

would produce a line consisting of 20 blanks followed by

```
PROGRAM TESTER FOR PHONES
```

at the top of the page or at the top of the screen.

If RN contained the value 0.713256783 at the time

```
WRITE (6, 602) RN
```

was executed with the format statement

```
602 FORMAT ('0', 'RN = ', F5.2)
```

the system would place on the output line

```
RN =   0.71
```

and nothing else.

Sometimes it is convenient to have a FORMAT-WRITE pair merely to insert two blank lines to separate lines of output. This may be done by the following:

```
WRITE(6, 690)

690 FORMAT('0')
```

The results of output directed to a terminal screen may vary from this, depending upon the particular system you are using.

4.8 RECORDS

Originally, when punched cards were used, a card was said to be one record. The FORTRAN input/output system was developed using the concept of a record. *A READ statement always reads at least one record.* (If it contains the slash edit specification, it will read more than one record.) The system does not provide any means of using two or more read statements to input data from the *same* record.

Most systems used cards that contained 80 columns of data. When punched cards were used, the operating system marked the end of a card (i.e., after the character in column 80 was read, a special character was added to indicate that this was the end of the record.) Unfortunately, when computer systems stopped using cards, the way the system detected the end of a data line on the screen was not standardized. Consequently, this information must be obtained for each system you use. However, if you think of a line on the screen as equivalent to a record, you should not experience difficulties if you write an edit specification list that explicitly includes specifications for all columns on your device.

4.9 STYLISTICS

As we have already mentioned, it is very desirable to keep in mind whether a FOR-MAT statement is used with a READ or with a WRITE. To assist in achieving this, we recommend the following conventions:

(1) Reserve unit 5 for input from the file opened as the INPUT file.

(2) Reserve unit 6 for output to the file opened as the OUTPUT file.

(3) Use format statement numbers in the 500s for any input from the INPUT file.

(4) Use format statement numbers in the 600s for any output to the OUTPUT file.

(5) Use statement numbers in the 500s and in the 600s for no other purpose.

Although FORMAT statements may appear anywhere within the unit that refers to them, we recommend that they be gathered together, ordered by their increasing value, and inserted just before the END statement of the unit in which they are used. We make this recommendation because it assists in increasing the rapid reading of the executable statements in a unit. (FORMAT statements are not executable; they merely supply information to the FORTRAN system.)

4.10 EXERCISES

In Exercises 1–5, assume that the first digit of a data line occurs in column 1. Further, assume that whenever there is a blank within the data line, there is exactly one blank. Assume that the system you are using will treat a blank within a numeric field as a zero. Finally, always assume that the edit specification is appropriate for the type of the variable. For each exercise, indicate the values assigned to all variables listed in the READ statement. Of course, these are to be the values you would expect immediately after the execution of the read statement. The FORMAT statements for Exercises 1–5 are collected and appear after Exercise 5.

1. Data line:

```
97235 941892071

        READ (5, 501, END = 901) HEIGHT, RADIUS
```

2. Data line:

```
97235 941892071

        READ (5, 502, END = 902) HEIGHT, RADIUS
```

3. Data line:

```
2139 2 21 7903

        READ (5, 503, END = 903) X, Y, Z
```

4. Data line:

```
1132122054280713

        READ (5, 504, END = 904) AMOUNT, RATE, TIME
```

5. Data line:

```
99.231-7.921600.03546271
```

```
         READ (5, 505, END = 905) PRES, TEMP, VOL, WEIGHT
```

FORMAT statements for Exercises 1–5 are as follows:

```
501 FORMAT (F5.4, 3X, F6.3)

502 FORMAT (I5, 3X, I3)

503 FORMAT (1X, F3.2, F2.0, F4.2)

504 FORMAT (F4.2, 2X, F3.2, 2X, F4.1)

505 FORMAT (F6.3, F5.2, 2X, F4.2, F5.2)
```

In Exercises 6–10, assume that the variables have the following values. In each case, assume that a listed value with a decimal point is type real and that a value without a decimal point is integer.

VARIABLE	VALUE
ANSWER	-7.965093
DIAM	27.921
HEIGHT	4.23
LENGTH	5724
RESULT	3.001
VOL	210.7982
WEIGHT	17.50
WIDTH	8042
X	-0.231758
Y	+ 3.103309
Z	-0.000001

For each of Exercises 6–10, give the output for each WRITE statement *exactly* as you would expect it to appear. This means you should indicate any and all blanks you would expect and indicate the first print column. The FORMATs appear after Exercise 10.

6. WRITE (6, 600)
7. WRITE (6, 601)
8. WRITE (6, 602) DIAM, HEIGHT, VOL, WEIGHT, ANSWER
9. WRITE (6, 603) X, Y, Z, ANSWER
10. WRITE (6, 604) LENGTH, WIDTH, RESULT

Format statements for Exercise 6–10 are as follows:

```
600 FORMAT ('1', 10X, 'VOLUME OF SPHERES')

601 FORMAT ('0', 2X, 'DIAMETER', 2X, 'HEIGHT', 4X, 'VOLUME', 4X, 'WEIGHT',

  1 'ANSWER')
```

(continues)

```
602 FORMAT ('0', 2X, F8.5, 2X, F6.2, 2X, F10.5, 2X, F6.2, 2X, F10.5)

603 FORMAT (' ', 'X = ', F8.5, 2X, 'Y = ', F8.5, 2X, 'Z = ', F8.5,

   1 'ANSWER = ', F10.5)
```

11. A program contained the specification

```
REAL RESULT
```

and the output statement and its FORMAT

```
WRITE (6, 601) RESULT

601   FORMAT (F4.1)
```

The coder noticed that sometimes the value of RESULT listed on the output was incorrect. Her consultant spotted the probable cause of the difficulty. You are to detect a probable cause of such a symptom, explain the difficulty, and suggest a correction.

12. The design segment

> input A, B, C

was coded as

```
READ (5, 501) A, B, C

501   FORMAT (I6, F10.7, F7.3)
```

which was found to lead to errors in data entry. The systems analyst observed the client using the program and decided that reading three numbers from the same line was too frequently leading to errors in the entry. Consequently, the analyst converted the design to the following:

> input A
>
> input B
>
> input C

Write the code for this alternative design segment, using the same edit specifiers as before.

5

The Design Chapter

5.1 INTRODUCTION

Up to this point in the text, you have been introduced to the ideas of the computer problem-solving process in a form primarily intended to introduce the vocabulary and concepts involved. In particular, although you probably could produce both a design and the code for that design, the program would have to be limited to one that was very similar to those we have used as illustrations in this text. Thus, we expect that at this point in your studies, you are limited to imitation. We consider this quite appropriate. But now we shall turn to a more detailed consideration of the first two steps in the computer problem-solving process. We again state that the computer problem-solving process is composed of the following steps:

(1) Defining the problem
(2) Designing a solution
(3) Coding the design
(4) Designing test data
(5) Testing the code using the test data
(6) Verifying that the code is a correct interpretation of the client's request

In this chapter, we will concentrate on (1) defining the problem and (2) designing a solution. These two steps will be taken as the two major sections of this chapter. The presentation in each section is predicated upon our view that for many individuals, if not for all, it is most efficient to have a clear goal in mind to direct both thinking and acting. We stress this, as our experience in teaching programming and in teaching writing repeatedly demonstrates that a learner who does not have a clear goal in mind is stymied. Some individuals even find themselves completely unable to begin. Symptoms of this problem include such statements as, I don't know where to begin, or I'm at a loss, as well as avoidance behavior.

We also stress the necessity for a clear understanding of the goal for another reason. This second reason for emphasizing the importance of having a clear and complete understanding of the goal, especially the goal in terms of an unambigious and thorough understanding of the problem, is more complicated. This second reason is related to the historical development of programming methodologies. The computer science profession has come to appreciate what is called *top-down step-wise refinement* as a method for developing programs. The phrase top-down is used to characterize the process of program development as one that is hierarchically ordered and as one in which the programmer works from the top down. Specifically, a programmer following this method would design the topmost level of the program first. Then, *before designing the next level down,* the programmer would implement and test this topmost level. Further, the phrase stepwise refinement implies that the design process proceeds via a systematic elaboration of each step. That is, a programmer practicing stepwise refinement initially states a section of the design in the most abstract form and then gradually refines this statement by making this same section more and more detailed.

We advocate this method for professionals. However, we have discovered an important qualification. We feel that a beginning student of algorithmic design should be very careful to complete the first step of the computer problem-solving process, i.e., defining the problem, before he or she attempts to design a solution.

We maintain that most individuals need a clear understanding of the task to be implemented before they begin to develop a method for computer implementation. Further, our experience strongly suggests that students need a clear, unambiguous, and precise criterion to use in determining whether or not they understand the problem. Without such a clear, easily operationalizable criterion, it is meaningless to recommend to a beginner that he or she needs to "understand" the problem. The student needs a specific action that he or she may do to assist in achieving understanding.

All too often we have encountered students who claim to understand the problem but experience extreme difficulty in developing an algorithm. When we have inquired of such students what they perceive to be the source of their difficulties, they are usually rather vague in their responses. However, when working with such students on an individual basis, we have discovered that they seldom have worked through the assigned problem with numerical values and, perhaps, with a calculator. Finally, we have come to realize that a major source of the difficulties of students in engineering and science in learning algorithmic design stems from not having a clear definition of the problem prior to attempting to create a design. The single most critical but missing element is an understanding of the problem at the same level as the level at which the program is to solve the problem. The program is to solve the problem at the numeric level. Thus, to gain an understanding of the problem *at the numeric level,* we must work through the problem using numerical data. To maximize the effectiveness of this step, the correct numerical answer to the problem should be available to verify the numeric computations.

When we say that a student must have a clear goal in mind before starting to design an algorithm, we are stating that to define the problem (i.e., Step 1), the student must have as his or her goal the acquisition of an understanding of how to solve the equations with numerical values. Further, we maintain that this goal can best be reached by solving the equations with numeric values! (Obviously, we imply that you would use noncomputer methods to solve the equations.) These ideas will become more apparent when we consider examples later in this chapter.

Unfortunately, instructors and authors of programming texts may have added to the student's frustration. They sometimes imply that asking about the solution before creating the design of the topmost level violates top-down stepwise refinement methodology. Indeed, when speaking at the design level, it appears to be a violation because the student is attempting to obtain the solution, which is the last thing to be done — that is, the lowest level — before the design, implementation, and testing of the higher levels. But this situation is a result of confusion by all parties. In fact, what the beginning student is trying to do is to understand the problem as part of what we have identified as the first step, to define the problem, *not* as part of the second step, to design a (computer) solution. The student, instructor, and authors of textbooks must keep in mind that defining the problem is the first step of the computer problem-solving process and, hence, *precedes the design step*. Further, our experience with beginning students suggests that frequently they do not understand — and, hence, cannot define — the problem, unless they have in fact correctly worked through one or more numerical examples using noncomputer methods.

5.2 DESIGNS AND THE PROCESS OF CREATING DESIGNS

When an individual who has not yet created a design is shown a computer design and the resulting computer code, it is not unusual for that person to jump to the incorrect conclusion that a design is computer code with boxes around it. Thus, when initially pressed to produce a design (when they do not know how to design) students may attempt to answer the question What is a design? instead of asking How do I design? It is therefore most helpful to distinguish between

the process of designing

from

the result of the process, i.e., a design.

We would like to point out that many individuals have had some experience following a design someone else has created. There are recipes in cookbooks. Instructions in using tools for home repair have been stated as recipes. Even prepared cake mixes come with a recipe on the box. However, we suspect that very few students have had the experience of creating a recipe, especially for some food item sensitive to proportions and technique. Have you ever tried to create a recipe for making a cake? We want to reassure you that the experience of creating a written design for someone else to use is probably new to almost all students. This text is designed for individuals who have never previously created a design. (Further, we hope that you have never had the experience of programming, since bad habits are hard to correct.)

In studying the material on designs, you may find it very helpful to keep in mind that the objective is to make a document (the design) such that it can be read by an optical reader of a computer and automatically coded. (We state this as a way of thinking; we believe something more complicated than this will come to replace the paper form of the design.) Also, you may find it helpful to have some of our answers to the question Why stress designs? The most important reason to stress designs is that designs are helpful in eliminating logical errors before they become incorporated into code. Thus, a design is an aid in obtaining a correct solution. Further, industry and government are convinced that money spent on designing is well spent because a good design keeps down the costs of developing and maintaining programs. Designs serve as a cost-effective means for comparing alternative solutions to the same problem without having to code and implement each design. Rapid and cost-effective problem solving requires that the problem solver eliminate some alternatives without the necessity of producing code and testing the code. Designs also serve as a very convenient method for communicating between humans, including communicating with someone who is not a programmer as well as with a programmer or systems analyst.

5.2.1 The Design Diagrams

A design consists of a combination of control structure diagrams. These component control structure diagrams represent the logical flow of the computations. That is, they convey meaning, and the major type of meaning they convey is the order in which the computations are to be carried out. Therefore, we refer to the design as a flow-of-control diagram as well as a design diagram.

When creating a design for implementation in FORTRAN using the style of programming we are presenting, a complete program consists of two or more *independent units*. Exactly one of these independent units must be a program unit. The other units are subprogram units — usually either a FUNCTION unit or a SUBROUTINE unit. (A FUNCTION unit computes only a single value, which then is associated with the FUNCTION name so that the name may be used in an arithmetic expression. A SUBROUTINE unit is usually used whenever it is desired to compute more than one value in a separate program unit.) As each unit is designed separately and is designed to be independent of other units (except as specifically designed to be coordinated), a separate design is prepared for each unit.

Figure 5.1 illustrates the fundamental structure of a design. There it may be seen that a design is a rectangle with double lines at the top and at the bottom but with little space between the double lines. The rectangle has major horizontal margins, which are the double lines at the top and the bottom. The vertical margins at the right and the left ends of the double lines are the major vertical margins. All four margins are required. Designs should be prepared on unlined paper with each of the four margins specifically drawn.

Figure 5.1 Fundamental Structure of a Design

As Figure 5.2 shows, a design consists of two sections. The first section is a preamble, and the second section is the flow-of-control. The preamble is part of the design. When both the preamble and the flow-of-control cannot be presented on one side of one sheet of paper, terminate the preamble on one sheet; then, on another sheet, present the flow-of-control. We do not recommend using both sides of the sheet of paper, as it is most useful to have these designs so that they may be examined without having to turn over any sheet. If they can be seen as a whole, then we may examine all the designs related to the problem, thereby gaining a better understanding of the whole.

The preamble contains eleven sections. It opens with the key design phrase, "preamble for the," followed by the kind of unit (program, integer function, logical function, real function, or subroutine), followed by the name of that unit.

The second section, beginning with the word ABSTRACT, contains a brief description of what this unit computes. The third section begins with the word INPUT and describes variables to be read during the execution of this unit. The fourth section begins with the word OUTPUT and describes anything to be written from the execution of this unit. It should be noted that both input and output refer only to the process of reading or writing. Neither refers to the communication of information between different units.

Sections 5, 6, and 7 refer only to communication between units. These sections do not refer to reading and writing. These sections always appear in each external function and in each subroutine, but they do not appear in a main program.

The fifth section begins with the phrase ENTRY VALUES and lists (in alphabetical order) those array and variable names that are used as entry values. Thus, the entry values are those that bring values into a subprogram from another unit. Consequently, entry values are the values of the arrays and variables in the argument list that are bringing values into the unit.

The sixth section begins with the phrase EXIT VALUES and lists (in alphabetical order) the array and variable names in the argument list that are being used to transmit values to the calling, or referencing, unit. Normally, there are no exit values in functions.

The seventh section begins with the phrase ENTRY AND EXIT VALUES and lists (in alphabetical order) the array and variable names that are being used both as entry and as exit values. It should be noted that, from the standpoint of good style, only large arrays would possibly be both entry and exit values.

The eighth section begins with the phrase DESIGN HISTORY and contains the list (in chronological order) of all individuals associated with the design of this unit and the dates of their involvement. The ninth section begins with the phrase CODING HISTORY and contains the list (in chronological order) of all coders of this unit and the date of their involvement. The tenth section begins with the word REFERENCE and is a section that lists appropriate references for further details. Thus, for example, if a statistical procedure is being implemented, the published article or book about the procedure is listed here.

The final section is the identifier dictionary, introduced by the phrase ID DICTIONARY. In this section, all identifiers (i.e., programmer-created names) are listed in alphabetical order. The type, meaning, and use are also listed. If some entry preamble for the

ABSTRACT:
INPUT:
OUTPUT:
DESIGN HISTORY:
CODING HISTORY:
REFERENCE:
ID DICTIONARY:
ID   TYPE   MEANING   USE

flow-of-control for

preamble goes here

specifications go here

END of

Figure 5.2   The Two Sections of a Design

is not applicable, this fact is indcated by the standard English abbreviation, NA. (This avoids leaving a blank, which raises the question of whether or not something was accidentally omitted.)

We specify that the list of identifiers be alphabetized in order to speed any subsequent references to the dictionary. In general, we can locate an item in an alphabetized list much more rapidly that in an unalphabetized one. In addition, if the list is alphabetized, it is much easier to locate any accidental omissions. The principle in creating this list is that each and every name you use in the flow-of-control section of this unit must be listed in the ID dictionary. Examples of preambles appear in the first chapter.

Figures 5.3 through 5.5 present the models, or templates, for the flow-of-control for a FORTRAN program unit, a FORTRAN function unit, and a FORTRAN subroutine unit. As you may verify in Figure 5.3, the flow-of-control for the program unit begins with the phrase flow-of-control for program, followed by the name of that program. The program unit closes with the three sections listed there, namely, the key phrases:

```
output 'Normal Program Termination'
STOP
END of PROGRAM _____
```

with the name of the program again appearing, but this time appearing in the location indicated by the blank line. As a note though, be sure to design your flow-of-control so that if you detect an error, you do not output the message 'Normal Program Termination.' (This may be done by writing a message describing the nature of the error you detected and then having an additional STOP section.)

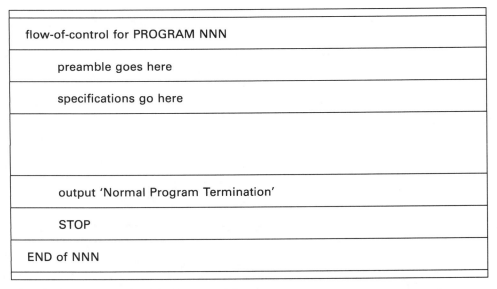

flow-of-control for PROGRAM NNN

preamble goes here

specifications go here

output 'Normal Program Termination'

STOP

END of NNN

Note: NNN should be replaced by the name of the program.

Figure 5.3   Template for the Flow-of-control for a PROGRAM Unit

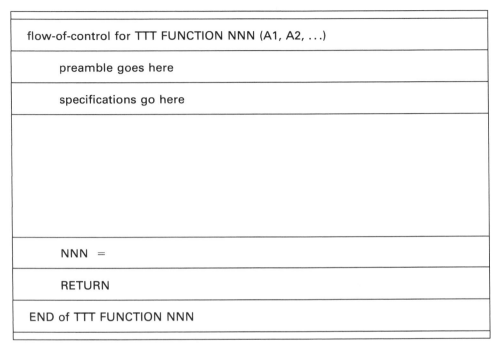

flow-of-control for TTT FUNCTION NNN (A1, A2, . . .)

preamble goes here

specifications go here

NNN =

RETURN

END of TTT FUNCTION NNN

Note: NNN should be replaced by the name of the function, TTT should be replaced by the type
(INTEGER, REAL, etc.) of the function, and A1, A2, . . . should be replaced by the
arguments.

Figure 5.4   Template for the Flow-of-control for a FUNCTION Unit

The major tasks to be accomplished in a program unit are the input of data and
the control of the sequence of execution of the remaining units. In other words, the
program unit controls the flow-of-control during the execution of the coded version
of the algorithm. There must be exactly one program unit in a job. Both in the set of
design units and in the set of code units, the program unit should be the first unit.

Figure 5.4 presents the template for the function unit. There you may see that
the opening flow-of-control section has been expanded to include the type of the
function and the list of the arguments to the function. The function unit closes with
three sections, the first with the name on the left-hand side of the replacement operator (recall that the replacement operator is the = symbol). The syntax of several
common programming languages requires that the name of any function appears
(without the argument list) on the left-hand side of the replacement operator. This
instruction assigns to the name of the function the result of the computations within
the function. We may think of this as assigning the result or the answer to the name.

Normally, immediately following this section will be a section consisting only
of the keyword RETURN, which is taken as a command to return to the unit that
used this function name, substituting the numeric value of the answer for the function name in that referencing unit.

flow-of-control for SUBROUTINE NNN (A1, A2, ...)

preamble goes here

specifications go here

RETURN

END of SUBROUTINE NNN

Note: NNN should be replaced by the name of the subroutine and A1, A2, ... should be replaced by the arguments.

Figure 5.5 Template for the Flow-of-control for a SUBROUTINE Unit

The final section contains the phrase END of _ _ _ _ FUNCTION _ _ _ _ , in which the first blank is the type of the function and the second blank repeats the name of the function.

A FUNCTION unit computes a single value. A programmer may reference the function (i.e., indicate that the function is to be executed) by using the name of the function *in some other unit*. The FUNCTION subprogram construction was provided to ease the task of implementing mathematical functions.

Important. A function that includes within it a command to reference itself is said to be **recursive.** Although some computer languages permit recursive functions, *recursive functions are prohibited in FORTRAN.*

The template for the flow-of-control for a subroutine is given in Figure 5.5. As might be expected, the first section opens with the phrase flow-of-control for SUBROUTINE _ _ _ _ _ , where the name appears in the space reserved by the blank. Following the name is the list of the arguments, enclosed in parentheses, with each argument separated from a succeeding argument (except the last) by a comma. Notice that no type is included for subroutines because subroutines do not have the attribute of type associated with their names.

Both the FUNCTION subprogram and the SUBROUTINE subprogram may be called *procedures*. Procedures are separate units that compute one or more values or do specific tasks. A procedure that is to return a single value may be designed and implemented either as a FUNCTION or as a SUBROUTINE. However, a procedure that is to return more than one value should always be implemented as a SUBROUTINE. There are other differences between FUNCTION subprograms and SUBROUTINE subprograms, but we will not consider them at this time.

Comparing each of the flow-of-control sections, you should observe that each opens with the phrase flow-of-control and each closes with a section starting with the keyword END. The name of the unit appears in both the opening section and in the closing sections. Subprograms (recall that FUNCTIONS and SUBROUTINES are subprograms) include the argument list in the opening section when argument lists will be used for communication of parameters between units.

5.2.2 Control Structure Diagrams

As we have mentioned, there are three general classes of control options available to a programmer, sequence, selection, and repetition. These are further subdivided, producing the following seven possible constructions:

(1) Sequence
(2) 1-alternative selection
(3) 2-alternative selection
(4) *n*-alternative selection
(5) Determinate repetition
(6) Pretested repetition
(7) Posttested repetition

The diagrams for these control structures are given here as Figures 5.6 through 5.12. A comparison of these diagrams should lead you to note the following points: First, each diagram is unique. Thus, each is different from each of the others. Second, each of the selection diagrams contains a dashed horizontal line fairly close to the top of the diagram. The diagram for the 1-alternative selection and the 2-alternative selection contains the word IF, as well as other keyword(s). Third, the shape of each of the diagrams for the alternatives indicating repetition contains an L shape. In one case, it is simply an L in a standard orientation. In another case, it is an inverted L. In the third case, two L's, one in the standard orientation and one inverted, overlap. This last case might be called a square C.

Figure 5.6   Control Structure Diagram for SEQUENCE

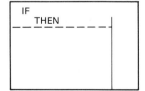

Figure 5.7   Control Structure Diagram for 1-alternative SELECTION

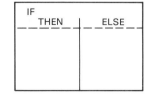

Figure 5.8   Control Structure Diagram for 2-alternative SELECTION

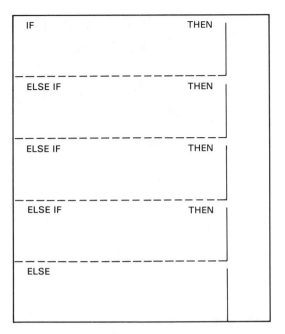

Figure 5.9   Control Structure Diagram for *n*-alternative SELECTION

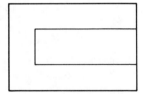

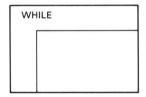

Figure 5.10   Control Structure Diagram for Determinate REPETITION

Figure 5.11   Control Structure Diagram for Indeterminate Pretested REPETITION

Figure 5.12   Control Structure Diagram for Indeterminate Postested REPETITION

5.2.2.1 Design contents: vocabulary to be used.   A designer may use standard mathematical notation where appropriate, but programmer-created names should be used for all constants and variables. A + is used to indicate addition, − is used to indicate subtraction, * is used to indicate multiplication, / is used to indicate division, and ** is used to indicate exponentiation. Notice that programming languages do not permit implied multiplication, so multiplication must be indicated using the * symbol.

An example of implied multiplication given *in algebraic notation* is

$$ax$$

This notation indicates that the value of the variable a is to be multiplied by the value of the variable x. This notation cannot be used in programming languages that permit AX to represent the name of a single variable because the language translator could not distinguish between the two notations if implied multiplication were permitted. Thus, the expression

$$ax$$

in algebraic notation must be represented as

$$A*X$$

in a design.

In addition to these constructs, the following words or phrases may be used in designs (a blank is used where the programmer-created name is to appear):

echo
ELSE
ELSEIF
END of integer function _ _ _ _ _ _
END of logical function _ _ _ _ _ _
END of real function _ _ _ _ _ _
flow-of-control for integer function _ _ _ _ _ _
flow-of-control for logical function _ _ _ _ _ _
flow-of-control for real function _ _ _ _ _ _
flow-of-control for PROGRAM _ _ _ _ _ _
flow-of-control for SUBROUTINE _ _ _ _ _ _
IF
input
output
preamble
preamble for integer function _ _ _ _ _ _
preamble for logical function _ _ _ _ _ _
preamble for real function _ _ _ _ _ _
preamble for PROGRAM _ _ _ _ _ _
preamble for SUBROUTINE _ _ _ _ _ _
prompt
RETURN
specifications
STOP
THEN
UNTIL
WHILE

When echo, output, or prompt are used, they probably will include some message to be written on the output device. The message should be surrounded by apostrophes. Items not surrounded by apostrophes in any list following the words will be interpreted as the names of variables for which the values are to be written on the output device. For example, in a design

```
output 'The value of X is ', X
```

is to be interpreted as a command to print the message

```
The value of X is
```

with a numeric value (taken to be the value of the variable X) appearing on the same line after the word is.

5.2.2.2 Design contents: vocabulary to be avoided. Just as certain words and phrases are to be expected in designs, there are some words, phrases, and constructions that should be avoided in designs. *Avoid the following words or phrases:*

CONTINUE
DO
FOR
GO TO
label
REPEAT

In addition, you should avoid any attempt to create a flow-of-control other than the seven listed earlier in this chapter. (If you have programmed before, you may already be conditioned to think in terms of a GOTO construction. The GOTO construction is not permitted in the design of a program in a structured programming methodology.)

5.2.3 Combining Flow-of-control Diagrams

There are only two ways to combine the flow-of-control diagrams. We can stack one upon another, or else we can nest one within another. However, there is a tendency for beginning students to nest too deeply. As a rule of thumb, if you find that you cannot write the design on a $8\frac{1}{2}$-in.-by-11-in. sheet of paper (oriented as a letter) because it is not wide enough, then you have probably created a design that is too deeply nested. A beginning student should not have to create a deeply nested structure. (We have seen a student create one 32 levels deep, which is asking for trouble!) There are tasks that are best treated by a series of nested selections, but these should be reserved for a programmer with more experience. At this point, if a student designs a program with more than three levels, the student is probably doing too complex a design. We would advise such a student to try to redesign the program to avoid this nesting.

5.2.4 Interpretation of Designs

You may recall our initial definition of a design:

> A design is a written description of the program in the form of a diagram, which can be given to a coder for translation into FORTRAN statements. Thus, a design represents an intermediate step in the programming process. It comes between the first

step, defining the problem, and the third step, coding. In this position in the programming process, a design should be decidedly simpler than the computer code to be generated, yet precise enough so than coding from the design is a straightforward task for a coder experienced in FORTRAN. At the same time, the design must be more detailed and more organized than the revised client's request.

Insofar as possible, the design should be relatively independent of the computer language used to code the program. Although we stated the initial definition in terms of implementation in FORTRAN, we have in fact attempted to keep the design structure independent of the specifics of any particular programming language designed for implementation of scientific problems in a structured manner. Thus, the designs could just as well be implemented in the programming languages Ada, ALGOL, or Pascal.

5.3 EXAMPLE 1

Suppose that we now have a personal computer and we want to develop an algorithm to balance a checkbook. To gain an understanding of the problem, we probably would begin by looking at last year's checkbook. There we would examine the section in which the amount of each check was recorded. Let us assume that we found in January there was a starting balance of $1,037.27. Then, during the month there were the entries

    101.73,   10.73,   23.75,   2.30,   10.00,   171.95,   230.55

representing the seven checks written during January and

            202.77,   205.34,   200.89,   198.65

representing four deposits.

Next, we might use a calculator to work out the balance at the end of the month. We would either have to turn on the calculator, or, if it was already on, clear the memory. Then we would enter each item, in chronological order, with a + sign before the starting balance and before each deposit and with a − sign before the value of each check. Following this method, the sequence would be:

$$+1037.27$$
$$-101.73$$
$$-10.73$$
$$-23.75$$
$$+202.77$$
$$-2.30$$
$$-10.00$$
$$+205.34$$
$$-171.95$$
$$+200.89$$
$$+198.65$$
$$-230.55$$

Then, we would depress the = button to obtain the end-of-the-month balance. If we had not made any errors, we would have the end-of-January balance as 1293.91 (dollars).

In this case, balancing the checkbook using a calculator is close to the way a computer would do it. The natural way to do this task using a calculator is to accumulate the current balance. (If we were doing this computation using paper-and-pencil methods, we would add all the deposits to the starting balance, add all the checks to obtain the sum of the withdrawals, and then subtract the withdrawals from the balance.)

5.3.1 Design of an Algorithm To Balance a Checkbook: An Initial Attempt

How do we convert the calculator method to a design for a computer program? Recall our design goal — we want to design a program unit that performs any required initialization of variables and then controls the rest of the computational process, leaving to subprogram units the arithmetical operations and all other operations required to compute the result. Further, recall that we always want to design the topmost level first. Consequently, when we reexamine our calculator method to look for the first task, we see that we either turned on the calculator or cleared the display. Then we entered the starting balance. This completed the initialization.

If we were to construct a design equivalent to this initialization, we might think of the calculator display as accumulating the balance. Naturally, when we moved to a design, we might represent this as a real variable, choosing, perhaps, BAL as the name of the variable. Then we might initialize BAL by the design segment

```
BAL = 0.0
```

which would be the analogue of clearing the display window. Then we might have the design seqment

```
input BAL
```

which would be used to enter the starting balance. (You may already be thinking ahead and, if so, you might have detected something odd about this decision. But for the moment, we are going to leave both of these design segments in our repertoire in order to continue the development of the design. Later, we may alter this design.)

Reexamining the steps used in the calculator method, we see that we next entered the transactions in chronological order. Consequently, to convert this to a design, we would want to input the amount of the transaction and then add this to the previous balance. But if we were to repeat "input BAL," we would destroy the previous value in the memory location reserved for the value of BAL, replacing it with the last value read. We want to accumulate the balance. This would necessitate our creating another variable, say AMOUNT, which would be used to take the new input. Then, later, we could add this value to BAL. Therefore, we have determined that we need an additional design section,

```
input AMOUNT
```

somewhere after the initialization by means of the input BAL section but before the section in which we add the new AMOUNT to the previous value of BAL.

But how are we to accumulate in BAL? Recall that we are practicing top-down design. This design philosophy would require that the computations be done at a lower level. Thus, let us merely create a section that would call a subroutine to perform the actual accumulation of the balance for all the transactions that occurred during the month of January. Thus, we would have the section

```
CALL ADDER(AMOUNT, BAL)
```

Recapitulating, we would have the segments

```
BAL = 0.0

input BAL
```

followed by the pair of consecutive sections

```
input AMOUNT

CALL ADDER(AMOUNT, BAL)
```

So far we have entered only two values, the starting balance and the first transaction. Obviously, we need to add the remaining values. We could accomplish this by using the SEQUENCE control structure repeatedly. If so, then we might attempt to accomplish this by making an appropriate number of explicit occurrences of the pair

```
input AMOUNT

CALL ADDER(AMOUNT, BAL)
```

which would look like the following:

| BAL = 0.0 |
| input BAL |
| input AMOUNT |
| CALL ADDER(AMOUNT, BAL) |
| input AMOUNT |
| CALL ADDER(AMOUNT, BAL) |

and so on, one pair of

| input AMOUNT |
| CALL ADDER(AMOUNT, BAL) |

for each transaction. This approach to the organization of the flow-of-control is constructed by using the SEQUENCE structure exclusively.

As you might suspect, this would work for a particular number of values—i.e., it would work for the case in which the number of pairs of

| input AMOUNT |
| CALL ADDER(AMOUNT, BAL) |

corresponded to the exact number of items to be entered. But if we had examined the list of transactions for February, we probably would have discovered that the number of transactions in February was not the same as the number of transacations in January. Consequently, we would have to redesign the program for each month. This is quite awkward, although it does require a programmer, and if you were in the programming profession you might like that!

But there is a better alternative. We recognize that we want to make the computer work for us. So we can let the computer itself determine how many times the pair

| input AMOUNT |
| CALL ADDER(AMOUNT, BAL) |

is to be repeated. Thus, we want to control the number of repetitions. Therefore, we abandon the SEQUENCE control structure and ask ourselves whether it is a SELECTION control structure (which alternative? or select an alternative.). The task does not lend itself to expression as a selection from a fixed list of alternatives. Consequently, we ask ourselves whether it can be expressed as a REPETITION (repeat or loop a number of times.). Because we have described it to ourselves as a repetition, we conclude that it probably would be represented as one of our varieties of repetition constructions. We then ask ourselves which kind, determinate or indeterminate? As this situation appears to be the very common one of wanting to command the computer to read data as long as data are present but terminate data reading after all of the data are used (at least all the entries for the month of January), we decide that it must be the common indeterminate repetition, WHILE-there-are-data, which is the same form as the pretested indeterminate repetition.

In terms of the control diagrams, this conclusion may be stated as requiring this control structure:

WHILE-there-are-data

But how is this section of the design to be related to those we have so far considered? That is, how do we assemble the following segments with the diagram for the pretested indeterminate repetition? Thus, the task is to organize the following in a manner that fulfills the needs of the task:

BAL = 0.0

input BAL

input AMOUNT

CALL ADDER(AMOUNT, BAL)

WHILE-there-are-data

If we examine this design, we can see that

BAL = 0.0

and

```
input BAL
```

must occur in the order given. However, we might now detect something odd about this pair of blocks. The first block assigns the value of zero to the variable, BAL. But the second member of the pair inputs a value and assigns this new value to BAL, replacing the 0.0 just assigned. Consequently, it is now apparent that we do not need to have the block that assigns zero to BAL. (The calculator analogy is not perfect.)

We desire the program to input AMOUNT each time and then accumulate AMOUNT in BAL. Thus, we need to have the input of the AMOUNT and the accumulation of BAL *inside* the repetition WHILE-there-are-data. Consequently, we are led to the following design segment:

```
input BAL

WHILE-there-are-data

     input AMOUNT

     CALL ADDER(AMOUNT, BAL)
```

All we have to do to represent the last step of the calculator design is to include a design section to represent the very last step, which, when using our calculator, is to depress the key with the = sign on it. The action on the calculator is to present in the display window the value of BAL, that is, the balance at the end of the month. As this corresponds to the command to output the value of BAL, we use the following diagram to do this:

```
output BAL
```

Again, we must ask where we place this in our design structure. Obviously, we want to place it after the last transaction for the month has been entered. Clearly, it must be inserted after the statement

```
CALL ADDER(AMOUNT, BAL)
```

but we have two possibilities. First, we could insert it immediately after CALL ADDER(AMOUNT, BAL) but within the repetition loop. This would appear in the diagrammatic form as

input BAL
WHILE-there-are-data
input AMOUNT
CALL ADDER(AMOUNT, BAL)
output BAL

and would have the effect of displaying the value of BAL after the first transaction was entered. A computer program using this method would give the value of BAL after *each* January transaction.

There is an alternative, which is to place the statement as the first block immediately after the completion of the pretested indeterminate loop. Consequently, in terms of the diagrams, this would result in the following structure:

input BAL
WHILE-there-are-data
input AMOUNT
CALL ADDER(AMOUNT, BAL)
output BAL

If the subroutine ADDER did not contain any output statements, this design would result in a computer program that would output a single value, namely, the value of BAL after the last data value was read.

We seem to have the main program complete. If so, the major remaining task is to design the procedure ADDER. Recall that we decided that ADDER was to have two arguments, AMOUNT and BAL. The purpose of procedure ADDER is to add the value of the transaction, given as the value of AMOUNT, to the current value of BAL. (Remember that if the value of AMOUNT is negative, the procedure will add a negative value, thereby subtracting the value of AMOUNT.) Consequently, the computation required would be designed as the following block:

BAL = BAL + AMOUNT

This would take the current value of BAL, add the value of AMOUNT to it, and then store this new value in the location associated with the variable, BAL.

At this point we have the major components of the designs for the main program and for the subroutine. We have yet to embed these components into the standard templates for a main program and for a subroutine. As these templates have already been given, we will not repeat them apart from the design we have been developing. Consequently, we may now assemble these decisions and present the flow-of-control section for the main program and for the subroutine subprogram. See Figure 5.13.

We have yet to complete this design process. We invite you to examine the designs in the earlier chapters to ascertain what remains to be done. If you examine the earlier designs, you would no doubt notice that we have yet to write the preamble for each of these program units. But we also have another addition to make. We are designing programs for eventual implementation in an interactive environment. Any interactive program that is designed to request an entry from the user at the terminal must include a prompt for the data. (This is necessary because otherwise the computer might be waiting for an entry from the user while the user is waiting for "something to happen.") We have combined these requirements and now are

flow-of control for PROGRAM CHKBAL
preamble goes here
specifications go here
input BAL
WHILE-there-are-data
input AMOUNT
CALL ADDER (AMOUNT, BAL)
output 'The balance is', BAL
output 'normal program termination'
STOP
END of PROGRAM CHKBAL

Figure 5.13 Flow-of-control for PROGRAM CHKBAL and for SUBROUTINE ADDER (First Design)

```
flow-of-control for SUBROUTINE ADDER (AMOUNT, BAL)

    preamble goes here

    specifications go here

BAL  =  BAL  +  AMOUNT

RETURN

END of SUBROUTINE ADDER
```

Figure 5.13   (continued)

prepared to present the final designs for CHKBAL and ADDER. These are shown in Figures 5.14 and 5.15.

5.4 DESIGN HINT: THE HEART OF THE MATTER

In developing designs for computer implementation of an algorithm, it is not difficult to lose sight of the big picture. We would like to remind you of this big picture

preamble for PROGRAM CHKBAL

ABSTRACT:		CHKBAL is an interactive program to compute the balance of your checking account at the end of a month	
INPUT:		starting balance followed by an entry for each transaction	
OUTPUT:		balance in your account at the end of the month	
DESIGN HISTORY:		Proud P. C. Owner, 12JUN83	
CODING HISTORY:		none	
REFERENCE:		none	
ID DICTIONARY:			
ID	TYPE	MEANING	USE
ADDER	NA		subroutine name (2 arguments)
AMOUNT	real	the starting balance or the amount of a transaction	variable
BAL	real	the accumulating or running balance	variable

(continues)

Figure 5.14   Preamble and Flow-of-control for PROGRAM CHKBAL (Final Design)

flow-of-control for PROGRAM CHKBAL
preamble goes here
specifications go here
prompt 'Give the starting balance. If negative, precede the first digit by a negative sign.'
input BAL
WHILE-there-are-data
prompt 'Give the amount of the transaction, preceded by a negative sign if the amount is to be subtracted from your current balance'
input AMOUNT
CALL ADDER (AMOUNT, BAL)
output 'The balance is', BAL
output 'normal program termination'
STOP
END of PROGRAM CHKBAL

Figure 5.14   (continued)

and then make a few additional comments about the design process before we consider a second design example.

The heart of computation is a three-step process:

INPUT—TRANSFORMATION—OUTPUT

which is to say that ultimately, computation is nothing more than the process of performing a series of transformations upon some input to produce the desired output.

This does not sound complicated, does it? Yet even experienced systems analysts sometimes lose sight of this fact! We urge you to remember this idea in the form of a basic question to consider when attempting to create a design. Thus, we

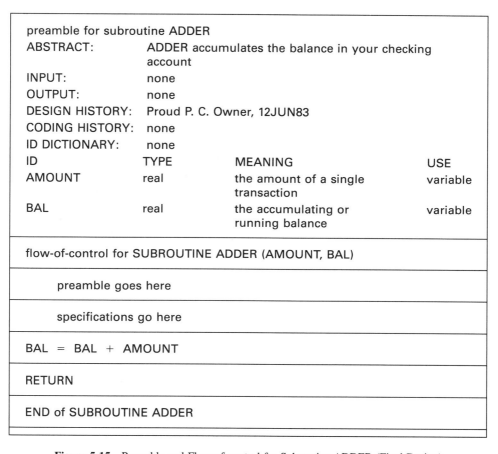

preamble for subroutine ADDER

ABSTRACT:	ADDER accumulates the balance in your checking account
INPUT:	none
OUTPUT:	none
DESIGN HISTORY:	Proud P. C. Owner, 12JUN83
CODING HISTORY:	none
ID DICTIONARY:	none

ID	TYPE	MEANING	USE
AMOUNT	real	the amount of a single transaction	variable
BAL	real	the accumulating or running balance	variable

flow-of-control for SUBROUTINE ADDER (AMOUNT, BAL)

preamble goes here

specifications go here

BAL = BAL + AMOUNT

RETURN

END of SUBROUTINE ADDER

Figure 5.15   Preamble and Flow-of-control for Subroutine ADDER (Final Design)

suggest you ask yourself,

> What is the INPUT-TRANSFORMATION-OUTPUT series needed to solve this problem?

5.5 DESIGN HINT: THE MATHEMATICAL DEFINITION OF THE PROBLEM

A large proportion of users of this text will be using programs to solve mathematical equations with numeric data. A beginning programmer is likely to neglect to ask, Are there any *mathematical limitations* on the input values? That is, are there any possible values that lead to undefined or meaningless mathematical expressions? If a mathematical expression is undefined, the computer transformations of input should not be expected to make sense. The most familiar example is the problem of division by zero. The process of dividing by zero is *not defined* in mathematics, but every process in a computer is designed to lead to a result, although some results are meaningless. What happens when a computer is instructed to divide by zero depends upon the particular computer system being used. But in all cases, the computer results are meaningless. It is important for all programmers to be cautioned about this type of a problem, because *there is no standard in the computer industry requiring that the user be notified when a meaningless computation has occurred.* Consequently, whenever a design is created, the resulting code should include provisions for detecting exceptional cases and taking whatever action is deemed appropriate. In the case of division, a denominator that is the result of computation should be tested for zero before attempting to use the value as a denominator.

Further, the units of measurement must be appropriate to the problem and consistent throughout the solution of the problem. Therefore, great care must be exercised to ensure that the specifications for each function supplied by the system (such as the square root function or the trigonometric functions) are meticulously observed. As an example, the values of some of the trigonometric functions available in the system library may require arguments in radians. If supplied arguments are in degrees, the results will be wrong, but the computer cannot inform the user that an error exists. In general, it is the responsibility of the designer to ensure that the requested transformations, given the input, make mathematical sense. Further, it is the designer's responsibility to alert the coder to any restrictions on the possible values for each input variable and to include in the design a means to verify that all input values satisfy all restrictions.

Another design matter related to the mathematics of the problem is that many problems fall into a few related but distinct cases. When this is the case, the designer should consider these cases separately in the initial stages of developing a numeric solution and in the initial stages of the construction of a design. If there are three distinct cases, then the designer should work through three distinct sets of data, one for each of the three cases. Likewise, when moving toward the design phase, the systems analyst should specifically examine to what extent the different cases are distinct. He or she should consider whether or not it would be useful to pull out some portion of the computation that is common to several cases and perform this computation in a separate unit. But it does not necessarily follow that because there are three separate mathematical cases, there should be three separate design units. Nor does it follow that the division into separate units should be the same as the mathematical division into distinct cases.

5.6 A SECOND DESIGN EXAMPLE

5.6.1 A Program Request

A program that computes the roots of a quadratic equation is needed.

5.6.1.1 Background.   A quadratic equation is of the form

$$y = ax^2 + bx + c$$

with roots (the value(s) of x, given values for the constants a, b, and c, that result in a y value of zero) given by the formula:

$$x = \frac{-b + \sqrt{b^2 - 4ac}}{2a}$$

and by

$$x = \frac{-b - \sqrt{b^2 - 4ac}}{2a}$$

There are either two distinct real roots, one real root, or two imaginary roots.

The roots are real if

$$b^2 > 4ac$$

The roots are degenerate (i.e., the two roots become one root) if

$$b^2 = 4ac$$

and the roots are imaginary if

$$b^2 < 4ac$$

5.6.1.2 The systems analyst's thoughts.   What is the INPUT-TRANS-FORMATION-OUTPUT series needed to solve a quadratic equation? For each equation to be processed, the inputs are the values of a, b, and c in the quadratic equation. The output consists of one of the three statements

There are two real roots.

There is one real root.

There are two complex roots.

together with one or two labeled numeric values representing the values of x that solve the quadratic equation. The transformations required to obtain these values of x are the two expressions given for x:

$$x = \frac{-b + \sqrt{b^2 - 4ac}}{2a}$$

and

$$x = \frac{-b - \sqrt{b^2 - 4ac}}{2a}$$

Evidently, there are three mathematically distinct cases. Consequently, we shall construct three different numerical examples to assist us in understanding the problem. In each case, we have to select a set of values for the constants a, b, and c. As nothing particular is said about the possible values for the constants, it appears that we could select almost any real values. However, if we consider the mathematical development of the equation, we see that a quadratic equation would no longer be a quadratic equation if the constant a were to take on the value zero. Consequently, we cannot assume that a takes on a zero value. We also notice that the constant a appears in the denominator of the formula that gives the solution. This too implies that the constant a cannot take on a value of zero. (If we recall the special characteristics of zero, we would be cautious about the use of zero as a constant in any attempt to construct a numerical example.)

In the construction of a numerical example, we want to make simple examples. In the case of the expressions that give the solution to the quadratic equation, we observe that we must take a square root. This leads us to try to construct a set of constants that make the expression under the square root sign a perfect square. Further, in the construction of the examples, we will use values for the constants that do not involve fractions. However, we must note that there is no mathematical restriction to whole numbers so that when we design and implement a program to obtain the solution, we must utilize variables that are type real for these constants. We shall consider the three cases separately.

5.6.1.3 Example 2: numerical example, case of two real solutions.   The mathematical discussion of the solution of the quadratic equation included the information that there are two (distinct) real solutions when

$$b^2 > 4ac$$

Consequently, we seek values for the constants that will produce a value of the square of b larger than the value for the product $4ac$. After a few attempts, we find that the values

$$a = 1, \quad b = 4 \quad \text{and} \quad c = 3$$

yield a perfect square for the expression

$$b^2 - 4ac$$

thereby producing a simple numerical example.

Evaluating the formula for the roots of a quadratic equation in which $a = 1$, $b = 4$, and $c = 3$ yields one solution of -1 and another of -3. We then verify our understanding and our calculations by evaluating the quadratic equation $x^2 + 4x + 3$ for $x = -1$ and $x = -3$. Both values of x should yield a value of zero for y, which they do. This affirms both that we understand the problem and that we have not made any calculation errors.

5.6.1.4 Example 2: numerical example, case of one real solution.   Again, we refer to the mathematical discussion of the quadratic equation. There is one solution to the quadratic equation when

$$b^2 = 4ac$$

Consequently, for the case of one real solution, we seek values of the constants for which the square of b is equal to the product $4ac$. Trial and error yields the values

$$a = 1, \quad b = 2, \quad c = 1$$

as having the properties we desire. Using these values, we solve for x, obtaining the solution

$$x = -1$$

We notice that because the factor under the radical sign is zero, we, in fact, can have only one solution. To be sure that we have understood the mathematics and have not made an arithmetical error, we use the set of constants for this case with a value of -1 for x to solve for y. Again, we obtain a value of zero for y, verifying our work to this point.

5.6.1.5 Example 2: numerical example, case of two imaginary solutions.
There are two imaginary solutions when

$$b^2 < 4ac$$

A little exploration gives the possible set of values

$$a = 1, \qquad b = 2, \qquad c = 2$$

Recalling that i is used as the indicator of the imaginary number in mathematics
and that

$$i^2 = -1$$

we indicate the square root of -4 (i.e., the value of the expression under the square
root sign in the formula for the root of the quadratic equation) by

$$2i$$

and then continue the evaluation of the formula to obtain as one solution

$$x = -1 + i$$

and, as the other,

$$x = -1 - i$$

Finally, using these solutions and the selected constants, we test to see whether or
not they result in a value of zero for y in each case. (Although they do so, we highly
recommend that you verify this for yourself.)

5.6.1.6 Example 2: design considerations.   We shall create several different designs. Each will have the same structure for the main program. But the remaining portion of the design will vary. We will begin with a design that is closest
to the logic of the mathematical statement of the problem, and then, in later designs,
consider different and more attractive alternatives. They are considered to be attractive because we will eventually implement the design on a computer and may wish
to consider alternatives that look as if they are more efficient. Thus, the second and
third design for the subprograms will be closer to a computer statement of the problem. At this point, we stress that there is nothing 'wrong' with any of these alternative designs. There are various trade-offs in using one rather than another.

Because the first version is closer to the mathematical statement of the problem, we anticipate that it will be easier for a student to understand the flow-of-control. Further, unless we begin with a version close to the mathematical statement of
the logic, we needlessly create the possibility the design process will look like a collection of unrelated "tricks" to be memorized and recalled upon demand.

5.6.1.7 Example 2: design of the main program.   We require a main
program to read an indefinite number of data sets. For each set, it must verify that
the constant a is not zero. If a is zero, an error message must be written. If a is not
zero, a procedure should be called to solve for the roots of the equation. We continue to assume that the program will be implemented as an interactive program. The
design for the main program is given in Figure 5.16. There it may be seen that we
chose to call this program QUAD1.

5.6.1.8 Example 2: design of SOLVE1.   SOLVE1 must do three tasks.
First, SOLVE1 must determine which of the three cases is implied by the values of

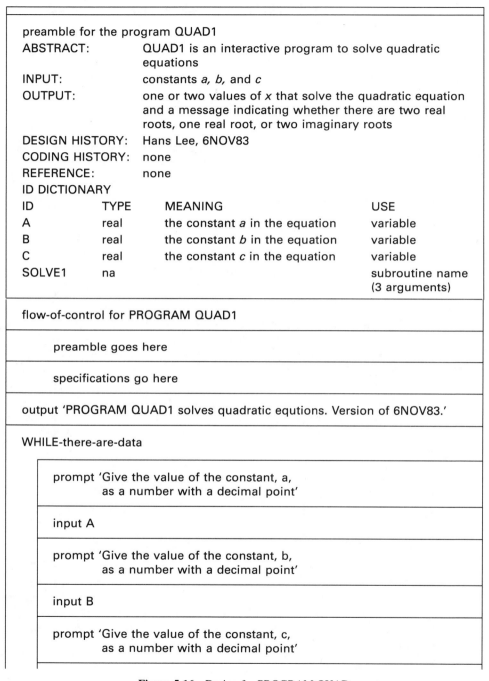

preamble for the program QUAD1

ABSTRACT:		QUAD1 is an interactive program to solve quadratic equations	
INPUT:		constants *a, b,* and *c*	
OUTPUT:		one or two values of *x* that solve the quadratic equation and a message indicating whether there are two real roots, one real root, or two imaginary roots	
DESIGN HISTORY:		Hans Lee, 6NOV83	
CODING HISTORY:		none	
REFERENCE:		none	

ID DICTIONARY

ID	TYPE	MEANING	USE
A	real	the constant *a* in the equation	variable
B	real	the constant *b* in the equation	variable
C	real	the constant *c* in the equation	variable
SOLVE1	na		subroutine name (3 arguments)

flow-of-control for PROGRAM QUAD1

preamble goes here

specifications go here

output 'PROGRAM QUAD1 solves quadratic equtions. Version of 6NOV83.'

WHILE-there-are-data

prompt 'Give the value of the constant, a,
    as a number with a decimal point'

input A

prompt 'Give the value of the constant, b,
    as a number with a decimal point'

input B

prompt 'Give the value of the constant, c,
    as a number with a decimal point'

Figure 5.16 Design for PROGRAM QUAD

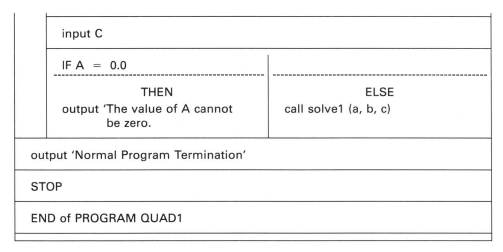

Figure 5.16   (continued)

the constants *a, b,* and *c.* That is, SOLVE1 must determine whether there are two distinct roots, one real root, or two imaginary roots. Second, SOLVE1 must output a message indicating the result of this determination. In other words, SOLVE1 must output "there are two real roots," "there is one real root," or "there are two imaginary roots." Third, SOLVE1 must obtain the root(s) of the equation. That is, SOLVE1 must obtain the value(s) of *x* that yield a value of zero for *y.*

The design for SOLVE1 is shown in Figure 5.17.

5.6.1.9 Example 2: discussion of SOLVE1.   We now should examine SOLVE1 to see whether there are any alternative designs. We notice that to determine which case we have, we must examine some or all of the following three relational expressions:

```
B*B > 4*A*C
B*B = 4*A*C
B*B < 4*A*C
```

In addition, we notice that within each selection we must compute the value of the following expression once or twice:

```
B*B - 4*A*C
```

Further, we must take either the real square root of this expression or else we must take the complex square root of this expression. We recall that in the mathematical description of the problem there are three distinct cases, depending upon the relationship of the value of b^2 to the value of $4ac$.

In light of the recurrence of these terms in the selection blocks, we are alerted to the need to reexamine the way b^2 and $4ac$ appear in the quadratic formula. We see that b^2 and $4ac$ are the sole constituents of the expression under the square root sign. We also note that they appear as $b^2 - 4ac$.

preamble for SUBROUTINE SOLVE1

ABSTRACT:	SOLVE1 solves the formula $(-b + \sqrt{b^2 - 4ac})/2a$ and the formula $(-b - \sqrt{b^2 - 4ac})/2a$ for x in a quadratic equation.		
INPUT:	none		
OUTPUT:	A message reporting whether there are one or two roots, whether the root(s) are real or imaginary, and the value(s) of the root(s).		
DESIGN HISTORY:	Hans Lee, 6NOV83		
CODING HISTORY:	none		
REFERENCE:			

ID DICTIONARY

ID	TYPE	MEANING	USE
A	real	the constant a in the equation	argument
B	real	the constant b in the equation	argument
C	real	the constant c in the equation	argument
CX1	complex	one complex root	variable
CX2	complex	the other complex root	variable
X1	real	one real root of the equation	variable
X2	real	the other real root (if there are two roots)	variable

flow-of-control for SUBROUTINE SOLVE1 (A, B, C)

preamble goes here

specifications go here

IF B * B > 4.0 * A * C
                            THEN
----
output 'There are two real roots.'

$X1 = (-B + \sqrt{B^2 - 4.0 * A * C})/(2.0 * A)$

$X2 = (-B - \sqrt{B^2 - 4.0 * A * C})/(2.0 * A)$

output 'X = ', X1, 'or X = ', X2

IF B * B = 4.0 * A * C
                            THEN

Figure 5.17 Design for SUBROUTINE SOLVE1

```
-------------------------------------------------------------------------------
output 'There is one real root.'
-------------------------------------------------------------------------------
X1  =  ( − B  +  √B² −  4.0 *A * C) * (2.0 * A)
-------------------------------------------------------------------------------
output 'X  =  ', X1
-------------------------------------------------------------------------------
IF B * B  <  4.0 * A * C
                              THEN
-------------------------------------------------------------------------------
output 'There are two imaginary roots.'
-------------------------------------------------------------------------------
                                              caution:
                                              complex
CX1  =  ( − B  +  √B² −  4.0 * A * C)/(2.0 * A)  root
-------------------------------------------------------------------------------
                                              caution:
                                              complex
CX2  =  ( − B  −  √B² −  4.0 * A * C)/(2.0 * A)  root
-------------------------------------------------------------------------------
output 'X  =  ', CX1, ' or X  =  ', CX2
-------------------------------------------------------------------------------
RETURN
-------------------------------------------------------------------------------
END of SUBROUTINE SOLVE1
-------------------------------------------------------------------------------
```

Figure 5.17   (continued)

Because the three cases and the determination of which case is which depend upon the relationship between b^2 and $4ac$, we could restate the criteria for recognizing the cases in terms of the value of the difference between b^2 and the value of the product $4ac$. To aid our thinking, we make Table 5.1.

TABLE 5.1   THE THREE CASES OF THE SOLUTION OF THE QUADRATIC EQUATION

Case	Solution Type	Stated Criterion	Corresponding Criterion in Terms of the Difference between b^2 and $4ac$
1	Two distinct real solutions	$b^2 > 4ac$	$b^2 - 4ac > 0$
2	One single real solution (degenerate)	$b^2 = 4ac$	$b^2 - 4ac = 0$
3	Two distinct imaginary solutions	$b^2 < 4ac$	$b^2 - 4ac < 0$

Reflecting upon these observations, we are led to consider an alternative design in which we introduce a new real variable, which we call TERM and which appears as follows:

```
TERM = B*B - 4*A*C
```

Then we could write, for the respective selection statements in the design,

```
IF TERM > 0.0
IF TERM = 0.0
IF TERM < 0.0
```

Then, we might be tempted to carry this reasoning a step further by the introduction of another variable, say, RTERM (for root of TERM), defined as:

```
RTERM = SQRT(TERM)
```

which is, evidently, an indication that the designer would like to take the square root of the value of TERM and assign the result to RTERM. (We have not discussed the collection of functions available in the FORTRAN system, but, in fact, there is such a collection, it does include a function to take the square root of a positive real-valued variable, and the way it is used is as shown.)

You might suspect that this would not work. But apart from the way we worded our discussion, there is another clue to potential design difficulties. We just indicated that the square root function will take the square root of a positive real value. But for the complex case, the value of TERM will not be positive. Consequently, a designer must resort to the use of another function supplied by the FORTRAN system, which will take the complex root. Such a function is available in standard FORTRAN. We will return to a consideration of this possibility later. At the moment, we will abandon the attempt to use

```
RTERM = SQRT(TERM)
```

and merely incorporate the first change introduced. We present this as the design of SOLVE2, given here in Figure 5.18. The only difference in the program unit is that SOLVE2 is substituted for SOLVE1 in invoking the procedure, so the program unit is not rewritten here.

5.6.1.10 Example 2: design of SELECT.
Suppose we now examine SOLVE2. We might now notice that it is rather long. Can we follow the recommended strategy of making units small? It looks as if we can if we extract the task of determining which of the three cases we have from the task of computing the solutions, given that we know which case is at hand. Consequently, we could imagine the introduction of a procedure, which we will call SELECT, that computes the value of TERM, selects which case we have, and then uses a specific procedure for the appropriate case. In other words, instead of a main program and the procedure SOLVE2, we would have a main program, a procedure, SELECT, and three additional procedures, say, CMPLXR for CoMPLeX Roots, RRONE for Real Root ONE, and RRTWO for Real Roots TWO.

preamble for SUBROUTINE SOLVE2

ABSTRACT:	SOLVE2 solves the quadratic formula for *x*		
INPUT:	none		
OUTPUT:	A message reporting whether there are one or two roots, whether the root(s) are real or imaginary, and the value(s) of the root(s).		
DESIGN HISTORY:	Hans Lee 7DEC83		
CODING HISTORY:	none		
REFERENCE:			
ID DICTIONARY:			

ID	TYPE	MEANING	USE
A	real	the constant *a* in the equation	argument
B	real	the constant *b* in the equation	argument
C	real	the constant *c* in the equation	argument
CX1	complex	one complex root	variable
CX2	complex	the other complex root	variable
TERM	real	$b^2 - 4*a*c$	variable
X1	real	one real root of the equation	variable
X2	real	the other real root (if there are two roots)	variable

flow-of-control for SUBROUTINE SOLVE2 (A, B, C)

preamble goes here

specifications go here

TERM = B $*$ B $-$ 4.0 $*$ A $*$ C

IF TERM $>$ 0.0

                          THEN
----

output 'There are two real roots.'

X1 = ($-$ B $+$ $\sqrt{\text{TERM}}$)/(2.0 $*$ A)

X2 = ($-$ B $-$ $\sqrt{\text{TERM}}$)/(2.0 $*$ A)

output 'X = ', X1, ' or X = ', X2

Figure 5.18   Design for SOLVE 2   *(continues)*

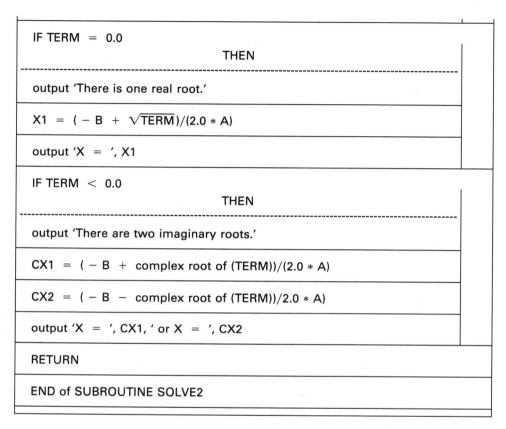

IF TERM = 0.0
                        THEN
----
output 'There is one real root.'

X1 = (− B + √TERM)/(2.0 ∗ A)

output 'X = ', X1

IF TERM < 0.0
                        THEN
----
output 'There are two imaginary roots.'

CX1 = (− B + complex root of (TERM))/(2.0 ∗ A)

CX2 = (− B − complex root of (TERM))/(2.0 ∗ A)

output 'X = ', CX1, ' or X = ', CX2

RETURN

END of SUBROUTINE SOLVE2

Figure 5.18   (continued)

We have created some of the appropriate designs and presented them here as Figures 5.19–5.20.

5.6.1.11 Example 2: another alternative.   Recall that we started to consider the possibility that we could create another alternative if we could take the square root of TERM in the procedure SELECT. However, we temporarily abandoned that idea because of the problem of taking the square root of a negative number. We now return to a consideration of yet another design in which we do take the root of TERM before we invoke the appropriate procedure to compute the value of the roots of the quadratic equation.

A reexamination of the three mathematical cases would show that only when we have the complex root do we have to be concerned about how to take a complex root of TERM. If this case were eliminated, then for all the remaining cases, we could merely use

$$RRTERM = SQRT(TERM)$$

preamble for subroutine SELECT (A, B, C)

ABSTRACT:		SELECT determines which of three solution cases for the quadratic equation is at hand	
INPUT:		none	
OUTPUT:		none	
DESIGN HISTORY:		Hans Lee, 7DEC83	
CODING HISTORY:		none	
REFERENCE:			

ID DICTIONARY

ID	TYPE	MEANING	USE
A	real	the constant a in the equation	argument
B	real	the constant b in the equation	argument
C	real	the constant c in the equation	argument
COMPLXR	na	the procedure that computes the complex roots	subroutine name (2 arguments)
RRONE	na	the procedure that computes the single (i.e., one) real root	subroutine name (2 arguments)
RRTWO	na	the procedure that computes the two real roots	subroutine name (2 arguments)
TERM	real	$B * B - 4 * A * C$	variable

flow-of-control for SUBROUTINE SELECT (A, B, C)

preamble goes here

specifications go here

TERM $= B * B - 4.0 * A * C$

IF TERM > 0.0
                                THEN

CALL RRTWO (B, TERM)

IF TERM $= 0.0$
                                THEN

CALL RRONE (B, TERM)

Figure 5.19   Design of SUBROUTINE SELECT   *(continues)*

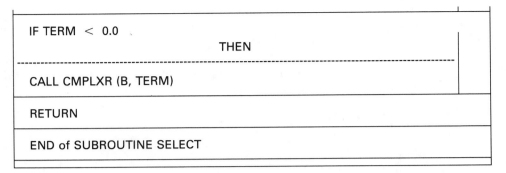

IF TERM < 0.0

THEN

CALL CMPLXR (B, TERM)

RETURN

END of SUBROUTINE SELECT

Figure 5.19   (continued)

preamble for SUBROUTINE CMPLXR

ABSTRACT: CMPLXR obtains the complex roots
INPUT: none
OUTPUT: A message reporting that there are two complex
                       roots together with the numeric values of each
                       root.
DESIGN HISTORY: Hans Lee 7DEC83
CODING HISTORY: none
REFERENCE: none
ID DICTIONARY:

ID	TYPE	MEANING	USE
A	real	the variable a in the equation	argument
B	real	the variable b in the equation	argument
CX1	complex	one complex root	variable
CX2	complex	the other complex root	variable
TERM	real	$b^2 - 4*a*c$	argument

flow-of-control for SUBROUTINE CMPLXR (A, B, TERM)

preamble goes here

specifications go here

output 'There are two imaginary roots.'

CX1 = (− B + complex root of TERM)/(2.0 ∗ A)

CX2 = (− B − complex root of TERM)/(2.0 ∗ A)

Figure 5.20   Design of SUBROUTINE CMPLXR

output 'X = ', CX1, ' or X = ', CX2
RETURN
END of SUBROUTINE CMPLXR

Figure 5.20   (continued)

meaning that we could indicate that the Real Root of TERM is to be assigned the value of the SQuare RooT of TERM. Thus, we might be led to consider rearranging the order of the selections and, at the same time, changing to a series of nested selections, starting with the complex case first. For the complex case, we would want to introduce a different variable, for instance, CRTERM (for Complex Root of TERM), as the name of the value of the complex root of TERM. To obtain this value, we would need to use an appropriate FORTRAN routine. For the design level, we will indicate that the complex root is wanted merely by stating the assigment statement as

```
CRTERM = complex root of TERM
```

which will be taken as sufficient to alert a FORTRAN coder to use the appropriate routine.

5.7 EXERCISES

1. A university assigns course grades of 0.0, 2.0, 2.5, 3.0, 3.5, and 4.0. Suppose an instructor designs a course so that a student might earn from 0 to 100 points during the term. You are to prepare a flow-of-control design segment that assigns a course grade on the basis of the total number of points a student has earned. The instructor used the following scale:

GRADING SCALE

Total Points	Course Grade
90–100	4.0
85–89	3.5
80–84	3.0
75–79	2.5
70–74	2.0
Below 70	0.0

For your design segment, you should use entirely selection control structures. You should use the variable names TOTAL and GRADE for the total number of points a student earned and for the corresponding course grade to be assigned. Notice that the instructor designed the course such that the maximum number of possible points a student could earn was 100. There was no way for a student to earn negative points. In Exercises 2–8 are various possible alternative designs for the grade-assignment task described in Exercise 1. Understanding of combinations of selection control structures requires careful attention to alternative possible control structures. To maximize your learning experience, we suggest that you first complete Exercise 1. Then, for each of the remaining selection exercises, we recommend that, *without trying out specific set of values of total earned points,* you examine each design, and, for each, *write down* whether you believe that the design is correct. Also, note any poor design features you find.

2.

| IF (TOTAL > 90) THEN |
| GRADE = 4.0 |
| IF (TOTAL ≥ 85) THEN |
| GRADE = 3.5 |
| IF (TOTAL ≥ 80) THEN |
| GRADE = 3.0 |
| IF TOTAL ≥ 75) THEN |
| GRADE = 2.5 |
| IF (TOTAL ≥ 70) THEN |
| GRADE = 2.0 |
| IF (TOTAL ≥ 70) THEN |
| GRADE = 0.0 |

3.

| GRADE = 0.0 |
| IF (TOTAL ≥ 70) THEN |
| GRADE = 2.0 |
| IF (TOTAL ≥ 75) THEN |
| GRADE = 2.5 |

IF (TOTAL ≥ 80) THEN
GRADE = 3.0

IF (TOTAL ≥ 85) THEN
GRADE = 3.5

IF (TOTAL ≥ 90) THEN
GRADE = 4.0

4.

GRADE = 0.0

IF (TOTAL ≥ 70) THEN
GRADE = 2.0

IF (TOTAL ≥ 75) THEN
GRADE = 2.5

IF (TOTAL ≥ 80) THEN
GRADE = 3.0

IF (TOTAL ≥ 85)	
THEN	ELSE
GRADE = 3.5	GRADE = 4.0

5.

```
IF (TOTAL ≥ 90) THEN
    GRADE = 4.0
ELSEIF (TOTAL ≥ 85) THEN
    GRADE = 3.5
ELSEIF (TOTAL ≥ 80) THEN
    GRADE = 3.0
```

```
----------------------------------------------------------------|
    ELSEIF (TOTAL ≥ 75) THEN
        GRADE = 2.5                                             |
----------------------------------------------------------------|
    ELSEIF (TOTAL ≥ 70) THEN
        GRADE = 2.0                                             |
----------------------------------------------------------------|
    ELSE
        GRADE = 0.0                                             |
```

6.

```
    IF (TOTAL < 70) THEN
        GRADE = 0.0                                             |
----------------------------------------------------------------|
    ELSEIF (TOTAL ≥ 70) THEN
        GRADE = 2.0                                             |
----------------------------------------------------------------|
    ELSEIF (TOTAL ≥ 75) THEN
        GRADE = 2.5                                             |
----------------------------------------------------------------|
    ELSEIF (TOTAL ≥ 80) THEN
        GRADE = 3.0                                             |
----------------------------------------------------------------|
    ELSEIF (TOTAL ≥ 85) THEN
        GRADE = 3.5                                             |
----------------------------------------------------------------|
    ELSE
        GRADE = 4.0                                             |
```

7.

```
    IF (TOTAL < 70) THEN
----------------------------------------------------------------|
        GRADE = 0.0                                             |
----------------------------------------------------------------|
    IF ( 70 ≤ TOTAL ≤ 74 ) THEN
----------------------------------------------------------------|
        GRADE = 2.0                                             |
----------------------------------------------------------------|
    IF ( 75 ≤ TOTAL ≤ 79 ) THEN
----------------------------------------------------------------|
        GRADE = 2.5                                             |
```

```
IF ( 80 ≤ TOTAL ≤ 84 ) THEN
------------------------------------------------------------
     GRADE = 3.0
IF ( 85 ≤ TOTAL ≤ 89 ) THEN
------------------------------------------------------------
     GRADE = 3.5
IF ( 90 ≤ TOTAL ≤ 100 )
              THEN                    |          ELSE
----------------------------------------------------------------
     GRADE = 4.0                      |   output error message
```

8.

```
IF (TOTAL < 70) THEN
     GRADE = 0.0
------------------------------------------------------------
ELSEIF ( 70 ≤ TOTAL ≤ 74 ) THEN
     GRADE = 2.0
------------------------------------------------------------
ELSEIF ( 75 ≤ TOTAL ≤ 79 ) THEN
     GRADE = 2.5
------------------------------------------------------------
ELSEIF ( 80 ≤ TOTAL ≤ 84 ) THEN
     GRADE = 3.0
------------------------------------------------------------
ELSEIF ( 85 ≤ TOTAL ≤ 89 ) THEN
     GRADE = 3.5
------------------------------------------------------------
ELSEIF ( 90 ≤ TOTAL ≤ 100 ) THEN
     GRADE = 4.0
------------------------------------------------------------
ELSE
     output error message with value of TOTAL
```

9. After you have completed the examination of the selection exercises in Exercises 2–8, we recommend that you return to Exercise 1 and then for it and all the other selection exercises, follow the flow-of-control for the following test data. It is important that for each value of POINTS you go through the *entire* control structure to determine the grade that structure would assign to that student.

TEST DATA FOR GRADE
ASSIGNMENT DESIGNS

Student	Total Points
Joe	0
Frank	75
Mary	82
Carol	91
Fran	61
Jo	103

10. The following design segment illustrates at least two errors. First, explain in detail what this segment does; second, explain why this is probably not what was intended; third, correct the design.

```
WHILE-there-are-data
    prompt for last name
    input last name
    prompt for first name
    input first name
prompt for grade
input grade
```

6

Arrays

6.1 INTRODUCTION

Up to this point, we have used only variables. Associated with a variable are a name, a value, a type, a location in memory, and, finally, an address. The *name* is the symbolic name created by the designer for that variable. The *value* is the value of that variable at a given point in time. The *type* is the specified type, for example, INTEGER or REAL. The *location* is a memory location where the computer system stores the value of the variable. The *address* is the address of the location in memory where the value of the variable is stored. A variable of either type INTEGER or type REAL occupies exactly one memory location. The symbolic name of a variable consists exclusively of a combination of up to six letters or digits, with the first character of the name restricted to being a letter.

In this chapter we introduce arrays. Unlike variables, arrays were designed to refer to a series of values. In mathematical notation an expression such as

$$x_1, x_2, x_3, x_4, x_5$$

involving *x*, here with subscripts 1, 2, 3, 4, and 5, probably would be represented in a computer program by a one-dimensional array. It would be natural to use X as the name of the array. But the specifications for an algorithm using X as an array would include the specifications that give the language translator the information it requires to reserve at least five or more locations for X. Obviously, the language syntax must also provide for some means to refer to any individual value. Thus, X serves as a family name, and the subscripts serve as modifiers that designate or point to individual members of the "X family." When FORTRAN was initially implemented, there was no easy way to represent subscripts as subscripts. That is, there was no way to write a symbolic name that included a variable number written below the line. The developers of FORTRAN chose to use a syntax that followed the symbolic name by parentheses, which enclosed the subscript. The symbolic name and the subscript, with the enclosing parentheses, are to be written on the same line, although they are still called subscripts. To use the computational capabilities of a computer in a reasonable manner, the subscripts may be INTEGER digits, such as 1, 2, 3, in X(1), X(2), X(3), and so on, or they may be INTEGER variables, such as I or ROW in X(I), X(ROW), or so on, where I or ROW are variables of type INTEGER and have values consistent with the number of memory locations reserved for the array X in its specification.

Associated with an array is a symbolic name, a subscript, a range of possible subscript values, several values, several memory locations, several addresses, and a type. The phrase *a type* indicates one very important property of any array in FORTRAN 77. *All values of a given array must be of the same type.*

Most of the discussion will focus on arrays with one or two dimensions. We begin with the one-dimensional array.

6.2 THE ONE-DIMENSIONAL ARRAY: NOTATION AND VOCABULARY

A one-dimensional array element is indicated by a symbolic name followed by parentheses, which enclose a single subscript. The subscript may be an integer or a variable that is of type INTEGER. Thus, if GRADE, NUMBER, S, X, Y, XY, and Z are specified to be one-dimensional arrays and if I, N, and NUM are type INTEGER, then the following are acceptable names, with subscripts for the designated array:

```
GRADE(10)
GRADE(12)
GRADE(1)
GRADE(I)
GRADE(N)
NUMBER(3)
NUMBER(81)
NUMBER(I)
NUMBER(N)
S(11)
S(37)
S(NUM)
X(1)
X(5)
X(I)
Y(6)
Y(9)
Y(I)
XY(1)
XY(2)
XY(N)
Z(33)
Z(88)
Z(N)
```

Consider the last example in the list, Z(N). Z is the symbolic name of a one-dimensional array. N is the symbolic name of a variable of type INTEGER.

Just as values may be assigned to variables, values may be assigned to arrays. In either case, this may be done by input or by assignment. Suppose that we used an assignment to give the value of 3.1416 to XY(2). This would be represented in a design as follows:

```
XY(2) = 3.1416
```

Such an assignment would be valid if the array XY had been specified to be type REAL. Be sure to distinguish between the value of the array and the subscript. In this example, the subscript is 2, and the value stored at the location indicated by XY(2) is 3.1416. Also, notice that a type is associated with the array, and a type is associated with any variable used for a subscript. Only integers or INTEGER variables should be used for subscripts.

Sometimes a beginning programmer jumps to the conclusion that each element of an array is automatically set to zero by the compiler without any specific instructions by the programmer to do so. Unfortunately, although setting all the elements of an array to zero automatically is a logically appealing idea, FORTRAN standards do not specify that this must be done. Thus, we strongly recommend that a programmer always supply appropriate values to all elements of an array that are going to be used. You know about two ways to assign values to an array — by input or by assignment. To set all values of a REAL one-dimensional array X to zero, where the specification for X was for X to have space reserved for a maximum of 100 values, we could use a determinate repetition. The design segment to represent this is as follows:

```
FOR I FROM 1 TO 100

    X(I) = 0.0
```

This design segment shows a determinate repetition, which controls the nested sequence. The effect of this segment would be first to assign the INTEGER variable I the value 1 and then to assign to X(1) the value 0.0; then I would be assigned the value 2, X(2) would be assigned the value 0.0, and so on, until eventually I would be assigned the value 100 and X(100) would be assigned the value 0.0, and the flow-of-control would leave this block.

Suppose that the specification for Y is that Y is to be a REAL one-dimensional array with space for 100 values. In a design to be implemented on an interactive system, a client might want to be able to input one value per line into the array Y. This could be done by the following design segment:

```
FOR J FROM 1 TO 100

    input Y(J)
```

A client may have occasion to use a program with an array but with the dimension varying from data set to data set. This is easy to accommodate. All that is required is that the specification for the array gives the *maximum* size that is expected. Then, as long as no data set exceeds the maximum size specified, all the client needs to do is to input the number of elements for each data set. The design of such a segment would be similar to the following:

```
prompt 'Give the number of values to be read.'

input NVALS

FOR K FROM 1 TO NVALS

    input XY(K)
```

For this to be correct, the maximum size that XY could assume must have been specified. The method for specifying the dimensional information will be presented later. The value assigned to K cannot exceed this maximum size. If, at any time, K does exceed the specified maximum size, an error situation will result. (The symptoms of such an error depend upon the particular FORTRAN compiler. In general, a programmer cannot depend upon a compiler to issue an error message in this situation.) The value given on input for NVALS cannot exceed the maximum size specified for the array XY. Consequently, it would be wise to have the prompt message for the value of NVALS indicate the range of possible values. Thus, the design segment for this prompt might better be as follows:

```
prompt 'Give the number of values (from 1 to 100 only) to be read.'
```

Of course, this prompt implies that the maximum size specified for the one-dimensional array XY is 100.

6.2.1 Use of Two or More One-dimensional Arrays

Just as a program may use more than one array, a program may use several one-dimensional arrays. However, the design considerations become more dependent upon the specifics of the application. One significant factor that leads to important design factors is the nature of the data. Specifically, the layout of the data governs the design of the input section. For example, if four different measurements are taken on each subject in a nutrition study, it is most likely that the data, before being input into the computer, are recorded as four numbers on a single line for each subject. Thus, if the four factors in the study were age, calories, height, and weight, each appropriately measured and preceded by an accompanying identification number, the data for a set of four subjects might appear as follows:

326	35	2146	73	180
327	43	2308	75	197
328	26	2532	71	173
329	39	1900	69	161

We urge our readers to take a few moments to sharpen their skills at making reasonable guesses about data by identifying each column in this sample portion of the data for the nutrition study. Being able to make educated guesses is a valuable skill for a designer, coder, or maintainer of programs, as well as for anyone else analyzing or using data. Such a skill frequently assists in spotting errors in the data or preventing the occurrence of errors in the design or implementation of programs.

If the client requests a program to assist in the subsequent analysis of these data, a designer could consider the use of five one-dimensional arrays. They might be called ID, AGE, CAL, HEIGHT, and WEIGHT. Further, we suggest that ID be type INTEGER, whereas all the others should be type REAL. Admittedly, though, there is no compelling reason that ID be type INTEGER. Presumably we have verified with the client (and also by inspection of the data) that the numbers used for the subject identification contain no fractional parts. But even if the subject identification numbers were all whole numbers, there still is no strongly compelling reason for the designer to make them INTEGER. But we will leave the design with ID of type INTEGER and the other arrays of type REAL. As the data were recorded by the researcher in the format given previously, it is natural to input the five values for one subject from a single line. Consequently, this would lead to the following design section:

```
input NSUBS

FOR N FROM 1 TO NSUBS

    input ID(N), AGE(N), CAL(N), HEIGHT(N), WEIGHT(N)
```

NSUBS would be an INTEGER variable that would be used to receive the number of subjects for which data are to be read. This particular form of a design for input of the five one-dimensional arrays probably would be used to read five values from each line. If this design segment were to be implemented as an interactive program, appropriate prompt messages would have to be added.

6.2.2 Mathematical Operations Using One-dimensional Arrays

Frequently, a researcher makes a series of observations on a number of factors, such as in the nutrition study described. As part of the analysis of such data, a number of statistical summary measures may be used, such as the mean and the standard deviation of each factor or the correlation between two or more factors. Although we do not elaborate on the statistical measures at this time, we use some of the required calculations as an example of mathematical computations with data recorded in one-dimensional arrays. Because these statistical calculations are usually described in terms of general abstract arrays, such as x or y, rather than HEIGHT or WEIGHT, we also describe the design in terms of abstract array names. We assume that there are n observations on two related factors, x and y. In mathematical notation, we can state this as two sets of observations:

$$x_1, x_2, x_3, x_4, \ldots, x_n$$

and

$$y_1, y_2, y_3, y_4, \ldots, y_n$$

The statistical measures will require that we obtain the following quantities, expressed in mathematical notation:

$$\Sigma x_i \qquad \Sigma y_i \qquad \Sigma x_i^2 \qquad \Sigma y_i^2 \qquad \Sigma x_i y_i$$

where summation for each, indicated by the uppercase Greek letter sigma, is over all values, that is, for

$$i = 1, 2, \ldots, n$$

for each quantity.

We will use

SUMX, SUMY, SUMXSQ, SUMYSQ, and SUMXY,

as the array names for the variables that will accumulate these sums.

There are two alternative ways to input the values and obtain the required quantities. In the first method, all the values are read before the sums are obtained. Obviously, this logical structure is quite clear. The design segment that illustrates this method is given as Figure 6.1.

As an alternative to reading all the values for x and y before obtaining the sums, an algorithm might specify that the sums are obtained after reading each pair x, y. The design for this alternative is given in Figure 6.2.

This second method may not appear very complicated. In fact, whether or not you conclude that the first method is logically simpler may be a matter of personal taste. Either method should produce the same numerical results. There may be a dif-

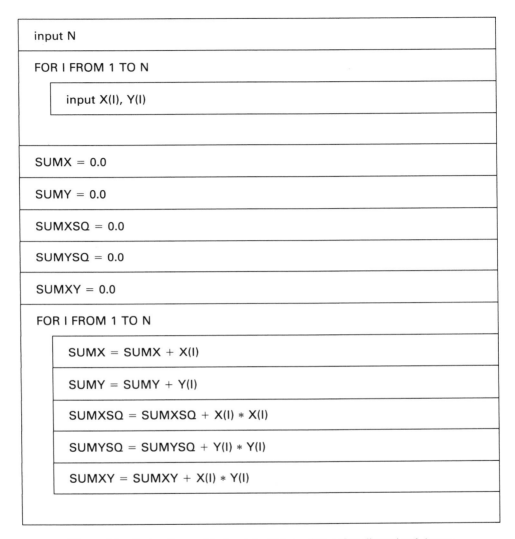

Figure 6.1   Design Segment to Input the Values of Two One-dimensional Arrays
and to Obtain Several Statistical Quantities

ference in the time required to execute each version, but without specific tests with almost each possible computer system, it would be difficult to judge in advance which is more efficient for the task. Further, which is more efficient may be dependent upon the number of elements in the array. But we feel that a student of this text should not be overly concerned about considerations of efficiency. As computer systems become more refined, it is preferable for a systems analyst to expect the system to be efficient. Instead of spending time on considerations of efficiency in execution, a better allocation of the student's time is to try to achieve a logically easy to understand design.

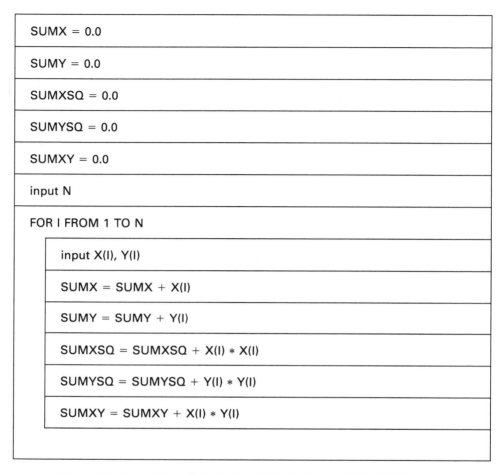

Figure 6.2   Design Segment for Another Method to Input the Values of Two One-dimensional Arrays and to Obtain Several Statistical Quantities

These design segments illustrate the use of one-dimensional arrays in arithmetic expressions. At this point in this text, we will leave the statistical quantities as they are and move on to consider arrays that have two dimensions.

6.3 TWO-DIMENSIONAL ARRAYS

A two-dimensional array is an array that has two subscripts. Thus, equations that have two subscripts may use two-dimensional arrays. However, arrays are an advanced variety of data structures in computer utilization. Thus, they lend themselves as a 'natural' means of representing and manipulating a variety of data. A two-dimensional array may be used to represent data in a table that has rows and columns. But a table is not the same thing as the mathematical entity known as a matrix. A matrix may appear to be the same as a table in some instances, but a matrix, which is studied in linear algebra, is treated as a unit. There are well-defined operations upon matrices, such as addition and multiplication. On the other hand, if the data are presented as a table with rows and columns, there are probably no meaningful operations on the entire table as a whole. Nonetheless, both tables and matrices may be represented as two-dimensional arrays. Much of the time, when a two-dimensional array is being used, we shall speak of an array with rows and columns, where rows are the horizontal components and columns are the vertical components. Mathematical texts (especially those published outside of the United States) may not follow this use of row to refer to the horizontal dimension and column to refer to the vertical dimension.

6.3.1 Input and Output of Two-dimensional Arrays

The input and output of two-dimensional arrays depend upon the data and the computational setting. When a two-dimensional array is used, the number of memory locations required is given by the product of the number of rows and the number of columns. Thus, an array with 4 rows and 5 columns requires that space for 20 elements be reserved. In many scientific applications, considerably larger arrays are required. It is not uncommon to see arrays with up to 100 rows and 100 columns or more. Such an array would require 10,000 memory locations. Typically, very large arrays are used in conjunction with programs written by professionals and may be designed for supercomputers. In any case, we do not discuss the design of input and output for very large arrays.

If the total number of elements in an array is small and if the program is to be developed for a microcomputer or for interactive use on a larger computer, the easiest method for input is to enter one element on each line, each in response to an appropriate prompt message. For example, if an array A has been specified to be a two-dimensional array with a maximum of 10 rows and 10 columns, a design might ask for NROWS, the number of rows actually needed for the particular data set to be entered, and NCOLS, the number of columns actually needed for the data set. (It is quite customary merely to specify a maximum size for an array. The user then needs to input the actual size used, as long as the required size is no larger than the maximum size actually reserved for the array.) A possible design for inputting a small array in this interactive situation is given in Figure 6.3.

On the other hand, some users might prefer to enter all elements of a row of the array as an entire line. Thus, for an array with four columns, for instance, such a user would want to enter four numbers on one line. A design segment to accomplish this is given in Figure 6.4.

6.3.1.1 A few operations on two-dimensional arrays.   We can set each element of a two-dimensional array to zero very easily. A design segment to accomplish this is shown in Figure 6.5.

The design segment presented in Figure 6.5 sets each element of an array to zero. The array, whose name is ARRAY, is assumed to be a REAL-valued array. The design assumes that MNROWS is an INTEGER-valued array giving the maxi-

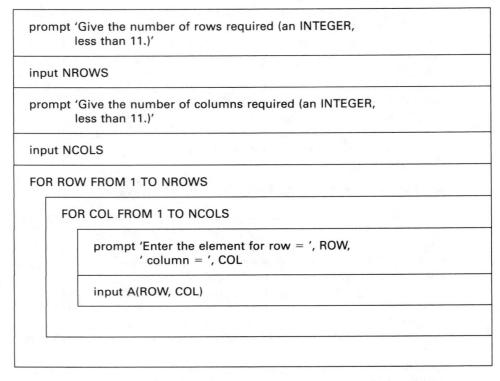

Figure 6.3 Design Segment to Input a Small Array by Entering One Number per Line

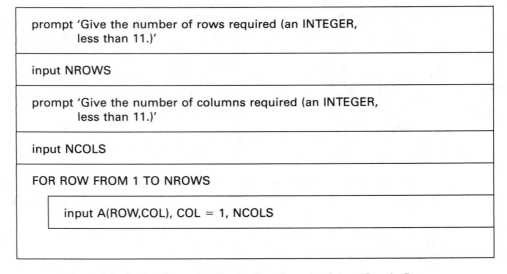

Figure 6.4 Design Segment to Input a Two-dimensional Array Row by Row.

```
FOR ROW = 1, MNROWS

   FOR COL = 1, MNCOLS

      ARRAY (ROW, COL) = 0.0
```

Figure 6.5   Design Segment to Set Each Element of an Array to Zero

mum number of rows in the ARRAY and that MNCOLS is an INTEGER-valued array giving the maximum number of columns in the ARRAY. Also, ROW and COL are assumed to be INTEGER-valued variables.

6.4 ARRAY SPECIFICATION

FORTRAN requires that the symbolic names and the dimensions of each array be specified in *each and every unit* in which the array name appears. Although FOR-TRAN provides two methods for specifying arrays, we show and use only one method. This method inserts the array-dimensioning information into the type specification for the array name by enclosing d, the **dimension declarator**, in parentheses and placing it immediately after the symbolic name of the array. The dimension declarator is of the form

$$[d_1 :] d_2$$

where

d_1 is the lower dimension bound

and

d_2 is the upper dimension bound.

In this notation, the square brackets indicate optional material. Consequently, as this general notation indicates, the lower bounds and the colon may be omitted. If the lower bound is omitted, it is assumed to be 1.

The dimension bounds should be INTEGERs. Although they may be constants, symbolic names of constants, or variables, we use constants. The following are examples of type specifications that contain some array specifications:

```
INTEGER I, J, K, LIST(100), MAXVAL, X(10,10)
REAL    A, MATRIX(12,12), MONE(50,100), MTWO(2,100), SUM(0:1000), Z
```

6.5 ARRAY VOCABULARY, RESTRICTIONS, AND SIZE

The symbolic name of an array is called the **array name.** One member of an array is called an **array element,** or an **element.** An array name qualified by a subscript is called an **array element name.**

All elements of an array must be of the same type.

The FORTRAN 77 standards do not state a requirement that the elements of an array be initialized. That is, the standards do not require that the elements of an array have any value other than "undefined" when they are created by the compiler. Although some FORTRAN 77 compilers may set each element of an array to zero, we recommend that *a programmer always initialize array elements before any other use of those elements.* Just as variables may be initialized by READing values into the elements or by assignment of values to the elements, so may array elements be initialized. Again, a word of caution: The use of an array element, or a variable for that matter, that has not been initialized may lead to an error that is very difficult to detect or for which it is very difficult to locate its cause. Beginning programming students frequently assume that array elements are set to zero when they are created by the compiler. Because the standards do not specify that this must be done, you should not be surprised to learn that some compilers do not initialize array elements to zero. But even if you are using a complier that initializes array elements to zero, we recommend that you use the code to set the array elements to zero.

The **size** of an array is the number of elements in the array. Thus, for the example array specifications used earlier,

```
INTEGER I, J, K, LIST(100), MAXVAL, X(10,10)
```

and

```
REAL A, MATRIX(12,12), MONE(50,100), MTWO(2,100), SUM(0:1000),Z
```

the array LIST is a one-dimensional array with size 100, and the array X is a two-dimensional array with size 100. All elements of LIST and X are of type INTEGER. Of course, I, J, K, and MAXVAL are INTEGER variables, not arrays. MATRIX is a two-dimensional array with size 144, MONE is a two-dimensional array of size 5000, MTWO is a two-dimensional array of size 200, and SUM is a one-dimensional array of size 1001 (notice that because the lower bound is zero, there are 1001 elements.) All elements of the arrays MATRIX, MONE, MTWO, AND SUM are of type REAL. A and Z are not arrays; both A and Z are variables. The elements of the array, say SUM, are SUM(0), SUM(1), SUM(2), SUM(3),..., SUM(999), SUM(1000). The elements of a two-dimensional array, say X, are X(1,1), X(1,2), X(1,3),..., X(1,9), X(1,10), X(2,1), X(2,2), X(2,3),..., X(10,10).

6.6 A BRIEF INTRODUCTION TO LINEAR ALGEBRA

The most important application of one- and two-dimensional arrays is to represent vectors and matrices, the fundamental entities in linear algebra. Consequently, we shall consider this application of arrays. However, before we do so, we have to introduce some of the mathematical definitions from linear algebra. Then, we present a short series of examples using mathematical operators with vectors and matrices. In this text, we shall reserve the words *vector* and *matrix* for use in the mathematical context of linear algebra. *Array* will be used as an alternative to the more cumbersome one-dimensional array or two-dimensional array. Thus, array is used in the context of computer programming. In addition, we occasionally use it in a very general sense to refer to a collection of numbers.

6.6.1 Some Basic Definitions in Linear Algebra

A **matrix** is a rectangular array of numbers. To indicate that the collection of numbers is to be treated as a whole, the array of numbers is surrounded by parentheses:

$$\begin{pmatrix} 3 & 124 & -23 \\ 12 & 0 & 1 \end{pmatrix} \quad \begin{pmatrix} -44 & 7 \\ 6 & 0 \\ 1 & -8 \end{pmatrix} \quad \begin{pmatrix} 11 \\ 4 \end{pmatrix}$$

The first matrix has two rows and three columns. The second matrix has three rows and two columns. The third matrix has two rows and one column. The numbers within a matrix are called the **elements** of the matrix. Thus, the third matrix has two elements, 11 and 4. The horizontal lines are called **rows** and the vertical lines are called **columns.** Sometimes the rows are called the row vectors and the columns are called the column vectors of the matrix. Uppercase boldface letters, such as **A, B, C,** are used to denote matrices.

The elements of **A** may be symbolically represented as

$$a_{11}, a_{12}, a_{13}, a_{14}$$

and so on. The general element may be represented as

$$a_{ij}$$

This notation may be extended to represent the entire matrix by enclosing the general element in parentheses:

$$(a_{ij})$$

The elements of **A** are a's, the elements of **B** are b's, and so on. When elements have two subscripts, the first subscript denotes the row and the second, the column.

A matrix that has only one row is called a **row matrix,** or a row vector. Similarly, a matrix that has only one column is called a **column matrix,** or column vector. Lowercase boldface letters are used to denote either a row matrix or a column matrix. If the number of rows in a matrix is equal to the number of columns, then that matrix is called a **square matrix.** (Square matrices have special importance.) The number of rows in a square matrix is called the **order** of the matrix. If n denotes the number of rows in a square matrix, the matrix is said to be of order n. The **principal diagonal** of a square matrix is the diagonal containing the elements

$$a_{11}, a_{22}, \ldots, a_{nn}$$

Mathematical operations have been defined for matrices, but some properties of such operations are not the same as operations on scalars. (**Scalars** are real numbers, that is, single numbers, not collections of numbers.)

6.6.2 Addition of Matrices

The addition of two matrices **A** and **B** is defined only when the number of rows in **A** is the same as the number of rows in **B** and the number of columns in **A** is the same as the number of columns in **B**. When this condition is satisfied, the sum of **A** and **B** is a third matrix **C** given by adding the corresponding elements. Thus,

$$c_{ij} = a_{ij} + b_{ij}$$

for $i = 1, 2, \ldots, m$ and $j = 1, 2, \ldots, n$.
This sum is written as

$$\mathbf{C} = \mathbf{A} + \mathbf{B}$$

Each of the three matrices **A**, **B**, and **C** is an $m \times n$ matrix. For example, if

$$\mathbf{A} = \begin{pmatrix} 4 & -1 & 0 \\ 6 & 0 & -1 \end{pmatrix} \qquad \mathbf{B} = \begin{pmatrix} 7 & 8 & -2 \\ -2 & 6 & 5 \end{pmatrix}$$

then

$$\mathbf{A} + \mathbf{B} = \begin{pmatrix} 11 & 7 & -2 \\ 4 & 6 & 4 \end{pmatrix}$$

6.6.3 Multiplication of Matrices

The multiplication of matrices is defined only when a specific relationship exists between the sizes of the two matrices. Further, *the order in which the multiplication is to be done, in general, affects the result.* If we let **A** be an $m \times n$ matrix and **B** be an $r \times s$ matrix, then the product **AB** (in that order) is defined only for the case when $r = n$; the product is the $m \times s$ matrix **C** with elements

$$c_{ij} = a_{i1}b_{1j} + a_{i2}b_{2j} + \cdots + a_{in}b_{nj}$$

which may be expressed in the more compact form using sigma notation as

$$\sum_{k=1}^{n} a_{ik}b_{kj}$$

This compact notation may be exemplified by the following symbolic example.

Let **A** be given by

$$\begin{pmatrix} a_{11} & a_{12} & a_{13} \\ a_{21} & a_{22} & a_{23} \end{pmatrix}$$

and **B** be given by

$$\begin{pmatrix} b_{11} & b_{12} & b_{13} \\ b_{21} & b_{22} & b_{23} \\ b_{31} & b_{32} & b_{33} \end{pmatrix}$$

Then, if **C** = **AB,** the matrix **C** is given by

$$\begin{pmatrix} c_{11} & c_{12} & c_{13} \\ c_{21} & c_{22} & c_{23} \end{pmatrix}$$

where

$$c_{11} = a_{11}b_{11} + a_{12}b_{21} + a_{13}b_{31}$$
$$c_{12} = a_{11}b_{12} + a_{12}b_{22} + a_{13}b_{32}$$
$$c_{13} = a_{11}b_{13} + a_{12}b_{23} + a_{13}b_{33}$$
$$c_{21} = a_{21}b_{11} + a_{22}b_{21} + a_{23}b_{31}$$
$$c_{22} = a_{21}b_{12} + a_{22}b_{22} + a_{22}b_{32}$$
$$c_{23} = a_{21}b_{13} + a_{22}b_{23} + a_{23}b_{33}$$

If **A** is given by

$$\begin{pmatrix} 1 & 2 & 3 \\ 4 & 5 & 6 \\ 7 & 8 & 9 \end{pmatrix}$$

and **B** is given by

$$\begin{pmatrix} 11 & 12 & 13 \\ 14 & 15 & 16 \\ 17 & 18 & 19 \end{pmatrix}$$

then the matrix $C = AB$ is a 3×3 matrix with the elements

$$c_{11} = 1 \times 11 + 2 \times 14 + 3 \times 17$$
$$c_{12} = 1 \times 12 + 2 \times 15 + 3 \times 18$$
$$c_{13} = 1 \times 13 + 2 \times 16 + 3 \times 19$$

$$c_{21} = 4 \times 11 + 5 \times 14 + 6 \times 17$$
$$c_{22} = 4 \times 12 + 5 \times 15 + 6 \times 18$$
$$c_{23} = 4 \times 13 + 5 \times 16 + 6 \times 19$$

$$c_{31} = 7 \times 11 + 8 \times 14 + 9 \times 17$$
$$c_{32} = 7 \times 12 + 8 \times 15 + 9 \times 18$$
$$c_{33} = 7 \times 13 + 8 \times 16 + 9 \times 19$$

Therefore, rewriting this in matrix form,

$$C = \begin{pmatrix} 90 & 96 & 102 \\ 216 & 231 & 246 \\ 342 & 366 & 390 \end{pmatrix}$$

6.7 DESIGN CONSIDERATIONS FOR MATRIX MULTIPLICATION

The name of an array may be thought of as a pointer that points to a set of memory locations. Nonetheless, both the name and the subscript values are required to point to a specific memory location. The memory location contains the representation of the value of that element of the array. Just as we have advised beginning programmers to work out a numerical example before preparing a design of an algorithm, we also advise beginning programmers to use paper-and-pencil methods to study the pattern of subscripts. In particular, it is *vital* to work out the subscripts *at the numerical level* prior to making a design. (Quite commonly, beginners will skip this step and instead try to design thinking of symbolic names only. When working with arrays having two or more dimensions, this frequently leads to the worst kind of errors — those that give incorrect numerical results not detected by the computer.)

Suppose that we have to design an algorithm to carry out matrix multiplication. Let us take as an example the multiplication of two 3×3 matrices, **A** and **B,** to yield a third, **C.** Let us assume that the order is

$$C = AB$$

One way to design such a program would be to use numeric subscripts throughout. Although this is not what we ultimately will want to do, a design segment to obtain a specific element is given here:

```
C(2,3) = A(2,1)*B(1,3) + A(2,2)*B(2,3) + A(2,3)*B(3,3)
```

We all agree that this would be difficult to design and to implement! It would require painful attention to each and every subscript to ensure that they were all correct. But even more of a problem is that this approach is specific to the given size of the matrix. We always want to strive for designs that are more general than this. Obviously, we want the computer to generate the subscripts. Thus, we want to create a design that uses the determinate repetition to specify the subscripts for us. But before we jump too quickly, let us use a determinate repetition to output the numeric values of subscripts, just so that we can study the pattern of subscripts at the numerical level.

The design segment to do this is as follows:

```
FOR ROW FROM 1 TO N

    FOR COL FROM 1 TO N

        output ROW, ',', COL
```

If N has the value 3, we would expect to see the following as the output from a correct implementation of this design segment:

```
1,1
1,2
1,3
2,1
2,2
2,3
3,1
3,2
3,3
```

As an important aside, we call your attention to a property of nested determinate repetitions. This property is that the inner determinate repetition is the one that increments (increases) faster.

Obviously, we could use a similar strategy to set each element of **C** to zero. The segment to do this is:

```
FOR ROW FROM 1 TO N

    FOR COL FROM 1 TO N

        C(ROW, COL)  =  0.0
```

Recall that when we wanted to sum the elements of a one-dimensional array, we first initialized an array, SUM, by setting SUM to zero. Then we used a determinate repetition to add each element of the array, element by element, to SUM. A design segment to accomplish this is given here:

```
SUM = 0.0

FOR I FROM 1 TO N

    SUM = VECTOR(I) + SUM
```

We want to try to use a similar strategy to obtain the sum of the element by element product of **B** and **C**.

Following our own advice, we first study the subscripts in the multiplication of our 3 × 3 matrices. We write the subscript patterns for this, using computer notation, as follows:

```
C(1,1) = A(1,1)*B(1,1) + A(1,2)*B(2,1) + A(1,3)*B(3,1)
C(1,2) = A(1,1)*B(1,2) + A(1,2)*B(2,2) + A(1,3)*B(3,2)
C(1,3) = A(1,1)*B(1,3) + A(1,2)*B(2,3) + A(1,3)*B(3,3)
C(2,1) = A(2,1)*B(1,1) + A(2,2)*B(2,1) + A(2,3)*B(3,1)
C(2,2) = A(2,1)*B(1,2) + A(2,2)*B(2,2) + A(2,3)*B(3,2)
C(2,3) = A(2,1)*B(1,3) + A(2,2)*B(2,3) + A(2,3)*B(3,3)
C(3,1) = A(3,1)*B(1,1) + A(3,2)*B(2,1) + A(3,3)*B(3,1)
C(3,2) = A(3,1)*B(1,2) + A(3,2)*B(2,2) + A(3,3)*B(3,2)
C(3,3) = A(3,1)*B(1,3) + A(3,2)*B(2,3) + A(3,3)*B(3,3)
```

Next, observe that for C(1,1) the sequence of products is:

```
A(1,1)*B(1,1)
A(1,2)*B(2,1)
A(1,3)*B(3,1)
```

and that for C(1,2) the sequence of products is:

```
A(1,1)*B(1,2)
A(1,2)*B(2,2)
A(1,3)*B(3,2)
```

and so on, until finally, for C(3,3) the sequence is:

```
A(3,1)*B(1,3)
A(3,2)*B(2,3)
A(3,3)*B(3,3)
```

If we consider C(1,1) fixed and scan the three products that have to be summed to obtain C(1,1) and compare with the three products that have to be summed to obtain C(1,2) when we consider C(1,2) fixed, we can detect a pattern. For, within the three products required to form a given element of C, we may observe that the first subscript of A has the same value as the first subscript of C. Likewise, if we compare the second subscript of B with the second subscript of C, we detect that these two subscripts have an identical value.

Let us represent these observations as a design segment, but for the moment, we leave the second subscript of A and the first subscript of B undetermined. We shall indicate this by using a question mark. See Figure 6.6.

Now we have to determine the correct way to produce the subscripts for which we temporarily used question marks. To do this, we return to a study of the patterns of numerical values for the subscripts, as displayed in the sequence of products. There we see that the values of the second subscript of A and the first subscript of B in any given product are the same. Consequently, we surmise that we can use an array for this subscript. Further, when we scan down the columns of the sequence of products, we see another portion of the pattern. We find that the values in sequence of the subscript are 1, 2, and 3. Finally, we detect that this sequence of 1, 2, and 3 as the value of the second subscript of A and the first subscript of B is repeated for each element of C.

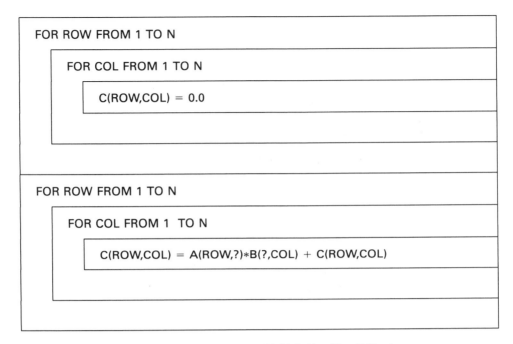

Figure 6.6   Design Segment to Multiply Two $N \times N$ Matrices

We already know how to produce a series of INTEGERs, 1, 2, and 3; namely, we use a determinate repetition. So, we have to consider how we nest this determinate repetition within the others that we employed to produce the subscripts for C and the other subscripts for A and B. Clearly, the 1, 2, 3 sequence for replacing the question mark is the sequence that increments most rapidly. Thus, recalling that it is the innermost repetition that increments most rapidly, we correctly conclude that we must position this repetition as the innermost one. Let us use K as the name for this innermost control variable in the determinate repetition. Then, we can complete the design. Here, we form the design as a subroutine. The complete design is shown in Figure 6.7 as the procedure MATMUT.

6.7.1 Squaring a Square Matrix

A square matrix may be multiplied by itself. The result is then called the square of the original matrix. In mathematical notation, this may be represented as

$$\mathbf{A}^2 = \mathbf{A}\mathbf{A}$$

and, as one might suspect, the order in which the multiplication is carried out does not effect the result. (Recall, though, that the order of the terms in the product of two matrices does, in general, make a difference in the results.)

The procedure MATMUT can be used to obtain the square of a square matrix. We simply have to set the value of the second argument, B, to the value of the first argument, A. Then, the execution of an implementation of MATMUT produces the

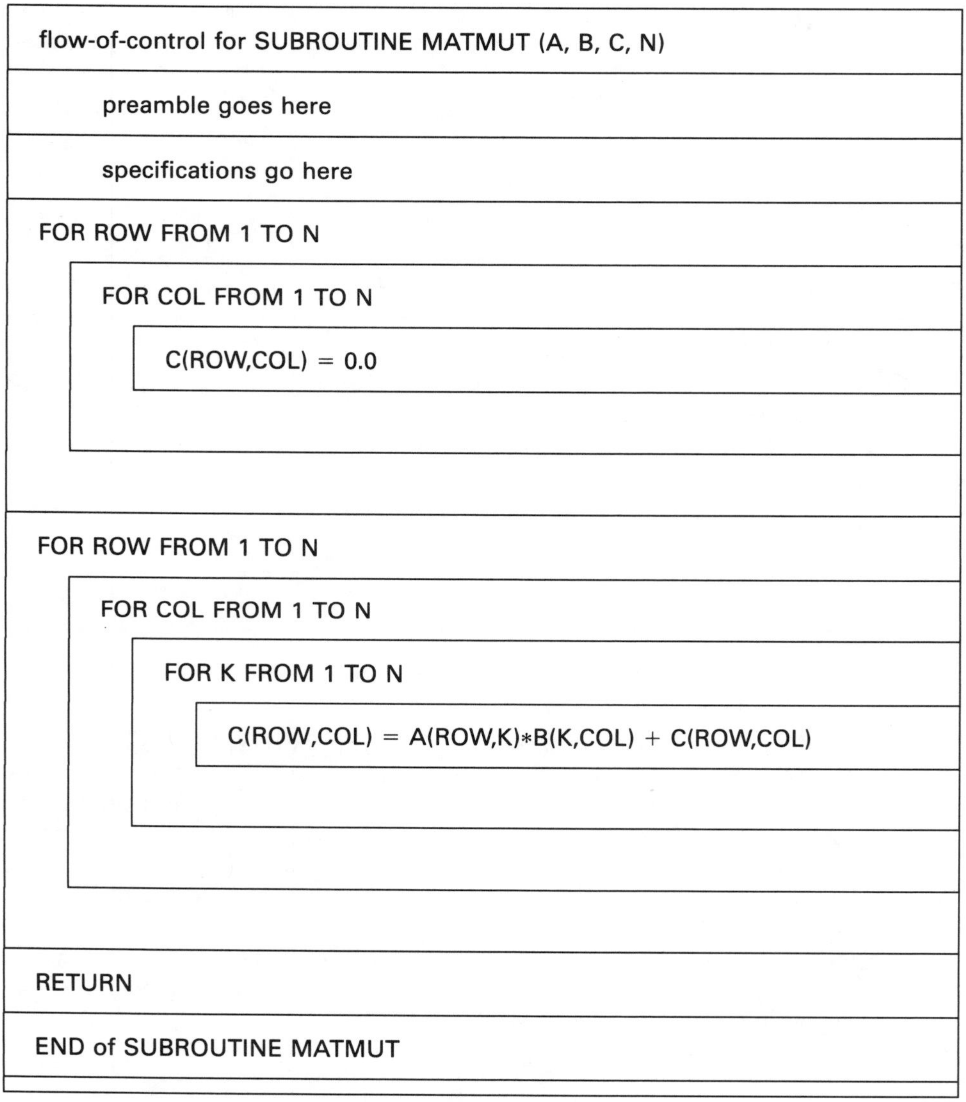

---

flow-of-control for SUBROUTINE MATMUT (A, B, C, N)

preamble goes here

specifications go here

FOR ROW FROM 1 TO N

    FOR COL FROM 1 TO N

        C(ROW,COL) = 0.0

FOR ROW FROM 1 TO N

    FOR COL FROM 1 TO N

        FOR K FROM 1 TO N

            C(ROW,COL) = A(ROW,K)*B(K,COL) + C(ROW,COL)

RETURN

END of SUBROUTINE MATMUT

Figure 6.7 Design for Flow-of-control for the Multiplication of Two Square Matrices

value of A squared as the value of C. Obviously, we could introduce the design elements to do this into MATMUT. If we were to do this, we should change the name of the procedure so that the procedure name would more appropriately reflect the computational task. We could also use MATMUT more directly by specifying as the argument list (A, A, C, N) when we invoked (called or used) the procedure. This too would assign A squared to C. However, there is yet another alternative, and it is this alternative we now describe.

We shall assume that we want to use MATMUT as it has been designed to square matrix **A.** We might, for example, choose to do this because we might want to use MATMUT later in the same program to multiply other matrices. We want to avoid twice entering the values in **A,** the matrix to be squared. If we could enter the values in **A** just once, we would save a considerable amount of work and also would not have to verify that both sets of values for **A** were correct. But, as we would like to preserve our ability to use MATMUT to multiply two different $N \times N$ matrices, we need to have a separate procedure to copy the values of **A** from input into the matrix **B.** Consequently, we will introduce another procedure, which we call MATAIB. This procedure will have three arguments, A, B, and N. A and B will be square matrices, each $N \times N$. The procedure will expect that A and N are **entry arguments** (meaning that the values associated with A and N will be made available from the unit that invokes MATAIB), whereas B is an **exit argument** (meaning that the procedure assigns values to B to be (presumably) used in the unit that invokes MATAIB. The purpose of the procedure is to copy the values of A into B. The design to do this is given in Figure 6.8.

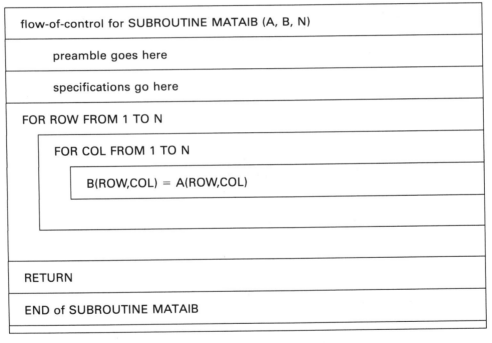

```
flow-of-control for SUBROUTINE MATAIB (A, B, N)

    preamble goes here

    specifications go here

FOR ROW FROM 1 TO N

    FOR COL FROM 1 TO N

        B(ROW,COL) = A(ROW,COL)



RETURN

END of SUBROUTINE MATAIB
```

Figure 6.8   Design of a Procedure to Copy Matrix **A** into Matrix **B**

Obviously, to produce the square of matrix **A** given these procedures, we would use a program that first inputs the values into **A,** then invokes the procedure MATAIB, and, finally, invokes the procedure MATMUT. Then, the value of A squared would be given as the value of C.

6.7.2 Raising a Square Matrix to Integer Powers

Square matrices have important use in applications. In some of these, a square matrix must be raised to an arbitrary integer-valued power. In some of these applications, the client might like to have all intermediate results. That is, the client would like to have

$$\mathbf{A}^2, \ \mathbf{A}^3, \ \mathbf{A}^4, \ \mathbf{A}^5, \ \mathbf{A}^6$$

and so on.

We claim that this can be done by applying a strategy similar to the one we used in designing a method for obtaining A squared. This time however, we shall copy C into B. To be consistent with our selection of names for our matrix manipulation procedures, we should call this MATCIB. However, because we recognize that it is very easy to make an error and confuse MATAIB with MATCIB, we have chosen the name CINTOB. CINTOB is a procedure with three arguments, B, C, and N. C and N are entry arguments, and B is an exit argument. The design for CINTOB is presented in Figure 6.9.

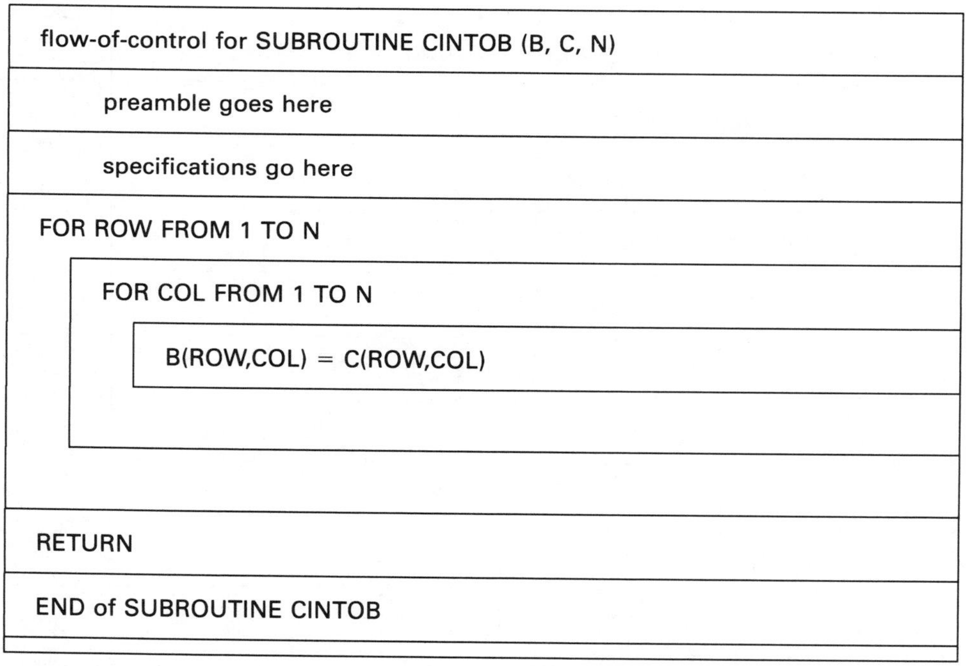

---

flow-of-control for SUBROUTINE CINTOB (B, C, N)

    preamble goes here

    specifications go here

FOR ROW FROM 1 TO N

    FOR COL FROM 1 TO N

        B(ROW,COL) = C(ROW,COL)

RETURN

END of SUBROUTINE CINTOB

Figure 6.9   Design of Procedure CINTOB, which Copies Matrix **C** into Matrix **B**

A design segment to carry out the entire process of raising a matrix **A** to an INTEGER power given by the value of POWER is given here as follows:

CALL MATAIB(A, B, N)

CALL MATMUT(A, B, C, N)

NREPS = 3, POWER

> CALL CINTOB(B, C, N)

> CALL MATMUT(A, B, C, N)

6.8 EXERCISES

1. Design, implement, and test a program to accept chemical symbols, molecular weights, and coefficients in the chemical reaction equation for reactants and products and for the amounts of reactants supplied. Find the limiting reactant, the grams of each product produced, and the percent excess of each reactant supplied.

   Supporting information. A chemical reaction equation has the form

   $$x_1 \,[\text{reactant 1}] \; + \; x_2 \,[\text{reactant 2}] \; + \; \cdots \rightarrow y_1 \,[\text{product 1}] \; + \; y_2 \,[\text{product 2}] \; + \; \cdots$$

   There must be at least one reactant and at least one product. The constants $x_1, x_2, \ldots, y_1, y_2, \ldots$ are the coefficients of the reaction. These indicate the proportions in which reactants must be suplied or products will be formed, in units of moles (mol). The conversion between mass, m, given in grams, and moles, n, is given by $n = m/w$, where w is the molecular weight of the compound (reactant or product). The molecular weight represents the mass in grams of 1 mol of the compound. When the moles of each reactant supplied and the coefficients are known, the limiting reactant is the reactant that has the smallest value of n/x (moles divided by the coefficient).

   Moles of any product formed are given by

   $$n_l(x_p/x_l)$$

   where l refers to the limiting reactant and p refers to the product in question.

   Percent excess of any reactant is given by

   $$[n_r - n_l(x_r/x_l)/n_l(x_r/x_l)]100$$

   The quantity $n_l (x_r/x_l)$ represents the required amount of reactant. The limiting reactant is always supplied in zero excess.

   A valid reaction equation will always obey the mass balance

   $$\sum_{i \,=\, \text{all reactants}} x_i W_i \;\; = \;\; \sum_{j \,=\, \text{all products}} x_j W_j$$

Input Specifications.   The input will have one of the forms

R

chemical symbol of the reactant

coefficient

molecular weight

grams supplied

P

chemical symbol of the product

coefficient

molecular weight

A

The input A means that all reactants and products have been entered, so analyze the data.

2. Design, implement, and test a program to determine the best possible I-beam that meets specified criteria.

   Supporting information: The diagram of a cross section of an I-beam is given in Figure 6.10. In the use of an I-beam, there are four factors to be considered: (1) shear stress; (2) bending stress; (3) amount of deflection; and (4) amount of material. We consider a concentrated load of 10,000 lb, for which the point of maximum stresses and deflection is in the center of the beam. This may be diagramed as in Figure 6.11.

   The shear stress is the force that will shear or break the beam. It is highest in the middle. The shear stress, in pounds per square inch (psi) is given by the equation:

$$\text{Shear stress} = \frac{10,000\,[AC + (BD/2)Y]}{TD}$$

where T, the moment of inertia, is

$$T = \frac{A(B + 2C)^3}{12} - \frac{2(A - D)B^3}{24}$$

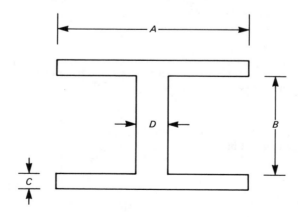

Figure 6.10   An I-beam.

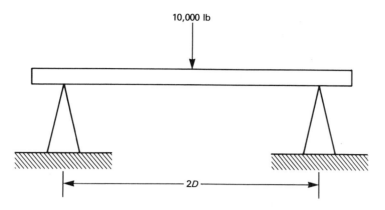

Figure 6.11   A Load-bearing I-beam.

and Y, the distance from central axis to the center of the area, is

$$Y = \frac{AC(B+ C)/2 + B^2D/4}{AC + (BD/2)}$$

The bending stress, in pounds per square inch, is

$$\text{Bending stress} = \frac{10{,}000 \times 10 \times 12BC}{2T}$$

The deflection, in inches, is

$$\text{Deflection} = \frac{10{,}000(20 \times 12)^3}{48 \times 3 \times 10^7 T}$$

The area, in square inches is

$$\text{Area} = BD + 2AC$$

For the particular situation under consideration, the architect specified that the steel beam must withstand a maximum shear stress of 6,500 psi, a maximum bending stress of 23,750 psi, and a maximum deflection of 0.45 in. The architect also stated that standard I-beams are manufactured with A in increments of 0.50 in., B in increments of 1.00 in., C in increments of 0.20 in., and D in increments of 0.15 in. The architect wants to determine what beams meet these requirements, have minimum area, and also satisfy the following range restrictions:

A is to be from 2.75 in. to 6.0 in.
B is to be from 8.90 in. to 10.2 inc.
C is to be from 0.58 in. to 0.95 in.
D is to be from 0.09 in. to 0.39 in.

Desired Output.   Your program is to explore all possibilities within the ranges of interest, using only standard I-beams. The desired output is a list of each combination of dimensions which meets all of the architects requirements, except minimum area. The program is to list each dimension, the obtained area, shear stress, bending stress, and the amount of deflection. In addition, the program is to indicate which combination(s) in fact have the minimum area. Because of this need to indicate which combination(s) have the minimum area, a two-dimensional array is to be used.

7

Expressions and Characters

7.1 INTRODUCTION

The basis of all the control structures except, of course, the implicit one, simple sequence, is some test. The test is stated in FORTRAN as an expression. Further, all mathematical computations are stated in FORTRAN as expressions. Consequently, expressions are fundamental language constructions. For this reason, we wish to re-examine expresssions and to present systematically the details of the construction and evaluation of expressions. In addition, we wish to present more information on the use of characters and character expressions.

7.2 EXPRESSIONS IN FORTRAN

In FORTRAN, an **expression** is formed from operands, operators, and parentheses. **Parentheses** are used as punctuation and as separators. In complicated expressions, they may be used to specify the order in which the expression is to be evaluated. **Operators** indicate the operation that is to be performed. The arithmetic operators and the character operator are expressed using nonalphabetical symbols, - , + , * , and /. The logical operators and the relational operators use **mnemonics** (aids to memory) constructed with characters of the alphabet but distinguished from possible programmer-created symbolic names by surrounding periods. **Operands** are the entities that are to be operated upon. There are four kinds of expressions: arithmetic expressions, character expressions, logical expressions, and relational expressions. When evaluated, arithmetic expressions produce a result that is one of the numeric types (complex, double precision, integer, or real); character expressions produce a result of type character; logical expressions produce a result of type logical; and, finally, relational expressions produce a result of type logical. The most common form of an expression is

> operand operator operand

Each of the following is an example of an expression:

```
A * B
A // B
A .AND. B
A .LT. B
```

The first is an arithmetic expression that indicates that A is to be multiplied by B. The second is a character expression that indicates that the strings A and B are to be concatenated (joined together to form one string—in this case, A first with B following A.) The third is a logical expression that indicates that the logical product of A and B is to be obtained. Finally, the last is a relational expression that indicates that the truth value of A less than B is to be obtained (that is, it is asking whether A is less than B; if it is less than B then the relational expression is true; otherwise, it is false.) Tables 7.1–7.3 summarize these types of operations.

Table 7.1 ARITHMETIC OPERATORS

Operator	Operation
**	Exponentiation
/	Division
*	Multiplication
−	Subtraction or negation
+	Addition or identity

Table 7.2 LOGICAL OPERATORS

Operator	Operation
.NOT.	Logical negation
.AND.	Logical conjunction
.OR.	Logical inclusive disjunction
.EQV.	Logical equivalence
.NEQV.	Logical nonequivalence

Note: The surrounding periods are required.

Table 7.3 RELATIONAL OPERATORS

Operator	Operation
.LT.	Less than
.LE.	Less than or equal
.EQ.	Equal
.NE.	Not equal
.GT.	Greater than
.GE.	Greater than or equal

Note: The surrounding periods are required.

7.3 SOME IMPORTANT REMARKS ABOUT EXPRESSIONS

Although it is syntactically correct, if the arithmetic operators .EQ. or .NE. are used with a real operand, incorrect results may be obtained. Real numbers are represented in the computer, and during computation, rounding or truncating can make real numbers inaccurate. Therefore, if a real operand is the result of some prior computation, then it should not appear in a relational expression that uses either .EQ. or .NE.

A relational expression may be used to compare the values of two arithmetic operands or expresssions, or to compare the values of two character operands or expressions. However, a relational expression *cannot* be used to compare a *character operand* with an *arithmetic operand*.

Be sure to keep in mind that the result of the evaluation of a relational expression is of type logical; that is, the result is either true or false.

A logical variable alone may be used as an expression. Thus, if a name, say BUG, is specified to be LOGICAL, a coder may write

```
IF (BUG) THEN
```

meaning if BUG has the value true, then carry out the instructions following the THEN.

7.4 CHARACTERS AND COMPUTATION WITH CHARACTERS

Up to this point, we have stressed computation using numeric values. Although we have used some alphabetical characters in the programs, these have appeared more frequently as labels for numeric values, such as in the FORMAT statements, where they were used with a WRITE statement. Here we present a fuller and a more systematic discussion of computation with characters.

7.5 THE FORTRAN 77 CHARACTER SET

The **FORTRAN 77 character set** consists of letters, digits, and special characters. It includes the 26 letters of the English alphabet (which appear as uppercase letters), the ten digits of the Arabic base ten number system, and the following thirteen special characters:

$$= + - * / ( ) , . \$ ' :$$

including the one character you cannot see, the blank character.

7.6 CHARACTER STRINGS

One or more contiguous characters is called a **string**, or a **character string.** A string is delimited on the left and on the right by an apostrophe. Be alert! An apostrophe is a single stroke. It should not be confused with an accent mark (´) nor with a quotation mark ("). Because an apostrophe is used to delimit a character string, the question immediately arises of how to represent an apostrophe within a string. FORTRAN 77 does permit the representation of an apostrophe within a string. This is done by using two consecutive apostrophes without an intervening blank. To enter this, the keyboard operator merely depresses the apostrophe key two consecutive times. (Again, be alert! The single character ", consisting of two lines and occupying one column, is not equivalent to the repeated apostrophe, '', which occupies two consecutive columns.)

An important property of character strings is their length. The **length** of a character string is an integer value that gives the number of characters in the string. The delimiting apostrophes are not included in the count of the number of characters. But the two consecutive apostrophes used to indicate an apostrophe within a string are counted as *one* character. FORTRAN 77 requires that the length of a character constant be greater than zero. Table 7.4 contains some examples of character strings and their length.

Table 7.4.   EXAMPLES OF CHARACTER STRINGS

String	Length
' '	1
' '	3
'A'	1
'ABC'	3
'FRANK THOMAS'	12
'GEORGIA O''KEEFFE'	16
'1985'	4
'$12.95'	6
'3.1416'	6
'OLAF TRYGVESSON'	15

Although the graphic (what appears on the screen or on paper) for an integer, say 3, is the same as the graphic for the character, 3, in a computer system, the integer 3 has a different internal representation from that used to represent the character 3. This means that the pattern of bits (binary digits) used to represent the integer 3 and the character 3 are different. Consequently, *arithmetic operations such as those denoted by* $+$, $-$, $/$, $*$, *and* $**$ *may be applied to integers but cannot be applied to characters*.

As we have seen in earlier chapters, a literal character string may be used in FORMAT statements to be used with a WRITE statement. Thus, we might label our output using

```
          WRITE (6, 600)
          WRITE (6, 601) X, Y, Z
  600     FORMAT ('1', 'PROGRAM TRIANGLE')
  601     FORMAT ('0', 'X =', F10.5, ' Y =', F10.5, ' Z =', F10.5)
```

In this example, we see the character string used to convey the carriage-control characters 1 and 0, in addition to a title and the labeling information for X, Y, and

Z. Notice that we specified that literal strings may appear in a FORMAT statement intended to be used in conjunction with a WRITE statement and also notice that such strings are delimited by apostrophes. Nothing was said about the use of literal strings in FORMAT statements designed to be used with input. In fact, the apostrophe edit descriptor cannot be used to input character data. The apostrophe edit descriptor can be used only in a FORMAT statement to output a character string.

In addition to the literal character strings just described, character strings may be associated with symbolic names representing arrays, constants, or variables. When this is done, the symbolic name must be declared using the type specification statement

```
CHARACTER
```

followed by a list of information that inludes the symbolic names and the maximum length for possible values. For instance, the specification

```
CHARACTER *10 A, B, CAT
```

defines three variables, A, B, and CAT, to be type character. It also specifies that each one of them can take on a maximum length of 10 characters.

A slightly different syntax may be used to specify differing lengths. Thus, the specification

```
CHARACTER FIRST*20, LAST*30, TITLE*80
```

specifies that FIRST, LAST, AND TITLE are to be type character. FIRST may have up to and including 20 characters; LAST may have up to and including 30 characters; and TITLE may have up to and including 80 characters.

7.7 HOW TO INPUT CHARACTER DATA

Character data may be supplied as input. When this is to be done, the READ statement is used along with a FORMAT statement. But an A edit descriptor is used in the FORMAT statement for character data. The complete form of this edit descriptor is

```
Aw
```

where w specifies the field width—that is, the number of characters to be associated with the symbolic name given in the list of arrays or variables in the READ statement. Of course, all symbolic names to be associated with character data must have appeared in a CHARACTER specification statement. For example, in a unit containing

```
CHARACTER TITLE*80
```

a string containing a maximum of 80 characters may be read using

```
      READ (5,507) TITLE
507   FORMAT (A80)
```

which would input a string of up to and including 80 characters. If a string is to be read or written by means of an associated FORMAT statement using an Aw edit specification, such as A80, the string is not delimited by apostrophes.

After the title has been read, it may be printed at the top of the page by executing the code

```
              WRITE(7,710) TITLE
       710    FORMAT ('1', A80)
```

(Notice the literal character string, '1', which is the carriage-control character indicating that the printing is to appear on the first line of the next page.)

7.8 CHARACTER STRINGS IN ASSIGNMENT STATEMENTS

Character strings may also appear on the *right-hand side* of the assignment operator. Thus, in a unit containing

```
CHARACTER SEX*6
```

the following might appear:

```
SEX = 'MALE'
```

In the case of the assignment of 'MALE', the internal respresentation would be the four characters, MALE, followed by two blanks. Thus, MALE would be left-justified in the six-column character field, and the remaining columns would be filled with blanks.

If a unit contained

```
CHARACTER*1 FIRST, SECOND
FIRST = 'A'
SECOND = FIRST
```

the value of SECOND would be the representation of the letter, A. Although the assignment operator may be used to assign a character value to a variable of type character, *noncharacter type values cannot be assigned to a character entity*.

7.9 COMPARISONS OF TWO STRINGS

Character strings may be compared easily using the relational operators .EQ. or .NE. If the two character strings are of unequal length, the system will perform the comparison as if a sufficient number of blank characters were added on the right end of the shorter operand to make its length to be the same as the length of the originally longer one. Two character strings are equal if and only if they have the same characters in the same order, but with the comparison operating as just described in the case that the two strings are of unequal length.

In a unit containing the specification

```
CHARACTER *10 CITY, CNTRY, NATION, STATE
```

the assignment of values could be made as follows:

```
CITY = 'CHICAGO'
CNTRY = 'USA'
NATION = 'USA'
STATE = 'ILLINOIS'
```

Comparisons could be made using

```
IF (CNTRY .EQ. 'USA') THEN
```

or using

```
IF (CNTRY .EQ. NATION) THEN
```

In either case, the relation would be true as long as no other changes to the value of CNTRY occurred between the assignment just given and the comparison. However, if the comparison were stated as

```
IF(CNTRY .EQ. 'U S A') THEN
```

the relation would be false because of the presence of the blanks. Similarily,

```
IF (CNTRY .EQ. ' USA') THEN
```

would be false because a blank precedes the letter U, whereas

```
IF (CNTRY .EQ. 'USA ') THEN
```

would be true because a blank follows the A in USA. The other relational operators (.LT., .LE., .GE., or .GT.) should not be used with character comparisons. Instead, the FORTRAN intrinsic functions described in the next section should be used.

7.10 INTRINSIC FUNCTIONS FOR CHARACTER VALUES

FORTRAN 77 includes some functions to compute particular values. These supplied functions are called intrinsic functions and will be described in a later chapter. There are four intrinsic functions for performing other character comparisons. Each of these has two character arguments and produces a result which is type logical. These are given in Table 7.5 below.

Table 7.5 INTRINSIC FUNCTIONS FOR LEXICAL COMPARISON OF STRINGS

Intrinsic Function	Specific Name
Lexically greater than or equal	LGE
Lexically greater than	LGT
Lexically less than or equal	LLE
Lexically less than	LLT

These intrinsic functions are based on the specified ordering of the characters (known as the collating sequence) contained in the document *ANSI* X3.4-1977. This collating sequence is the American Standard Code for Information Interchange, or ASCII, collating sequence.

The intrinsic functions for performing lexical comparisons may be used within an IF - THEN statement. For example, in a unit containing

```
CHARACTER*30 NAME
DIMENSION NAME(10)
```

the programmer might write

```
IF (LLT(NAME(1), NAME(2))) THEN
```

which would be true if the character string represented in the location NAME(1) precedes the character string represented in the location NAME(2). Otherwise, the function would return false. Such lexical comparisons are necessary so that lists of names and the like may be alphabetized.

7.11 ADDITIONAL INTRINSIC FUNCTIONS FOR USE WITH STRINGS

FORTRAN 77 contains four additional intrinsic functions for use with character strings. Two of these are described in the standards as "type conversion," but this way of classifying them may be misleading. They might better have been described as *character-to-position* (in the collating sequence of the *processor*) and *position-to-character*. Both are defined with reference to the *collating sequence of the processor* and, hence, vary from computer to computer. See Table 7.6.

Table 7.6   ADDITIONAL INTRINSIC FUNCTIONS FOR USE WITH STRINGS

Intrinsic Function	Specific Name	Type of Argument(s)	Function
Type conversion to character	CHAR(a)	Integer	Character
Type conversion to integer	ICHAR(a)	Character	Integer
Index of substring (location of substring a2 in string a1)	INDEX(a1, a2)	Character	Integer
Length of string	LEN(a)	Character	Integer

The results of referencing the intrinsic functions CHAR(a) and ICHAR(a) depend upon the collating sequence of the processor being used. Hence, they must be used with caution. CHAR(j) is designed to return the character in the jth position of the processor's collating sequence. For ICHAR(c), c is type character and of length 1. When evaluated, the function ICHAR() gives the position of the character (denoted by the argument) in the collating sequence of the processor. For both CHAR()

and ICHAR(), the first character in the processor's collating sequence is designated position 0. The last position is designated $n - 1$, where n is the number of characters in the collating sequence. A safe use of these functions is

```
CHAR(ICHAR('A') + 1)
```

which yields 'B' whatever character coding sequence is used.

The value of LEN(a) is an integer that is the length of the string given by the value of the argument. INDEX(a1, a2) gives an integer that is the position in a1 at which the first occurrence, if any, of the substring a2 starts. If the substring a2 does not appear in a1, the function returns zero. The function will always return zero if the length of a1 is less than the length of a2.

7.12 SUBSTRING REFERENCE

Recall that a string consists of one or more characters. The length of a string is the number of characters in the string. Each character in a string is said to occupy a character **position.** The character positions are denoted by the sequence of integers 1, 2, . . . , starting with 1 for the first, or leftmost, character in the string. For example, the string

```
'FORTRAN'
```

occupies the respective character positons indicated by the integers in the second line:

```
FORTRAN
1234567
```

A portion of a string is called a **substring.** The definition also includes the possibility that an entire string may be a substring of itself. In FORTRAN 77, a substring is indicated by the name of the string followed by parentheses, which enclose a pair of integers or integer expressions separated by a colon. The integer value preceding the colon indicates the character position of the first character of the substring, whereas the integer value that follows the substring indicates the character positon of the last character of the substring. The notation includes the possibility of indicating that the substring is the entire original string. If a substring is shorter than the maximum value specified, the substring characters are left-justified into the created string, and the remaining character positions in the created string are set to the blank character.

Let us consider a unit containing the following:

```
CHARACTER *12 ALPHA, BETA, GAMMA, STRING
STRING = 'ABCDEFGHIJKL'
ALPHA = STRING(1:1)
BETA = STRING(2:4)
GAMMA = STRING(1:12)
```

We would expect that the value of ALPHA would be the single visible character A followed by eleven blanks, that the value of BETA would be the three visible characters BCD followed by nine blanks, and that the value of GAMMA would be the character string ABCDEFGHIJKL.

7.13 CONCATENATION

Concatenation of two character strings is the joining together of the two character strings. The character operator to do this in FORTRAN 77 is //. Thus, two consecutive slashes indicate that two character strings, one on the left of the operator and one on the right, are to be joined. The result is a character string whose length is the sum of the lengths of the two constituent strings. For example,

```
RESULT = 'CAT' // 'DOG'
```

produces 'CATDOG' as the value of RESULT. Of course, RESULT must have been specified to be of type CHARACTER.

We feel that the manipulation of characters in FORTRAN 77 is only minimally satisfactory. If an entire computational task involves the manipulation of characters, some alternative computer language such as SNOBOL should be considered.

7.14 EXERCISES

1. Design, implement, and test a program to obtain the final composition and temperature of mixtures of ice at its freezing point and water at various temperatures.

   Supporting information.   The heat of fusion is the amount of energy required to melt a given mass of ice. The numerical value of the heat of fusion is 80 cal/g. The melting point of ice is 0°C. The heat capacity is the amount of energy required to raise the temperature of a given mass of water by a given number of degrees. The numerical value of the heat capacity is 1 cal/g °C. Liquid water exists at temperatures between 0 and 100°C. When two samples of water are mixed, energy will be exchanged until the temperatures are equal.

$$T = \frac{g_1 T_1 + g_2 T_2}{g_1 + g_2}$$
$$G = g_1 + g_2$$

   When ice is mixed with water, the energy given up by the water as it cools is equal to the energy absorbed by the ice as it melts.

$$\Delta E_{\text{water}} = g_{\text{water}}(T - T_{\text{water}})$$
$$\Delta E_{\text{ice}} = g_{\text{ice}} \Delta H_{\text{fusion}} = 80 g_{\text{ice}}$$

   Input specifications.   The input will be of the form:

```
'I'
grams of ice
```

or

```
'W'
grams of water
temperature of water
```

or

```
'A'
```

An indefinite number of data sets is to be processed. Each data set will contain an indefinite number of the first two types of input shown. When the input 'A' is received, output the final mixture temperature and composition.

2. Design, implement, and test a program to obtain one of the three variables (pressure, temperature, volume), given values of the other two variables for an ideal gas. The calculations are to be made for a sample of one mole of an ideal gas.

   Supporting information.   An ideal gas obeys the relationship
   $$PV = nRT$$
   where

   P = absolute pressure
   V = volume
   n = number of moles of gas
   R = universal constant
   T = absolute temperature

   Units.   When P is in atmospheres, V is in liters, and T is in Kelvin, the numerical value of the universal constant, R, is 0.08206.

8

Intrinsic and External Functions

8.1 INTRODUCTION

The standards for FORTRAN 77 contain specifications for functions such as the absolute value function, the square root function, trigonometric functions, and so on. Consequently, these functions are automatically supplied with the FORTRAN system. Therefore, they are called **intrinsic functions.** These intrinsic functions are predefined and available to any user of the FORTRAN processor merely by using the name of the intrinsic function followed by its arguments enclosed within parentheses. In FORTRAN, the process of using a function is more properly described as a *function reference.*

As an example of an intrinsic function, we will take the square root function. To obtain the square root of

$$b^2 - 4ac$$

a coder would merely use the name of the function (obtained from Table 8.1 on page 148 or from the FORTRAN Reference Manual for the system being used),

```
SQRT
```

with the single argument, the arithmetic expression

```
B*B - 4.0*A*C
```

enclosed within parentheses. Thus, the FORTRAN code would be

```
SQRT(B*B - 4.0*A*C)
```

which could be combined with other parts of an arithmetic expression or used alone in an assignment statement such as

$$ROOT = SQRT(B*B - 4.0*A*C)$$

as might be required by the task.

The description of the SQRT function in the FORTRAN Reference Manual states that the possible values of the argument are restricted to values greater than or equal to zero. Consequently, a defensive coder would test the value of

$$b^2 - 4ac$$

prior to referencing the SQRT function.

8.2 THE ANSI-SPECIFIED INTRINSIC FUNCTIONS

Table 5, Intrinsic Functions, in the publication *American National Standard Programming Language FORTRAN, ANSI* X3.9–1978 lists 32 intrinsic functions. A majority of these functions have both a single generic name and two or more specific names. A reference using the specific name requires argument(s) of a specific type. However, a reference using the generic name allows some flexibility in the type of the argument(s). As a reference to an intrinsic function that uses the generic name will return the results with a type that is the type of the argument(s) supplied, coders use the generic name. In some cases, one of the specific names is also a generic name. (The older versions of FORTRAN did not incorporate the generic concept for intrinsic functions. The specific names that were used in older versions of FORTRAN are retained in FORTRAN 77 in order to minimize the amount of work required to convert programs in older FORTRAN to FORTRAN 77.)

The distinction between the generic and the specific form may be illustrated by the common logarithm function. The generic name of the common logarithm function is

LOG10

where the first three characters are the letters of the alphabet and the last two characters are digits. LOG10 will accept either real or double-precision arguments and will return a result that has the same type as the argument used in the reference. This may be contrasted with the specific forms

ALOG10

and

DLOG10

which also may be used to obtain the common logarithm. But ALOG10 is designed to be used with a type real argument, and it will return a type real result. DLOG10 is designed to be used with a double-precision argument and it will return a double precision result.

8.3 ADDITIONAL SYNTAX AND GRAMMAR OF INTRINSIC FUNCTIONS

There is a type associated with the result of the evaluation of each intrinsic function *and* with each argument of the function. If an intrinsic function has more than one argument, then the FORTRAN standards specify that all arguments in a given reference of that function be of the same type. The FORTRAN IMPLICIT statement does not change the type of an intrinsic function.

Recall that *referencing* is the process of using a function. The appearance of the name of the function followed by parentheses surrounding the arguments of the function is a **function reference.** Such a function reference results in the evaluation of the function. More precisely, a function reference first causes the evaluation of the argument(s). This is followed by the evaluation of the function. Finally, function evaluation terminates by the flow-of-control being returned to the continued evaluation of the arithmetic expression that contained the function reference.

In the example

```
ROOT = SQRT(B*B - 4.0*A*C)
```

first the argument,

```
B*B - 4.0*A*C
```

is evaluated. Then the square root is obtained. (But if the value of the argument were less than zero, an error condition would result, and the execution would terminate with an error message.) Finally, the result (of taking the square root of the argument) is assigned to the variable, ROOT.

In keeping with the intentions of the designers of FORTRAN, arguments of intrinsic functions are always only *entry* arguments. This means that the argument(s) are used only to supply values to the function; that is, arguments are *not* used to return values to the referencing expression. Further, good programming practice dictates that the arguments themselves must not be changed by the evaluation of the function.

8.4 A LIST OF SOME INTRINSIC FUNCTIONS

Some of the commonly used intrinsic functions are listed in Table 8.1, which contains a description of the function, the reference form (i.e., the name of the function), the type of the argument(s), and the type of the result.

8.5 INTRODUCTION TO EXTERNAL FUNCTIONS

The concept of a function is probably the single most important concept in mathematics. Therefore, it should come as no surprise that the designers of FORTRAN included the predefined, or intrinsic, functions. Nor should it be surprising to learn that they also included the linguistic structures required to permit a coder to define

Table 8.1 SOME COMMONLY USED INTRINSIC FUNCTIONS

Function Description	Reference Form or Name	Type of Argument	Type of Result
Absolute value	ABS(a)	C, D, I, R	C, D, I, R
Common logarithm	LOG10(a)	D, R	D, R
Cosine	COS(a)	C, D, R	C, D, R
Exponential	EXP(a)	C, D, R	C, D, R
Natural logarithm	LOG(a)	C, D, R	C, D, R
Remaindering	MOD(a1, a2)	C, I, R	C, I, R
Sine	SIN(a)	C, D, R	C, D, R
Square root	SQRT(a)	C, D, R	C, D, R
Tangent	TAN(a)	D, R	D, R
Type conversion	INT(a)	C, D, I, R	I
Type conversion	REAL(a)	C, D, I, R	R

Notes:

1. The lowercase letter *a* stands for argument. For those functions with two arguments, a1 denotes the first argument and a2 denotes the second argument.
2. C stands for complex, D stands for double, I stands for integer, and R stands for real.
3. The angles for the trigonometric functions must be supplied in radians. (Multiply an angle in degrees by $\pi/180.0$ to obtain the value of the angle in radians.)
4. MOD(a1,a2) performs modular arithmetic on a1 with modulus a2. The standards define MOD(a1,a2) as the result of evaluating a1 - INT(a1/a2)*a2.
5. The result of the MOD function is a1 if a1 $<$ a2. The result of the MOD function is undefined if the second argument is zero.
6. The argument for SQRT must be greater than or equal to zero; otherwise, an error condition will result.

additional functions. Indeed, the required structures are present. In FORTRAN, a user defined function is called an **external function.** The qualifier *external* might be thought of as a means to differentiate such functions from intrinsic functions. Thus, intrinsic functions are intrinsic, meaning intrinsic to (i.e., supplied with) the FORTRAN compiler. On the other hand, external may be interpreted as meaning "external to the compiler" or, in other words, not supplied with the compiler. In this chapter we describe the two steps required to implement an external function — namely, the definition of the function and the referencing of the function.

8.6 A TASK NEEDING AN EXTERNAL FUNCTION

A client submitted the following program request:

I want a program that will compute
$$P(v \text{ successes in } n \text{ trials})$$

which is given by

$$\binom{n}{v} p^v q^{n-v}$$

where

$$p = \text{denotes the probability of a success in one trial}$$

$$q = 1 - p$$

$$\binom{n}{v} = \frac{n!}{v!\,(n - v)!}$$

with the factorial, $n!$, defined as $n! = 1 \times 2 \times \cdots \times n$ and 0! defined to be 1.

When the systems analyst read this program request, she noticed that factorials are required. She recognized that the factorial function returned a single value and that it would be used within a mathematical expression. Consequently, she decided that the program should also use a function to compute the factorial. She checked the list of intrinsic functions only to confirm her recollection that there was no factorial function included in the list. Therefore she specified that the factorial was to be computed by an external function.

She also obtained the following needed information: (1) as p and q each are probabilities, each is a real variable defined between 0 and 1, inclusively; (2) n and v are integer variables; (3) n must be greater than or equal to v; and, (4) n, p, v are entry values.

8.7 THE DEFINITION OF AN EXTERNAL FUNCTION

FORTRAN contains the syntactic structures that permit a coder to define an external function or a subroutine. Unlike a subroutine subprogram, a function subprogram was designed (1) to return only a single value and (2) to be referenced within an arithmetic expression. As an external function was designed to return a single value in connection with the evaluation of an arithmetic expression, the function subprogram has (3) a type associated with the function name.

Each unit of a FORTRAN job, main program, external function, or subroutine, may be thought of as a separate independent program. (In fact, each unit is compiled independently of all other units within the same job.) For these separate and independent units to work as a whole, it is necessary to provide explicit means of communication between units. Arguments are the means we stress in this text for communication between units. Keeping with the intended use of a function to return a single value by means of associating the result of the evaluation of the function with the symbolic name of the function, all arguments in the definition of an external function should be entry-only arguments. That is, each argument is used only to communicate values to the function from the referencing unit.

The first statement in a unit that defines an external function contains the keyword FUNCTION preceded by the type, followed by the symbolic name of the function, and terminated by parentheses surrounding zero or more arguments. This statement is followed by the code that defines the computations to be performed by the function. The unit that defines the function, like all units in a FORTRAN job, terminates with the END statement. However, after the opening FUNCTION statement but before the END statement, there must be two other statements. The first of these is an assignment statement with the name of the function but without the parentheses or arguments on the left-hand side of the replacement operator. On the right-hand side of the replacement operator is some expression whose value is taken to be the result of the evaluation of the function. This assignment statement is followed by the RETURN statement. The keyword RETURN indicates the point during the execution of the function at which the flow-of-control is to return to the referencing unit. (Although the syntax of FORTRAN permits a subprogram to contain more than one RETURN, the use of more than one RETURN in the same unit violates the modularity of the structuring by creating more than one exit from the unit. Because a design can be changed to avoid the use of more than one RETURN within any given subprogram, we insist on the stylistic requirement of having *exactly one* RETURN in each subprogram.)

A skeleton of an external function definition is given in Figure 8.1. This skeleton contains several FORTRAN statements that have not yet been discussed. These statements will be presented later. For the time being, it is quite appropriate simply to include them as they appear here whenever you write a FUNCTION subprogram.

A function unit is designed to return a single value when it is referenced in some other unit. The form of the reference is simple. It consists of the function name followed by the list of the function arguments. The arguments are enclosed in parentheses. The function reference may appear in an output list, although this use is rather infrequent. More commonly, the reference appears on the right-hand side of an assignment statement, frequently within an arithmetic expression. Suppose that

```
SLOPE(X,Y,Z)
```

is the name of a function that has been defined as an external real function. Then the following are samples of references to this function:

```
RESULT = SLOPE(X, Y, Z)
ANSWER = HEIGHT*SLOPE(X, Y, Z)
```

In the first example, the right-hand side of the assignment statement consists only of a reference to the function SLOPE with the arguments X, Y, and Z. In the second example, the function reference appears in an arithmetic expression, which, when executed, has the effect of forming the product of HEIGHT and the value computed in the function, SLOPE, using the current values of X, Y, and Z.

We again call attention to the fact that a function unit is intended to return a single value, not more than one value. (This also implies that the arguments are entry-only arguments and that a function does not return an array of values; only a simple variable is returned.) There is a type associated with this value.

The type associated with the function name appears before the keyword FUNCTION in the function definition. It does not appear within the body of the function in a type statement. *However, the function name must be typed in any unit that references the function.*

Just before the RETURN statement in the function definition is another *required* syntax structure. The name of the function must appear on the left-hand side of an assignment statement. Notice that the name appears on the left-hand side of the

```
        type FUNCTION name (  )
C
        preamble goes here
C
        IMPLICIT LOGICAL (A − Z)
        remaining type specifications go here
        COMMON /BUGBLK/BUG
        remaining specifications go here
C
        IF (BUG) THEN
          WRITE (  )        to output 'entering function name'
          WRITE (  )        to output labeled list of arguments
        ENDIF
C
          .
          .
          .
C
        IF (BUG) THEN
          WRITE (  )        to output 'leaving function name'
          WRITE (  )        to output labeled list of arguments
        ENDIF
C
        name = . . .
        RETURN
C
        formats go here
C
        END
```

Figure 8.1   Code Skeleton for a FUNCTION unit

assignment operator but without the arguments enclosed in parentheses. It is this assignment statement that commands the computer to store the single value computed by the right-hand side in the location designated by the function name.

8.8 DESIGN OF A JOB THAT USES A FUNCTION

We return to the task of making a design for a job to consist of a main program and a function that will compute the the probability of v successes in n trials. The program will be for an interactive environment. The design for the main program is given in Figure 8.2. As usual, the main program inputs the major data items. For this application, the main program will input p, v, and n. It then computes the com-

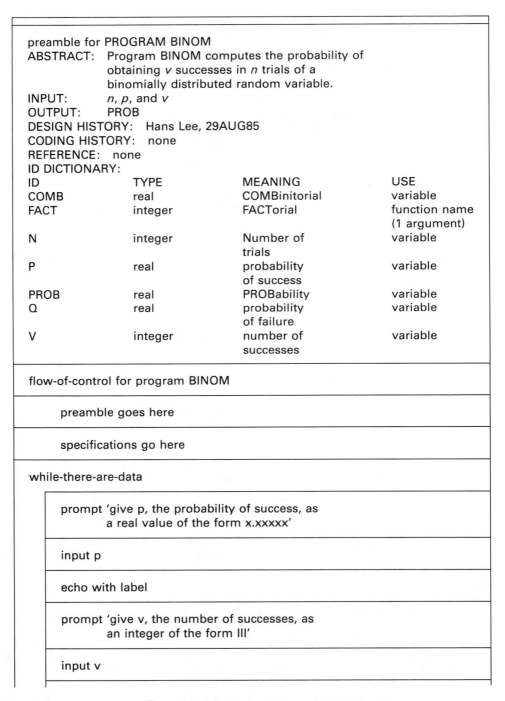

preamble for PROGRAM BINOM
ABSTRACT: Program BINOM computes the probability of
             obtaining *v* successes in *n* trials of a
             binomially distributed random variable.
INPUT: *n*, *p*, and *v*
OUTPUT: PROB
DESIGN HISTORY: Hans Lee, 29AUG85
CODING HISTORY: none
REFERENCE: none
ID DICTIONARY:

ID	TYPE	MEANING	USE
COMB	real	COMBinitorial	variable
FACT	integer	FACTorial	function name (1 argument)
N	integer	Number of trials	variable
P	real	probability of success	variable
PROB	real	PROBability	variable
Q	real	probability of failure	variable
V	integer	number of successes	variable

flow-of-control for program BINOM

    preamble goes here

    specifications go here

while-there-are-data

    prompt 'give p, the probability of success, as
           a real value of the form x.xxxxx'

    input p

    echo with label

    prompt 'give v, the number of successes, as
           an integer of the form III'

    input v

Figure 8.2   The Design of Program BINOM

echo with label
prompt 'give n, the number of trials, as   an integer of the form III'
echo with label
Q = 1.0 − P
COMB = FACT(N)/(FACT(V) ∗ FACT(N − V))
PROB = (COMB) ∗ (P∗∗V) ∗ (Q∗∗(N − V))
output PROB

output 'normal program termination'

end of program BINOM

Figure 8.2   (continued)

binatorial using the function FACT, which will be defined in another unit, shown here as Figure 8.3. As may be seen in the design, we have two assignment statements, one that obtains the value of the combinatorial and the other that uses it to compute the probability we desire. The two assignment statements could have been written as one, but this would have made it a very long and complex one. Such long and complex expressions should be avoided, as they are quite likely to contain errors. The use of the intermediate variable COMB and the second assignment operation is well worth the cost, as it makes the logic clearer and makes it much easier to read the expressions; hence errors may be detected much more easily.

8.9 DISCUSSION OF FACT AND OF FUNCTIONS IN FORTRAN

We should always check on the effects of all possible values that might be assumed by entry parameters. There is one possible point of confusion, speaking as system designers. A system designer must be careful to distinguish between what a user might supply as values from what are mathematically acceptable as values. For example, the factorial function is defined for all positive integer values, including zero. Consequently, the design for the function should include a test for possible negative values. It should provide a message and then terminate execution if a negative value is supplied as an argument. The behavior of the function then should be

preamble for integer function FACT(N)
ABSTRACT: The function, FACT, returns the factorial
             of the value of its argument.
INPUT: none
OUTPUT: none
ENTRY VALUE: N
EXIT VALUE: FACT
ENTRY AND EXIT VALUES: none
DESIGN HISTORY: Hans Lee, 28AUG85
CODING HISTORY: none
REFERENCE: none
ID DICTIONARY:

ID	TYPE	MEANING	USE
FACT	integer	FACTORIAL	function name
I	integer	I	variable
N	integer	N	variable
TEMP	integer	TEMPorary	variable

flow-of-control for integer function FACT(N)

preamble goes here

specifications go here

TEMP = 1

if N is less than zero then
----
output 'factorial function not defined for
       values less than zero. Argument of
       N had value of ', N

STOP

for I from 1 to N in steps of 1

TEMP = TEMP * I

Figure 8.3   Design of Integer FUNCTION FACT(N)

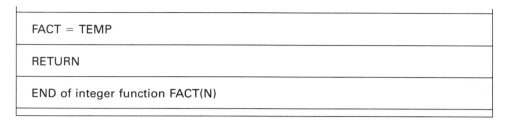

FACT = TEMP

RETURN

END of integer function FACT(N)

Figure 8.3   (continued)

verified for 0!, which is defined to be the integer 1. When we examine the antici-
pated execution for the function referenced with a zero argument, we see that TEMP
is initialized to the integer 1. The following determinate repetition specifies 'for the
control variable, I, from 1 to N.' But when translated into FORTRAN 77, the system will evaluate the N and, in the case it is 0, simply omit the execution of the entire determinate repetition. Therefore, execution will continue by assigning to FACT
the value of TEMP, which is 1; then execution will return to the referencing program. Thus the function will apparently behave correctly for a zero argument.

The factorial function also may be defined as

$$n! = n(n - 1)!$$

which is called a *recursive definition,* since it defines the factorial function in terms
of itself. This is perfectly acceptable as long as some terminating value is defined. In
the case of the factorial function, 1! is defined as 1, and 0! is defined as 1. Consequently, the recursion will terminate.

The meaning of the notation is best illustrated with an example: 4! is evaluated
as follows:

$$4(3!)$$
$$4(3(2!))$$
$$4(3(2(1!)))$$

However, because 1! is defined as 1, we may write

$$(4(3(2(1))))$$

Thus, 4! = 24.

Although some computer languages include facilities for writing recursive subprograms, in FORTRAN *recursion is prohibited.* No function may reference itself.
This implies that, within a function definition, the name of that same function with
parentheses surrounding its argument list may *not* appear on the right-hand side of a
replacement operator. It also means that no chain of function references may result
in a recursive function reference. A chain of function references might be based on
two or more functions, say FNA and FNB. If FNA references FNB and if FNB contains a reference to FNA, then a recursive reference has been made. *This is prohibited in FORTRAN.*

Caution.   In the FORTRAN standards, there is no specification that the system must check for the possibility of recursion. Thus, the writers of the FORTRAN
system need not include a check and commonly do not check for this. If you violate

this prohibition against recursion, the results are unpredictable. You might want to try it to see what happens with a few different examples.

Recursion is not permitted with subroutines either.

8.10 EXERCISES

1. Design and implement a program to determine the kinetic energy of a weight, w, that has fallen a distance d feet.

Supporting Information.   The energy of an object due to its motion is called its *kinetic energy,* abbreviated K.E. It is given by

$$\text{K.E.} = \tfrac{1}{2}mv^2$$

where m is the mass and v is the velocity. The mass of an object may be obtained from

$$F = mg$$

in which F is the force, m is the mass, and g is the acceleration due to gravity. From this, we can obtain

$$m = \frac{F}{g}$$

The distance an object falls is given by

$$d = \tfrac{1}{2}gt^2$$

where t is the time the object falls. We may solve this expression for the numerical value of the mass. The velocity is given by

$$v = gt$$

We can combine this information to express the velocity as

$$v = \sqrt{2gd}$$

We can then substitute the distance in this expression for the velocity. Then we use this numerical value for the velocity and the mass in the expression

$$\text{K.E.} = \tfrac{1}{2}mv^2$$

Constant. g is 32 ft/s^2.

Units.   If the distance is in feet and the weight is in pounds, then the mass is in slugs, the velocity is in feet per second, and K.E. is in foot-pounds.

Program Specification.   The program is to process an indefinite number of data sets. Each data set consists of a pair of values, w, the weight of the object, and d, the distance the object has fallen. The output should echo w and d and give the kinetic energy for these values.

Data Sets.   Test your program using the following data sets:

$$
\begin{array}{ll}
w = 10.0 \text{ lb}, & d = 50.0 \text{ ft} \\
w = 10.0 \text{ lb}, & d = 100.0 \text{ ft} \\
w = 50.0 \text{ lb}, & d = 6.5 \text{ ft} \\
w = 50.0 \text{ lb}, & d = 0.0 \text{ ft} \\
w = -2.5 \text{ lb}, & d = 4.0 \text{ ft} \\
w = 0.0 \text{ lb}, & d = -5.0 \text{ ft}
\end{array}
$$

2. This problem is another version of the kinetic energy problem. Follow the instructions given in Exercise 1, except, instead of supplying data as a set of specific values, input an

indefinite number of ranges of values and use nested determinate repetition to explore the kinetic energy for these ranges.

3. Find the tension in two cables that are used to suspend a traffic light over the middle of an intersection. The light weighs w pounds and the cables form an angle, α, as in Figure 8.4. The angle is given in degrees.

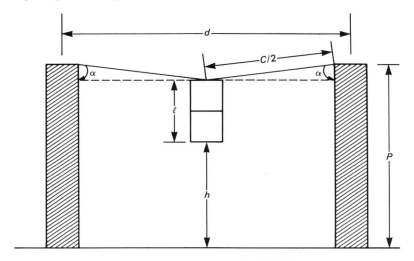

Figure 8.4   A Suspended Traffic Light

Supporting Information.   The tension, T, is given by

$$T = \frac{w}{2\sin(90 - \alpha)}$$

Units.   The tension, T, is in the same units as w, the weight of the light.

Program Specification.   The program is to input pairs of values, α and w.

Data sets.   Traffic lights can vary in weight. Systematically explore various values, say between 50 lb and 150 lb. Considering the nature of the problem, there are "reasonable" and "unreasonable" values for α. Build in program tests for unreasonable values. Explore various combinations of reasonable values for α with the values you selected for the weight of the traffic light.

4. This problem is based on Exercise 3. Refer to that problem for the diagram and additional detail.

Task.   In the traffic light problem, allow α to vary over the range $50° \leq \alpha \leq 85°$ in 5° increments. Also calculate the length of cable and post required.

Supporting Information.

$$C = \frac{d}{\cos(90 - \alpha)}$$

and

$$P = h + l + \left(\frac{d}{2}\right)\tan(90 - \alpha)$$

9

Developing Designs with Sketch Diagrams

9.1 INTRODUCTION

At this point we would like to reconsider the process of developing a design. In this chapter we reexamine several of the essential ideas involved in developing a design and introduce a few new ones. One of the new concepts is the use of an organizational chart to diagram the **units** (main program, external functions, and subroutines) and their interrelationships. Another new idea is the use of what we call the *sketch diagrams* for the seven control structures. These sketch diagrams are to be used to jot down preliminary design ideas *prior* to the preparation of a formal design utilizing the design diagrams already presented.

We believe that these sketch diagrams provide a reasonably good means for representing the thoughts of a systems analyst working in the early phases of developing a design. These diagrams are especially convenient for the tasks required in this early phase because they represent most of the aspects of the control structures in a form that is both fairly easy to record and fairly easy to modify. In less academic terms, our sketch diagrams are intended to be used in "scratch work." Thus, although we use them in this text to display the thought processes involved in the development of a design and although we ourselves do develop designs by using these diagrams, we believe that they are *only* for the designer to use in the scratch-work phase of developing a design. They are *not* intended for communication to others. Further, they are not meant to be kept over any period of time, nor are they intended to become a replacement for the formal design diagrams introduced in earlier chapters. They are not as good as the formal diagrams in sharply and unambiguously displaying graphically all of the details of a program. Further, they are not, to our knowledge, used in other texts or programming manuals. In summary, these sketch diagrams are a preliminary and temporary device, but one that is especially convenient for displaying design ideas and reflecting how we ourselves develop a design and how we suspect others go about the process of preparing a design.

We shall illustrate the use of these sketch diagrams by considering a client's program request. In creating a design to meet the specifications contained in the client's program request, we shall illustrate what is meant by the phrases design by stepwise refinement and top-down design. Of course, we continue to stress modular structured programming.

9.2 ORGANIZATIONAL CHARTS

In discussing the structure of organizations such as corporations or universities, sociologists present a diagram that they call an *organizational chart*. This chart presents the various administrative positions and their interrelationships from the top down. Part of such a chart is presented here as Figure 9.1. Such a chart is drawn by using rectangles for the relevant positions, offices, or committees. These are arranged with the chief corporate (or legal) body at the top and all other subsidiary positions below, arranged to show the levels within the organization and the flow-of-command from the top down to the lowest position in the organization. These charts imply a hierarchical structuring of the positions within the organization.

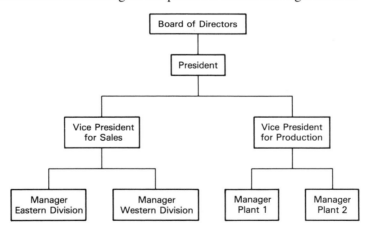

Figure 9.1   Organizational Chart for a Small Manufacturing Firm

An analogous hierarchical arrangement of the units of a computer program is a usual characteristic of almost all but the most simple program. Therefore, similar organizational charts are useful for conveying the organization of the main program and subprograms. In such a representation, each rectangle represents a unit of the program. The chart as a whole displays the levels of the units and the interrelationship between the units. The topmost level is always a main program. In programs of any complexity, the main program is used with one or more subprograms. When a main program is used primarily to reference a series of subprograms, it is called a **driver.** As it is customary to strive to construct programs that are as general as possible, a program is usually designed to process an indefinite number of data sets. This implies that the main program routinely takes on the form of a driver constructed as a while-there-are-data module containing the necessary subprogram references. Finally, as a matter of modular style, we strive to construct the main program so that it conforms to the modular criteria of one entrance and one exit (the normal program termination message or an error message) followed by the termination of execution (commanded by the STOP).

Just as we strive to construct a main program that conforms to the criteria of a module, we strive to construct each unit so as to conform to the criteria of a module. Because of the importance of these criteria, we review them in a slightly different form than in our earlier definition:

(1) Conceptually speaking, a module executes a single task.
(2) The flow-of-control can enter a module only at one place — the top of the module.
(3) The flow-of-control can exit from a module only at one place — the bottom of the module.
(4) There is a *single* exception. When an error is detected, it is appropriate to output an informative message and immediately terminate execution.

We also call attention to the fact that each of the following seven control structures is a module:

Sequence
1-alternative selection
2-alternative selection
n-alternative selection
Determinate repetitition
Pretested indeterminate repetition
Posttested indeterminate repetition

We might choose to call these the fundamental modules and then to conceive of a module as either a fundamental module or a structure constructed out of fundamental modules. Although there is nothing in the syntax of FORTRAN to force the units of a program to conform to the criteria of a module, as a matter of style, we strive to construct all units so that each conforms to the criteria of a module.

You may have wondered about the first criterion, which speaks of a module executing just one task. We claim that to execute one task, the task may require the execution of several steps. But the task should be characterizable by one basic goal. This should be reflected in the name chosen by the analyst for the unit. A fairly satisfactory intuitive definition of a task that, conceptually speaking, "does one thing" is that you should be able to describe the task in a single — although perhaps complex — sentence. An example is, This main program reads an indefinite number of data sets and, for each data set, references three subroutines: SOLVE, INSCR, and CIRCUM.

9.3 SKETCH FORMS OF THE CONTROL STRUCTURES

Sketch diagrams are constructed from the fundamental form, a rectangle, and consist of horizontal separators, called **full bars** and **right bars**, and vertical boundaries, called **left** and **right margins.** These features are illustrated in Figure 9.2. When used in the specific sketch diagrams, these separators, along with indentation of inserted material, emphasize the logic of the flow-of-control. The individual sketch diagrams for each of the control structures are illustrated in Figure 9.3. These contain the **indicator words** or **phrases** that serve to assist the user in associating the sketch diagram with the respective control structure.

When standing alone, each sketch diagram has a full bar across the top and another across the bottom. As we construct a full sketch design of a program unit, we either stack the sketch diagrams, each one on top of another one, or else nest them within one another. When we stack them on top of one another, only one full bar is used to separate consecutive diagrams. When we nest a sketch diagram within another, the full bar is replaced by the right bar. Then the burden of making the logic clear is shared among the user, the right bar, and indentation, as the left margin is omitted from the sketch diagrams when they are nested within another diagram. Consequently, *it is imperative to draw the right bars with a given length for each level of nesting and to be very meticulous about preserving indentation in order*

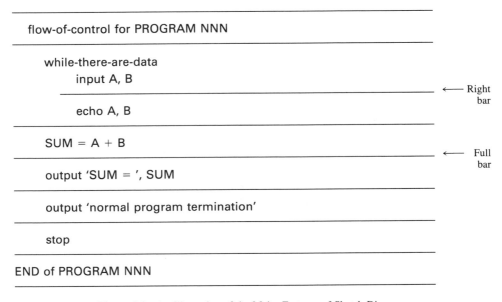

Figure 9.2   An Illustration of the Major Features of Sketch Diagrams

sequence

_____

_____

1-alternative selection

if ( ) then
    statement

_____

2-alternative selection

if ( ) then
    statement

_____

else
    statement

_____

----

n-alternative selection

for n = 1
    statement

_____

for n = 2
    statement

_____

    ⋮

_____

----

determinate repetition

repeat
    statement

_____

    statement

_____

----

pretested determinate repetition

while
    statement

_____

    statement

_____

----

posttested determinate repetition

    statement

_____

    statement
until

_____

Figure 9.3 Control Structure Sketch Diagrams

to appropriately match the levels of nesting. Neither the exact length of the right bars nor the exact depth of indentation is of great concern. The critical factor is that the user can see the relative depth of the nesting. Thus, a quick glance permits the immediate detection of the level of nesting. Consistency is the major criterion we use to determine the depth of indentation or the length of the right bars. The right bar and the indentation should be the same throughout a given design for any given level of nesting; but each different level must have an easy means of discriminating it from every other level.

9.4 THE USE OF SKETCH DIAGRAMS

When developing a design, we use the indicator words or phrases contained within the forms presented in this chapter. These indicator words are supplemented by English words and phrases and by mathematical notation. In the development of a design, we strive to *avoid* thinking in code or writing in code. But we do attempt to develop the symbolic names as early in the design process as possible. As we select the symbolic names, we use them from that point on in the designs. We shall illustrate the use of sketch diagrams by a case study that we call Circles and Triangles.

9.4.1 Circles and Triangles: A Client's Request

A client wants a program that will process an indefinite number of data sets. Each data set will consist of real values for the lengths of the sides of a triangle. The client wants the following output:

The area of the triangle

The circumference and area of the circle inscribed in the triangle

The circumference and area of the circle that circumscribes the triangle

The client supplied the following notation and formula: Let a, b, and c denote the sides of a triangle. Further, let $s = 0.5(a + b + c)$.

(1) The area of this triangle, A, is given by
$$A = \sqrt{s(s - a)(s - b)(s - c)}$$

(2) The radius of a circle, r, inscribed in any triangle is given by
$$r = \frac{\sqrt{s(s - a)(s - b)(s - c)}}{s}$$

(3) The radius of a circle, r, that circumscribes a triangle is given by
$$r = \frac{(abc)}{4\sqrt{s(s - a)(s - b)(s - c)}}$$

(4) The circumference, C, of a circle with radius r is given by
$$C = 2\pi r$$

(5) The area of a circle, A, is given by
$$A = \pi r^2$$

9.4.2 The Design of the Topmost Level

The systems analyst, as is always the case, started to sketch out the program by considering the topmost unit, a main program. As is customary, he conceived of the main program as a driver that would input the data, perform any necessary checks on the data, and then reference other units to carry out the remaining computations. He decided to use CIRTRI as the name of the main program. His initial sketch of CIRTRI is reproduced here as Figure 9.4.

---

program CIRTRI

an indefinite repetition

to read one data set (three real numbers to be
sides of a triangle)

to verify that the three numbers are indeed the sides
of a triangle

if the three numbers are a triangle,
to reference a subroutine to solve for the
requested areas and circumferences

if the three numbers are not a triangle,
to output a message, and go on to the next
three values

to loop back to process the next three values

when there are no more data, to terminate

Figure 9.4   First Sketch of Main PROGRAM CIRTRI

In the next step, the systems analyst rewrote this first version. He selected the names A, B, and C, for the variable names for the values of the sides of the triangles. Because his sketch included the idea for using an indefinite repetition based upon the desire to enable the program to input an indefinite number of data sets, he began the second sketch of the main program with a pretested indefinite repetition (while-there-are-data). To be sure that no error was made in reading the data, he also decided to echo it. (To **echo** input is to output the input immediately after the values were read in order to be sure no error was made. If the output is directed to a printer, it is always a good practice to echo the values of variables; for arrays, we recommend that you echo the first three values and the last three values.) Figure 9.5 shows the use of the sketch design for this.

He decided that because there were several possibilities for errors in the data, the checking of the data values should be done in another unit. The outcome of that checking would be either, Yes, the three values form a triangle or No, the three values do not form a triangle. He reasoned that because the result of the evaluation was to be used in a logical or relational expression in a test in the main program, the data-checking unit ideally should be a logical function. Thus, the result of the evaluation of the function would be either true or false, and this value could be employed in the test in the main program. He also decided to call this function TRI, with the

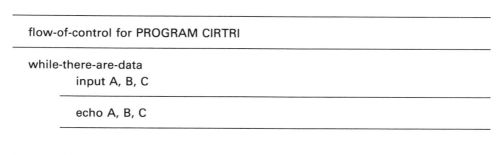

Figure 9.5   Second Sketch of Main PROGRAM CIRTRI

connotation that the function would return true if the values of A, B, and C formed a TRIangle. (At this point, he did *not* consider further the details of the yet-to-be-designed function TRI.)

When the analyst reexamined the client's program request, he noted that it was somewhat complicated and jotted down a reminder (in red ink) to be careful because the notation could lead to errors that would be difficult to detect. He made notes to be sure to retain the distinctions between the dual uses of *r* for both the inscribed and circumscribed radius as well as the use of *A* for the area of the triangle, for the area of the circle, and as the symbolic name for one of the sides of the triangle. After making these notes to himself on the working copy of the client's request, he continued the consideration of the main program.

The analyst reasoned that if the three numbers indeed formed a triangle, then another unit would be referenced that would solve the various equations for the results requested by the client. This unit would be a subroutine with the name SOLVE. Further, he determined that SOLVE would require three arguments, A, B, and C. Now, at this point, he entered these decisions in the sketch of the main program using a 1-alternative selection to reference SOLVE if TRI returned *true*. This resulted in the design in Figure 9.6.

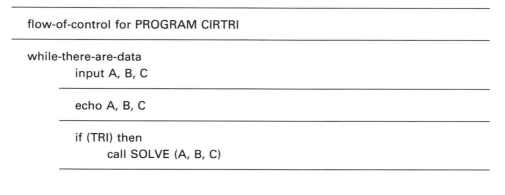

Figure 9.6   Third Sketch of Design of Main PROGRAM CIRTRI

Finally, the analyst reexamined the first sketch design and there saw that the only remaining tasks for the main program were to output a "normal program termination" message and terminate the execution. Then he completed the sketch design of the main program (see Figure 9.7). Notice that the last right bar of Figure 9.6 becomes a full bar in Figure 9.7.

flow-of-control for PROGRAM CIRTRI
while-there-are-data
      input A, B, C

      echo A, B, C

     if (TRI) then
          call SOLVE (A, B, C)

output 'normal program termination'

stop

END of PROGRAM CIRTRI

Figure 9.7 Fourth Sketch of Main PROGRAM CIRTRI

9.4.3 The Formal Design of Program CIRTRI

The next step, the translation of the sketch diagram into the formal design for Program CIRTRI, was simple and quite straightforward. To do this, the systems analyst had to write the preamble and had to translate the sketch diagram into the formal design. The result is the formal design in Figure 9.8. If he did not have a coder available, he would translate the design into code at this time and test the code. We will assume that he had a coder available and, therefore, was able to continue working on the design by going on to design the next unit.

preamble for program CIRTRI
ABSTRACT: Given the length of each side of a triangle,
                  CIRTRI computes the area of the triangle,
                  the area and circumference of a circumscribed
                  circle and the area and circumference of an
                  inscribed circle.
INPUT: the length of each of the three sides of a
                  triangle

Figure 9.8 Design of PROGRAM CIRTRI

OUTPUT:		echo of the three sides of the triangle	
DESIGN HISTORY:		Trina Lee, 12MAR85	
CODING HISTORY:		none	
REFERENCES:		Burington, Richard Stevens.	
		Handbook of Mathematical Tables and Formulas.	
		Sandusky, Ohio: Handbook Publishers, Inc.	

ID DICTIONARY:

ID	TYPE	MEANING	USE
A	real	side A of a triangle	variable
B	real	side B of a triangle	variable
C	real	side C of a triangle	variable
CIRTRI	NA	CIRcles and TRIangles	program name
SOLVE	NA	solve for results	subroutine name (3 arguments)
TRI	logical	TRIangle (returns true if A, B, C are the sides of a triangle)	function name (3 arguments)

---

flow-of-control for PROGRAM CIRTRI

---

    preamble goes here

---

    specifications go here

---

while-there-are-data

    input A, B, C

---

    echo A, B, C

---

    if (TRI)
          then
- -
    call SOLVE (A, B, C)

---

output 'normal program termination'

---

stop

END of PROGRAM CIRTRI

Figure 9.8   (continued)

9.4.4 Developing the Design of the Logical Function TRI

The systems analyst decided to verify that the three values given as input form the sides of a triangle. This could be done in a logical function for which he chose the name TRI. But, little needed to be done to design this function. It must be a function, specifically, a logical function. Further, it is obvious that the values to be transmitted to the function are the three values that are to be considered as the values of the sides of the triangle. The question to be answered by the execution of the function is, Do these three values form a triangle? His initial sketch of the design may be seen in Figure 9.9.

logical function TRI (A, B, C)

the function is to return true if A, B, and C
form a triangle; it is to return false if they
do not form a triangle

Figure 9.9 Initial Design of Logical Function TRI

There was no specific formula included with the client's request for verifying that the three values were indeed the sides of a given triangle. So, the systems analyst had to develop the appropriate tests. Certainly if any of the values are zero or are negative, it cannot be a triangle. Then he thought about the construction of a triangle. If the longest side were on a horizontal axis, then the sum of the other two sides would have to be longer than the longest side. This could be programmed as two tests. He realized, though, that this would require several statements, in addition to the computations required to determine which side was the longest. Before he started making more notes on this method, he thought about the problem further. He became convinced that there was a simpler way to determine whether three values, a, b, c, formed a triangle. The three values could not form a triangle if any one value was larger than the sum of the other two values, for each combination of values. Thus, if any *one* of the three values a, b, or c were larger than the sum of the other two values, the function should return *false*. Otherwise, the function should return *true*. That is, the function should return *false* if $a > (b + c)$, if $b > (a + c)$, or if $c > (a + b)$. He noted that the same restrictions could be formed with reverse logic by having the function return *true* if *all* the three inequalities, $a \le (b + c)$, $b \le (a + c)$, and $c \le (b + a)$ were true.

The test could be performed as a single 2-alternative selection. Only one flow-of-control structure would be necessary, but the test would require a complicated relational expression. This complexity is manageable in this case, but simpler tests are preferable as they are less likely to be incorrect. The systems analyst sketched out the design using the 2-alternative selection, as shown in Figure 9.10.

Another possibility would be to use a series of 1-alternative selections, one for each of the inequalities. But in this case, the test using the logical connective *or* must be used. He also prepared this form of the design, so that he could compare the two approaches. This design is shown in Figure 9.11.

flow-of-control for logical function TRI (A, B, C)

if (((A ≤ (B + C)) and (B ≤ (A + C)) and (C ≤ A + B)) then
    TRI = true

else

    output 'the three values do not form a triangle'

    TRI = false

RETURN

END

Figure 9.10   Sketch Design of Logical Function TRI Using 2-alternative Selection

Which approach is better? Unfortunately, each of the two approaches has some advantages and some disadvantages. The shortness of the design that uses the 2-alternative selection is offset by the complexity of the relational expression that must be evaluated. The simplicity of the design using the 1-alternative selection is offset by the length of the design. The major criterion our systems analyst uses is logical simplicity. In contrasting these two designs, he felt that they were about

flow-of-control for logical function TRI

TRI = true

if A > (B + C) then
    TRI = false

    output 'the three values do not form a triangle'

    output 'A is larger than B + C'

if B > (A + C) then
    TRI = false

    output 'the three values do not form a triangle'

    output 'B is larger than A + C'   *(continues)*

Figure 9.11   Sketch Design of Logical Function TRI Using Three 1-alternative Selections

```
if C > (A + B) then
    TRI = false
```

---

output 'the three values do not form a triangle'

---

output 'C is larger than A + B'

RETURN

END

Figure 9.11   (continued)

equal in logical simplicity, but he recognized that he had a slight preference for the method using the 1-alternative selection. He felt that the simpler relational expressions made the logic much clearer, that giving explicit error information was slightly better, and that the designs would be easier to update. Consequently, he chose the method using the 1-alternative selection. He next converted this sketch into a polished design. The result is shown in Figure 9.12.

preamble for logical function TRI (A, B, C)

ABSTRACT: When the three values, A, B, and C form a
                     triangle, the function, TRI, returns true.
                     If A, B, and C do not form the sides of a
                     triangle, the function returns false.
INPUT: none
OUTPUT: Output is made only if the values do not
                     form a triangle.
ENTRY VALUES: A, B, C
EXIT VALUES: TRI
ENTRY AND EXIT VALUES: none
DESIGN HISTORY: Trina Lee, 12MAR85
CODING HISTORY: none
REFERENCE: none
ID DICTIONARY:

ID	TYPE	MEANING	USE
A	real	the A side of a triangle	variable
B	real	the B side of a triangle	variable
C	real	the C side of a triangle	variable
TRI	logical	TRIangle	function name (3 arguments)

Figure 9.12   Design of Logical Function TRI

flow-of-control for logical function TRI (A, B, C)

preamble goes here

specifications go here

TRI = true

if A > (B + C)
   then
--   ------

   TRI = false

   output 'the three values do not form a triangle'

   output 'A is larger than B + C'

if B > (A + C)
   then
--   ------

   TRI = false

   output 'the three values do not form a triangle'

   output 'B is larger than A + C'

if C > (A + B)
   then

   TRI = false

   output 'the three values do not form a triangle'

   output 'C is larger than A + B'

RETURN

END of logical function TRI

Figure 9.12   (continued)

9.4.5 Design of Subroutine SOLVE

As the design is emerging, when execution reaches subroutine SOLVE, there will be three values that have been verified to be the sides of a triangle. Further, these are the only data values that must be made available to the subroutine. Also, the subroutine does not need to return any data to the referencing unit. Thus, there would be an argument list consisting of the three values, A, B, and C. The analyst noted that the remaining computations made extensive use of the value of s and of the more complicated expression that appears under the square root sign in several different equations, so he decided that these would have to be computed before obtaining the areas and circumferences. He decided to use the symbolic name S to stand for s and the symbolic name ROOT to stand for the square root of the expression given in the formula under the square root sign. One possibility for the design would be to compute S and ROOT in separate functions, since each returns a single value and each appeared in an arithmetic expression. However, he rejected this possibility because he noted that S and ROOT appeared in several places; if they were implemented as functions and directly referenced each time that S and ROOT appeared in these other formulas, several reevaluations of the same function using the same values for the arguments would be required. In addition, he reasoned that if he implemented them as functions but referenced them just once at the beginning of subroutine SOLVE, he would not be referencing them in arithmetic expressions but merely in an assignment statement. Thus, if they were to be implemented in another unit or in two other units, one of the motivations for using a function rather than a subroutine did not seem applicable. Further, if he used functions for both, he would have to reference the function that evaluated S and supply the result to the function that would compute ROOT. Thus, the logic would become somewhat more complicated, and the choice of functions would not be well motivated. He therefore rejected the idea of implementing them as two functions. He considered the possibility of implementing the unit to compute S as a function and the unit to compute ROOT as a subroutine. But again, the unit that would compute ROOT would have to reference the function to obtain S or else the value would have to be supplied as an argument. Again, he rejected this mixed approach because it made the logic unnecessarily unwieldy. Next, he considered the alternative of evaluating both S and ROOT in a single subroutine. This seemed a reasonable alternative. But he compared this strategy with merely evaluating them directly within the subroutine SOLVE. When he considered the contrast between the single subroutine and direct evaluation within SOLVE, he could not see any strong arguments for preferring one way over the other. Wisely, he reasoned that the decision in part depended upon what additional computations would be done in SOLVE. So, before making a decision as how to evaluate S and ROOT, he turned to another examination of the client's request. He noted the annotations in red that cautioned about the two distinct uses of r and the three distinct uses of A. Also, he noted that the remaining computations really appeared to be logically divided into three components: (1) the area of the triangle; (2) the area and circumference of the circle inscribed in the triangle; and (3) the area and circumference of the circle circumscribing the triangle. He observed that if a new subroutine were used for the inscribed circle and another new subroutine were used for the circumscribed circle, the potential problems with the multiple use of R would disappear, and some of the potential problems with the multiple use of A would be alleviated. Consequently, he decided that he would indeed use two subroutines for these tasks. One he elected to name CIRCUM and the other, INSCR. Each would require A, B, C, ROOT, and S as entry values.

Finally, he considered the computation of the area of the triangle. The formula for the area of the triangle shows that the value of the area is given directly by the expression computed for the value of ROOT. Thus, no computations would be required, only an output statement. Suddenly, the design of SOLVE seemed to fall into place. After the computation of S and ROOT, the subroutine would have to have an output statement for the area of the triangle; then there would be two subroutine calls, which would complete the tasks for SOLVE. Further, because the output statement and the subroutine calls were quite simple and because nothing more was to be done in SOLVE, he decided that S and ROOT would be computed directly within the subroutine rather than in a separate unit for this purpose. After these decisions had been made, the sketch of the design of subroutine SOLVE was complete. See Figure 9.13.

```
SUBROUTINE SOLVE (A, B, C)
computes S
computes ROOT, the expression under square root sign
output the area of the triangle (given by the value of ROOT)
call CIRCUM (A, B, C, ROOT, S)
call INSCR (A, B, C, ROOT, S)
return
end of SUBROUTINE SOLVE
```

Figure 9.13   First Sketch Design of SUBROUTINE SOLVE

The sketch of the design of SOLVE next has to be refined by moving toward a polished design. Thus, the statements in English given in Figure 9.13 are converted to the sketch design form. The system analyst does this step by step, starting at the top of SOLVE and working down to the end of the subroutine. As each of the steps in SOLVE is a sequence and there are no other structures, we present only the design after it has been completely converted to the sketch form (see Figure 9.14).

The next step is to translate the sketch design presented in Figure 9.14 to a polished design form. Again, as this is a very simple unit, only the result is given. It is shown in Figure 9.15.

9.4.6 Design of SUBROUTINE CIRCUM

The systems analyst had already decided that CIRCUM would be a subroutine with entry-only arguments, A, B, C, ROOTS, and S. He designed it to compute the radius, the area, and the circumference of the circle that circumscribes the triangle. He was alerted by his red ink comments to be sure to double-check on the use of the flow-of-control for subroutine SOLVE (A, B, C)

S = 0.5(A + B + C)

ROOT = S(S − A) (S − B) (S − C)

output 'the area of the triangle is', ROOT

call CIRCUM (A, B, C, ROOT, S)

call INSCR (A, B, C, ROOT, S)

return

end of subroutine SOLVE

Figure 9.14 Sketch Design of SUBROUTINE SOLVE

preamble for subroutine SOLVE (A, B, C)

ABSTRACT:	SOLVE computes S, ROOT, calls CIRCUM and INSCR.
INPUT:	none
OUTPUT:	ROOT, which gives the area of the triangle
ENTRY VALUES:	A, B, C
EXIT VALUES:	ROOT, S
ENTRY AND EXIT VALUES:	none
DESIGN HISTORY:	Trina Lee, 12MAR85
CODING HISTORY:	none

ID DICTIONARY:

ID	TYPE	MEANING	USE
A	real	side A of a triangle	variable
B	real	side B of a triangle	variable
C	real	side C of a triangle	variable
CIRCUM	NA	CIRCUMscribed	subroutine name (5 arguments)
INSCR	NA	INSCRibed	subroutine name (5 arguments)
ROOT	real	square ROOT	variable
S	real	S	variable
SOLVE	NA	SOLVE	subroutine name (3 arguments)

Figure 9.15 The Design Sketch of SUBROUTINE SOLVE

flow-of-control for subroutine SOLVE (A, B, C)
preamble goes here
specifications go here
S = 0.5 * (A + B + C)
ROOT = S * (S − A) * (S − B) * (S − C)
output 'the area of the triangle is', ROOT
call CIRCUM (A, B, C, ROOT, S)
call INSCR A, B, C, ROOT, S
RETURN
END

Figure 9.15   (continued)

letter *r* for the radius of the circumscribed and the inscribed circles. Consequently, he was very careful to choose the correct formula, and he double-checked that it was indeed correct. However, before he computed the radius of the circle, he specified that he would use PI as the name of π and, further, that the value of PI would be specified as a constant. As the design of this unit was quite simple, involving only a series of sequences, he wrote out the sketch form quite quickly. The result is presented here in Figure 9.16.

SUBROUTINE CIRCUM (A, B, C, ROOT, S)
specify PI as a constant
compute radius of circumscribed circle
compute area of this circle
output area
compute circumference of this circle
output circumference
return
end

Figure 9.16   Design in English of SUBROUTINE CIRCUM

flow-of-control for SUBROUTINE CIRCUM (A, B, C, ROOT, S)

specify PI as a constant with value 3.1415

R = (A * B * C)/(4.0 * ROOT)

AREA = PI * R * R

output 'the area of the circle is', AREA

CIR = 2.0 * PI * R

output 'the circumference of the circle is', CIR

return

end of SUBROUTINE CIRCUM

Figure 9.17 Sketch Design of SUBROUTINE CIRCUM

It was a straightforward task for the analyst to convert the preliminary statement of the design of subroutine CIRCUM to sketch form. The result of this conversion is included here as Figure 9.17. As may be seen there, the analyst chose the name CIR for the circumference and the name AREA for the area. The sketch design was easy to convert to the polished design. The polished design is given here in Figure 9.18.

preamble for subroutine CIRCUM (A, B, C, ROOT, S)	
ABSTRACT:	CIRCUM obtains the radius of a circle circumscribed about a triangle, then obtains the area and circumference of the circle.
INPUT:	none
OUTPUT:	AREA, CIR
ENTRY VALUES:	A, B, C, ROOT, S
EXIT VALUES:	none
ENTRY AND EXIT VALUES:	none
DESIGN HISTORY:	Trina Lee, 12MAR85
CODING HISTORY:	none
REFERENCE:	Client's Program Request

Figure 9.18 Design of SUBROUTINE CIRCUM

ID DICTIONARY:

ID	TYPE	MEANING	USE
A	real	side A of a triangle	variable
B	real	side B of a triangle	variable
C	real	side C of a triangle	variable
CIR	real	CIRcumference	variable
CIRCUM	NA	CIRCUMference	subroutine name (5 arguments)
PI	real	PI (3.1415)	constant
R	real	Radius	variable
S	real	S	variable

flow-of-control for SUBROUTINE CIRCUM (A, B, C, ROOT, S)

preamble goes here

specifications go here

R = (A * B * C)/(4.0 * ROOT)

AREA = PI * R * R

output 'the area of the circle is', AREA

CIR = 2.0 * PI * R

output 'the circumference of the circle is', CIR

RETURN

END of SUBROUTINE CIRCUM

Figure 9.18   (continued)

9.4.7 The Design of INSCR

The analyst had no difficulties in the design of INSCR. It required very little effort, and the decisions came almost automatically (except he was well aware that this is just the time that something could go wrong.) But he produced the preliminary statement of the design in English, then the sketch form, and finally the polished form. The preliminary statement of the design is given in Figure 9.19. The sketch form is given in Figure 9.20. The polished design is not presented.

```
subroutine INSCR (A, B, C, ROOT, S)
specify PI as a constant
compute the radius of the inscribed circle
compute the area of this circle
output the area
compute the circumference of the circle
output the circumference
return
end
```

Figure 9.19   Preliminary Design of SUBROUTINE INSCR

flow-of-control of SUBROUTINE INSCR

specify PI as a constant with the value 3.1415

R = ROOT/S

CIR = 2.0 * PI * R

output 'the circumference is', CIR

AREA = PI * R * R

output 'the area is', AREA

return

end of SUBROUTINE INSCR

Figure 9.20   Sketch Design of SUBROUTINE INSCR

9.5 THE ORGANIZATION OF THE PROGRAM

Because we wanted to develop the design of the program in great detail, we did not also illustrate how the organizational chart for the program was developed. But now we can show the final result, as given in Figure 9.21. The analyst developed this as the respective units were developed.

In Figure 9.21 we see that the program has three levels. At the topmost level is the PROGRAM unit CIRTRI. The next level down consists of two units, the logical

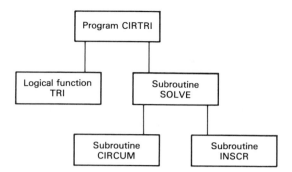

Figure 9.21   The Organization Chart for PROGRAM CIRTRI

FUNCTION TRI and the SUBROUTINE SOLVE. The bottom level also consists of two units, the SUBROUTINE CIRCUM and the SUBROUTINE INSCR. We also see in the figure that only SOLVE references CIRCUM and INSCR. In addition, only CIRTRI references TRI and SOLVE. Such an organization chart is a required part of the documentation of any large program. The process of developing such a chart is a helpful task for the analyst because, especially in larger programs, it can sharpen any logical difficulties or possibly unwanted complexity in the interrelationships between units.

9.6 TOP-DOWN DESIGN AND DESIGN BY STEPWISE REFINEMENT

In this text, we have stressed structured programming, meaning that only sequence, selection, and repetition flow-of-control structures are used. Further, we have stressed the use of a modular approach; that is, the program is broken up into a series of modules, each with flow-of-control entering at the top and leaving at the bottom. At this point, we now have designed a larger program, meaning that it consists of several units on different levels. In doing this, we have illustrated two additional aspects of program design. We have used top-down design in this text, although it has been possible to make the point vivid only in this chapter, where we have a sufficiently complex set of units. In **top-down design**, the topmost unit is designed first, and units at lower levels are left undesigned until the topmost level is completely designed. Only after the topmost level is designed is the next level designed. Only after all units on the next level are designed is the next level down designed, and so on, with the units in any one level systematically and completely designed before the design of any unit at a lower level is begun.

We have also illustrated another component in our repertoire of design techniques. We carefully began the design of each unit with a written sketch in English. Then, continuing with the design of this same unit (and before commencing the design of any other unit) we translated the English statements step by step into the sketch design statements. Then we translated these into the final, or polished, designs. This systematic approach, concentrating on one unit before beginning to consider another unit, starting with a statement in English and gradually refining this by a series of translations until a complete design is obtained, is called **design by stepwise refinement.** Although not all authors strive to make the distinction between the technique of top-down design and design by stepwise refinement, we do because we believe that it is helpful to do so. Thus, we conceive of top-down as referring to the levels of the program, designing the top level first, and then level by level down the organizational strcuture. Thus, top-down refers to the vertical aspect of designing down the organizational structure. We contrast this with the strategy of designing a given unit, step-by-step translating from English statements to design statements, or stepwise refinement, which we conceive of as the horizontal aspect of design. Certainly, we agree that these two design techniques are interrelated. It is conceivable that one method could be employed without the other; however, in most computer science applications, both are used, and we highly recommend that they be used together.

9.7 EXERCISES

1. This problem requests additional information for the traffic light problem, which should have been solved previously. (See Exercise 3 in Chapter 8.)

   Task.   In addition to the results originally requested, include the following: (1) Provide as input the cost of cable per foot and the cost of the post per foot; (2) provide as input the maximum allowable tension in the cable; and (3) find the configuration that gives the minimum cost of materials as a function of the angle between cable and post. To find this minimal cost configuration, start with an angle of 89° and decrease the angle in 1° decrements. The number of cables used must be sufficient to support the tension due to the weight of the light.

2. This problem is a continuation of the traffic light problem. The original problem appeared as Exercise 3 in Chapter 8, and the modifications to that program appeared as Exercise 1 in Chapter 9. Both must be solved prior to this one.

   Task.   Instead of varying the angle to locate the minimum cost configuration, vary the number of cables, beginning with one cable and incrementing by one cable until the minimum is found. Determine the angle corresponding to a given number of cables by assuming that the tension is exactly the amount that could be supported by that many cables.

3. This problem is a continuation of the traffic light problem. The original problem appeared as Exercise 3 in Chapter 8. The first variation appeared as Exercise 1 in Chapter 9. The second variation appeared as Exercise 2 in Chapter 9.

   Task.   In this continuing traffic light problem, make the following four modifications: (1) Instead of a single input for height, input a minimum and a maximum allowable height. (2) Instead of allowing posts of any length, assume that the posts must be selected to be a multiple of some standard size, such as 2 ft, 4 ft, 6 ft, and so on. Of course, include an input that gives this standard size. (3) Instead of varying the number of cables to find the minimum cost, vary the post length. Begin with the shortest possible post that allows the minimum height of the light to be achieved. For each post length, calculate the cost for the configuration having the fewest cables that satisfies the height criterion. (4) Instead of printing the tension, output the height of the light.

10

Sorting

10.1 INTRODUCTION

In this chapter, you will further develop your design skills, especially those skills of analysis that are used in the design method known as stepwise refinement. Thus, the chapter provides examples from an important class of programs used to sort lists of data as another case study of the design process. We also use the programs to introduce the notion of an algorithm, a fundamental concept in computer science. Finally, we use the discussion of these sorting programs to consider what has come to be called the computational complexity of an algorithm.

10.2 SOME OBSERVATIONS ON THE DESIGN OF PROGRAMS

A design of a computer program is something like a mathematical theorem. If you see the finished design or the published theorem, you see the end product of a long and frequently messy process. But the end product appears to be neatly organized. Again, we wish to emphasize that the polished and neatly linearized organization of a design is an important basis of good computer programs. However, it may be very counterproductive for anyone to try to produce the finished design in the first step. Human thinking is generally quite nonlinear when dealing with a novel task. Begin by recording notes to yourself on paper as initial scratch work. These initial notes are then revised, and additional organization of the computational process takes place. A good final design is the result of much work, which is usually never seen by anyone other than you. We believe that it is quite unfortunate that this preliminary work is not frequently illustrated in textbooks, as the omission creates the false impression that the design process involves merely drawing the final design on paper without this scratch work and without much preceding thought. Just as the preparation of a well-organized academic paper or an industrial report requires the rough draft versions, which are revised by the author before submission, the designs of computer programs require draft versions and revisions.

10.3 OVERALL DESIGN STRATEGY

For a large number of design tasks, there is a strategy that we feel can commonly be used. We use it, and we have observed others using it. We again emphasize that early in the process we should attempt to solve the problem using paper and pencil methods. Once we can do it, we then attempt to sketch how to do it by computer. We first do it for one case, usually the first or easiest case. We record, on paper, in English, each step. Next, we generalize each step as much as possible. Finally, we insert the generalized steps into an encompassing indefinite (while-there-are-data) repetition. Within this process, we must identify suitable termination criteria.

10.4 THE SORTING PROBLEM

In many applications, a major component of the computational task is to order data in some manner. If the data are alphabetical, such as a list of names, a common task is to alphabetize the names. If the data are numeric, a common task is to arrange them in either increasing value or decreasing value. When done by computer, the process of arranging data so that they appear in a specified order is called **sorting.** There are many different ways to sort data. We first consider a method close to what a human might use to sort a short list on paper. Later, we consider a method better suited for use on a computer.

10.5 PAPER-AND-PENCIL PHASE

We use a list of ten integer items as our example. For simplicity, we will assume that each item is either zero or a positive integer. Here is our list:

$$19$$
$$3$$
$$72$$
$$0$$
$$8$$
$$31$$
$$6$$
$$19$$
$$95$$
$$19$$

We take as our task the production of a list of these values in decreasing order.

When we do this by paper-and-pencil methods, we scan the entire list to locate the largest value. When we have checked all ten values, we take the largest, write it as the first item on the new list, and delete the item from the original list. Observe that there may be more than one occurrence of any given value. If this happens, we delete only the first occurrence. Then we must be sure to look for the largest value on the original list in such a manner that we allow for the possibility of repeated values. We show below the result of doing this five times:

Original List	Sorted List
—	95
3	72
—	31
0	19
8	19
—	
6	
—	
—	
19	

In the case of this example, we would know that we were done when we had crossed off all values from the original list.

10.6 OUTLINE OF THE DESIGN PHASE FOR A SORT PROGRAM

Although our paper-and-pencil-problem was just a sample and was, therefore, short, we eventually want to produce a design that will process an indefinite number of data lists. It is customary to use a one-dimensional array for a such a list. As we want to be able to process lists of unknown, but reasonable, length, we must provide for treating the length as an input value to be specified before reading the data for that list. Because FORTRAN does, in fact, require the specification of a specific value for the dimension of the array, before we can code the design, we must specify what is a maximum "reasonable" value. This should be determined in conference with the client. Here we will arbitrarily say that the reasonable maximum is 9999 elements. This information will not be needed until later.

We will require two arrays, one will be the input list, which will receive the values as they are read. This array we shall call INLIST. The second array will be the values sorted in decreasing order. This list we shall call SORTED. Following our usual custom, we shall design the program unit to perform the input tasks and to invoke a subroutine to perform the sorting. We choose to call the subroutine SORTIT. We shall have the sorted list as an exit parameter from the subroutine. Then we shall defer the output of the sorted list to the calling unit. The sketch of the program unit is as follows:

sketch of PROGRAM SORT
while-there-are-data

(1) Input N, the number of elements in a list

(2) Input N elements, assigning them to INLIST, a one-dimensional array

(3) Invoke subroutine SORTIT, with arguments N and INLIST

(4) Output the sorted list

output 'normal program termination'

In SUBROUTINE SORTIT, we will start by simulating the steps we just did for the paper-and-pencil solution. Thus, the first sketch of SORTIT would be as follows, shown with our notes to ourselves:

---

(1) Determine the largest value in INLIST

(2) Insert the largest value into the first unassigned location in SORTED

(3) Delete the first occurrence of the largest value from INLIST

(4) Repeat or stop

Now we systematically expand each step. The expansion of Step 1 follows:

1.1 Create a temporary variable, call it TEMP, and assign to TEMP the value of INLIST(1).

1.2 Compare the value of TEMP with each remaining N elements of INLIST, that is, with INLIST(2), INLIST(3), . . . , INLIST(N). We use I as the subscript variable. Then, if TEMP is less than INLIST(I), assign TEMP the value of INLIST(I). Notice that after TEMP has been compared to INLIST(N) and, if necessary, TEMP has been assigned the value of I LIST(N), the value of TEMP is the largest value on INLIST.

1.3 For conceptual clarity, we shall assign LARGE the value of TEMP when we have determined that TEMP has the largest value.

Next, we must expand Step 2; insert the largest value into the next location in SORTED. It sounds rather innocuous and easy to grasp. We want to insert the value on the list stored in SORTED at the first location that does not contain a value or, in other words, at the first "empty" location. Thus, we need to keep track of the next available location. This means that we need to have the value of the subscript available and that we must update this value each time we add another data value to SORTED. To gain access to the value of the subscript, we must create a variable. Here, we decide to call it I. Obviously, it will be type integer. The value of I must be initialized. We have two alternatives. We could initialize I to 0, as it were, before we increment it by 1 each time we insert a data value into SORTED. On the other hand, we could initialize I to 1, and then we would increment it by 1 after each insertion. We choose to initalize I to zero, so that each time we insert the next data item into the list, we increment I just before we perform the insertion. This has a slight advantage, because I will always have the value of the last item on the list during each pass. The sketch for the expansion of Step 2 is as follows:

2.1 Initialize I to zero.

2.2 Increment I by one just before making an insertion into SORTED

2.3 Insert LARGE into SORTED(I)

Now we must expand our initial Step 3; delete the first occurrence of the largest value from INLIST. Recall that we had decided to use LARGE as the name of an integer variable whose value would be the largest value found on INLIST. We might have avoided the introduction of this additional variable, but we decided to introduce it for conceptual clarity. We mention this again because we recommend the use of a simple variable in situations such as this in order to make the logic much clearer to the designer, coder, maintainer, and client. (We hope you realize that we could have used TEMP and avoided the use of LARGE.)

We shall continue the use of LARGE, and, therefore, we can say that we want to delete the first occurrence of the value stored in LARGE from the list stored in INLIST. We said that we want to delete the first occurrence of the value from IN-LIST. The selection of the "first" occurrence is a result of thinking in terms of being systematic in starting at the top of the list (that is, with the first element of the list) each time we scan the contents of the list. Further, it becomes rather natural for a designer to think of this in terms of a computational process being controlled by a determinate repetition.

In the computer method we are using, instead of crossing off a value to remove that value from the list, we replace the value to be removed by a special value. In this case, we have chosen to use -99999 as the special value because it is a negative value, and we have said that the possible values will always be zero or positive. Also, we selected five 9s because they will stand out when we scan the list. This idea of using -99999 as a special value is common in programming. We might want to consider other alternatives later. However, we will employ -99999 as our special value, and, further, we will code it as a constant using the symbolic name USED. The expanded Step 3 is as follows:

3.1 Locate the first element of INLIST that has the the value of LARGE.

3.2 Assign the value of the subscript of the element of INLIST containing the value of LARGE to a simple integer variable that we now choose to call TARGET.

3.3 Assign the value of USED to INLIST(TARGET), thereby crossing off, or deleting, that element.

In developing our design through stepwise refinement, we next start generalizing these steps, employing the design terminology. This, again, is scratch-paper work that is for the use of the designer alone.

generalize 1.

1.1   sequence
          TEMP = INLIST(1)

1.2   determinate repetition
          for I = 2 to N by 1   N must be initialized

              one alternative selection
              if TEMP is less than INLIST(I) then
                  TEMP = INLIST(I)

1.3   sequence
          LARGE = TEMP

generalize 2.

          sequence
          I = 0   must go before loop

          sequence
          I = I + 1

          sequence
          SORTED(I) = LARGE

generalize 3.

          sequence
          TARGET = 0

3.1   posttested indeterminate repetition
          sequence
          TARGET = TARGET + 1
3.2   until INLIST(TARGET) = LARGE
3.3   INLIST(TARGET) = USED   USED must be initalized

We now integrate these sections and reorganize any required portions. The result should be a workable preliminary version of the final design. After we obtain this preliminary version, we shall study it with the objective of trying to determine whether it can be improved. But to be effective, this review should come at least 1 day after the preparation of this version. When working on a design, you should give yourself a day off without looking at the design before you review it.

The preliminary polished version of the design is given in Figure 10.1.

preamble for SUBROUTINE SORTIT

ABSTRACT:	SORTIT sorts a list of the integers which must be zero or positive into a new list in which the numbers appear in decreasing value.
INPUT:	none
OUTPUT:	none
ENTRY VALUES:	INLIST, N
EXIT VALUES:	SORTED
ENTRY AND EXIT VALUES:	none
DESIGN HISTORY:	Hans Lee, 30JUL85
CODING HISTORY:	none
REFERENCE:	none

ID DICTIONARY:

ID	TYPE	MEANING	USE
I	integer	I points to next location in SORTED	variable
INLIST	integer	INputLIST	1-dimensional array
LARGE	integer	LARGEST value found in INLIST on one pass	variable
LOC	integer	LOCation INLIST (subscript) where LARGE was found	variable
N	integer	Number of elements on INLIST	variable
SORTED	integer	SORTED list	1-dimensional array
SORTIT	NA	SORT IT	subroutine name
TEMP	integer	TEMPorary	variable
USED	integer	indicates value moved to SORTED	constant = − 99999

flow-of control for SUBROUTINE SORTIT (INLIST, N, SORTED)

Figure 10.1   Design of SUBROUTINE SORTIT

preamble goes here

specifications go here

I = 0

<table>
<tr><td>/////</td><td>TEMP = INLIST(1)</td></tr>
<tr><td></td><td>LOC = 1</td></tr>
<tr><td></td><td>for I = 2 to N step by 1</td></tr>
<tr><td></td><td>if TEMP is less than INLIST(I) THEN

TEMP = INLIST(I)

LOC = I</td></tr>
<tr><td></td><td>LARGE = TEMP</td></tr>
<tr><td></td><td>I = I + 1</td></tr>
<tr><td></td><td>SORTED(I) = LARGE</td></tr>
<tr><td></td><td>INLIST(LOC) = USED</td></tr>
</table>

UNTIL (I equals N)

RETURN

END of SUBROUTINE SORTIT

Figure 10.1   (continued)

10.7 DISCUSSION OF SORTIT

In SUBROUTINE SORTIT we used a procedure that was based upon a method commonly used by humans to order such lists. In this computer design we have used two arrays. Thus, if the lists were long, we might have some space problems because the space required for this list might exceed the amount of space available in central memory. Or, as in some large mainframe computers, we might substantially increase the execution costs if a charge for central memory usage is included in the charges. Or, again as in some systems, we might want to change the execution priority of our job if the amount of central memory required is a factor in the priority assignment. The alternative is that we might be able to avoid having all the arrays in memory at one time, depending upon the facilities available in the computer system being used. For example, if extended memory or if disk or tape storage were available, the design could be arranged to use these resources. But this change would increase the complexity of the program and would also decrease the speed of execution of the job. Most likely, the use of secondary storage would also increase the cost of the ordering of large lists.

In addition to the use of two arrays, notice that we have to pass through IN-LIST a total of $n(n - 1)$ times. Therefore, as the length of the list, N, increases, the amount of execution time increases significantly, thereby causing the cost of execution to increase substantially as a function of the number of elements on the list.

Given a moment's reflection on the frequency of such operations and the amount of data in the form of lists that have to be alphabetized or numerically ordered, it should not be surprising to learn that sorting procedures have been extensively investigated by computer scientists. Considerable progress has been made in the development of efficient methods for sorting. But which particular method is preferred depends upon the details of each particular situation. Some methods are better for short lists, whereas other methods are better for long lists. The choice of a method depends upon other factors, such as whether or not much of the data are already sorted, whether other associated data are to be sorted, whether it is possible to keep all the data in central memory at the same time, and so on. Thus, there is no one single best method for sorting data. The method we have just considered is about the worst method that could be used for any but the most trivial case. The methods that are more frequently used have one interesting characteristic; namely, they are not a method a systems analyst would devise without considerable thought. Typically, they do not appear to be obvious methods. We now consider a sightly more sophisticated method, which is called a bubble sort, because of the similarity to the idea of a bubble in water, which bubbles up to the surface. (Sometimes it is referred to as a rock sort, because of the analogy to a rock that sinks to the bottom.)

10.8 THE BUBBLE SORT

The **bubble sort** is one instance of a class of sorting procedures known as exchange sorts. In an exchange sort, pairs of values are examined to ascertain whether or not each element of the pair is in the desired order. If they are not, the two elements of the pair are exchanged. In this method, items 1 and 2 are compared and, if necessary, exchanged. Then items 2 and 3 are compared and, if necessary, exchanged. The process continues until items $n - 1$ and n are compared and, if necessary, exchanged. At this point, item n will be in the correct position. Therefore, in the next pass item n need not be examined. The result is that in each pass, the number of items that must be examined is reduced by one.

Here is a list of five items to be arranged in descending order:

3

0

7

4

7

We illustrate the bubble sort on this list. We label the results using *Pass,* followed by the pass number to indicate which pass through the list is shown. We indicate which comparison is being made both in the label *Pair,* followed by the pair number, and by an asterisk after each member of the pair being "looked at" at this stage. In each case, the column headed B is the list before the pair is examined, and the column headed A is the list after any required exchange has taken place.

PASS 1

Pair 1		Pair 2		Pair 3		Pair 4	
B	A	B	A	B	A	B	A
3*	3	3	3	3	3	3	3
0*	0	0*	7	7	7	7	7
7	7	7*	0	0*	4	4	4
4	4	4	4	4*	0	0*	7
7	7	7	7	7	7	7*	0

PASS 2

Pair 1		Pair 2		Pair 3	
B	A	B	A	B	A
3*	7	7	7	7	7
7*	3	3*	4	4	4
4	4	4*	3	3*	7
7	7	7	7	7*	3
0	0	0	0	0	0

PASS 3

Pair 1		Pair 2	
B	A	B	A
7*	7	7	7
4*	4	4*	7
7	7	7*	4
3	3	3	3
0	0	0	0

PASS 4

Pair 1	
B	A
7*	7
7*	7
4	4
3	3
0	0

10.9 DESIGN FOR A BUBBLE SORT

If N is the number of items on the list to be sorted, then we observe that there will be $N - 1$ passes. Also, we note that after each pass, there will be one less comparison to be performed. We might note this in the form of a table:

Pass	Number of Comparisons
1	4
2	3
3	2
4	1

We determine that we have completed the sorting process when we have completed the $(N - 1)$st pass, which requires just one comparison. From the example, we see that we must perform $N - 1$ passes and that on the first pass, we must perform $N - 1$ comparisons. Because we had numbered the comparisons by the number of the pair being compared and, logically from this, labeled the columns in our example by the word pair, we shall use the symbolic name NPAIRS for the number of pairs to be examined in a given pass. For the first pass, NPAIRS would have to be initialized to $N - 1$. Then, on each consecutive pass, NPAIRS would be decreased by 1. We use the symbolic name PAIR to designate a particular pair to be examined. PASS is used as the symbolic name to designate a given pass. Because we wish to use as little memory as possible and as the objective is to reorder a list of values, we will use just one list, which we choose to call LIST. Notice that LIST will be both an entry and exit argument for the subroutine. Of course, we shall use N as an entry-only argument. To perform the exchange, we will have to use a temporary variable that we will call TEMP. Notice that we cannot use the sequence of statements

$$A = B$$
$$B = A$$

because in the second statement, the A that appears on the right-hand side of the replacement operator contains the value of B, which had been stored in the location for A by the first assignment statement. Hence, we must use a temporary variable, as in the design we present.

The sketch of the design is as follows:

---

(1) Initialize NPAIRS, the number of pairs, to $N - 1$.

(2) In a determinate repetition

    for PASS from 1 to N - 1

        2.1 in a determinate repetition

            for PAIR from 1 to NPAIRS

                2.1.1 in a 1-alternative selection

                      if the first element of a pair is

                      less than the second element of

                      the pair, exchange the two values

        2.2 decrement NPAIRS by 1

(3) Return to the calling unit.

The design for this subroutine, which we call BUBBLE, is given in Figure 10.2.

preamble for subroutine BUBBLE

ABSTRACT:		BUBBLE sorts a list of numbers so that the list is returned with the numbers appearing in the order of their decreasing value.	
INPUT:		none	
OUTPUT:		none	
ENTRY VALUES:		N	
EXIT VALUES:		none	
ENTRY AND EXIT VALUES:		LIST	
DESIGN HISTORY:		Hans Lee, 7AUG85	
CODING HISTORY:		none	
REFERENCE:		none	

ID DICTIONARY:

ID	TYPE	MEANING	USE
LIST	integer	list of numbers	1-dimensional array
N	integer	Number of items on the list	variable
NPAIRS	integer	Number of PAIRS	variable
PAIR	integer	PAIR number	variable
PASS	integer	PASS number	variable
TEMP	integer	TEMPorary	variable

Figure 10.2 Design of SUBROUTINE BUBBLE

10.10 DISCUSSION OF THE BUBBLE SORT

Because the bubble sort uses only one array, it is preferable to the selection sort presented earlier in this chapter. But the bubble sort is better than the selection sort for another reason: On each pass through the unsorted list, the number of comparisons decreases by 1. Thus, the maximum number of comparisons would be

$$(n - 1) + (n - 2) + \cdots + 2 + 1$$

This sum is

$$\frac{n(n - 1)}{2}$$

Therefore, the maximum number of comparisons required to perform the bubble sort is one-half of the $n(n - 1)$ comparisons required in the selection sort we have illustrated. This is a decided improvement.

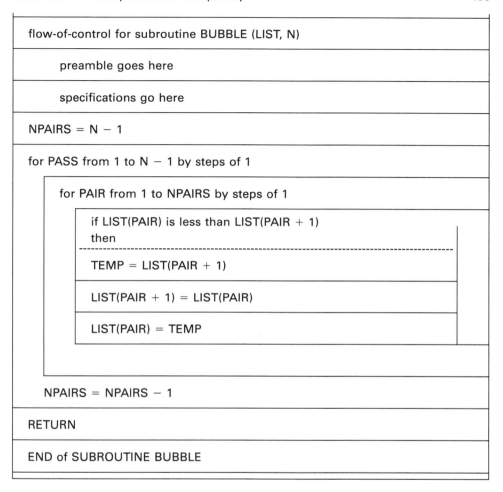

flow-of-control for subroutine BUBBLE (LIST, N)

preamble goes here

specifications go here

NPAIRS = N − 1

for PASS from 1 to N − 1 by steps of 1

for PAIR from 1 to NPAIRS by steps of 1

if LIST(PAIR) is less than LIST(PAIR + 1) then
- -
TEMP = LIST(PAIR + 1)

LIST(PAIR + 1) = LIST(PAIR)

LIST(PAIR) = TEMP

NPAIRS = NPAIRS − 1

RETURN

END of SUBROUTINE BUBBLE

Figure 10.2   (continued)

10.11 COMPUTATIONAL COMPLEXITY

Although the bubble sort is a considerable improvement over the selection sort, it may not be possible to use it for many applications because it is too slow. Other sorting methods have been developed that, on the average, are much faster. Methods are available that require

$$n \log_2 n$$

comparisons. Suppose that a university has 40,000 students and that each student is enrolled in five classes. In this example, n is 200,000. If the task included the preparation of a grade report for each student from these 200,000 grades, a present-day mainframe computer using an $n(n-1)$ sort might require 20 days of computation; an $n(n-1)/2$ sort, 10 days of computation; and an $n \log n$ sort, 12 to 15 min! The study of the time required to execute a given method for solving a problem based on such considerations as the number of comparisons required is called the study of the **computational complexity** of the method. (See Donald E. Knuth, 1973.) The computational complexity of a method is based upon an analysis of the operations performed in it. Thus, the computational complexity of a method may be studied without executing the program. The computational complexity of a method is developed as a function of *n,* the number of data items. The analysis is in terms of the amount of time or space required to carry out the computations.

10.12 THE CONCEPT OF AN ALGORITHM

In the field of computer science it is common to speak of an algorithm to do a particular task. In this chapter we have developed designs for two different algorithms to sort data. To a computer scientist, the word **algorithm** is used to designate a computational procedure specifically intended for use on a computer. The word algorithm is usually used in an abstract sense. Any algorithm has the following characteristics: Each step in the process must specify exactly what is to be done. Each step must, in fact, be executable on the computer. The algorithm must terminate in a reasonable amount of time, either by reporting the result or by issuing a statement that the answer cannot be obtained. In other words, an algorithm must include a stopping rule. Of course, to be useful, the algorithm must be correct. The study of algorithms and their properties, including their computational complexity, is a fundamental activity of computer scientists.

11

Defensive Programming with Good Style

11.1 THE GOOD PROGRAM

The criteria of a good program are that the program

(1) Either correctly solves the problem or clearly explains why it is unable to do so;

(2) Is easy to modify; and

(3) Is easy to maintain.

These criteria have led programming professonals to advocate defensive programming with good style.

11.2 WHAT IS DEFENSIVE PROGRAMMING AND WHY PRACTICE IT?

The phrase *defensive programming* was probably derived from the phrase defensive driving. The idea behind defensive driving is that you, as the driver of a car, try to defend against the possible unexpected conditions that might produce an accident, especially trying to keep alert to road conditions and what the drivers of other vehicles are doing. Defensive programming is the use of a number of strategies to anticipate possible error conditions before they occur or to minimize the effects of an error if it does occur. A classical example is to test the values of denominators to be sure that they are not zero. If a zero denominator is detected, then the program must contain code to output a message, giving additional information so that the source of the problem can be easily and quickly determined.

The computer professional's concern about defensive programming with good style has its source in costs associated with computer use. We consider the reduction of costs to be the overall objective of defensive programming. We identify the following list of costs:

(1) The costs associated with the initial development and testing of a program

(2) The costs associated with maintaining a system after it is accepted into the routine production status

(3) The costs associated with updating a system to meet newly identified needs or changing external factors

(4) The costs associated with using an incorrectly working program

(5) The costs associated with executing a correctly working program that uses more computer resources (execution time or memory) than is necessary

Using an incorrectly working program can be exceedingly expensive. Defensive programming with good style contributes to desk checking of the code to assist in verifying that the program is correct. Some of the defensive programming techniques assist in the identification of trouble. Matters of style contribute to program correctness and cost reduction by increasing the readability of the program listing and of the output. Under considerations of style, we include methods that make the logical structure more apparent to the human reader. This, in turn, enables the systems analyst or the coder to

(1) Anticipate possible error conditions before they occur;

(2) Detect unanticipated errors as soon as possible after they occur; and

(3) Locate in the listing of the code where the error occurred.

Thus, defensive programming with good style is an aid to the determination of the three W's of error correction: What happened? Where did it happen? When did it happen? Included in answering these questions is the recognition of information about what were the conditions: data values, system parameters, and so on. The intent of defensive programming is to provide information to the analyst or coder that may be used to repair errors quickly and without undue strain. The specific recommendations we make in this chapter are based on our experience. Part of the source of these recommendations is our own problems in program development and maintenance — the errors we made and the changes we wanted to make. Part of the source is observing others make errors. Some of the things we recommend may seem obvious to some of our readers, yet bizarre to others. We would like to discuss some of the assumptions beginning programmers sometimes make that may be misleading and that, if not understood, make our recommendations nothing but academic ritual. We consider only a few of these assumptions.

11.3 TROUBLESOME ASSUMPTIONS SOMETIMES MADE BY STUDENTS OF PROGRAMMING

In a number of cases, we have observed students who have made erroneous assumptions about how a language translator works or how a computer works. Some of these assumptions lead to incorrect results that are very difficult to correct. Unfortunately, it is not too practical to explain many of the important features of a computer and of language processors before studying some programming. But, at this point we feel that it is worthwhile to describe a few of these assumptions so that you may appreciate the motivation for the general concern among computer system managers in business, government, and industry as well as academic computer scientists about defensive programming with good style.

From our perspective, one of the strangest — but yet rather common — erroneous assumptions is that the computer can obtain mathematical results from operations that are not defined mathematically. The classical example of an operation that is not defined is division by 0. Yet we encounter students who think the computer will do something sensible when it is commanded to divide by 0. The students may know that it does not actually divide by 0, but they still think that it does something sensible. Some might believe that the computer sets the result to zero, but others have suggested that it might set the denominator to 1, or to a number that is very very small, that is, that approaches 0.

But what does a computer do when division by zero is executed? There is no standard answer to this question. In the CDC (Control Data Corporation) CYBER series of computers, a special value is inserted as the result. But nothing more is done. In particular, the system does not report that the program attempted to divide by 0. If at some later time in the execution of the program, an attempt is made to use the special value that was inserted into the memory location where the result was stored, the system will report that an attempt to divide by 0 was detected. The important fact to note is that the system does *not* report that an attempt to divide by 0 was made *at the time the attempt to divide by* 0 *was in fact made*. Thus, the error message that division by 0 was detected cannot be depended upon to show which statement was executing when the attempted division occurred. This separation of the time of attempted execution of an undefined operation from the time of notification of the user of a pathological condition means that it may not be easy to locate the cause of the error.

Another serious set of problems can arise from the fact that numeric data are represented in a computer, and some of the representations are not exact. We discuss some of these problems in a following chapter. But one assumption some students make related to the nature of computer arithmetic is that it always makes sense to test for the equality between two real numbers when one or both are the result of prior computations. (Perhaps it is not appropriate to state that students assume this. A possibly more appropriate characterization is to point out that students may not even consider the possibility of any problem in the testing for the equality between two real values.) However stated, the important point is that

The testing for equality between two real numbers is not appropriate when one or both are the result of prior computations.

This statement is a direct consequence of the fact that real values are represented in computer systems and that the representations are frequently inexact. Therefore, a programmer must test whether one number is greater than or equal to another real number or else test whether a real number is less than or equal to another real number. Note further that just as it is not appropriate, in general, to test real values for equality, it is not, in general, appropriate to test real values for strict inequality.

Another assumption we have encountered is that when the computer is instructed to input numeric data from a field that is blank (that is, does not contain any visible numeric character), the computer will notify the user. This is not necessarily true. Worse yet, what will be done may depend upon the computer, the operating system, an installation-specified option, a user-specified option, or the language. Thus, it is impossible to say, in general, what will happen. However, under some circumstances, a blank field may be read as numeric 0. This is frequently what will happen if a blank field is read as numeric data and the user has not specified a compiler option to do otherwise. The single most important fact to consider is to know how a blank is treated when the code specifies that a numeric value is to be read as data. You will have to obtain this information from your instructor or from your installation consultants.

There are other computational situations that may best be called "unusual or exceptional cases." We have concluded that the best advice we can offer is the following:

> Avoid making assumptions about how the computer treats unusual or exceptional cases. Always find out exactly what to expect. Guard against the possible occurrence of any exceptional or unusual cases by giving the user a message describing possible trouble and indicating the location in the program where these unusual conditions were detected.

There is an additional and very troublesome complication that must be mentioned. In many cases, different vendor's computers or different vendor's software may resolve unusual or exceptional cases differently. Further, even different versions of a language such as FORTRAN may treat exceptional cases differently on the same vendor's computer. In addition, when the resolution depends upon the local installation-specified options or the local operating system, the resolution may change, even though you may be under the impression that the system you used last month — when your program worked correctly — is the same as the one you are using today, when your program no longer is working correctly. About all that we can recommend is to guard against exceptional cases and be sure to know what your system does to resolve exceptional cases. We have said enough about why we personally feel that the recommendations we are about to make are important to follow. The exceptional cases we have mentioned only illustrate the kinds of unanticipated circumstances that may be encountered in computation. The recommendations we make in the material that follows have been found by us in our own programming, by our consultants in their consulting with students in our courses, and by our students to be helpful and well worth using.

11.4 RECOMMENDATIONS

11.4.1 Anticipate Undefined Computations

Insofar as possible, anticipate any illegal, inappropriate, or undefined computation. Thus, verify that denominators are not 0 before using code that requires division. Verify restrictions on all intrinsic functions. Notice, for example, that the square root function requires nonnegative values. Therefore, verify that the argument of the square root function meets this condition before the execution reaches the reference to the square root function. Of course, in each case, if an exceptional case is detected, output a message with information stating what is about to occur. This information is useful to the programmer in locating where the error occurred.

11.4.2 Maximize Probability of Error Detection

Whenever specific restrictions exist but cannot be directly detected by computation, devise tactics to minimize the user's producing erroneous results, and devise tactics to maximize the probability of the user's detection of an error if it occurs. Consider the intrinsic trigonometric functions. Each specifies that the angle to be supplied as the function argument is to be in radians. In general, there is no way that a program can detect whether an argument is in degrees or in radians. Similarily, there is no way, in general, for a program to verify that the correct units of measurement are used.

   If the program is to be executed interactively, the program can ask which units are used for each measurement, and when the user supplies the data, the program can be designed to make any appropriate transformations. The program can also ask what units are wanted for the output. Then, when the output is given, if properly designed, the output values are labeled with the correct units. If the program is not interactive, the user can still be asked to supply the units as character data and to supply the units desired for the output quantities. Thus, in either case, for the trigonometric functions, for example, input would include the value of the angle and either RADIANS or DEGREES. The program then would read either RADIANS or DEGREES into a character variable. The program would test the value of this character variable and, when necessary, carry out the transformation from degrees to radians before referencing the required trigonometric function.

   A programmer also has an obligation to protect a user from herself or himself. Thus, in some cases, the computations may be correct with respect to the numeric values as long as the user has been consistent in the use of either metric or English units. But even in these cases, it is preferable to ask for the units used and to report these along with the numeric values.

11.4.3 Use IMPLICIT LOGICAL (A–Z) in Each Unit

FORTRAN does not require a program to specify the type of arrays and variables. If no type is specified, FORTRAN will make any symbolic name starting with I, J, K, L, M, or N type integer. Also, it will make any symbolic name starting with some other letter type real. However, this **default typing** is a dangerous feature of a programming language. If a symbolic name of an incorrect type is used, the results are unpredictable. Therefore, the detection of an error or the diagnosis of the cause of an error may be exceedingly difficult. Type problems can be minimized by the inclusion of the specification IMPLICIT LOGICAL (A–Z) in each unit of a job. If it is included, the FORTRAN compiler will **flag** (give an output message for) any symbolic name that has not been specified in a type statement when the unspecified array name or variable appears in a context that implies some nonlogical type. When a programmer specifies the type of all symbolic names, there is much less likelihood that he or she will use a symbolic name of an incorrect type. Thus, the use of the IMPLICIT LOGICAL (A–Z) statement will assist in detecting symbolic names that were not specifically typed.

11.4.4 Choose Symbolic Names with Care

There are some helpful guidelines for the choice of symbolic names. The intent is always to make it easier for the human reader of the program to follow the logic of the program and, in general, to understand the program. Names should be chosen in relation to the problem. Thus, if the problem is primarily related to stating equations for the computer to solve and the mathematical notation is fairly well standardized, names should be chosen to be consistent with the usual mathematical notation. Symbolic names should also be chosen for their mnemonic value; that is, they should be chosen in order to aid in the recall of their meaning. In general, symbolic names should be chosen to avoid confusion with other symbolic names in the same unit. Within the same unit, all names longer than one or two characters should differ from one another by at least two characters. Further, if two or more names differ by only two characters, the two characters that are being distinguished should be at the start of the name or at the end of the name. We would admit to an exception, which is when a unit contains several names whose terminating characters are digits. Then, we would use a single terminating digit that would distinguish the different names. Thus, we might use CASE1, CASE2, CASE3 and so on. We recommend that no symbolic name contain embedded digits. Thus, we would not use A1A, WT1GM, WT2GM, and so on. Humans can note differences most easily when they occur at the beginning of a name but usually detect them almost as well when they occur at the end of a name, as long as the differing characters consist of two consecutive characters.

There are several characters that should be used only rarely. The letter *O* is particularly bad unless it is used in a name that completely spells some meaningful word. Thus, we would use ROW as a symbolic name, but we would not use *O* as a single character name. The letter *O* is too easily confused with the digit zero. In some type faces, the letter *Q* is difficult to distinguish from letter *O* or digit zero.

For this reason, *Q* should not be used alone as a symbolic name. The letter *L* is another bad letter because it can be confused with the digit one.

There are some common programming practices that might be thought of as conventions. The single letters *I, J,* and *K* are frequently used as names of the index variables in the determinate repetition construction and as the names of the array subscripts. TEMP is used as a TEMPorary, or holding, variable, especially when a value is being exchanged in a sequence of a few consecutive statements. The letter *N* by itself is frequently used in mathematics and statistics, in data analysis, and in tables and figures presenting data to signify the number of persons, items, and the like used in the data. If statistics on a class of students, for instance, are reported, the *N* is reported as part of the statistical analysis. The *N* here would be the number of students for whom data were collected.

11.4.5 Use Meaningful Comments

Meaningful comments are so very important that we feel that a unit without meaningful comments should be rejected as unacceptable. We say meaningful comments because comments that do not clarify or that say in words exactly what the code does are bad. We have formalized some of the routinely necessary comments in the section we call the preamble. The preamble of the design is to be inserted in the code at the location reserved by the phrase "preamble goes here." The preamble is inserted as comments in columns 1 through 80.

We also recommend another type of comment, which we call *code annotation*. The intent of these is twofold. As implied by the phrase we have chosen, they are intended to annotate, or explain, the code. In particular, we mean comments that appear in the executable portion of the code. As required by the FORTRAN syntax, comments must begin with a C in column 1 (although some systems permit an asterisk in column 1 in place of the C.) But on code-annotation comments, we leave columns 2 through 39 blank. Consequently, the printing characters appear in columns 40 through 80, with, of course, the C in column 1. The effect of this is to increase dramatically the readibility of the program, as the human reader may now scan down columns 1 through 39 to study the code without being distracted by comments. The comments can be scanned in a similar manner, thereby making them useful as a means of locating sections of code more quickly. Thus, the code-annotation comments become an index to the code itself.

As a matter of style, some programmers start using lines of dashes or of asterisks to separate sections of the code. We do not recommend this, as it in fact interrupts the vertical scanning of either the code or the comments. Instead, we believe that a line that has a C in column 1 but is otherwise blank serves as a better separator of sections of code.

Beginning programmers frequently request some guidelines about an appropriate number of comments. We usually say that about one annotation comment for every four to six executable statements is satisfactory. The number may vary somewhat depending upon the nature of the computational task and the expected readership of the code.

11.4.6 Use Indentation of the Code to Convey Logical Structure

We highly recommend the use of indentation to assist the reader in following the logical structure of the code. Most of the specific recommendations appear in the Code and Style Manual included as an appendix to this text. Judicious and systematic use of indentation sharpens the logical structure, thereby making it easier for the human reader to follow the logic of the program. It also serves to alert the coder to some kinds of errors before they become incorporated into the code. The major principle underlying our indentation recommendations is that all statements that are controlled by some other statement should be indented with respect to the controlling statement. A secondary principle is that as one moves to being under the control of other statements, the controlled statements move to the right; but as statements leave control of other statements, the leaving statements move to the left. In all cases, the effect is that the vertical alignment of statements returns to the same column as the column from which it started.

11.4.7 Label All Output

Often beginning programmers will give numeric output without labels or, if it is scientific output in which the units of measurement are significant, without the units of measurement. This should be avoided. Always label values with the units of measurement.

11.4.8 Report All *N*'s Used

Whenever statistics or data are reported, also include in the output the number of observations or the number of subjects (the N's) actually used.

11.4.9 Incorporate Your Own Tracing by Use of a Debug Mechanisim

Once something goes wrong in the computations, the single most important aid leading to a diagnosis of the cause is a readable and attractively presented output consisting of informative messages and the labeled output of the values of arrays and variables. Thus, what is most helpful is a set of clues. Especially helpful are clues that permit the programmer (1) *quickly* to ascertain that an error has taken place; (2) *quickly* to ascertain the first time the error has occurred; and, (3) *quickly* to detect any patterns in the errors. The emphasis on *quickly* is very important. Detection of errors and diagnosis of their causes should not require days of study of the output. Time is money, at least for the professional programmer and his or her employer.

Before we present our recommendations for making a useful set of output that usually provides helpful cues, we must mention something that all programmers, including us, have a tendency to do but that seems, after some reflection, to be illogical. When we detect some error condition, we humans seem to proceed as if guided by a desire to determine which statement in the program must be changed to make the error go away. Although it is very sensible to go from output to an exami-

nation of the code, it is not logically reasonable to stop there. The errors we are discussing are *logical errors,* not syntax errors. *The appropriate place to consider
logical errors is in the design.* Thus, we strongly recommend that you be sure to
study the design and ask where the logical error occurred. Of course, we feel that
correction of logical errors proceeds by first correcting the design and then replacing
the offending section of code with the code generated from the corrected design.

11.5 CAREFULLY DESIGNED OUTPUT AS THE SOURCE OF DIAGNOSTIC CLUES

As the coder translates the design into code, he or she should add additional output
statements. Some of these are designed to anticipate errors, such as division by 0,
and warn the user of trouble. Most of them, however, are designed to be of use to
the coder to determine the cause of the difficulty in terms of where the error occurred. The general principle that serves as a guideline to a professional programmer
is to insert clue-producing output (most frequently called **debugging output**) close
to where errors are most likely to occur.

Where are errors most likely to occur? What output is particularly useful —
that is, what output becomes a good clue to the nature of the difficulty? Some errors
occur because the data are in error. In fact, this occurs so often that in computations
on large data sets, it is routine to have the computer check the data. This has become
known as **data cleaning,** presumably because the data have to be cleaned up before
being analyzed. We consider data cleaning to be beyond the scope of this text, so we
do not explain further. Instead, we recommend that the value given as input to variables always be echoed immediately after input. For arrays, we recommend that the
first three values and the last three values for each dimension be echoed.

Some very nasty errors occur "between units." The problem is quite simple,
namely, that something is not correct with the data communicated from one unit to
another. That is, in one unit, the data appear to be correct. But in another unit, to
which these data are communicated, they appear to be incorrect. The probable cause
of such errors is not in fact, between the units. The cause of such conditions lies
within one of the units. Possibilities include incorrect dimensioning of arrays being
communicated (i.e., arrays that appear in the argument lists of functions or subroutines) or inconsistent typing of arrays, variables, or functions being communicated.

To provide clues for these types of errors, a coder should insert statements that
will provide output that (1) indicates that execution is entering a unit or leaving a
unit; (2) supplies the name of the unit; (3) indicates the kind of unit, function or subroutine; and (4) gives the values of the arguments. In the case of arrays, we recommend that the first three and last three values for each dimension be given. For
variables, the value of each variable should be given. Of course, the values should
be labeled completely.

When using function references, it is preferable to compute what is to be given
as the argument(s) before computing the function reference itself. For example, if
the square root of

$$b^2 - 4ac$$

is required, it is preferable to evaluate what is to be the argument in a separate assignment statement followed by the function reference. Thus, the preferred code is

```
ARG = B * B - 4.0 * A * C

ROOT = SQRT(ARG)
```

with an output of the value of ARG inserted between the two statements, rather than to have

```
ROOT = SQRT(B * B - 4.0 * A * C)
```

which does not permit the verification of the correct computation of the argument. This example is almost too simple and, is, therefore, unlikely to contain an error that would be difficult to detect. But the principle of breaking up complicated expressions and producing several less complicated statements, with the output of the evaluation of the various parts, is recommended. Merely coding complicated expressions as a series of less complicated assignment statements itself sometimes prevents the occurrence of errors.

Other errors occur within a unit or a control structure. Errors within a simple sequence are most often due to an expression that is logically incorrectly constructed. To assist in detecting these types of conditions, it is always better to break up a complicated expression formed as a single sequence (that is, formed as a single statement) into two or more sequence constructions (that is, into two or more statements.) Also, it is wise to output the partial result of each statement. For example, if the task is the computation of a long arithmetic equation that has a complicated expression for a numerator and another complicated expression for the denominator, it is preferable to compute the numerator in one assignment statement and the denominator in another rather than to compute the entire equation in one statement.

There are two kinds of logical errors most likely to occur with a selection. One possibility is that the relational expression used as the test may not be correct. Again, the strategy is to compute a complicated expression as a separate statement before it is to be used in the selection statement (that is, before the IF statement.) Then, its value can be given as debugging output before entering the selection control statement.

The other kind of error occurs at the end of the selection segment. Sometimes a selection segment will exclude one or more statements that should have been included or include one or more statements that should have been excluded. If the selection segment is long, it is worthwhile to output a message, with the value of some relevant variable(s) if appropriate, immediately after the selection block, thereby producing additional debugging output.

Insofar as repetitions are concerned, if a complicated expression is to be evaluated for the relational expression used to control the repetition, the complex relational expression might be incorrect. When possible, the relational expressions should be evaluated outside of where they occur in the loop to assist in the detection of this fact. Then, to be useful, their values should be produced as debugging output.

11.6 TURNING OFF THE DEBUGGING (CLUE-PRODUCING) OUTPUT

As a programmer would quickly discover, if all the recommended output for debugging were produced, the output would be very long. Also, the programmer would soon be told by the systems analyst or by the client directly that all the output is not wanted. We agree, but the output *is* still useful.

The answer is that we must recognize that much of the debugging output is for the use of the professional coder or systems analyst, not for the client. Therefore, we need to construct a mechanism that enables the coder to turn on and off the debugging output. In our programs we have used a specific mechanism to accomplish this. It is particularly suited to small programs. The idea is that as each unit is coded, a logical variable, BUG, is included. Also included in each unit is the statement

```
COMMON/BUGBLK/BUG
```

which is a means of sharing the value of BUG among all units. Then the value of BUG is set to true when the coder is developing the program or running it when an error has been detected. BUG is merely a programmer-created symbol, like any other symbol. It is NOT any special variable in the FORTRAN system. Like any logical variable, BUG can be set true by the assignment statement of the form

```
BUG =   .TRUE.
```

in which the periods surrounding true are a required part of the FORTRAN syntax.

Finally, the output statements to be controlled by the value of BUG are to be in a 1-alternative selection. Thus, a segment of code to do this would be as follows:

```
IF (BUG) THEN
WRITE ( . . . ) . . .
```

where the WRITE statement gives the debugging messages and labeled values.

When a unit is apparently working correctly or a large segment of a unit is working correctly, the coder may insert

```
BUG =   .FALSE.
```

at the beginning of the unit to turn the debugging output off and

```
BUG =   .TRUE.
```

at the end of the unit to turn the debugging output back on. Also, whenever an error is detected, BUG may be set to be true in each unit; then execution output may be obtained that is specific to the problem and that will probably lead to detecting the cause of the error. A more advanced technique is to store the value of BUG in a temporary logical variable, say TBUG, set BUG to false; then, just before leaving the unit, set BUG to the value of TBUG. This will turn off the debug printing within this unit but will not affect the value of BUG in other units.

12

Representation and

Computer Arithmetic

12.1 INTRODUCTION

When things go wrong, we need to be able to locate the source of the difficulty. In computation with numerical values, it is possible to produce errors that are a result of computer arithmetic. In some situations the computer system is able to warn the user of problems. In others, it cannot. In fact, even though the results are not meaningful, the computer is not, technically, making errors. It is simply using computer arithmetic. The problem is that we neither appreciate nor anticipate the implications of computer arithmetic. The purpose of this chapter is to give a brief overview of computer arithmetic so that you may be more aware of potential problems and so that you may better be able to understand some error messages.

Before execution begins, each unit of the FORTRAN program has been converted to machine language. It then consists of a sequence of computer instructions, each consisting entirely of 1s and 0s. These instructions are stored in consecutive words in memory. Further, all data (characters, logical values, or numbers) have also been converted to computer words consisting entirely of 1s and 0s. Consequently, the result of the conversion from what we regard as data is a binary **representation** of the data. The details of the representation used by any particular computer depend upon the the computer manufacturer and upon the particular model. Because there are several important implications for computations involving computer arithmetic, we will describe how the CDC (Control Data Corporation) 6000 series and 700 series mainframe computers represent data. For all computers, the representation of many real quantities, including double-precision and complex data, is not, in general, exact. The fundamental source of this inexactness is that humans use a base ten number system and the computers use a base two number system. As 10 is not a power of 2, fractional values expressed in one system cannot be expressed exactly in the other system.

In addition to the problems introduced by representation, there are other significant problems related to computer arithmetic arising from the different types of arithmetic available and from rounding or truncating intermediate results. For example, extensive use is made of integer arithmetic on a computer. We are not as likely to be familiar with integer arithmetic and, consequently, may find ourselves making errors because of this lack of familiarity. In this chapter, we will discuss computer arithmetic and the process of representation of data. We must begin by a review of the process of translating a FORTRAN program into its executable form, emphasizing the implications of type.

12.2 COMPILATION AND TYPE

When a unit of a FORTRAN program is given to the computer for the first time, the computer translates the unit into a lower-level language, either by translating it into an assembly-level language followed by translating the assembly-level language version into a machine-level language or by directly translating it into a machine-level language. Since this translation is performed by a computer program known as the FORTRAN **compiler,** this process of translation is usually called **compilation.** We also speak of the **compile phase** when we wish to distinguish it from the **execution phase.** *Each unit of a FORTRAN job is compiled independently of all other units.* This method requires that the separate units be linked together as another step between compilation and execution. This linking together of the various units, obtaining and inserting intrinsic functions, and making assignments of data to memory locations is done by another system program called a **loader.** The process itself is called **loading.**

Type specifications as well as some of the other nonexecutable statements are used during the compile phase of preparing a FORTRAN program for execution. To carry out the compilation, the computer scans the FORTRAN program many times. One FORTRAN compiler we have used made about 32 passes through the FORTRAN program before it had completed the compilation process. Early in the compile phase, the type of each array, function, and variable is determined from the results of analyzing the code and the specification statements. This knowledge of the type of the arrays, functions, and variables is used, together with the arithmetic or logical expressions in which the arrays, functions, and variables appear, to determine the appropriate translation of the arithmetic or logical expressions. As we shall see in somewhat more detail, the computer has separate instructions, corresponding to separate hardware circuits, to carry out integer and real arithmetic. Consequently, the type information and the exact expressions are both required to perform the translation of the FORTRAN code to machine code.

In order to provide the maximum flexibility in the input and output of data, FORTRAN provides FORMAT statements that may be used with some input and output statements. The details of the data are described in the FORMAT statements by the **edit descriptors.** When the data are read or written, these edit descriptors are used to guide the choice of the appropriate representation. The representation of an integer value in the computer is different from the representation of a real value. Further, *there is nothing stored in the computer word or associated with the computer word that indicates what type is to be associated with the sequence of 1s and 0s.* After compilation has been completed, the translated version of the FORTRAN program is prepared for execution. Once execution begins, the FORTRAN version of the program is no longer available. Consequently, there is no information available except the edit descriptors, which may be used to guide the correct interpretation of the input data or the output representations. *Unfortunately, the FORTRAN standards do not include a requirement that the FORTRAN system verify that the edit descriptors be consistent with the type specifications given for the array, function, or variable.* If a compiler does not detect type inconsistency, an error will probably occur sometime later during execution without a specific informative message pointing to the source of the problem. In the most literal sense of the phrase, we may say that "the results are unpredictable" when there are type mismatch problems. Therefore, *it is the programmer's responsibility to ensure that the edit descriptors and the type of arrays and variables correspond.*

In the following material, we need to distinguish between explicit and implicit. *Explicit* means *as stated* and *implicit* means *as implied.* The distinction will become clearer as we proceed. The FORTRAN compiler determines the type of an array or a variable from the following: (1) an explicit type specification statement (CHARACTER, COMPLEX, DOUBLE PRECISION, INTEGER, LOGICAL, or REAL); (2) implicit type specification using either the IMPLICIT statement or the **default naming convention,** or **implied naming convention.** This naming convention is that if an array, function, or variable starts with an I, J, K, L, M, or N, then that array, function, or variable is type integer. If the symbolic name starts with any other letter, then that name is type real. The explicit type specification takes precedence over the implicit specification methods. But within the implicit methods, the IMPLICIT statement takes precedence over the default naming convention.

To illustrate the significance of the concept of the type, we have included the programs TPINT and TPREAL. TPINT stands for TyPe INTeger, and TPREAL stands for TyPeREAL. Figure 12.1 is the FORTRAN version of TPINT, and Figure 12.2 is the resulting assembly language version when translated into CDC's assembly language, COMPASS. Figure 12.3 is the FORTRAN version of TPREAL, and Figure 12.4 is the COMPASS version. These FORTRAN programs are odd, as neither has any input or output. We deliberately omitted everything but the statements required to make our point. Input and output could be added, but the point we are about to make would not be changed. A comparison of these two FORTRAN programs reveals that the type specifications differ from one program to another, but the assignment statements are the same. In TPINT, all the variables are integer. In TPREAL, all the variables are real. The important point is to notice that the compiled code for the two programs uses different assembly-level instructions. This may be seen by comparing the two assembly-language versions. In the COMPASS version of TPINT, there is a line that reads

```
      PROGRAM TPINT
C
C     PREAMBLE FOR PROGRAM TPINT
C
C     ABSTRACT: TPINT ILLUSTRATES THAT DIFFERENT MACHINE INSTRUCTIONS
C               ARE GENERATED FROM THE SAME FORTRAN STATEMENT,
C               DEPENDING ON THE TYPE OF THE VARIABLES INVOLVED
C
C     INPUT:   NONE
C
C     OUTPUT:  NONE
C
C     DESIGN HISTORY: M. MISOVICH, 4JAN86
C
C     REFERENCE: NONE
C
C     ID DICTIONARY:
C
C     ID       TYPE         MEANING              USE
C
C     I        INTEGER                           VARIABLE
C     J        INTEGER                           VARIABLE
C     K        INTEGER                           VARIABLE
C
C     SPECIFICATIONS
C
      IMPLICIT LOGICAL (A-Z)
C
      INTEGER I,J,K
C
      I=J+K
C
      STOP
      END
```

Figure 12.1   The FORTRAN Version of TPINT

```
*                        LINE 31
```

which refers to the FORTRAN program. The asterisk indicates a comment. Line 31 refers to line 31 in the FORTRAN code, which is the FORTRAN statement

```
      I = J+K
```

Returning to the COMPASS version of TPINT, we see another comment indicating line 33. Thus, the code between these two comment lines is the translation of the FORTRAN statement

```
      I = J+K
```

Let us briefly explain the COMPASS instructions for this FORTRAN statement.

```
                 IDENT   TPINT
TPINT            TRACE.
FILVEC.          BSS     0
                 ADDR    0,1
                 PLIM    50000
                 USE     LITERL.
CON.             CON        00000000000000000000000B
                 USE     FORMAT.
                 USE     APLST.
AP.1             BSS     0
                 APL     0000,CON.+0
                 USE     IOAPL.
                 USE     NAMLST.
                 USE     CODE.
*                                      LINE 31
                 SBO     B2+0+37B
                 SA1     J
                 SA2     K
                 IX7     X2+X1
                 SA7     I
*                                      LINE 33
                 SBO     B2+0+41B
                 SA1     AP.1
                 RJT     =XSTOP5.,41B
*                                      LINE 34
                 SBO     B2+0+42B
                 BSS     0
                 USE     START.
                 SBO     B2+0-24B
                 SBO     B2+TRACE.
TPINT            BSS     0
                 SA1     FILVEC.
                 RJ      =XQ5RPV.
                 BSS     0
                 USE     TEMPS.
ST.              BSS     0
CT.              BSS     0
IT.              BSS     0
OT.              BSS     0
VD.              BSS     0
LC.              BSS     0
                 USE     BUFER.
LENP.            EQUN
                 END     TPINT
```

Figure 12.2   Assembly Language Version of TPINT

```
        PROGRAM TPREAL
C
C       PREAMBLE FOR PROGRAM TPREAL
C
C       ABSTRACT: TPREAL ILLUSTRATES THAT DIFFERENT MACHINE INSTRUCTIONS
C                 ARE GENERATED FROM THE SAME FORTRAN STATEMENT,
C                 DEPENDING ON THE TYPE OF THE VARIABLES INVOLVED
C
C       INPUT:   NONE
C
C       OUTPUT:  NONE
C
C       DESIGN HISTORY: M. MISOVICH, 4JAN86
C
C       REFERENCE: NONE
C
C       ID DICTIONARY:
C
```
(continues)

Figure 12.3   FORTRAN Version of TPREAL

```
C     ID       TYPE         MEANING              USE
C
C     I        REAL                              VARIABLE
C     J        REAL                              VARIABLE
C     K        REAL                              VARIABLE
C
C     SPECIFICATIONS
C
      IMPLICIT LOGICAL (A-Z)
C
      REAL I,J,K
C
      I=J+K
C
      STOP
      END
```

Figure 12.3 (continued)

```
         IDENT   TPREAL
TPREAL   TRACE.
FILVEC.  BSS     0
         ADDR    0,1
         PLIM    50000
         USE     LITERL.
CON.     CON        00000000000000000000B
         USE     FORMAT.
         USE     APLST.
AP.1     BSS     0
         APL     0000,CON.+0
         USE     IOAPL.
         USE     NAMLST.
         USE     CODE.
*                          LINE 31
         SBO     B2+0+37B
         SA1     J
         SA2     K
         RXO     X2+X1
         NX7     XO
         SA7     I
*                          LINE 33
         SBO     B2+0+41B
         SA1     AP.1
         RJT     =XSTOP5.,41B
*                          LINE 34
         SBO     B2+0+42B
         BSS     0
         USE     START.
         SBO     B2+0-24B
         SBO     B2+TRACE.
TPREAL   BSS     0
         SA1     FILVEC.
         RJ      =XQ5RPV.
         BSS     0
         USE     TEMPS.
ST.      BSS     0
CT.      BSS     0
IT.      BSS     0
OT.      BSS     0
VD.      BSS     0
LC.      BSS     0
         USE     BUFER.
LENP.    EQUN
         END     TPREAL
```

Figure 12.4   Assembly Version of TPREAL

                    SB0   B2+0+37B

A 'do nothing' instruction placed here for later possible use by the system traceback routines.

                    SA1   J

Fetches the contents from the location J in memory and puts them into register 1 in the arithmetic unit.

                    SA2   K

Fetches the contents from the location K in memory and puts them into register 2.

                    IX7   X2+X1

Performs an integer addition, adding the contents of register 2 and register 1, leaving the sum in register 7.

                    SA7   I

Stores the contents of register 7 in the location I in memory.

In the assembly code for TPREAL, the first instruction that is different from the instructions for TPINT is

                    RX0   X2+X1

The rounded floating-point add instruction. The sum is left in register 0.

The remaining instructions are as follows:

                    NX7   X0

Normalizes the contents of register 0 and leaves the result in register 7.

                    SA7   I

Stores the contents of register 7 in the location I.

In comparing these two assembly-language translations of the FORTRAN programs, we see that the type specifications in the FORTRAN version governs which assembly-level instructions are generated. This illustrates the point that the type of an array or variable determines the type of assembly instructions required to translate the operations. We have seen that the symbol + in FORTRAN results in different assembly instructions, depending on the type of the operands.

The computer cannot determine the type of an array or variable from the contents of the location(s) in memory where they are stored. Therefore, if the correct translation from FORTRAN to the assembly instructions is to be made, the FORTRAN program must contain the appropriate type specifications. (Recall that the type of an array or a variable is not communicated from one unit to another unit.) If the type of an array or a variable is inconsistent with the type of the representation used to store the values of the array elements or variables, computation will produce incorrect results, for which it may be very difficult to determine the cause.

It may be obvious that a computer will have different machine instructions to execute what appears at the FORTRAN level to be the standard mathematical operations of addition, subtraction, multiplication, and division, respectively, represented by the symbols $+$, $-$, $*$, and $/$. But it is far from obvious that the $+$ symbol, for example, should be translated into different instructions depending upon the something called type. But it is! A large computer has the following separate machine-level instructions: complex addition, double-precision addition, integer addition, and real addition; similar subdivisions exist for each basic mathematical operation.

The compiler must consider both the type of all arrays, functions, or variables used in a FORTRAN statement *and* the actual operations in a FORTRAN statement to determine which machine instructions should be selected. To explain further, we must consider the **precedence rules** (the rules that give the order in which an arithmetic expression is evaluated) and two additional features of arithmetic in FORTRAN. One feature is called *mixed-mode arithmetic* and the other, *automatic type conversion*.

We can think of the translation of an arithmetic expression in FORTRAN as being done in separate pieces. Each sum or difference may be thought of as a separate piece. Within each piece, the translator considers the operators, the types of each operand (an **operand** is that which the operators "operate upon"), and the rules of precedence. FORTRAN, like our arithmetic, uses the following precedence rules: (1) exponentiation is done first; (2) multiplication and division are done next; and (3) addition and subtraction are done last. Exponentiation is done from right to left, whereas each of the other operators are evaluated from left to right. If parentheses are present, the compiler evaluates the expression from inside the innermost pair to the outermost pair.

Now, let us consider a fairly simple example, the translation of the assignment statement

$$ANSWER = A/B$$

in a unit in which A, B, and ANSWER are type integer. For this situation, the compiler will generate an instruction to perform integer division. But what will the compiler do if either A or B is real? In such a situation, the compiler will automatically generate code to form the real representation of the integer operand and then generate the instructions to perform real division. Notice that we had to refrain from saying that the compiler converted integer A, for instance, to the real representation A. A is not changed. The process is done as if another variable (that is, another memory location) had been created and then the real representation of the value of A had been stored in this temporary variable. The fact that either A or B is real causes the compiler to form the real representation of the other operand and causes the compiler to use real division. Nothing about the type of ANSWER influences these actions so far described. But as ANSWER is type integer, the compiler will automatically take the result of the real division, discard any fractional part of the result, and form the integer representation thereof. This integer representation will be stored in the location associated with the variable, ANSWER. We will show shortly how this leads to major errors.

When the FORTRAN system must evaluate expressions involving arrays or variables of different types, it is said to perform **mixed-mode arithmetic.** It does this automatically by performing type conversions on the values to be used within a subexpression so that all values have the same type. (The values as they are represented in memory remain unchanged in memory.) Also, if necessary, the FORTRAN system generates the appropriate code to perform **automatic type conversion** in the assignment operation (that is, if the left-hand side of the replacement operator is of one type and the right-hand side is of a different type, the system will form the representation of the right-hand side that is suitable for the type of the left-hand side.)

The FORTRAN system does not produce any indication that type conversion has been used. Although many professionally written programs rely on automatic type conversion, both in mixed-mode arithmetic and in the assignment operation, we do not recommend reliance upon it because errors can occur for which it is very difficult to diagnose the cause. A preferable alternative is to employ the intrinsic functions to perform explicitly any required type conversions. The presence of the intrinsic function(s) in your program will remain as a constant reminder to any programmer about the type considerations in the code.

Observe that whenever a value that is real is converted to integer, the fractional part is lost, although with some systems, it may be rounded to the appropriate integer value. Exactly what happens depends upon the system you are using.

Type conversion in the assignment operation is illustrated by the FORTRAN program TPMIX2 (Figure 12.5) and its assembly version (Figure 12.6). The point of the illustration is that the evaluation of the FORTRAN statement on line 32,

$$I = J+K$$

```
      PROGRAM TPMIX2
C
C     PREAMBLE FOR PROGRAM TPMIX2
C
C     ABSTRACT: TPMIX2 ILLUSTRATES THAT DIFFERENT MACHINE INSTRUCTIONS
C               ARE GENERATED FROM THE SAME FORTRAN STATEMENT,
C               DEPENDING ON THE TYPE OF THE VARIABLES INVOLVED
C
C     INPUT:    NONE
C
C     OUTPUT:   NONE
C
C     DESIGN HISTORY: M. MISOVICH, 4JAN86
C
C     REFERENCE: NONE
C
C     ID DICTIONARY:
C
```
                                                              (continues)

Figure 12.5 FORTRAN Version of TPMIX2

```
        C       ID          TYPE         MEANING          USE
        C
        C       I           REAL                          VARIABLE
        C       J           INTEGER                       VARIABLE
        C       K           INTEGER                       VARIABLE
        C
        C       SPECIFICATIONS
        C
                IMPLICIT LOGICAL (A-Z)
        C
                INTEGER J,K
                REAL I
        C
                I=J+K
        C
                STOP
                END
```

Figure 12.5   (continued)

```
              IDENT   TPMIX2
TPMIX2        TRACE.
FILVEC.       BSS     0
              ADDR    0,1
              PLIM    50000
              USE     LITERL.
CON.          CON         000000000000000000000B
              USE     FORMAT.
              USE     APLST.
AP.1          BSS     0
              APL     0000,CON.+0
              USE     IOAPL.
              USE     NAMLST.
              USE     CODE.
*                               LINE 32
              SBO     B2+0+40B
              SA1     J
              SA2     K
              IXO     X2+X1
              PXO     XO
              NX7     XO
              SA7     I
*                               LINE 34
              SBO     B2+0+42B
              SA1     AP.1
              RJT     =XSTOP5.,42B
*                               LINE 35
              SBO     B2+0+43B
              BSS     0
              USE     START.
              SBO     B2+0-24B
              SBO     B2+TRACE.
TPMIX2        BSS     0
              SA1     FILVEC.
              RJ      =XQ5RPV.
              BSS     0
              USE     TEMPS.
ST.           BSS     0
CT.           BSS     0
IT.           BSS     0
OT.           BSS     0
VD.           BSS     0
LC.           BSS     0
              USE     BUFER.
LENP.         EQUN
              END     TPMIX2
```

Figure 12.6   Assembly Version of TPMIX2

where J and K are integer but I is real, requires that the result of the addition must be converted to floating-point representation before storage. This is done in assembly instructions as follows:

```
IX0     X2+X1
```

Performs integer addition, leaving the sum in register 0.

```
PX0     X0
NX7     X0
```

Together convert the contents of register 0 to floating-point representation in register 7.

```
SA7     I
```

Stores the contents of register 7 in the location I.

Program TPMIX1 illustrates type conversion both in mixed-mode arithmetic and in the assignment process. The FORTRAN version of TPMIX1 (Figure 12.7) contains line 32:

```
I = J+K
```

where both I and K are integer and J is real. Thus, the assembly version (Figure 12.8) must convert K to floating-point, then perform the real addition, and finally convert the resulting sum to the integer representation before storing the sum in I. The COMPASS instructions that accomplish this are as follows:

```
SA1     K
```

Fetches K (which is an integer) from memory and puts it into register 1.

```
PX0     X1
NX0     X0
```

Together, these instructions convert the contents of register 1 (which is the value of K represented as an integer) to the floating-point representation, leaving the result in register 0.

```
SA2     J
```

Fetches J (which is real) from memory and puts it into register 2.

```
RX1     X2+X0
```

Performs rounded floating-point addition, leaving the result in register 1.

```
NX6     X1
```

Normalizes contents of X1, leaving the result in register 6.

```
UX2     B6,X6
LX7     B6,X2
```

```
      PROGRAM TPMIX1
C
C     PREAMBLE FOR PROGRAM TPMIX1
C
C     ABSTRACT: TPMIX1 ILLUSTRATES THAT DIFFERENT MACHINE INSTRUCTIONS
C               ARE GENERATED FROM THE SAME FORTRAN STATEMENT,
C               DEPENDING ON THE TYPE OF THE VARIABLES INVOLVED
C
C     INPUT:   NONE
C
C     OUTPUT:  NONE
C
C     DESIGN HISTORY: M. MISOVICH, 4JAN86
C
C     REFERENCE: NONE
C
C     ID DICTIONARY:
C
C     ID        TYPE         MEANING              USE
C
C     I         INTEGER                           VARIABLE
C     J         REAL                              VARIABLE
C     K         INTEGER                           VARIABLE
C
C     SPECIFICATIONS
C
      IMPLICIT LOGICAL (A-Z)
C
      INTEGER I,K
      REAL J
C
      I=J+K
C
      STOP
      END
```

Figure 12.7   FORTRAN Version of TPMIX1

Together, these instructions convert the contents of register 6 to integer, leaving the result in register 7.

SA7   I

Stores the contents of register 7 in I.

Before we continue, we should supply a few examples of integer arithmetic to be sure you appreciate why we are concerned about mixed-mode arithmetic, automatic type conversion, and integer arithmetic. If 5/10 were evaluated using integer arithmetic, the answer would be 0; if 10/5 were evaluated using integer arithmetic,

```
              IDENT   TPMIX1
TPMIX1        TRACE.
FILVEC.       BSS     0
              ADDR    0,1
              PLIM    50000
              USE     LITERL.
CON.          CON         00000000000000000000000B
              USE     FORMAT.
              USE     APLST.
AP.1          BSS     0
              APL     0000,CON.+0
              USE     IOAPL.
              USE     NAMLST.
              USE     CODE.
*                                             LINE 32
              SBO     B2+0+40B
              SA1     K
              PXO     X1
              NXO     XO
              SA2     J
              RX1     X2+XO
              NX6     X1
              UX2     B6,X6
              LX7     B6,X2
              SA7     I
*                                             LINE 34
              SBO     B2+0+42B
              SA1     AP.1
              RJT     =XSTOP5.,42B
*                                             LINE 35
              SBO     B2+0+43B
              BSS     0
              USE     START.
              SBO     B2+0-25B
              SBO     B2+TRACE.
TPMIX1        BSS     0
              SA1     FILVEC.
              RJ      =XQ5RPV.
              BSS     0
              USE     TEMPS.
ST.           BSS     0
CT.           BSS     0
IT.           BSS     0
OT.           BSS     0
VD.           BSS     0
LC.           BSS     0
              USE     BUFER.
LENP.         EQUN
              END     TPMIX1
```

Figure 12.8   ASSEMBLY Version of TPMIX1

the answer would be integer 2, as one would expect. Suppose that ANSWER is type real. Then, when

$$ANSWER = 15/2$$

is evaluated, integer division will produce integer 7 as the value of the right-hand side. This will be converted to the real representation, in which the fractional part will have the value 0. Thus, we would expect to find the real representation of 7.0 stored in the location reserved for the variable ANSWER.

The evaluation of arithmetic expressions depends upon how the expression is stated. Evaualtion of expressions involving only multiplication and division are evaluated from left to right. Thus, consider

$$ANSWER = A/B * C$$

and

$$RESULT = A * C/B$$

when A has the value of 1, B has the value of 3, and C has the value of 6. If these are integers, then ANSWER will have the value of zero, as integer 1 divided by integer 3 produces a quotient of zero as a direct result of integer division. But, with the same values and still using integer arithmetic, RESULT will have the value 2, because the evaluation starts on the left of the expression by first multiplying A by C before carrying out the integer division by B.

Although FORTRAN automatically carries out appropriate type conversions while doing mixed-mode arithmetic, we recommend that a coder always utilize the appropriate intrinsic functions to perform any necessary type conversions explicitly. The reason we recommend explicit type conversion is that it tends to highlight the logic and therefore contributes to the reduction of errors stemming from mixed-mode arithmetic.

Up to this point, we have discussed the fact that the type of arrays, functions, and variables, together with the operators used to combine them in arithmetic expressions, govern which machine instructions are produced by the compiler. We next consider how type affects the representation of data.

12.3 TYPE AND REPRESENTATION

A computer represents the following information:

> Instructions
> Character data
> Logical data

as well as

> Complex numbers
> Double precision numbers
> Integer numbers
> Real numbers

In contexts such as the present one, the notion of represented entities usually includes the associated concept that there are different assembly- or machine-level instructions that operate on data of different types. There are not always different circuits corresponding to each different assembly-level instruction. The details vary from computer to computer and are not important for our discussion. If there is no assembly instruction corresponding to a given type in a language, the language processor contains the appropriate code to perform the computations with those instructions it has available. Also, some more recent computer languages provide the means for a user to define additional types. Of course, there are neither special codes nor special circuits to implement these user-defined types. The user must write the appropriate code for processing user-defined types.

12.4 THE IEEE STANDARDS FOR BINARY FLOATING-POINT ARITHMETIC

The Standards Committees of the IEEE (The Institute of Electrical and Electronics Engineers, Inc.) Computer Society developed standards for binary floating-point arithmetic. These standards are known as *The IEEE Standards for Floating-point Arithmetic*. These standards were developed to aid in moving a program from computer to computer, to aid in numeric computations, and to aid in the detection and reporting of anomalies and results that are nonnumbers (NaNs.) Although these standards are developed in terms of binary floating-point arithmetic, they include specifications for the conversion between binary floating-point numbers and decimal strings. Any processor that claims to follow these standards is required to support the single format standard they present. The single-format standard specifies that the correctly rounded binary-decimal range is to be

$$\pm M \times 10^{\pm N}$$

where the integer M can be a maximum of 10^9 - 1 and the integer N can be a maximum of 13.

Several vendors of FORTRAN 77 for microcomputers are following these IEEE standards. We recommend that you consider whether or not a FORTRAN system follows these standards whenever you consider the purchase of a FORTRAN compiler. We consider the standardization of computer arithmetic to be extremely important.

12.5 REPRESENTATION OF NUMBERS AND COMPUTER ARITHMETIC ON THE CYBER

We present the details of representation using as our example the CDC (Control Data Corporation) 6000 and 700 (or CYBER) series of mainframe computers designed for scientific applications. Binary means that its fundamental hardware is designed to operate on the electronic equivalent of binary numbers, that is, sets of 1s and 0s. Fixed word length means that the same fixed number of binary digits, in the case of the CYBER, 60 binary digits, function as a whole. Thus, the CYBER is designed to manipulate all 60 bits as a whole. Such groups of consecutive binary digits are called a **computer word.** Thus, each location in memory stores exactly one word. Different computers frequently use different word lengths.

If each digit can be only one of two values, 0 or 1, then there are

$$2^n$$

distinct patterns, where n is the number of digits in the computer word. A major design consideration is to produce a computer system that maximizes the range of values that can be represented by these patterns.

12.6 THE REPRESENTATION OF INTEGERS

Let us examine the case of the representation of integer numbers. We have to be able to represent negative, positive, and zero values. The representation of zero posed no problem for the computer engineer. The obvious representation is a word consisting of 60 zeros. To represent positive integer 1, a word starting with 59 zeros followed by a 1 is used. Then, each consecutive positive base ten integer can be produced by adding binary 1 to the preceding binary value. Thus, the representation of 0 and the positive (base 10) integers, 1, 2, and 3, for the CYBER is

000000000000000000000000000000000000000000000000000000000000
000000000000000000000000000000000000000000000000000000000001
000000000000000000000000000000000000000000000000000000000010
000000000000000000000000000000000000000000000000000000000011

As you can see, the binary form of the integers is cumbersome to write. Consequently, we are prone to make errors when we use the binary form. There is a better way. The trick is to recognize that higher powers of two are more convenient to use as a base and have the important property that numbers in this form have a one-to-one correspondence to those in the binary form. For most modern computers, either 2^3 or 2^4 is used, depending on other design considerations. Since $2^3 = 8$, a notation using this form is called octal. Similarily, the system using 2^4, which is 16, is called hexadecimal. Here we discuss the octal representation. Three consecutive binary digits are required to represent the eight octal digits. This may be seen in Table 12.1.

TABLE 12.1.   BINARY, OCTAL, AND DECIMAL
INTEGERS, 0 THROUGH 7

Binary	Octal	Decimal
000	0	0
001	1	1
010	2	2
011	3	3
100	4	4
101	5	5
110	6	6
111	7	7

This can be extended by observing that to represent decimal 8, we need to add one octal position to the left of the present one. But adding one octal position requires three binary positions. The result is shown in Table 12.2.

The range of patterns of 60 binary digits, or **bits,** starts with a word consisting entirely of 0s,

000000000000000000000000000000000000000000000000000000000000

which is of course a pictorial way to represent a specific electronic energy state of the computer circuitry. All patterns can then be generated by adding binary 1 until a word consisting entirely of 1s,

111111111111111111111111111111111111111111111111111111111111

is obtained. Any 60-bit word can be mapped onto a 20-octal-digit word (each octal digit uses three bits.) This mapping is one-to-one, so that groups of three consecu-

Table 12.2.   BINARY, OCTAL, AND DECIMAL INTEGERS, 0 THROUGH 18

Binary	Octal	Decimal
000000	00	00
000001	01	01
000010	02	02
000011	03	03
000100	04	04
000101	05	05
000110	06	06
000111	07	07
001000	10	08
001001	11	09
001010	12	10
001011	13	11
001100	14	12
001101	15	13
001110	16	14
001111	17	15
010000	20	16
010001	21	17
010010	22	18

tive binary digits can be converted by *inspection* to one octal digit using the binary-to-octal correspondence given in Table 12.1. For example, the 60-bit pattern

111001001010110111010100101010101000010101010101010101010101

can be presented as the 20-octal-digit pattern

71126724525025252525

without changing in its information content. Both the 60-binary-digit form and the 20-octal-digit form denote the same number.

The computer works with electronic circuits that are in one of two distinct states, either on or off. Consequently, the on-off condition is the binary signal condition used by the computer, and we think of it as corresponding to binary digits. But for most situations, humans find it much easier to use the octal representation. Because of the one-to-one correspondence between the binary and octal forms, there is always an exact equivalence between the binary representation and the octal representation of the same pattern. Before we consider how real values are represented using these possible patterns, we shall consider the representation of negative integers.

There are several ways that negative integers may be represented by a computer. The CDC 700 series computers use the system known as the 1's complement method. To form the **1's complement** of a 60-bit word, simply subtract each bit from 1, which can be accomplished by inspection simply by replacing each 0 in the original by 1 and replacing each 1 in the original by 0. If the original 60-bit word was the integer representation of a positive integer, then the 1's complement of the original 60-bit word is the integer representation of the negative. For example, the decimal integer 18 is represented as an integer in the CYBER as

000000000000000000000000000000000000000000000000000000010010 so

    111111111111111111111111111111111111111111111111111111101101

is the integer representation of the decimal integer -18.

Consider a complete systematic display of all possible 60-bit patterns produced by starting with a word consisting entirely of 0s and adding 1 to produce the next consecutive value. Eventually, such a tableau of numbers will produce the last unique value, a 60-bit word consisting entirely of 1s. Further, this tableau may be split in half at the middle. Where it splits in half would be easy to identify because the split occurs when the leftmost digit changes from 0 to 1. If we were to pause a moment and consider this tableau, we would realize that the half starting with 0 represents positive integers, whereas the half starting with 1 represents negative integers. In addition, we would notice that the top of the list represents 0, +1, +2, +3, ... For consistency, when we start at the bottom of the list and work up, we say that the last element in the tableau represents 0; and then, working up the list, -1, -2, -3, . . . are represented. This results in a situation in which there are two different patterns that represent zero. The zero represented by a word consisting entirely of 1s is said to be the representation of negative zero. The CDC CYBER is designed to recognize this situation. As far as the human is concerned, each pattern is zero.

Finally, the middle of the tableau has another important characteristic. On one side of the middle is the representation of the largest positive integer value; on the other side is the largest (in magnitude) negative integer value. Integer values outside this range cannot be represented as integers in the CYBER. Attempting to produce integers outside this range will yield unpredictable results. Further, at least on the CYBER, out-of-range errors will *not* produce an error message. Yet the computations are certainly wrong.

So far, we have discussed the tableau of integers in terms of binary notation. Any word in this tableau will have either a 0 bit or a 1 bit as its leftmost bit. If the leftmost bit is a 0, the integer representation is of a positive value. If the leftmost bit is a 1, the integer representation is of a negative value. Observe in Table 12.1 that a leftmost octal digit of 0, 1, 2, or 3 corresponds to a leftmost 0 bit, whereas a leftmost octal digit of 4, 5, 6, or 7 corresponds to a leftmost 1 bit. Thus, if we were using octal notation, we would say that an integer starting with octal 0, 1, 2, or 3 would be the representation of a positive integer, but an integer starting with octal 4, 5, 6, or 7 would be the representation of a negative integer. This is true because octal 0, 1, 2, and 3 correspond to binary 000, 001, 010, and 011, respectively. Consequently, the first four octal digits correspond to the case in which the leftmost bit of the 60-bit word is a zero. Similarily, octal 4, 5, 6, and 7 correspond to binary 100, 101, 110, and 111, respectively. Therefore, these four octal digits correspond to a 60-bit word in which the leftmost bit is a binary 1. Type integer is used to represent whole numbers or, in other words, to represent numbers without any fractional part. No **radix point** (decimal point, octal point, binary point) is associated with an integer. Nonetheless, in computer science, the integer representation is sometimes called a **fixed-point** representation. Perhaps less appropriately, integers are sometimes called fixed-point numbers. The phrase *fixed point* is better understood after we consider the representation of real numbers.

We have prepared a short program called REPINT, meaning REPresentation of INTegers, which is included here as Figure 12.9. The output from the execution of this program is given in Figure 12.10. The purpose of these figures is to display the representation of some typical integer values and to show how they would be printed using alphabetical and real edit specifications. Here we have also used the nonstandard O edit specification to present the bit patterns using octal notation. One important point is that if a type inconsistency is present and if the contents of a computer word that is the representation of an integer were printed or were used as a

```
      PROGRAM REPINT
C
C     PREAMBLE FOR PROGRAM REPINT
C
C     ABSTRACT: REPINT ILLUSTRATES SOME ASPECTS OF MACHINE
C               REPRESENTATION
C
C     INPUT:    NONE
C
C     OUTPUT:   REPRESENTATIONS OF SOME INTEGERS PRINTED ACCORDING
C               TO VARIOUS EDIT DESCRIPTORS.
C
C     DESIGN HISTORY: H. LEE, 4JAN86
C
C     REFERENCE: NONE
C
C     ID DICTIONARY:
C
C     ID        TYPE        MEANING               USE
C
C     N         INTEGER     VALUES -10 TO 10      VARIABLE
C
C     SPECIFICATIONS
C
      IMPLICIT LOGICAL (A-Z)
C
      INTEGER N
C
      OPEN(6,FILE='OUTPUT')
C
      WRITE(6,600)
      DO 1 N=-10,10,1
         WRITE(6,601)N,N,N,N
1     CONTINUE
      STOP
C
600   FORMAT('1','GENERATED AS INTEGERS')
601   FORMAT('0',I3,2X,O20,2X,F20.5,2X,A10)
      END
```

Figure 12.9   Program REPINT

GENERATED AS INTEGERS

-10	7777777777777777765	.00000	;;;;;;;;;;_
-9	7777777777777777766	.00000	;;;;;;;;;;!
-8	7777777777777777767	.00000	;;;;;;;;;;&
-7	7777777777777777770	.00000	;;;;;;;;;;'
-6	7777777777777777771	.00000	;;;;;;;;;;?
-5	7777777777777777772	.00000	;;;;;;;;;;<
-4	7777777777777777773	.00000	;;;;;;;;;;>
-3	7777777777777777774	.00000	;;;;;;;;;;@
-2	7777777777777777775	.00000	;;;;;;;;;;\
-1	7777777777777777776	.00000	;;;;;;;;;;^
0	0000000000000000000	.00000	
1	0000000000000000001	.00000	A
2	0000000000000000002	.00000	B
3	0000000000000000003	.00000	C
4	0000000000000000004	.00000	D
5	0000000000000000005	.00000	E
6	0000000000000000006	.00000	F
7	0000000000000000007	.00000	G
8	0000000000000000010	.00000	H
9	0000000000000000011	.00000	I
10	0000000000000000012	.00000	J

Figure 12.10   Output from the Execution of REPINT

real, many integer values would behave as a real value of 0.0. This, of course, can create serious errors. Another point illustrated by the output is that many integer values also have the same bit patterns as characters. The output should convince you that knowledge of the bit pattern of a computer word does not give information as to what that word is, in fact, representing. Professional programmers can make good guesses, but they are not always correct.

12.7 THE REPRESENTATION OF REALS

The method used to represent values in the computer that are type real is similar to the method we call scientific notation. Further, the methods for calculation in a computer have some features in common with calculations using values expressed in scientific notation. In scientific notation, the values are given as

$$m \times b^e$$

where m is the mantissa, b is the base, and e is the exponent. Thus, we might have

$$5.13 \times 10^1$$
$$2.973 \times 10^3$$

as a pair of values stated in scientific notation. If we were to add these, we would adjust the values so that each had the same exponent. This would enable us to obtain the sum by simply adding the mantissas and affixing the base and exponent. Thus, we would rewrite the pair and add as follows:

$$\begin{array}{r} 0.0513 \times 10^3 \\ + \ 2.973 \ \times 10^3 \\ \hline 3.0243 \times 10^3 \end{array}$$

Suppose that we had to subtract, such as in the following example:

$$\begin{array}{r} 1.61 \times 10^3 \\ - \ 8.9 \ \times 10^2 \\ \hline \end{array}$$

To subtract, we write the values so they both have the same exponent as before; then we subtract the mantissas:

$$\begin{array}{r} 1.61 \times 10^3 \\ - \ 0.89 \times 10^3 \\ \hline 0.72 \times 10^3 \end{array}$$

Although the result is numerically correct, we usually write numbers in scientific notation, so that any value has exactly one nonzero digit to the left of the decimal point. This is called the **normal form.** The process of creating the normal form is called **normalization.** Consequently, we rewrite the difference as

$$7.2 \times 10^2$$

Normalization is performed to avoid any leading zeroes and to maximize the proportion of nonzero digits. Zero is a special case and cannot be normalized.

The method of representation for reals that is used in the CYBER is designed to maximize the range of values that can be represented. Because all values are in binary, the base value of 2 is understood. (Therefore, it is not stored in the representation.) CYBER represents reals as **floating-point numbers** in the form

$$k \times B^n$$

where k is the coefficient, B is the base, and n is the exponent. Control Data Corporation engineers labeled the bit positions starting with bit position 0 on the right-hand side of the word to bit position 59 on the left-hand side of the word. Although this appears strange at first, this still produces a 60-bit word. The CYBER (CDC 750) computer uses the following 60-bit floating point format:

Bit 59 (the leftmost bit) is the sign of the coefficient;

Bits 48–58 contain what is called the biased exponent; bit 58 may be called the sign of the exponent or the bias.

Bits 0–47 contain the coefficient.

The binary point is assumed to be to the right of the 0 bit. This implies that the coefficient is shifted in order to have 48 bits to the left of this assumed binary point. Because the binary point is assumed, no bit need be allocated for it.

When the sign bit for the coefficient, bit 59, is zero, a positive coefficient is represented. When bit 59 is 1, a negative coefficient is represented.

Eleven bits are used to represent the exponent. However, the exponent is stored in a special form known as a *biased exponent*. This may be thought of as scaling the exponent. It simply shifts its value over the range that is possible within the limits of 11 bits.

The process of converting a real base ten value to its CYBER representation is called **packing.** The method involves converting a base ten number into a base two number and then shifting the binary point to its assumed position at the right of the least significant bit. This shifting requires appropriate changes in the exponent. Before the exponent may be inserted into bit positions 48–58, it must be scaled or biased. For example, if the coefficient is positive and the exponent is positive, the biased exponent is obtained by adding the magnitude of the exponent to 2000 octal.

The representation of some common real values is illustrated by the program REPRLA, a short version of REPresentation of ReALs. The program is presented in Figure 12.11 and the output from the execution of the program is given in Figure 12.12. In the output we can see that commonly encountered real values also could be interpreted as very large integer numbers. Although type errors can occur by interpreting a value that is expressed in floating-point representation as an integer, the mistake usually is quite apparent because many floating-point patterns are large-valued integers; hence, the error is easy to detect because many applications do not use such large integers.

We would like to illustrate some of the things that may occur in computations with numeric values using floating-point representation. We first consider Program ZERONE, given here as Figure 12.13. ZERONE stands for ZERO and ONE because the intent of the program is to produce 0s and 1s as a result of computation, using the real representations and real arithmetic. The designer of this program has used a O20 edit specification. This nonstandard edit specification produces the contents of an entire 60-bit computer word using octal notation, which requires 20 octal digits. As you can determine by studying the code, the real variable ONE should have the real value 1.0, and the real variable ZERO should have the value 0.0 for each and every pass through the DO loop. However, an examination of the output from this program, given here as Figure 12.14, shows that reality is quite startling. If an F edit specification is used to specify a small number of digits, the results appear reasonable. But when an F20.15 edit specification is used to produce the output, we observe that the first six pairs are what we would expect; yet, the remaining values give evidence of something occurring that we had not expected. What is happening is known as the **accumulation of truncation errors.** This, in fact, is in addition to the initial inaccuracies in the representation of the real values.

There are two factors related to the production of some of the strange features of the output. One factor is that an algorithm is used to produce the "best possible" representation of the contents of the computer for the real variables. This algorithm does a very careful analysis of each situation and produces good interpretations as long as it is able to do so. Thus, it can do quite well for small edit specifications but

```
      PROGRAM REPRLA
C
C     PREAMBLE FOR PROGRAM REPRLA
C
C     ABSTRACT: REPRLA ILLUSTRATES SOME ASPECTS OF MACHINE
C               REPRESENTATION
C
C     INPUT:   NONE
C
C     OUTPUT:  REPRESENTATIONS OF SOME REALS PRINTED ACCORDING
C              TO VARIOUS EDIT DESCRIPTORS.
C
C     DESIGN HISTORY: H. LEE, 4JAN86
C
C     REFERENCE: NONE
C
C     ID DICTIONARY:
C
C     ID       TYPE       MEANING             USE
C
C     N        REAL       VALUES -1.0 TO 1.0   VARIABLE
C
C     SPECIFICATIONS
C
      IMPLICIT LOGICAL (A-Z)
C
      REAL N
C
      OPEN(6,FILE='OUTPUT')
C
      WRITE(6,600)
      DO 1 N=-1.0,1.0,0.1
         WRITE(6,601)N,N,N,N
1     CONTINUE
      STOP
C
600   FORMAT('1','GENERATED AS REALS')
601   FORMAT('0',F5.2,2X,O20,2X,I20,2X,A10)
      END
```

Figure 12.11　FORTRAN Program REPRLA

cannot do so well for larger edit specifications. This algorithm is invoked only to produce output. It is not used between each assembly-level instruction. The second factor underlying the understanding of the output is that the computer is using a register longer than the 60-bit register one might imagine. This explains why the output seems to show a sudden change in the values for 0 and 1. In fact, in the less significant bits, a change in values is gradually and steadily occuring with each pass through the loop. We are unable to detect the change until it becomes large enough to appear in the portion of register given as output.

GENERATED AS REALS

-1.00	60573777777777777777	-274860314757955584	#.4;;;;;;;
-.90	60600631463146314631	-274691429771929190	##FY-Y-Y-Y
-.80	60601463146314631463	-274663282274258124	##L:L:L:L:
-.70	60602314631463146315	-274635134776587058	##SL:L:L:M
-.60	60603146314631463147	-274606987278915992	##Y-Y-Y-Y*
-.50	60610000000000000003	-274438102292889596	#[C
-.40	60611463146314631466	-274381807297547465	#[L:L:L:L!
-.30	60613146314631463151	-274325512302205334	#[Y-Y-Y-Y (
-.20	60621463146314631471	-274100332320836806	#]L:L:L:L?
-.10	60631463146314631501	-273818857344126142	#:L:L:L:MA
.00	16407400000000000000	261472661178155008	N5@
.10	17146314631463146334	273818857344126172	OL:L:L:L:1
.20	17156314631463146325	274100332320836821	OM:L:L:L:U
.30	17164631463146314636	274325512302205342	ON-Y-Y-Y-3
.40	17166314631463146321	274381807297547473	ON:L:L:L:Q
.50	17174000000000000002	274578839781244930	OO5 B
.60	17174631463146314634	274606987278915996	OO-Y-Y-Y-1
.70	17175463146314631466	274635134776587062	OO=:L:L:L!
.80	17176314631463146320	274663282274258128	OO:L:L:L:P
.90	17177146314631463152	274691429771929194	OO?-Y-Y-Y)

Figure 12.12   Output from the Execution of REPRLA

PROGRAM SUMRLS (Figure 12.15), which illustrates the representation problems of reals, attempts to obtain the sum of 1000 one-tenths. We would expect that this sum should be 100.0. The best floating-point representation of 100 is printed for comparison purposes. Although the outputs produced using an F10.5 edit specification for SUM and HUND are the same, the outputs of the two values using the octal specification shows that, in fact, the values are different, as may be seen in Figure 12.16. Consequently, we must expect that any test of the form

$$(SUM\ .EQ.\ HUND)$$

would be false because the relational operator compares all 60 bits. If the bit patterns in the two locations are not the same, the expression evaluates to false. Notice that

```
      PROGRAM ZERONE
C
C     PREAMBLE FOR PROGRAM ZERONE
C
C     ABSTRACT: ZERONE ILLUSTRATES SOME ASPECTS OF MACHINE
C               REPRESENTATION AND ITS EFFECT ON COMPUTATIONS.
C
C     INPUT:   NONE
C
C     OUTPUT:  REAL AND OCTAL REPRESENTATIONS OF ZERO AND ONE
C              WHEN CALCULATED IN VARIOUS WAYS.
C
C     DESIGN HISTORY: M. MISOVICH, 7JAN86
C
C     REFERENCE: NONE
C
C     ID DICTIONARY:
C
C     ID          TYPE          MEANING              USE
C
C     N           INTEGER       INDEX                VARIABLE
C     ONE         REAL          CALCULATED VALUE 1   VARIABLE
C     SUM         REAL          SUM OF N 0.1'S       VARIABLE
C     TENTH       REAL          VALUE 0.1            VARIABLE
C     ZERO        REAL          CALCULATED VALUE O   VARIABLE
C
C     SPECIFICATIONS
C
      IMPLICIT LOGICAL (A-Z)
C
      INTEGER N
      REAL ONE,SUM,TENTH,ZERO
C
      OPEN(6,FILE='OUTPUT')
C
      WRITE(6,600)
      SUM=0.0
      TENTH=0.1
      DO 1 N=1,10
         SUM=SUM+TENTH
         ZERO=N*TENTH-SUM
         ONE=(N*TENTH)/SUM
         WRITE(6,601)ZERO,ZERO,ZERO,ONE,ONE,ONE
1     CONTINUE
      STOP
C
600   FORMAT('1','PROGRAM ZERONE')
601   FORMAT('0','ZERO = ',F5.2,F20.15,2X,O20,
     +      /' ','ONE  = ',F5.2,F20.15,2X,O20)
      END
```

Figure 12.13 FORTRAN Program ZERONE

```
PROGRAM ZERONE

ZERO  =  .00     .000000000000000   0000000000000000000000
ONE   = 1.00    1.000000000000000   1720400000000000000000

ZERO  =  .00     .000000000000000   0000000000000000000000
ONE   = 1.00    1.000000000000000   1720400000000000000000

ZERO  =  .00     .000000000000000   0000000000000000000000
ONE   = 1.00    1.000000000000000   1720400000000000000000

ZERO  =  .00     .000000000000000   0000000000000000000000
ONE   = 1.00    1.000000000000000   1720400000000000000000

ZERO  =  .00     .000000000000000   0000000000000000000000
ONE   = 1.00    1.000000000000000   1720400000000000000000

ZERO  =  .00     .000000000000000   0000000000000000000000
ONE   = 1.00    1.000000000000000   1720400000000000000000

ZERO  =  .00    -.000000000000004   6137377777777777777777
ONE   = 1.00     .999999999999993   1717777777777777777776

ZERO  =  .00    -.000000000000004   6137377777777777777777
ONE   = 1.00     .999999999999993   1717777777777777777776

ZERO  =  .00    -.000000000000004   6137377777777777777777
ONE   = 1.00     .999999999999993   1717777777777777777776

ZERO  =  .00    -.000000000000007   6136377777777777777777
ONE   = 1.00     .999999999999993   1717777777777777777776
```

Figure 12.14 Output from the Execution of ZERONE

```
PROGRAM SUMRLS
C
C    PREAMBLE FOR PROGRAM SUMRLS
C
C    ABSTRACT: SUMRLS ILLUSTRATES SOME ASPECTS OF MACHINE
C              REPRESENTATION AND ITS EFFECT ON COMPUTATIONS.
C
C    INPUT:    NONE
C
C    OUTPUT:   REAL AND OCTAL REPRESENTATIONS OF 0.1, 100.0 (AS A
C              CONSTANT), AND 100.0 (AS A SUM OF 1000 0.1'S).
C
C    DESIGN HISTORY: H. LEE, 4JAN86
C
C    REFERENCE: NONE
C
C    ID DICTIONARY:
C
C    ID       TYPE       MEANING                USE
C
```
(continues)

Figure 12.15 FORTRAN Program SUMRLS

```
C      HUND       REAL        VALUE ONE HUNDRED    VARIABLE
C      N          INTEGER     INDEX                VARIABLE
C      SUM        REAL        SUM OF 1000 0.1'S    VARIABLE
C      TENTH      REAL        VALUE 0.1            VARIABLE
C
C      SPECIFICATIONS
C
       IMPLICIT LOGICAL (A-Z)
C
       INTEGER N
       REAL HUND,SUM,TENTH
C
       OPEN(6,FILE='OUTPUT')
C
       SUM=0.0
       TENTH=0.1
       HUND=100.0
       DO 1 N=1,1000
          SUM=SUM+TENTH
1      CONTINUE
       WRITE(6,600)
       WRITE(6,601)TENTH,TENTH,HUND,HUND,SUM,SUM
       IF(HUND.EQ.SUM)THEN
          WRITE(6,602)
       ELSE
          WRITE(6,603)
       ENDIF
       STOP
C
600    FORMAT('1','PROGRAM SUMRLS')
601    FORMAT('0','TENTH = ',F10.5,2X,O20,
      +       /'0','HUND  = ',F10.5,2X,O20,
      +       /'0','SUM   = ',F10.5,2X,O20)
602    FORMAT('0','HUND AND SUM ARE EQUAL')
603    FORMAT('0','HUND AND SUM ARE NOT EQUAL')
       END
```

Figure 12.15   (continued)

```
PROGRAM SUMRLS

TENTH =      .10000   17146314631463146315

HUND  =  100.00000   17266200000000000000

SUM   =  100.00000   17266177777777777603

HUND AND SUM ARE NOT EQUAL
```

Figure 12.16   Output from the Execution of SUMRLS

this is true even if you output the values of SUM and HUND and these printed values are the same. Of course, in many real-world problems, these representation and truncation errors can be very serious. It is the user's responsibility to know his or her problem thoroughly and to be alert to the problems stemming from representation and from computer arithmetic. For many applications, considerable knowledge is available about numerical methods. This material should be examined for specific techniques. This material is usually indexed under the subject heading "numerical methods." Professionally designed and implemented systems for doing numerical computations usually, but not always, employ reasonably good numerical methods.

The details of how a real number is converted to its packed floating-point format are not too important. But there are several things about the representation of real numbers that are important. First, because the base ten number is converted to a base two number and ten is not an integer power of two, the representations are not, in general, exact representations. This may contribute to inaccurate numerical computations. Second, because there are a fixed number of binary digits available to represent an exponent, there is a limitation on the range of real values that may be represented. A value outside of this range may be produced in computations. Such a value is an error. In such circumstances, CYBER usually inserts the endpoint of the range in the word that is in error. The system is able to detect these errors, and when erroneous values are encountered, the system outputs an error message. Unfortunately, the error messages are not meaningful to the beginning programmer because they appear as a short message in the dayfile, which is a record of the sequence of executed control statements. The dayfile is printed with the output of the job. One such message is

```
                              ERROR MODE= 2.
```

which is given when the system encounters an infinite operand. This is the result either of an attempted division by zero or the use of a value that was too large to be represented.

12.8 OVERFLOW, UNDERFLOW, OR INDEFINITE

Overflow, underflow, or indefinite values can occur with floating-point computations. **Overflow** occurs when calculations lead to a result requiring an exponent larger than the largest positive value in the range. The CYBER documentation and some execution-time error messages use the phrases *positive overflow* or *negative overflow*.

Underflow occurs when calculations produce a value for the exponent equal to or smaller than the smallest exponent that can be represented. Either positive or negative underflow can occur. On the CYBER, underflow may not produce any error message.

Whenever the CYBER cannot resolve a calculation, such as an attempted division when both divisor and dividend are zero, the CYBER calls this either a positive or negative indefinite value. When such errors occur, a special value is inserted into the computer word. When the system attempts to use such a special value, it writes a mode error message in the dayfile and terminates execution.

─────── *13* ───────

Gauss-Seidel

13.1 INTRODUCTION

The purpose of this chapter is to stress the importance of searching for patterns in the symbolic form of mathematical equations as an aid to the design of a program. We also wish to emphasize the disciplined approach to the design of a program for a complex mathematical problem. The problem is to obtain the solution to a set of simultaneous linear equations. Such systems of equations are used to model the forces operating on a structure, such as a bridge. Or, they may be used to model the flow of current in an electric circuit. Although there are several known methods to solve a system of linear equations, we consider only one, the Gauss-Seidel method.

We begin by considering the problem of obtaining a numeric solution to the set of simultaneous equations

$$x_1 + x_2 = 3 \qquad\qquad (1)$$

$$x_1 + 3x_2 = 7 \qquad\qquad (2)$$

Using the Gauss-Seidel method, the first step is to verify our understanding of the method by working a simple example using a calculator or paper and pencil. Next, we shall study the mathematics of the method at a more general, or symbolic, level. In doing this, we shall look for patterns in the form of the solution. We shall also make a list of the possible errors that might arise. Only after we feel that we understand the method for solving these equations, have a clear idea of the patterns involved in obtaining the solutions, and have a list of possible errors will we begin to design a program to solve such equations. We shall use the developmental forms for the control structures, translate these into a formal design, translate the design into FORTRAN code, and, finally, test the resulting program.

13.2 A NUMERIC SOLUTION

Equations (1) and (2) are two equations in two unknowns,

$$x_1 \quad \text{and} \quad x_2$$

The Gauss-Seidel method is an iteration method for obtaining the solution to such a set of simultaneous equations. This **iteration method** for solving these equations is to solve equation (1) for

$$x_1$$

using an initial trial value, say 0, for

$$x_2$$

and then solving equation (2) for

$$x_2$$

using the just-obtained result for

$$x_1$$

Going through a set of simultaneous equations once, solving the first equation for

$$x_1$$

solving the second equation for

$$x_2,$$

and so on through the entire set is said to be **one iteration.**

To solve the system of equations almost always requires many iterations, but each time we obtain the solution to one of the equations, we use the latest values for each of the other unknowns. We always systematically solve the first equation for

$$x_1$$

the second equation for

$$x_2$$

and so on. The Gauss-Seidel method is not guaranteed to produce a solution.

13.2.1 Iteration 1

We repeat the equations here:

$$x_1 + x_2 = 3 \tag{1}$$
$$x_1 + 3x_2 = 7 \tag{2}$$

We solve equation (1) for

$$x_1$$

using a trial value of 0.0 for

$$x_2$$

as follows:

$$x_1 + x_2 = 3$$
$$x_1 + 0 = 3$$
$$x_1 = 3$$

Then we solve equation (2) for

$$x_2$$

using the latest value for

$$x_1$$

(which is 3):

$$x_1 + 3x_2 = 7$$
$$3 + 3x_2 = 7$$
$$x_2 = 1.33333$$

which completes the *first* iteration.

13.2.2 Iteration 2

We now solve equation (1) for

$$x_1$$

using the value of 1.33333 for x_2:

$$x_1 + x_2 = 3$$
$$x_1 + 1.33333 = 3$$
$$x_1 = 1.66667$$

and then solve equation (2) for

$$x_2$$

using the value of 1.66667 for x_1:

$$x_1 + 3x_2 = 7$$
$$1.66667 + 3x_2 = 7$$
$$x_2 = 1.77776$$

which completes the *second* iteration.

We continue in this fashion for several more iterations. The results are tabulated in Table 13.1. There we see that the iterations apparently are converging to the solution values of

$$x_1 = 1.0 \quad \text{and} \quad x_2 = 2.0$$

TABLE 13.1   RESULTS OF THE FIRST
EIGHT ITERATIONS

Iteration	x_1	x_2
1	3.00000	1.33333
2	1.66667	1.77776
3	1.22224	1.92592
4	1.07408	1.97531
5	1.02499	1.99083
6	1.00917	1.99694
7	1.00306	1.99898
8	1.00102	1.99966

The Gauss-Seidel method for solving simultaneous equations is said to converge to a solution of the equations if certain necessary conditions are satisfied. We leave a discussion of the necessary conditions for the convergence to others. But we can state a sufficient condition for convergence, which is known to be more stringent than the necessary condition. A sufficient condition for convergence is that the absolute value of the main diagonal term in each equation is larger than all other terms in that equation. (The first term is the **main diagonal term** in the first equation. The second term is the main diagonal term in the second equation, and so on.) Obviously, the order in which the equations appear may determine whether or not a solution is obtained.

13.2.3 General Form of the Solution

As we have stated, our final goal is to produce a computer program that applies the Gauss-Seidel iteration method to obtain the solution to a system of simultaneous equations. Further, as is the usual practice in programming, we desire a program to be fairly general. In the case of solving simultaneous equations, we would want to be able to solve a system of 2, 3, 4, . . . , n equations. For the next step in moving toward our goal, we need to write out the symbolic form for a system of simultaneous equations in as general a form as necessary so that we can detect any possible patterns in the solutions. *A search for patterns is an important technique in developing a design intended for computer solution.*

To assist our detection of possible patterns in the form of the solution, we restate the equations in a more symbolic form. We use

$$a_{ij}$$

for the coefficients of the unknown

$$x_i's$$

Further, we replace the constant on the right-hand side of the equation by

$$a_{ij}$$

This notation is similar to matrix notation, where the first subscript represents the row number and the second subscript represents the column number.

The general form for a system of two simultaneous equations in two unknowns is:

$$a_{11}x_1 + a_{12}x_2 = a_{13} \tag{1}$$

$$a_{21}x_1 + a_{22}x_2 = a_{23} \tag{2}$$

(In this compact notation, usable only for matrices less than 10×10, 11 means row 1, column 1; 12 means row 1, column 2, etc.) We solve equation (1) for

$$x_1$$

indicating the latest value by an apostrophe. Thus, we may indicate the solutions as follows:

$$x_1' = \frac{a_{13} - a_{12}x_2}{a_{11}}$$

$$x_2' = \frac{a_{23} - a_{21}x_1'}{a_{22}}$$

We realize that as yet there are no visible patterns in the form for the solution. Consequently, we shall continue our search for patterns by examining the notation for three equations in three unknowns:

$$a_{11}x_1 + a_{12}x_2 + a_{13}x_3 = a_{14}$$
$$a_{21}x_1 + a_{22}x_2 + a_{23}x_3 = a_{24}$$
$$a_{31}x_1 + a_{32}x_2 + a_{33}x_3 = a_{34}$$

The solution is as follows:

$$x_1' = \frac{a_{14} - a_{12}x_2 - a_{13}x_3}{a_{11}}$$

$$x_2' = \frac{a_{24} - a_{21}x_1' - a_{23}x_3}{a_{22}}$$

$$x_3' = \frac{a_{34} - a_{31}x_1' - a_{32}x_2}{a_{33}}$$

In order to increase the possibility that we may be successful in the detection of any patterns in the form of the solutions, we examine the system of equations for four equations in four unknowns:

$$a_{11}x_1 + a_{12}x_2 + a_{13}x_3 + a_{14}x_4 = a_{15}$$
$$a_{21}x_1 + a_{22}x_2 + a_{23}x_3 + a_{24}x_4 = a_{25}$$
$$a_{31}x_1 + a_{32}x_2 + a_{33}x_3 + a_{34}x_4 = a_{35}$$
$$a_{41}x_1 + a_{42}x_2 + a_{43}x_3 + a_{44}x_4 = a_{45}$$

The indicated solutions are

$$x_1' = \frac{a_{15} - a_{12}x_2 - a_{13}x_3 - a_{14}x_4}{a_{11}}$$

$$x_2' = \frac{a_{25} - a_{21}x_1' - a_{23}x_3 - a_{24}x_4}{a_{22}}$$

$$x_3' = \frac{a_{35} - a_{31}x_1' - a_{32}x_2 - a_{34}x_4}{a_{33}}$$

$$x_4' = \frac{a_{45} - a_{41}x_1' - a_{42}x_2 - a_{43}x_3}{a_{44}}$$

Before you continue studying the exposition, we strongly recommend that you search for the patterns that exist among all these to see if you can find a clue that will lead to a solution. Further, if you feel confident that you perceive the patterns, we urge you to rewrite the solutions in a more compact form using the summation symbol, Σ (sigma). If you are not too sure that you perceive the patterns, we suggest that you write out the equations and the indicated solutions for a system of five equations in five unknowns and then attempt to see the pattern and to rewrite the indicated solutions using sigma notation.

13.2.3.1 Patterns in the solutions.   We search for patterns in the indicated solutions, that is, in the expressions given for

$$x_1', x_2', x_3', x_4'$$

by comparing these expressions for the trial solutions with the original set of equations. The most outstanding feature we can observe is that for each trial

$$x_i'$$

the denominator consists solely of the coefficient of

$$x_i'$$

which is always of the form

$$a_{ii}$$

Next, we detect that the first term of the numerator is the value of the constant term given on the right-hand side of the equality sign in the ith equation. Finally, recalling that a trial solution in this symbolic form is nothing more than the algebraic solution to the equation for

$$x_i'$$

we realize that the remaining terms, each of which is being subtracted from the constant term, are the terms from the left-hand side of the equality symbol that did not contain

$$x_i$$

Both to assure ourselves that we have a sufficiently detailed understanding of the Gauss-Seidel method and to facilitate eventually moving towards the design and code for a computer implementation of the method, let us carry the generalization somewhat further. Thus, let us indicate the forms of the equations and the forms for the trial values for the unknowns for n equations in n unknowns. In addition, we will use the general notation

$$a_{ij}$$

where

$$i = 1, 2, \ldots, n$$

and

$$j = 1, 2, \ldots, n$$

We may write the general symbolic form for a system of n simultaneous equations in n unknowns as follows:

$$a_{11}x_1 + a_{12}x_2 + a_{13}x_3 + a_{14}x_4 + \cdots + a_{1,n}x_n = a_{1,n+1}$$
$$a_{21}x_1 + a_{22}x_2 + a_{23}x_3 + a_{24}x_4 + \cdots + a_{2,n}x_n = a_{2,n+1}$$
$$a_{31}x_1 + a_{32}x_2 + a_{33}x_3 + a_{34}x_4 + \cdots + a_{3,n}x_n = a_{3,n+1}$$
$$a_{41}x_1 + a_{42}x_2 + a_{43}x_3 + a_{44}x_4 + \cdots + a_{4,n}x_n = a_{4,n+1}$$
$$\vdots$$
$$a_{n,1}x_1 + a_{n,2}x_2 + a_{n,3}x_3 + a_{n,4}x_4 + \cdots + a_{n,n}x_n = a_{n,n+1}$$

In such a system, the solutions may be indicated using the summation notation, as follows:

$$x_1' = \frac{a_{1,n+1} - \sum\limits_{j=2}^{n} a_{1,j} x_j}{a_{11}}$$

$$x_2' = \frac{a_{2,n+1} - a_{21} x_1' - \sum\limits_{j=3}^{n} a_{2,j} x_j}{a_{22}}$$

$$x_i' = \frac{a_{i,n+1} - \sum\limits_{j=1}^{i-1} a_{1,j} x_j - \sum\limits_{j=i+1}^{n} a_{i,j} x_j}{a_{i,i}}$$

Mathematicians write this with an even more compact notation, as follows:

$$x_i' = \frac{a_{i,n+1} - \sum\limits_{i \neq j} a_{i,j} x_j}{a_{i,i}}$$

where the sigma notation implies that the summation is over all possible values of i but excluding the case in which j has the value i. If you did not figure out the solution and if you did not understand our solution, you need to review the material above before continuing.

13.2.4 Termination Criteria and Solution Accuracy

All well-designed computer programs must include provisions to terminate. Consequently, before we move into the actual design of our program, we must obtain termination criteria. We have already mentioned that the Gauss-Seidel method may not converge to a solution. If any program uses an indefinite (data-dependent) iteration procedure to obtain a solution, an almost universal strategy is used to prevent an excessive expenditure of computer time in a possibly hopeless pursuit of a solution. The strategy is merely based upon the number of iterations. The *user* is asked to specify the maximum number of iterations wanted. This number would be supplied as input to the program. Then, during the execution of the program, it would check at the end of each iteration to be sure that the number of iterations already computed did not exceed the value specified by the user as the maximum value. If the iteration count, as it is called, did not exceed the maximum, the execution would continue by performing another iteration. On the other hand, the first time the iteration count (which is incremented after each iteration) exceeded the specified maximum, the program would output a message to this effect, state the values obtained for the iteration count and the unknowns, and, finally, terminate. Obviously, this iteration count procedure would guarantee eventual termination of execution.

But consider for a moment what we do when solving a set of equations using paper-and-pencil methods and a calculator. We compare the newest solution set to the previous one. We continue iterating until the newest differs from the previous set by only a "small" amount. In fact, we may notice that it is sufficient to examine the value of the single

$$x_i'$$

that has the largest difference in absolute value from its previous value. The difference between a trial solution for an unknown on one iteration and the trial solution for it on the next iteration is called the **residual.** Consequently, we can state another termination criterion in terms of these residuals. Again, we would require that the user specify the maximum largest (in absolute value) acceptable residual. Whenever the largest computed residual drops below the user-specified value for the largest acceptable residual, the program would cease iterating and output the results.

Finally, before we start the design phase, we should examine the equations to determine whether any unacceptable error conditions could arise. When we examine the equation for the trial solution, we observe that each involves the division by

$$a_{ii}$$

Consequently, after we have read all the data for one system of equations, we should ascertain whether one or more of the

$$a_{ii}\text{'s}$$

is zero. If such an error were detected, we should output an informative message, omit trying to obtain a solution to this system of equations, and continue by reading the next system of equations. A better approach would be to rearrange the equations in order to remove the zero element from the main diagonal.

13.3 THE DESIGN OF A PROGRAM FOR THE GAUSS-SEIDEL METHOD

The work we have done so far in this chapter is all *preliminary* to the actual design of a computer program to carry out the Gauss-Seidel method for the solution of a system of simultaneous linear equations. These vital steps included working out a numerical example using a calculator, obtaining the general pattern of the solution to the equations in symbolic form, and defining the criteria that are to be used to terminate the iterative search for the solution. As we have just completed these tasks, we can begin the design of a computer program to implement this method. Again, we shall decompose the design process into a sequence of steps. First, we shall describe in English the computations to be done in the PROGRAM unit. Then we shall restate these using the sketch design notation. Finally, we shall translate the sketch design into the formal design. These steps will then be repeated for the first subroutine unit. After the first subroutine unit has been designed, we shall design the next unit, and so on.

13.3.1 The PROGRAM Unit

We almost always design a program to process an indefinite number of data sets, using the PROGRAM unit as a driver. We shall follow this strategy here as well. The written program request indicates that the resulting program is to be able to process a system of up to 50 equations. In addition, the client indicated that in systems with a large number of equations, it is common for many of the terms to be zero. Consequently, two alternative methods for input would be desirable. In one method, all the terms, including the zero ones, would be required for input. In the other method, only the nonzero terms would be required. Therefore, we shall ask the user to specify how the data are to be read. We shall use a character variable, HOWRD, with expected input of either 'ALL' or 'NONZERO,' which then would be used to select a subroutine. We shall have two subroutines to input the values for the array, A, which, of course, will contain the values of the coefficients and constants represented in the mathematical notation by

$$a_{ij}$$

We shall call one subroutine RDALL and the other RDNZ.

For each data set, we will input a data set identification. This will be one line of up to 80 characters. This will be the first line to be read for each data set. Following this identification line will be the following parameters, each parameter on a separate line: HOWRD, N, MAXIT, and MAXRES. (N is the number of equations in this data set. MAXIT is the maximum acceptable number of iterations before termination of the computations for this data set. MAXRES is the maximum acceptable residual for this data set.) The remaining input for the data set will be the values to be read by the appropriate subroutine into the matrix A. We have implied that for each data set, the main program will perform all the input except for the values of the matrix A.

After the first data set is read, the program should verify that no error condition has appeared in the data. Recall that we will have to divide by each

$$a_{ii}$$

Consequently, none of these may be zero. If none are zero, we shall call a subroutine, SEIDEL, which will carry out the iterations until one of the two terminating criteria is met. These steps will be repeated as long as any data sets remain to be processed. After the last data set has been processed, the program should write the normal program termination message and then quit execution. These considerations lead to the first sketch of the PROGRAM, which we call GAUSS and present here as Figure 13.1.

The first sketch of the program unit GAUSS is quite straightforward, except possibly for the choice of the 'elseif' instead of the equivalent nested 2-alternative selection. We favor the n-alternative selection rather than nesting 2-alternative selections in a 2-alternative selection because we feel that the logic is easier to follow; furthermore, the resulting code is easier to modify. You may notice that we have chosen to input an item and then echo that item before going on to input the next item and echo it. We believe that this is preferable to the alternative of reading all items before echoing any item, for if anything goes wrong during reading, more information will be available sooner to diagnose the situation. In particular, we would know which item was in error. As this unit seems quite simple, we will present only the final design. It appears as Figure 13.2.

PROGRAM GAUSS
output program title headings
while-there-are-data
    input and echo
        data set identification
        HOWRD
        N
        MAXIT
        MAXRES
        call selected subroutine to input A(I,J)
    check for possible error (any A(I,I) = 0.0 is an error)
    if no error, call SEIDEL, which will perform the iterations
output 'normal program termination'
quit

Figure 13.1   The First Sketch of Program Unit GAUSS

preamble for program GAUSS
ABSTRACT: GAUSS uses the Gauss-Seidel method to obtain
               the solution to a system of simultaneous
               linear equations or reports reaching a user-
               specified maximum number of iterations.
INPUT: DATAID, HOWRD, MAXIT, MAXRES, and N
OUTPUT: error message if A(I,I) is zero with value
               of I
DESIGN HISTORY: Hans Lee, 3May85
CODING HISTORY: none
REFERENCE: none
ID DICTIONARY:

ID	TYPE	MEANING	USE
A	real	A, the coefficients and constant term	array (2 dimensional)
DATAID	character	DATA IDentification	variable
ERRAII	logical	ERROR in A(I,I)	variable
HOWRD	character	HOW ReaD	variable
I	integer	array and loop Index	variable
MAXIT	integer	MAXimum acceptable number of ITerations	variable
MAXRES	real	MAXimum acceptable RESidual	variable

Figure 13.2   Design of Program Unit GAUSS   *(continues)*

N	integer	Number of unknowns	variable
RDALL	NA	ReaD ALL elements into A(,)	subroutine (2 arguments)
RDNZ	NA	ReaD NonZero elements into A(,)	subroutine (2 arguments)
SEIDEL	NA	SEIDEL is called once for each data set to iterate for a solution	subroutine (4 arguments)

flow-of-control for program GAUSS

preamble goes here

specifications go here

output 'Program GAUSS uses the Gauss-Seidel method
to solve a system of linear equations,
Programmed by H. Lee, 3May85.'

while-there-are-data

> input DATAID
>
> echo DATAID
>
> input HOWRD
>
> echo HOWRD
>
> input N
>
> echo N
>
> input MAXIT
>
> echo MAXIT
>
> input MAXRES
>
> echo MAXRES
>
> IF (HOWRD is 'ALL') THEN
>   call RDALL(A, N)

Figure 13.2   (continued)

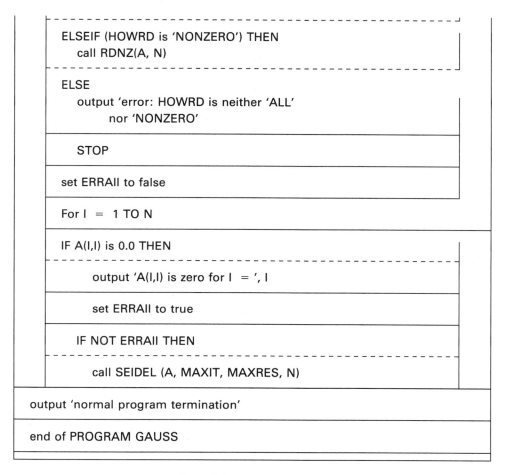

ELSEIF (HOWRD is 'NONZERO') THEN
    call RDNZ(A, N)

ELSE
    output 'error: HOWRD is neither 'ALL'
          nor 'NONZERO'

  STOP

set ERRAll to false

For I = 1 TO N

IF A(I,I) is 0.0 THEN

    output 'A(I,I) is zero for I = ', I

    set ERRAll to true

IF NOT ERRAll THEN

    call SEIDEL (A, MAXIT, MAXRES, N)

output 'normal program termination'

end of PROGRAM GAUSS

Figure 13.2   (continued)

13.3.2 Design of SUBROUTINES RDALL and RDNZ

The SUBROUTINE RDALL will read all elements of $A(I, J)$. As long as either the number of values to be read is small or as long as most of the values are nonzero, this is the preferred method to input $A(I, J)$. The procedure is quite simple. If all values were to be read, the reading probably would have been done in the PROGRAM unit. However, as the client desired to have the program input only the nonzero elements, which requires that the zero elements be initialized by the program, the input of $A(I, J)$ was assigned to two different subroutines. The reading of only the nonzero elements of $A(I, J)$ is to be done, along with the initialization of $A(I, J)$ to zero, by the SUBROUTINE RDNZ. Each subroutine has two arguments, A, the exit argument, and N, the number of unknowns. As each is short, we have not presented the sketch versions. The final designs are presented as Figures 13.3 and 13.4.

preamble for subroutine RDALL (A, N)

ABSTRACT:	RDALL reads all (including zero-valued) elements into array A(,).
INPUT:	A(,)
OUTPUT:	none
ENTRY VALUES:	N
EXIT VALUES:	A(,)
ENTRY AND EXIT VALUES:	none
DESIGN HISTORY:	Hans Lee, 3MAY85
CODING HISTORY:	none
REFERENCE:	none

ID DICTIONARY:

ID	TYPE	MEANING	USE
A	real	A(,) coefficients and constant term	array (2 dimensional)
COL	integer	COLumn array subscript and index	variable
N	integer	Number of unknowns	variable
ROW	integer	ROW array subscript and index	variable

---

flow-of-control for SUBROUTINE RDALL (A, N)

---

preamble goes here

---

specifications go here

---

for ROW = 1 to N

> input A(ROW,COL), COL = 1, N + 1

RETURN

END of SUBROUTINE RDALL

Figure 13.3   Design of SUBROUTINE RDALL

```
preamble for subroutine RDNZ (A, N)
    ABSTRACT:                      RDNZ( , ) reads nonzero terms into A( , )
    INPUT:                         A, ROW, COL
    OUTPUT:                        A( , )
    ENTRY VALUES:                  N
    EXIT VALUES:                   A( , )
    ENTRY AND EXIT VALUES:  none
    DESIGN HISTORY:                Hans Lee, 3MAY85
    CODING HISTORY:                none
    REFERENCE:                     none
    ID DICTIONARY:

    ID          TYPE             MEANING                          USE
    A           real             A( , ) the coefficients          array
                                 and constant terms               (2 dimensional)
    COL         integer          COLumn array subscript           variable
                                 and index
    N           integer          Number of unknowns               variable
    ROW         integer          ROW array subscript              variable
                                 and index
```

```
flow-of-control for SUBROUTINE RDNZ(A, N)

    preamble goes here

    specifications go here

for ROW = 1 to N

        for COL = 1 to N + 1

            A(ROW, COL) = 0.0




 ////    input ROW, COL, A(ROW, COL)

until ROW is −1

RETURN

END
```

Figure 13.4 Design of SUBROUTINE RDNZ

13.3.3 Design of SUBROUTINE SEIDEL

SUBROUTINE SEIDEL will be called once for each error-free data set. It will iterate for a solution until either a solution with a residual less than the value specifed
by the user as the maximum acceptable residual, MAXRES, is obtained or the number of iterations reaches the value specified by the user as the maximum acceptable
number of iterations, MAXIT. As the iteration is to continue until either one of two
terminating criteria is reached, the major control structure will be a posttested indefinite repetition. This may be stated as the first sketch of the subroutine, given here as
Figure 13.5.

The subroutine SEIDEL requires especially careful attention to the initialization of some of the arrays and variables it uses. Some must be initialized before the
indefinite posttested repetition is begun. Others must be initialized after it has begun
but before the determinate repetition is entered. And still others must be initialized at
the start of the determinate repetition. Thus, there are three levels of the control
structures, and an array of one or more variables must be initialized at the beginning
of each level. This is the major complexity in the design of the subroutine SEIDEL,
once the method for obtaining the solution is understood. The second sketch design
for SEIDEL is given in Figure 13.6, which necessarily reflects these levels of control structures.

The formal design makes the control structures somewhat more apparent. The
complete design of the subroutine is presented here as Figure 13.7.

13.4 SOME DESIGN CONSIDERATIONS REVIEWED
AND EXTENDED

In this chapter, we have either emphasized design techniques that were introduced in
earlier chapters or have introduced new ones. As the complexities of the Gauss-
Seidel method tend to obscure these design techniques, which we think are of much

---

SUBROUTINE SEIDEL will be based on an indefinite
posttested repetition, which will iterate for a solution
to a set of simultaneous linear equations until
either
    the residual is less than the maximum acceptable
    value specified by the user
or
    the iteration count reaches the maximum acceptable
    value specified by the user
After the iterations terminate, the subroutine will
output the values for the unknowns along with the
iteration count and the residual. The execution will
return to the calling program.

Figure 13.5   First Sketch of SUBROUTINE SEIDEL

SUBROUTINE SEIDEL (A, MAXIT, MAXRES, N)

initialize ITER to 0

for I = 1 to N
  initialize X(I) to 0.0

begin indefinite posttested repetition
    increment ITER by 1

  initialize RESID to 0.0

  for I = 1 to N
      initialize SUMONE to 0.0

    initialize SUMTWO to 0.0

    for J = 1 to I − 1
        SUMONE = SUMONE + A(I, J) ∗ X(J)

    for J = I + 1 to N
        SUMTWO = SUMTWO + A(I, J) ∗ X(J)

    XNEW = (A(I, N + 1) − SUMONE − SUMTWO)/A(I, I)

    DIF − ABS(XNEW − X(I))

    if DIF is greater than RESID then
        RESID = DIF

    X(I) = XNEW

UNTIL ((RESID is greater than or equal to MAXRES)
    or (ITER is equal to MAXIT))

for I = 1 to N
  output I, X(I)

output ITER, RESID

end of SUBROUTINE SEIDEL

Figure 13.6   Second Sketch of SUBROUTINE SEIDEL

preamble for subroutine SEIDEL (A, MAXIT, MAXRES, N)

ABSTRACT:		SEIDEL solves a system of linear equations by an iteration method. Iteration is terminated either when a user-specified criterion, called a residual, is reached or when the user-supplied maximum number of iterations is reached.
INPUT:		none
OUTPUT:		I, ITER, RESID, X( )
ENTRY VALUES:		A, MAXIT, MAXRES, N
EXIT VALUES:		none
ENTRY AND EXIT VALUES:		none
DESIGN HISTORY:		Hans Lee, 11MAY85
CODING HISTORY:		none
REFERENCE:		none

ID DICTIONARY:

ID	TYPE	MEANING	USE
A	real	Array of coefficients and constants	array (2 dimensional)
ABS	real	ABSolute value	intrinsic function
DIF	real	absolute value of the DIFference between XNEW and X(I)	variable
I	integer	Index, array subscript	variable
ITER	integer	ITERation count	variable
J	integer	index, array subscript	variable
MAXIT	integer	MAXimum number of ITerations	variable
MAXRES	real	MAXimum RESidual	variable
N	integer	Number of equations	variable
RESID	real	RESIDual	variable
SUMONE	real	SUM ONE	variable
SUMTWO	real	SUM TWO	variable
X	real	X, the unknowns	array (1 dimensional)
XNEW	real	the NEW value of X(I)	variable

flow-of-control for subroutine SEIDEL (A, MAXIT, MAXRES, N)

preamble goes here

specifications go here

Figure 13.7 Design of SUBROUTINE SEIDEL

```
ITER = 0

for I = 1 to N

    X(I) = 0.0


////   ITER = ITER + 1

       RESID = 0.0

       for I = 1 to N

           SUMONE = 0.0

           SUMTWO = 0.0

           for J = 1 to I − 1

               SUMONE = SUMONE + A(I, J) * X(J)


           for J = I + 1 to N

               SUMTWO = SUMTWO + A(I, J) * X(J)


           XNEW = (A(I, N + 1) − SUMONE − SUMTWO)/A(I, I)

           DIF = ABS(XNEW − X(I))

           IF DIF is greater than RESID then
           ---------------------------------------------------
           RESID = DIF

           X(I) = XNEW
```

Figure 13.7 (continued)

UNTIL ((RESID is less than or equal to MAXRES)
        or (ITER is equal to MAXIT))

for I = 1 to N

        output I, X(I)

output ITER, RESID

RETURN

END of SUBROUTINE SEIDEL

Figure 13.7   (continued)

greater importance than the Gauss-Seidel method itself, we emphasize the design aspects by asking and answering a series of questions.

Question.   How do I know that I understand the mathematics of the problem?

Answer.   You solve a few example problems for the numeric answers using paper, pencil, and a hand calculator. Obviously, you need to be able to verify that your answers are correct by some means or you need to have numeric examples with the correct answers available.

Question.   Evidently the design of a computer program requires that I know the patterns of regularity in the forms of the solutions. Further, it appears that I need to know these patterns for a very general case. Is this correct? If so, when and where do I look for such general patterns?

Answer.   Indeed, you are correct. You do need to look for general patterns in the form of the solutions. You should search for the patterns before you start to design the program. You look for the patterns in the most general symbolic statement of the mathematics of the problem, and especially, in the general symbolic statement of the solutions.

Question.   How do I input an indefinite series of values when the input of these values is nested within a pretested indefinite repetition ('while-there-are-data' construction)?

Answer.   If there are values that are not possible values in the data but are still feasible values for the variable, you can use a specific value to indicate that there are no more values in this data set. In our example, subroutine RDNZ, we use a value of -1 for an array subscript to indicate that this is the end of this data set. This is called a **sentinel** value.

Question.   On what basis do I decide to terminate an iteration process?

Answer.   You should give the responsibility to the user for setting parameters that control the termination. The user should know the most about his or her problem and what are reasonable results. In our example, we asked the user to specify both the value for maximum acceptable residual and the value for the maximum acceptable number of iterations.

Question.   If there is an indication that there is a logical error in a program, where do I look for further information and what should I do?

Answer.   If you suspect a logical error, you should, of course, verify that the design was correctly coded. If it was, then you should study the design itself. If something is wrong with the design, you should change the design first and then change the code. We stress this because we have noticed perhaps a natural tendency for programmers to attempt to repair logical errors by looking only at the code. This quickly leads to a number of "patches" in a program. If several of these are inserted into the same unit of a program, then that program becomes exceedingly difficult to maintain and usually becomes unstructured.

13.5 Exercises

1. **Task.** Design, implement, and test a program to obtain the amount a steel shaft is deformed by a weight, w. Assume that the amount deformed is only due to torsion.

   Supporting Information. A steel shaft of length L and diameter D is presented in Figure 13.8. An end view, with weight W attached at distance R, shows the shaft deformed in torsion by having one end twisted through an angle A. The end view is given as Figure 13.9. Given D, L, W, and R, the angle A may be obtained by solving for A in the equation

$$WR \cos A - 113{,}000\left(\frac{AD^4}{L}\right) = 0$$

The Newton-Raphson iteration method is to be used to solve for the value of A.

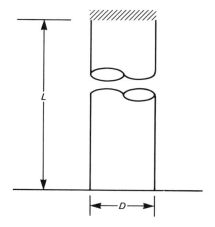

Figure 13.8 A Steel Shaft

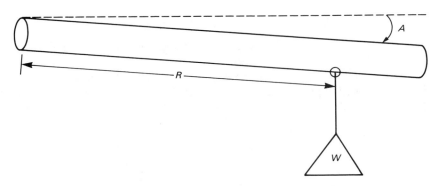

Figure 13.9   Side View of a Bar Bent Through Angle A by Weight W Applied at Distance R

The Newton-Raphson Iteration Method. The Newton-Raphson iterative method for solving for the roots of high-order polynomials or for the roots of equations that are not polynomials, such as

$$\sin \alpha - \alpha = 0$$

is also known as Newton's method. The strategy is based on the general form of the recursion

$$x_{n+1} = x_n - \frac{f(x_n)}{f'(x_n)}$$

where x_n is an initial (or the previous) estimate of the solution and x_{n+1} is a calculated improved estimate.

This improved value, in turn, is used on the right-hand side of the relation. The repetitions can be repeated until a satisfactory result is obtained.

Application to the Angle of Deformation. When the equation for the angle of deformation is written as required by the general form for the Newton-Raphson method, the result is

$$A_{n+1} = \frac{A_n + WR \cos A_n - 113{,}000\,(A_n D^4/L)}{WR \sin A_n + 113{,}000\,(D^4/L)}$$

$$= A_n - \frac{WR \cos A_n - 113{,}000\,(A_n D^4/L)}{-WR \sin A_n - 113{,}000\,(D^4/L)}$$

Assume that an estimate for A is satisfactory if the difference between

$$A_n \quad \text{and} \quad A_{n+1}$$

is less than α degrees. However, the procedure should be limited to a user-specified maximum number of iterations.

Program Specification. The program is to process an indefinite number of data sets. For each, input α; MAXIT, the maximum number of iterations to be used; A, the initial guess for the angle A; and D, L, W, and R.

Suggested Values. MAXIT $= 50$; $A = 5$; $D = 2$; $L = 30$; $W = 25$; $R = 7$. Explore each of these values for α: 0.000049; 0.00001; and 0.001.

14

Closing Comments and Advice

14.1 INTRODUCTION

In this last chapter, we shall make some closing comments. Among other things, the purpose of this chapter is to give us an opportunity to share some information we feel you should have. Thus, we shall now tell you about alternatives to the design and implementation of programs — namely, the use of professionally written programs. We also would like to let you know about special-purpose computer languages in case you may become interested in computations that would benefit from the selection and use of such languages. In this chapter we present a brief discussion of the portability of computer programs. Finally, we would like to recommend some additional classes for you to take.

14.2 SOFTWARE

Software, a professionally written program, is available for many diverse applications. Quite a few of these software systems or languages are of interest to engineers and scientists. Usually a computer user in these fields can locate professionally developed and written procedures. Most of these are more reliable and better tested than those a user might write. We highly recommend the use of these software systems. In this chapter, we will mention a few such systems. Most of these have been used for many years, are well tested, and are reasonably well documented. Each may be considered to be reliable. Some of these are available both on mainframes and micros. But some have only portions implemented on micros.

The **IMSL** (International Mathematics and Statistics Library) consists of FORTRAN subprograms that compute various mathematical functions, perform most of the computational tasks in linear algebra, solve equations, and so on.

There are two widely available systems for information processing and statistical computations, **SAS** and **SPSS** (Statistical Package for the Social Sciences.) In addition to these, there are many other statistical systems, but it is difficult to evaluate their reliability.

There are more specialized systems, such as **ENPORT-6,** which is a bond graph processor for problems in nonlinear systems. **SPICE** is a program for use in electrical engineering designed to solve circuit problems.

All these systems solve problems stated in terms of numeric data. There are several software products of interest to engineers and scientists that help solve symbolic (that is, nonnumeric) problems. These include the **SNOBOL, SPITBOL,** and **ICON** languages. SNOBOL and its faster version, SPITBOL, are especially designed languages to process character data; hence, they may be called *character-manipulating languages,* although they are more usually characterized as *string-processing languages.* ICON is a much broader language system, but it includes extensive character-manipulating facilities. The **LISP** language is another language designed for nonnumeric computations. It is extensively used in the computer science field of artificial intelligence. Many programs that prove theorems, parse languages, play games, and so on are written in LISP or have major portions written in LISP.

There are many software systems for performing symbolic mathematical computation. These systems perform algebraic and more advanced computations on equations. Such systems can multiply two polynomial equations and simplify the result. Although they are used directly to obtain results, they also serve a very useful function because they are the ideal research assistant to verify algebraic computations. **MAXSYMA, MATHEMATICA,** and **SMP** (Symbolic Manipulation Program) are examples of these systems. **REDUCE** is a symbolic mathematical system especially designed to solve symbolic problems in theoretical physics.

Most university computing centers have several of these systems available for use by faculty and students. It is important to ascertain what supporting services accompany their use. It is of utmost importance that consulting be available. The symbolic mathematical systems work best with special printers and special computers that display the mathematical expressions in forms close to the standard mathematical notation.

14.3 THE PORTABILITY OF FORTRAN 77 PROGRAMS

In this text we have selected some of the FORTRAN 77 statements and features for use by a beginning programmer. We have attempted to choose a minimum set of FORTRAN 77 statements. Also, we have attempted to introduce only FORTRAN statements and constructions that are available in most versions of FORTRAN 77. To accomplish this we have used features of the language that achieve the highest degree of portability as is reasonably possible. A program is **portable** to the degree that the same program can be executed using different FORTRAN systems but yet produce the same results. However, any FORTRAN system is embedded in an *environment,* which contains features that may lessen the portability of a FORTRAN program.

To maximize the portability of programs, we have used only FORTRAN 77 as described in the document *American National Standard Programming Language FORTRAN, ANSI* X3.9–1978. These standards describe both the Full Language and the Subset Language. Almost all our text describes features for FORTRAN 77 that appear in both the Full Language and in the Subset Language. We executed all the FORTRAN programs in this text using the following FORTRAN processor:

Control Data Corporation, FORTRAN Version 5.   These programs were executed using the HUSTLER Operating System of Michigan State University, which is closest to CDC's NOS/BE 1 Operating System. In all cases, the CYBER (CDC 750) computer was used. For all programs except one, we set the ANSI flag so that any construction inconsistent with the FORTRAN 77 standards would cause a fatal error. On this basis, we claim that the programs in this text conform to the Full Language version of these standards. Unfortunately, the standards permit the construction of programs that remain machine dependent. Machine dependencies are most likely to occur either in the use of some constructions for manipulating characters or in some input/output processes.

It is very desirable to use only standard FORTRAN in order to maximize the portability of programs. Also, it is desirable to avoid any machine-dependent constructions. The reason for the desirability of a high degree of portability of programs is that it is very expensive to change programs each time a computer or FORTRAN processor is changed. Obviously, computers age and are replaced. Also, they are subject to failure. A user needs to be able to run a program on a different machine or using a different FORTRAN processor more frequently than you might imagine. In addition, a new approach to using computers is emerging in engineering and science. In these fields, a user may develop and maintain a FORTRAN program on a microcomputer. But at times when an especially large data set is to be processed, this same program may be executed on a mainframe.

Although our programs were executed on a CDC mainframe, a similar environment can be created for other mainframes. Thus, for the IBM VM/SP CMS, the desired environment for compiling and executing a program with the name *test* may be specified by the following:

```
global txtlib vsf2fort
global loadlib vsf2load
fortvs2 test (fips(f))
load test
genmod test
filedef input terminal
filedef output terminal
test
```

which would treat your terminal keyboard as the input device and the terminal screen as the output device.

Similarly, to compile and execute a program with the name *test* on the VAX/ VMS system, the following would create an appropriate environment:

```
fortran/list/standard test
link test
define input sys$input
define output sys$output
run test
```

Other systems would require other specifications.

One source of difficulties in porting a program from one FORTRAN system to another is how blanks are treated in numeric fields. In the Full Language, a file for formatted input OPENed using

```
OPEN(UNIT=5,FILE='INPUT',BLANK='NULL')
```

will treat any blanks read from unit 5 using a format statement as if the blanks were not there. That is, blanks would be ignored. However, if the entire field were blank, the field would be interpreted as zero. The BLANK='NULL' is the standard default value for a file for the Full Language *when the OPEN statement is used for that file*.

If the Subset Language is used, the way a file is OPENed must be changed from the Full-Language version we have used throughout this text. For the Subset Language,

```
OPEN(5)
```

should be used. The OPEN statement in the Subset Language does not implement some of the parameters available in the Full Language.

Before we can describe this further, we must describe the **blank significance property.** This property may be illustrated by the following example. If the digit 2 appeared alone on a line read using an I3 edit specification, the value would be 2 if read from a file OPENed using BLANK='NULL'. On the other hand, the digit 2 appearing alone on a line read using an I3 edit specification would have the value 200 if read from a file OPENed using BLANK='ZERO'. In the standards, this is called the blank significance property. In the Full Language, if an OPEN statement is not used, the blank significance property is determined by the vendor. In the Subset Language, blank characters in a numeric field, other than leading blanks, are interpreted as zeros. (See *ANSI* X3.9–1978 (1978), Section 13.5.8.)

It should also be noted that when a BN edit specification appears in a format statement, subsequent numeric values read using I, F, or E edit specifications will be interpreted as if blanks were null. The BN edit specification applies only to the remaining edit specifications in the format statement in which the BN appears.

The BZ edit specification causes the remaining numeric fields in a format statement to be read as if any nonleading blanks were zero. The BZ edit specification controls only numeric fields read by an I, F, or E edit specification. The BN and BZ edit specifications have no effect when the format statement is used for output.

To maximize portability, the blank significance property should not be left to the default, which the vendor specifies. If you use the Full Language, use the

OPEN statement we have illustrated with the BLANK='NULL'. If you are using the Subset Language, begin each format statement used for input with the BN edit specification.

A final way for enhancing the possibility that a program will give the "same" results on different FORTRAN systems is to use the FORTRAN systems that implement the IEEE standards for REALs. Unfortunately, these standards are not implemented on all FORTRAN systems.

14.4 CLOSING ADVICE

14.4.1 Use Professionally Written Software Systems

It is very expensive to develop major programs. Many programming tasks already have been programmed and tested. It is almost always preferable to spend the time locating a software product that meets your needs than to write the program yourself. Further, user-written programs usually do not get tested enough to be reliable. Finally, computational tasks in engineering or science frequently involve complicated issues in numerical analysis. Most of the potential problems in numerical analysis have been addressed by the group or corporation that maintains the major systems we have mentioned in this chapter.

14.4.2 Study More Computer Science, Mathematics, Numerical Analysis, and Statistics

In most fields of engineering and in many fields of science, students study mathematics through calculus and also have at least one course in linear algebra. We recommend that after you complete your course in linear algebra, you take course work in numerical analysis. We also strongly recommend that students in these fields take at least a year-long calculus-based course on probability and statistics.

14.4.3 Increase Your Communications Skills

Unfortunately, a far too common criticism of students by employers is that the students do not have good communications skills. Skills in both oral and written presentations are required. These skills can be acquired and enhanced by course work specifically designed to accomplish this objective. Active participation in classroom discussions in other courses also contributes to your communications abilities. Philosophy departments usually offer courses in logic, reasoning, and ethics. We stress the importance of such training for engineers and scientists. Most courses in philosophy also require papers, which contribute to your communications skills.

14.4.4 Be Suspicious of all Computer Output

For some reason human beings seem to come equipped with an unhealthy tendency to believe in computer results merely because they are the result of computations using a computer. *This can be disastrous!* There are too many known examples of errors in computer results to sustain any faith in computer output. Careful computation requires constant attention to details, checking, and vigilance. Absolutely never accept computer results on faith.

Appendix A

A Manual of Coding Style

A.1 INTRODUCTION

Businesses and organizations engaged in computer programming develop and use a manual of programming style. The reasons for using such a manual stem from experience in designing, implementing, and maintaining programs. When programs are not the product of a single person but rather a number of individuals working over several years, it becomes especially apparent to management that standardizing how code is to be written is very desirable. Ultimately, the economic factor is the single most important reason for the utilization of a code and style manual. Software systems, and to a lesser degree user programs, are very expensive. Because government and industry have found that the cost of maintaining a programming system is over 50% of the total cost of the system, the savings in having programs both correct and standardized cannot be ignored.

The specific conventions covered in a style manual vary, of course, from organization to organization. Many such manuals cover similar topics, and more and more insist on structured programming using internal documentation (appropriate comments within the code) and on using indentation of code to indicate the logical structures of the code. The manual in this appendix is the one we have prepared for your use. Although there is nothing sacred about the particular recommendations, we believe you should learn to follow *some* set of guidelines. Just as other organizations employing programmers insist that their programmers follow their manual, we require all students in our FORTRAN course to follow this manual.

We suspect that there is another factor motivating the use of a style manual, although we have yet to see it being mentioned in discussions of software engineering. This factor is related to the personality of the individual programmer. We certainly have encountered students who comment that following a style manual takes away their creativity. Many programmers have strong personal involvement with their programs. They like to think of them as their creative productions. Unfortunately, this often implies that these creative productions are very difficult for some other programmer to understand. However, we feel that understanding the objectives will resolve the issue. The objective of structured programming is to solve the client's problem with a computer program that can be coded quickly, works correctly, warns of possible error conditions before the error occurs, is easy for other programmers to understand, is easy to maintain, and is easy to modify as the needs of the client change over time. Thus, from our point of view, a programmer who is concerned with the "mechanical" nature of the coding process (i.e., lack of opportunity to be creative) is misguided. Specifically, we feel that *coding* should be *a mechanical process,* given a good design. The human creative component properly appears in the design phase. We anticipate that within the next few years, more and more of the mechanical task of coding will be done by the computer system itself. We admit that there seems to be a personal reward from getting code to work, but we also have experienced a different type of personal reward from making alternative designs and especially from seeing that something we thought to be "straightforward," was, upon a fuller consideration of design alternatives, quite different from our original, uncritical straightforward design. If you haven't before seen designing as creative, try it. We hope you'll like it.

The major sections of the manual are as follows:

(1) Skeleton of a FORTRAN job
(2) Code skeletons for PROGRAM, FUNCTION, and SUBROUTINE
(3) Code skeletons for flow-of-control structures
(4) Stylistic conventions

We have attempted to make the sections as independent as possible, except that the code skeletons implicitly contain the indentation specifications for the code used.

A.2 SKELETON OF A FORTRAN JOB

Unfortunately, there is no easy way to refer to all the necessary components of a computer program as a whole that use an agreed-upon standard terminology. We speak of a program, but in FORTRAN a program is divided into a number of units. The first unit of any program should be a PROGRAM unit. Thus, a computer program will consist of only a PROGRAM unit or a PROGRAM unit followed by one or more subprogram units. Technically, we might find ourselves speaking of a PROGRAM program unit along with a SUBROUTINE program unit, and so on. To avoid this cumbersome terminology or resulting confusion, we need a way to refer to the computer program as a whole, that is, to refer to the PROGRAM unit and to all other units that collectively constitute the FORTRAN program. Consequently, we shall use the phrase, FORTRAN job, or merely the word job, for this purpose. The situation is further complicated by the fact that the required components of a job vary from operating system to operating system. The FORTRAN code usually is organized similarly in different operating environments, but the remaining components vary from one system to another. A typical skeleton of a FORTRAN job is given in Figure A.1.

The FORTRAN code section begins with the PROGRAM statement. It contains each unit of the FORTRAN program. (Here we have merely indicated the opening and closing keywords of each unit. For the detailed model, see the skeleton for the respective unit, which appears in Section A.3.) Each unit terminates with the FORTRAN statement, END. Observe that nothing else appears between an END of one unit and the opening FORTRAN statement that is the first statement of the next unit (either FUNCTION or SUBROUTINE.) As a matter of style, all units (except the PROGRAM unit, which should be first) are to be ordered alphabetically by the name of the unit created by the programmer. This makes it very easy to locate the unit in the listing. In the determination of the order, the words FUNCTION or SUBROUTINE are not considered; only the name of the unit is used to determine the alphabetical order in which the units appear after the PROGRAM unit.

```
[possible system-dependent control statement(s) go here]

    program



    end
    subroutine A (    )



    end
    subroutine B (   )



    end
    real function C (   )



    end

[possible system control statement(s) go here]

data go here
```

Figure A.1   Skeleton of a FORTRAN 77 Job

A.3 CODE SKELETONS FOR PROGRAM, FUNCTION, AND SUBROUTINE

In each of the skeletons, uppercase text is to appear just as given. Lowercase text either supplies additional information or represents material you will insert. The word *name* indicates the name of the unit created by the designer. Figure A.2 gives the code skeleton for a PROGRAM unit.

The code skeleton for a FUNCTION unit is given in Figure A.3. This skeleton includes a BUG mechanism for assisting in testing and debugging the code. Because the syntax of a FUNCTION unit requires that the name of the function (without following parentheses) appear on the left-hand side of the replacement operator, this is included just before the RETURN statement. The BUG mechanism includes an output statement to give the names and the values of the arguments. If the arguments are dimensioned variables, then only the first three elements and the last three elements should be listed if there are more than a few elements.

Figure A.4 gives the code skeleton for a SUBROUTINE unit, which is very similar to a FUNCTION. However, there are two very important differences. There is no type associated with the SUBROUTINE name. Also, the name of the SUBROUTINE does not appear on the left-hand side of a replacement operator.

```
        PROGRAM name
C
C       insert preamble here
C
        IMPLICIT LOGICAL (A-Z)
        remaining type specifications
        COMMON /BUGBLK/ BUG
        remaining specifications
        OPEN statement(s)
C
C
        BUG = .TRUE.
        WRITE ( )   to output program name etc.
           .

           .

           .
C
        WRITE ( )  to output 'Normal Program
                   Termination'
        STOP
C
        formats in increasing order of statement numbers
C
        END
```

Figure A.2   Code Skeleton for a PROGRAM Unit

```
      type FUNCTION name ( )
C
C     insert preamble here
C
      IMPLICIT LOGICAL (A-Z)
      remaining type specifications
      COMMON /BUGBLK/ BUG
      remaining specifications
C
      IF (BUG) THEN
        WRITE ( ) to output 'function name entered'
        WRITE ( ) to output labeled list of arguments
      ENDIF
C
          .
          .
          .
C
      IF (BUG) THEN
        WRITE ( ) to output 'leaving function name'
        WRITE ( ) to output labeled list of arguments
      ENDIF
C
      name = ...
      RETURN
C
      formats
C
      END
```

Figure A.3   Code Skeleton for a FUNCTION Unit

A.4 CODE SKELETONS FOR CONTROL STRUCTURES

The figures giving the implementation of the control structures in FORTRAN code have similar structures. Within each figure, the code appears between a solid horizontal line at the top of the code and another solid horizontal line at the bottom of the code. Above the top line are the numbers 1, 7, and 9, which indicate column 1, column 7, and column 9, respectively. Below the bottom line, these numbers are repeated in their respective columns. This makes it easier to use these figures to illustrate both the FORTRAN code and the indentation of the code that is to be used.

The first and last line of each control structure is a line containing a C in column 1 that is otherwise blank. This is intentional and is used to make the control structure more visible to the reader of the listing of the code. We prefer a C in column 1 rather than merely leaving the entire line blank so that when the code is examined at a later time, there is no concern that something was accidently omitted. In

```
      SUBROUTINE name ( )
C
C     insert preamble here
C
      IMPLICIT LOGICAL (A-Z)
      remaining type specifications
      COMMON /BUGBLK/ BUG
      remaining specifications
C
      IF (BUG) THEN
        WRITE ( ) to output 'SUBROUTINE name entered'
        WRITE ( ) to output labeled list of arguments
      ENDIF
C
        .
        .
        .
C
      IF (BUG) THEN
        WRITE ( ) outputs 'leaving SUBROUTINE name'
        WRITE ( ) outputs labeled list of arguments
      ENDIF
C
      RETURN
C
      formats
C
      END
```

Figure A.4   Code Skeleton for a SUBROUTINE Unit

addition, some FORTRAN systems may not accept a totally blank line. We strongly recommend that the coder avoid using a printed character, such as an asterisk or a dash, to separate sections of code. Such lines are not conducive to easy scanning of the code, whereas blank lines (with the C in column 1) are exceptionally easy to scan.

We use

statement(s)

to indicate that one or more statements would be expected here. Each statement would appear below the other at the same level of indentation. Thus, if there were three statements, here represented as statement A, statement B, and statement C, the line in the skeleton

statement(s)

represents

> statement A
> statement B
> statement C

Because several of the structures used in structured programming do not have a single (or a single pair) of corresponding FORTRAN statements to be used to implement them in FORTRAN, these structures must be constructed from available FORTRAN statements. Thus, we may speak of these structures as being simulated in FORTRAN. When we simulate these structures, we are, however, constrained by the logic of the structure. Consequently, no statements may be inserted at the top or at the bottom of the code where indicated.

A control structure controls the flow of execution of the program. Thus, the control structure controls other statements. The statements to be controlled must be indicated. Obviously, it is desirable to be able to distinguish easily and quickly between the portion of code doing the controlling and the portion of code that is being controlled. A natural way to do this is to have the syntax of the control structure be composed of two statements. One statement is at the top of the structure, and the other is at the bottom of the structure. Then, these two statements *bracket* the statements being controlled. (For example, in FORTRAN, the IF THEN is an opening statement and the ENDIF is the closing statement of a selection structure.) Finally, the statements being controlled are indented with respect to this pair of bracketing statements. This combination of opening and closing controlling statements with indentation of the controlled statements in between makes the logic of the structure quite visible to the reader.

Although FORTRAN has the statements for directly implementing the 1-alternative selection, the 2-alternative selection, the *n*-alternative selection, and the determinate repetition, it does not have an opening and closing pair of statements to implement the two indeterminate repetition structures, and, consequently, a coder is forced to use a set of statements to implement these. But these statements may be thought of as a whole—that is, they may be thought of as representing a single statement. We have inserted a right square bracket around the top set of statements to be thought of as the single opening statement. Similarily, we have inserted another series of right square brackets around the bottom set of statements to be thought of as the single closing statement of the control structure. *No other statements are to be inserted within the bracket*. These brackets are only to point out that no statements are to be inserted between any two consecutive lines containing a right square bracket. These square brackets will be seen in the code skeletons for the indeterminate repetitions when they appear later in this chapter. Because the square brackets are not part of FORTRAN syntax, the square brackets are not to appear in any FORTRAN code intended for execution.

A.4.1 Code Skeletons for Selection Structures

The code skeleton for the 1-alternative selection is directly implemented using the block IF construction without an ELSE. The code is given in Figure A.5.

```
1    7 9
```

```
C
     IF ( ) THEN
      statement(s)
     ENDIF
C
```

```
1    7 9
```

Figure A.5 The Code Skeleton for the 1-alternative Selection

The 2-alternative selection is directly implemented using the block IF statement with an ELSE. The complete skeleton is given in Figure A.6.

Another 2-alternative selection may be nested inside a 2-alternative selection. This is called a *nested structure*. It may be coded in as an extension of the single 2-alternative selection, as is done in Figure A.7. However, instead of nesting a

```
1    7 9
```

```
C
     IF ( ) THEN
      statement(s)
     ELSE
      statement(s)
     ENDIF
C
```

```
1    7 9
```

Figure A.6 The Code Skeleton for the 2-alternative Selection

```
1    7 9
```

```
C
     IF ( ) THEN
      statement(s)
     ELSE
      IF ( ) THEN
       statement(s)
      ELSE
       statement(s)
      ENDIF
     ENDIF
C
```

```
1    7 9
```

Figure A.7 Nested 2-alternative Selection

2-alternative selection within a 2-alternative selection, we recommend the use of the *n*-alternative selection.

The *n*-alternative selection is implemented directly in FORTRAN using the block IF with ELSEIF and ELSE, as shown in Figure A.8. This structure should always include the ELSE alternative as the very last alternative. Frequently, the ELSE alternative in the nested version serves as an error case to cover any situation not explicitly expected to occur.

A.4.2 Code Skeletons for Repetition Structures

Except for the determinate repetition, all other repetition structures must be simulated in FORTRAN. For the pretested repetition, there are two skeletons; one is for the WHILE-there-are-data form and the other is for all other WHILE structures.

The determinate repetition is directly implemented in code using the DO statement with the CONTINUE statement. Figure A.9 gives this skeleton.

Because there are no statements provided in FORTRAN to implement directly the indeterminate repetition structures, these must be simulated.

```
1    7 9

C
     IF ( ) THEN
      statement(s)
     ELSEIF ( ) THEN
      statement(s)
     ELSEIF ( ) THEN
      statement(s)
     ELSEIF ( ) THEN
      statement(s)
     ELSE
      statement(s)
     ENDIF
C

1    7 9
```

Figure A.8   Code Skeleton for the *n*-alternative Selection

```
1    7 9

C
     DO 123 ...
      statement(s)
123  CONTINUE
C

1    7 9
```

Figure A.9   Code Skeleton for the Determinate Repetition

The implementation of the pretested indeterminate repetition is done in one of two ways. If the structure is an instance of WHILE-there-are-data, that is, an instruction to repeat the input of data while any data remains to be processed, it is implemented using the END= parameter in the READ statement. The code skeleton to do this is shown in Figure A.10. If the WHILE structure to be implemented is not WHILE-there-are-data, then it is simulated using several statements, including the block IF (without an ELSE) and the GOTO statement. This skeleton is given in Figure A.11. The comment statements are to be aligned with the other FORTRAN statements exactly as shown in these skeletons.

The posttested indeterminate repetition is simulated using a nonblock IF statement with a GOTO. Be sure to observe the .NOT. appearing in the logical expression within the IF statement. The skeleton is given here in Figure A.12.

```
1    79

─────────────────────────────────────────────────────────────────
C                                                       ]
C      BEGINWHILE                                       ] no
1      CONTINUE                                          ] inserts
       prompts, if required                             ] except
       READ ( , , END=2) ...                            ] prompts
         statement(s)
       GOTO 1                                           ]
2      CONTINUE                                          ] no
C      ENDWHILE                                          ] inserts
C
─────────────────────────────────────────────────────────────────

1    79
```

Figure A.10 Code Skeleton for Pretested Indeterminate Repetition (for Implementing the WHILE-there-are-data Structure)

```
1    79

─────────────────────────────────────────────────────────────────
C
C      BEGINWHILE                                       ]
1      CONTINUE                                          ] no
       IF ( ) THEN                                       ] inserts
         statement(s)
       GOTO 1                                           ]
       ENDIF                                             ] no
C      ENDWHILE                                          ] inserts
C
─────────────────────────────────────────────────────────────────

1    79
```

Figure A.11 Code Skeleton for Pretested Indeterminate Repetition

```
1   7 9

C
C    BEGINUNTIL                                    ] no
1    CONTINUE                                      ] inserts
      statement(s)
     IF (.NOT.( )) GOTO 1                          ] no
C    ENDUNTIL                                      ] inserts
C


1   7 9
```

Figure A.12 The Code Skeleton for the Posttested Indeterminate Repetition

A.5 STYLE AND STYLISTIC CONVENTIONS

The FORTRAN compiler ignores blanks in columns 7 through 72 (except in character strings) and ignores comment lines. Yet the use of comment lines and the use of indentation (which requires blanks) in code are important. The reason that such features of style are important is that properly used blanks, comments, and indentation makes the code easier for the human reader to understand. Thus, the stylistic conventions given here are to assist the original coder, especially if he or she has been away from the program for a period of time, or other coders who maintain the program to see the logical structure of the entire unit of code at a glance. Therefore, the conventions make extensive use of blank lines (except for the C in column 1) to separate structures. Also, the conventions include the use of indentation of code.

In maintaining a program (or in consulting on a program), it is very important to be able to locate a specific section of code quickly. Also, it is important to be able to verify quickly that specifications are present and correct for the variables. Students of some of these issues have been able to show that a language user is able to locate a particular target word in a list of words more quickly if the words in the list are arranged in alphabetical order. Consequently, the specifications require you to alphabetize lists.

(1) **Use blank lines (except for the C in column 1) to separate sections of code.** One or two blank lines, with a C in column 1, greatly improve the legibility of a program. To be maximally effective, separate the first statement of a unit from the preamble; separate the preamble from the specification statements; separate the specification statements from the executable statements; and isolate the END statement from the statement that precedes it. Within the executable code, except for consecutive sequence structures, separate each flow-of-control structure from the next one by a blank (except for a C in column 1) line.

(2) **Leave columns 73 through 80 blank.** FORTRAN ignores columns 73 through 80. However, beginning programmers sometimes are unaware that a statement extends into column 73 or beyond. We require that these columns be left blank, even in comments, to assist a programmer in detecting any statement that extends beyond column 72.

(3) On any comment line, use C in column 1 to indicate a comment and leave column 2 blank.   We require a C in column 1 rather than other comment indicators that may be acceptable alternatives on your system because not all processors permit an alternative. We require column 2 to be blank to aid the reader in seeing the fact that line is a comment line.

(4) On comment lines before the first executable statement, you may use columns 3 through 72 for comments.

(5) On comment lines after the first executable statement, restrict the comment (except for the C in column 1) to columns 40 through 72.   The intent of this requirement is to increase the readability of program listings. By keeping columns 2 through 39 blank on comment lines that occur within the section of the code containing executable statements, a reader will be able to scan down either of approximately two columns; the left column will contain only executable statements, and the right column will contain only comments. In addition, if the code is appropriately commented in this fashion, a reader may scan down the right column to index (locate) a particular section of the executable code. Later in these requirements, we specify that FORMAT statements are to appear collected at the bottom of the unit. This requirement also facilitates ease in scanning down the left column.

Note.   This requirement does not apply to the comments given in the code skeletons, which we view as part of the code itself. Those comments that appear as part of a skeleton should be included just as given in the skeleton.

(6) Alphabetize the elements of lists.   FORTRAN makes extensive use of lists. The dimension and type specification statements include the lists of the variables affected. The lists in these specification statements always should be alphabetized.

(7) Use OPEN(5,FILE = 'INPUT',BLANK = 'NULL')   We reserve statement numbers in the 500s for use with FORMAT statements that are associated with a READ statement that obtains input from unit 5. *Note:* A file is opened only once in the entire job. This should be done in the PROGRAM unit.
   If your system implements only the Subset Language, use OPEN(5).

(8) Use OPEN(6,FILE = 'OUTPUT')   This is the convention we use for associating unit 6 with the file OUTPUT. We also reserve statement numbers in the 600s for use with FORMAT statements that are associated with any WRITE statements that send output to unit 6. *Note:* A file is opened only once in the entire job. This should be done in the PROGRAM unit.
   If your system implements only the Subset Language, use OPEN(6).

(9) OPEN any other file you require   Always open each file you use. Check with your system concerning conventions for unit numbers and file name conventions. If possible, use a systematic format numbering convention, following the same principle as given before for the INPUT and OUTPUT files.

(10) Gather all FORMAT statements together near the END of the unit. FORMAT statements usually extend over many columns. If they are intermixed with executable statements, they then clutter the appearance of the code and obscure the logic of the flow-of-control. In addition to collecting the FORMAT statements in one location, the numbering conventions and associations with the respective OPEN statements should be observed. These are as follows:

(1) Reserve statement numbers in the 500s for FORMAT statements used with input from unit 5.

(2) Reserve statement numbers in the 600s for FORMAT statements used with output to unit 6.

(3) List the FORMAT statements in the order of the numeric values of the statement numbers.

(4) Locate all FORMAT statements after the last executable statement in the unit but before the END statement.

(11) Use names uniquely in a job. For the sake of consistency and to avoid possible confusion by the programmer, any symbolic name should be used with only one meaning throughout the unit.

(12) Avoid the use of a FORTRAN keyword for any other purpose. FORTRAN is designed to be forgiving if a coder uses a keyword in a sense other than as defined by FORTRAN. In some situations, nothing disastrous will happen. But in general, you as a coder should *never* deliberately use a FORTRAN keyword for any purpose other than the purpose defined by the FORTRAN standards.

(13) Avoid the redefinition of any FUNCTION supplied by the FORTRAN system. If you define a subprogram with a name that happens to be the same as the name of a FUNCTION supplied by the FORTRAN system, you have made the supplied FORTRAN FUNCTION unavailable to your program. A coder should always verify that any subprogram names he or she creates are not the names of the FUNCTIONS included in the FORTRAN system. This requires that you check in the FORTRAN Reference Manual for the names of the functions included in your implementation.

(14) Never assume the value of an uninitialized variable. Values are assigned to variables when the variable name appears on the left-hand side of the replacement operator in an assignment statement; when the variable is included in the successful execution of a READ statement; or when the variable is assigned a value by any system supplied test. If a variable has not been assigned a value, then that variable contains meaningless material, usually called *garbage*. (Beginning programmers sometimes think that FORTRAN assigns the value zero to the elements of an array or a variable before it is used. The FORTRAN standards do not require that array elements be initalized to zero or any other value.) You as coder are responsible for assigning a value to a variable before that variable is used for any purpose other than to be the receiver of a value.

(15) Use IMPLICIT LOGICAL (A–Z) in each program unit. Very nasty errors may result if a variable of the wrong type is used. In some more recent programming languages, the language compiler checks to be sure that each variable explicitly appears in a type statement. FORTRAN does not do this. However, if the IMPLICIT LOGICAL (A–Z) statement is used, the FORTRAN compiler will output an error message for any variable in the unit that is used in any manner other than as a logical variable. Thus, all variables that are not explicitly typed but are used other than as a logical variable will be noted in a message in the listing of the output from the compiler.

(16) Specify the types of all arrays and variables.   The use of IMPLICIT LOGICAL (A–Z) necessitates that the programmer specify the types of all arrays and variables except that of a logical array or variable. As a matter of consistency, specify the type of logical arrays and variables.

(17) Specify the dimension information for each array in the TYPE specification for that array.   FORTRAN 77 requires the specification of the dimension information for any array. We use one method only — namely, the inclusion of the dimension specifications in the TYPE statement for the array. This method has the advantage over the alternative method (using an additional FORTRAN statement, which we do not describe) of avoiding the scattering of the complete specification for an array over two kinds of statements. Further, the use of the method we advocate reduces the possibility of errors.

(18) Use explicit numeric (integer) values to specify the maximum array size.   For a beginning programmer, we recommend that in each unit (PROGRAM, FUNCTION, or SUBROUTINE) in which the symbolic name of an array appears, the *same explicit integer values* be used to specify the maximum array size. Of course, for different arrays, different maximum sizes may be specified.

(19) Use a main program as driver with subprograms.   All jobs are to use a main program as a driver to read an indefinite number of data sets and then use one or more subprograms.

(20) Use argument lists for communication between units.   All communication between program units is to be by the use of arguments in argument lists, except for the COMMON/BUGBLK/BUG statement.

(21) Use only READ and WRITE with FORMAT statements.   For all input and output, use only READ and WRITE with FORMAT statements.

(22) Use all the code as given in the code skeletons.   In general, use all of the FORTRAN code and all of the other structural features exhibited in the code skeletons.

(23) Use only the FORTRAN statements given in the list for beginning programmers.

(24) Avoid the use of the GOTO statement.   The GOTO statement is required to implement the pretested or the posttested repetition and therefore must be used in these structures *as given in their respective code skeletons. Other than this necessary use of GOTO in the indefinite repetitions, do not use the GOTO statement.*

Appendix B

Preamble Guidelines

The preamble is to assist anyone who reads the design or program to become oriented quickly to that unit. The preamble in the design, which is reproduced in the program, serves to communicate information to the first coder and to anyone who must later maintain or use the program. A preamble is required in each unit. In a design, the preamble appears first, preceding the flow-of-control section. When recorded in the code, the preamble appears immediately after the opening FORTRAN statement. In the code, each line of the preamble is entered as a comment and, therefore, begins with a C in column 1. Column 2 is left blank throughout the preamble.

A preamble is to have the following sections, although some sections only appear in subprograms. Each section is to appear in the order listed in this description. Words such as *first* and *second* that are used in this description are not to appear in the preamble itself.

The first section begins with whichever of the following phrases is appropriate:

Preamble for program
Preamble for type function
Preamble for subroutine

Each of the phrases is completed by giving the name of the unit followed by the argument list, enclosed in parentheses. If the unit is a function, the type of the function appears instead of the word *type* in the phrase.

The second section begins with ABSTRACT:. It contains a brief description of what the unit computes.

The third section begins with INPUT:. It lists and describes the arrays and variables that are to be read during the execution of the unit. (Input refers only to the process of reading. Input does not refer to the communication of information between different units.) If the unit has no input, write *none*.

The fourth section begins with OUTPUT:. It lists and describes the arrays and variables that are to be written by this unit. Messages without values, however, are not listed or described. (Output refers only to the process of writing. Output does not refer to the communication of information between different units.) If the unit produces no output, write *none*.

The fifth, sixth, and seventh sections refer only to communication between units. These sections do not refer to reading and writing. These sections appear in each external function and in each subroutine, but none of them appear in a program unit.

The fifth section begins with ENTRY VALUES:. It lists (in alphabetical order) the array and variable names in the argument list that are being used as entry values — that is, those arrays or variables that are bringing values into the unit from another unit. Those arguments listed in this section are entry-only arguments. The values of the entry-only arguments are not to be changed within the unit. If there are no entry values, write *none*.

The sixth section begins with EXIT VALUES:. It lists (in alphabetical order) the array and variable names that are in the argument list and that are being used as exit values, that is, are values to be transmitted to the calling or referencing unit. Note that because functions are intended to return a single value by association with the name of the function, the only exit value of a function is that associated with the name of the function. For a subroutine, if there are no exit values, write *none*.

The seventh section begins with ENTRY AND EXIT VALUES:. It lists (in alphabetical order) the array and variable names in the argument list that are being used both to bring values into the unit and to return values to the calling unit. If there are none, write *none*. (From the standpoint of good style, using variables as both entry and exit arguments should be avoided. Similarly, for small arrays, the use of arguments that are both entry and exit arguments should be avoided. However, it is sometimes necessary to use large arrays as both entry and exit arguments to avoid duplicating such arrays in the unit. The duplicating process itself may be expensive, and the additional space required for the duplicated array may be more than is available or may be very expensive.)

The eighth section begins with the phrase DESIGN HISTORY:. It contains the list (in chronological order) of all individuals who designed this unit and the dates of their involvement.

The ninth section begins with the phrase CODING HISTORY:. It contains the list (in chronological order) of all coders of the unit, including the dates of their involvement. In the design itself there is no coder, so state *none*.

The tenth section begins with the phrase REFERENCE:. This section contains references. It may contain, for example, references to published works that were consulted. As the first reference, however, it should contain a reference, including the date, of the client's initial program request. This should be followed by the dates and identifying information for any updates to the program request. These should be listed in chronological order prior to references to published works.

The eleventh section is the identifier dictionary, introduced by the phrase ID DICTIONARY:. In this section, all identifiers (that is, programmer-created names), except the name of the program unit, are listed. The name of any external function, intrinsic function, or subroutine appears in the ID dictionary of each unit that references the function or calls the subroutine. The name of an external function also appears in the ID dictionary of the unit that defines that function because the function name always appears on the left-hand side of the assignment operator somewhere in the unit. But the name of a subroutine does not appear in the ID dictionary of the unit that defines the subroutine.

For each identifier, the type, meaning, and use are also listed. If one of these entries is not applicable, this fact should be indicated by the standard English abbreviation NA. This avoids leaving a blank, which raises the question in a reader's mind about whether or not something was accidentally omitted.

We specify that the list of identifiers be alphabetized in order to speed up any subsequent references to the dictionary. We can locate an item in an alphabetized list much more rapidly than in an unalphabetized one. Also, it is much easier to locate any accidental omissions in an alphabetized list. The general principle for creating this list is that each and every symbolic name used within the unit is to be listed in the ID dictionary.

The following are some additional notes and examples:

Under MEANING, if the ID is an otherwise unintelligible mnemonic, be sure to indicate here what the characters stand for. Thus, if the ID is FTC, standing for Fahrenheit to Celsius, state Fahrenheit To Celsius under Meaning.

Under USE, if the ID is the name of an external function or a subroutine, state the number of arguments. Thus, if FTC were the name of a subroutine with one argument, state under USE:

```
SUBROUTINE NAME
(1 ARGUMENT)
```

Under USE, if the ID is the name of an array, give the number of dimensions. Thus, if MATRIX is the name of a two-dimensional array, state under USE:

```
ARRAY
(2-dimensional)
```

If the array is used as an argument for the function or subroutine unit, state under USE:

```
ARRAY ARGUMENT (2-dimensional)
```

Under USE, if the ID is the name of a variable, state VARIABLE or, if it is used as an argument for the function or subroutine unit, state VARIABLE ARGUMENT.

Under USE, if the ID is the name of a constant (that is, specified in a PARAMETER statement), state, under USE, CONSTANT; and if space permits, give the value of the constant.

Appendix C

FORTRAN Implementations of Designs

Chapter 5 Programs

PROGRAM CHKBAL
SUBROUTINE ADDER
output from CHKBAL/ADDER

PROGRAM QUAD1
SUBROUTINE SOLVE1
output from QUAD1/SOLVE1

PROGRAM QUAD2
SUBROUTINE SOLVE2
output from QUAD2/SOLVE2

PROGRAM QUAD3
SUBROUTINE CMPLXR
SUBROUTINE RRONE
SUBROUTINE RRTWO
SUBROUTINE SELECT
output from QUAD3/CMPLXR/RRONE/RRTWO/SELECT

PROGRAM QUAD4
SUBROUTINE CMPLXR
SUBROUTINE RRONE
SUBROUTINE RRTWO
SUBROUTINE SELECT

```
        PROGRAM CHKBAL
C
C       PREAMBLE FOR PROGRAM CHKBAL
C
C       ABSTRACT: CHKBAL IS AN INTERACTIVE PROGRAM TO COMPUTE THE
C                 BALANCE OF YOUR CHECKING ACCOUNT AT THE END OF A MONTH.
C
C       INPUT:    THE STARTING BALANCE FOLLOWED BY AN ENTRY FOR EACH
C                 TRANSACTION.
C
C       OUTPUT:   THE BALANCE IN YOUR ACCOUNT AT THE END OF THE MONTH.
C
C       DESIGN HISTORY: PROUD P.C. OWNER, 12JUN83
C
C       REFERENCE: NONE
C
C       ID DICTIONARY:
C
C       ID        TYPE          MEANING               USE
C
C       ADDER     NA                                  SUBROUTINE NAME
C                                                     (2 ARGUMENTS)
C       AMOUNT    REAL          THE STARTING BALANCE  VARIABLE
C                               OR THE AMOUNT OF A
C                               TRANSACTION
C       BAL       REAL          THE ACCUMULATING OR   VARIABLE
C                               RUNNING BALANCE
C
C       SPECIFICATIONS
C
        IMPLICIT LOGICAL (A-Z)
C
        REAL AMOUNT,BAL
C
        OPEN(UNIT=5,FILE='INPUT',BLANK='NULL')
        OPEN(UNIT=6,FILE='OUTPUT')
C
        WRITE(6,600)
        READ(5,500)BAL
C
C       WHILE THERE ARE DATA
5           CONTINUE
            WRITE(6,601)
            READ(5,500,END=10)AMOUNT
            CALL ADDER(AMOUNT,BAL)
            GO TO 5
10          CONTINUE
C       ENDWHILE
```

```
C
      WRITE(6,602)BAL
      WRITE(6,603)
      STOP
C
500   FORMAT(F10.2)
600   FORMAT(' ','GIVE THE STARTING BALANCE.  IF NEGATIVE, PRECEDE THE',
     +' FIRST DIGIT BY A NEGATIVE SIGN.')
601   FORMAT(' ','GIVE THE AMOUNT OF THE TRANSACTION, PRECEDED BY A ',
     +'NEGATIVE SIGN IF THE AMOUNT IS TO BE SUBTRACTED FROM YOUR ',
     +'CURRENT BALANCE.')
602   FORMAT('0','THE BALANCE IS ',F10.2)
603   FORMAT('0','NORMAL PROGRAM TERMINATION')
      END


      SUBROUTINE ADDER(AMOUNT,BAL)
C
C     PREAMBLE FOR SUBROUTINE ADDER
C
C     ABSTRACT: ADDER ACCUMULATES THE BALANCE IN YOUR CHECKING ACCOUNT
C
C     INPUT:   NONE
C
C     OUTPUT:  NONE
C
C     ENTRY VALUES: AMOUNT
C
C     EXIT VALUES: NONE
C
C     ENTRY AND EXIT VALUES: BAL
C
C     DESIGN HISTORY: PROUD P.C. OWNER, 12JUN83
C
C     REFERENCE: NONE
C
C     ID DICTIONARY:
C
C     ID        TYPE       MEANING              USE
C
C     AMOUNT    REAL       THE AMOUNT OF A      VARIABLE
C                          SINGLE TRANSACTION
C     BAL       REAL       THE ACCUMULATING OR  VARIABLE
C                          RUNNING BALANCE
C
C     SPECIFICATIONS
C
      IMPLICIT LOGICAL (A-Z)
```

```
C
      REAL AMOUNT,BAL
C
      BAL=BAL+AMOUNT
      RETURN
      END
1037.27
-101.73
-10.73
-23.75
202.77
-2.30
-10.00
205.34
-171.95
200.89
198.65
-230.55
      PROGRAM QUAD1
C
C     PREAMBLE FOR PROGRAM QUAD1
C
C     ABSTRACT: QUAD1 IS AN INTERACTIVE PROGRAM TO SOLVE QUADRATIC
C               EQUATIONS.
C
C     INPUT:    THE CONSTANTS A, B, AND C.
C
C     OUTPUT:   THE ONE OR TWO VALUES OF X WHICH SOLVE THE QUADRATIC
C               EQUATION, AND A MESSAGE INDICATING WHETHER THERE ARE
C               TWO REAL ROOTS, ONE REAL ROOT, OR TWO IMAGINARY ROOTS.
C
C     DESIGN HISTORY: HANS LEE, 6NOV83
C
C     REFERENCE:
C
C     ID DICTIONARY:
C
C     ID      TYPE        MEANING             USE
C
C     A       REAL        THE CONSTANT A IN   VARIABLE
C                         THE EQUATION
C     B       REAL        THE CONSTANT B IN   VARIABLE
C                         THE EQUATION
C     C       REAL        THE CONSTANT C IN   VARIABLE
C                         THE EQUATION
C     SOLVE1  NA                              SUBROUTINE NAME
C                                             (3 ARGUMENTS)
C
C     SPECIFICATIONS
C
      IMPLICIT LOGICAL (A-Z)
C
      REAL A,B,C
```

```
C
      OPEN(UNIT=5,FILE='INPUT',BLANK='NULL')
      OPEN(UNIT=6,FILE='OUTPUT')
C
      WRITE(6,600)
C
C     WHILE THERE ARE DATA
5        CONTINUE
         WRITE(6,601)
         READ(5,500,END=10)A
         WRITE(6,602)
         READ(5,500,END=10)B
         WRITE(6,603)
         READ(5,500,END=10)C
         IF(A.EQ.0.0)THEN
            WRITE(6,604)
         ELSE
            CALL SOLVE1(A,B,C)
         ENDIF
         GO TO 5
10       CONTINUE
C     ENDWHILE
C
      WRITE(6,605)
      STOP
C
500   FORMAT(F10.2)
600   FORMAT('1','PROGRAM QUAD1 SOLVES QUADRATIC EQUATIONS.  VERSION OF',
     +' 6NOV83.')
601   FORMAT(' ','GIVE THE VALUE OF THE CONSTANT, A, AS A NUMBER WITH',
     +' A DECIMAL POINT')
602   FORMAT(' ','GIVE THE VALUE OF THE CONSTANT, B, AS A NUMBER WITH',
     +' A DECIMAL POINT')
603   FORMAT(' ','GIVE THE VALUE OF THE CONSTANT, C, AS A NUMBER WITH',
     +' A DECIMAL POINT')
604   FORMAT('0','THE VALUE OF A CANNOT BE ZERO.')
605   FORMAT('0','NORMAL PROGRAM TERMINATION')
      END



      SUBROUTINE SOLVE1(A,B,C)
C
C     PREAMBLE FOR SUBROUTINE SOLVE1
C                                                     2
C     ABSTRACT: SOLVE1 SOLVES THE FORMULA (-B+SQRT(B -4AC))/2A AND THE
C                                     2
C               FORMULA (-B-SQRT(B -4AC))/2A FOR X IN A QUADRATIC
C               EQUATION.
C
C     INPUT:   NONE
C
C     OUTPUT:  A MESSAGE REPORTING WHETHER THERE ARE ONE OR TWO ROOTS,
C              WHETHER THE ROOT(S) ARE REAL OR IMAGINARY, AND THE
C              VALUE(S) OF THE ROOT(S).
```

```
C
C      ENTRY VALUES: A,B,C
C
C      EXIT VALUES: NONE
C
C      ENTRY AND EXIT VALUES: NONE
C
C      DESIGN HISTORY: HANS LEE, 6NOV83.
C
C      REFERENCE:
C
C      ID DICTIONARY:
C
C      ID        TYPE        MEANING              USE
C
C      A         REAL        THE CONSTANT A IN    ARGUMENT
C                            THE EQUATION
C      B         REAL        THE CONSTANT B IN    ARGUMENT
C                            THE EQUATION
C      C         REAL        THE CONSTANT C IN    ARGUMENT
C                            THE EQUATION
C      CMPLX     COMPLEX     CONVERT REAL TO      INTRINSIC FUNCTION
C                            COMPLEX
C      CSQRT     COMPLEX     COMPLEX SQUARE ROOT  INTRINSIC FUNCTION
C      CX1       COMPLEX     ONE COMPLEX ROOT     VARIABLE
C      CX2       COMPLEX     THE OTHER COMPLEX    VARIABLE
C                            ROOT
C      SQRT      REAL        SQUARE ROOT          INTRINSIC FUNCTION
C      X1        REAL        ONE REAL ROOT OF THE VARIABLE
C                            EQUATION
C      X2        REAL        THE OTHER REAL ROOT  VARIABLE
C                            (IF THERE ARE TWO
C                            ROOTS)
C
C      SPECIFICATIONS
C
       IMPLICIT LOGICAL (A-Z)
C
       REAL A,B,C,X1,X2
       COMPLEX CX1,CX2
C
       IF(B*B.GT.4.0*A*C)THEN
          WRITE(6,600)
          X1=(-B-SQRT(B*B-4.0*A*C))/(2.0*A)
          X2=(-B+SQRT(B*B-4.0*A*C))/(2.0*A)
          WRITE(6,601)X1,X2
       ENDIF
       IF(B*B.EQ.4.0*A*C)THEN
          WRITE(6,602)
          X1=(-B+SQRT(B*B-4.0*A*C))/(2.0*A)
          WRITE(6,603)X1
       ENDIF
       IF(B*B.LT.4.0*A*C)THEN
          WRITE(6,604)
          CX1=(-B-CSQRT(CMPLX(B*B-4.0*A*C)))/(2.0*A)
```

```
          CX2=(−B+CSQRT(CMPLX(B*B−4.0*A*C)))/(2.0*A)
          WRITE(6,605)CX1,CX2
       ENDIF
       RETURN
C
600    FORMAT('0','THERE ARE TWO REAL ROOTS.')
601    FORMAT(' ','X = ',F10.4,' OR X = ',F10.4)
602    FORMAT('0','THERE IS ONE REAL ROOT.')
603    FORMAT(' ','X = ',F10.4)
604    FORMAT('0','THERE ARE TWO IMAGINARY ROOTS.')
605    FORMAT(' ','X = ',2F10.4,' OR X = ',2F10.4)
       END
1
4
3
1
2
1
1
2
2
```

```
PROGRAM QUAD1 SOLVES QUADRATIC EQUATIONS.  VERSION OF 6NOV83.
GIVE THE VALUE OF THE CONSTANT, A, AS A NUMBER WITH A DECIMAL POINT
GIVE THE VALUE OF THE CONSTANT, B, AS A NUMBER WITH A DECIMAL POINT
GIVE THE VALUE OF THE CONSTANT, C, AS A NUMBER WITH A DECIMAL POINT

THERE ARE TWO REAL ROOTS.
X =    −3.0000 OR X =    −1.0000
GIVE THE VALUE OF THE CONSTANT, A, AS A NUMBER WITH A DECIMAL POINT
GIVE THE VALUE OF THE CONSTANT, B, AS A NUMBER WITH A DECIMAL POINT
GIVE THE VALUE OF THE CONSTANT, C, AS A NUMBER WITH A DECIMAL POINT

THERE IS ONE REAL ROOT.
X =    −1.0000
GIVE THE VALUE OF THE CONSTANT, A, AS A NUMBER WITH A DECIMAL POINT
GIVE THE VALUE OF THE CONSTANT, B, AS A NUMBER WITH A DECIMAL POINT
GIVE THE VALUE OF THE CONSTANT, C, AS A NUMBER WITH A DECIMAL POINT

THERE ARE TWO IMAGINARY ROOTS.
X =    −1.0000  −1.0000 OR X =    −1.0000    1.0000
GIVE THE VALUE OF THE CONSTANT, A, AS A NUMBER WITH A DECIMAL POINT

NORMAL PROGRAM TERMINATION


       PROGRAM QUAD2
C
C      PREAMBLE FOR PROGRAM QUAD2
C
```

```
C       ABSTRACT: QUAD2 IS AN INTERACTIVE PROGRAM TO SOLVE QUADRATIC
C                 EQUATIONS.
C
C       INPUT:    THE CONSTANTS A, B, AND C.
C
C       OUTPUT:   THE ONE OR TWO VALUES OF X WHICH SOLVE THE QUADRATIC
C                 EQUATION, AND A MESSAGE INDICATING WHETHER THERE ARE
C                 TWO REAL ROOTS, ONE REAL ROOT, OR TWO IMAGINARY ROOTS.
C
C       DESIGN HISTORY: HANS LEE, 6NOV83
C
C       REFERENCE:
C
C       ID DICTIONARY:
C
C       ID        TYPE          MEANING               USE
C
C       A         REAL          THE CONSTANT A IN     VARIABLE
C                               THE EQUATION
C       B         REAL          THE CONSTANT B IN     VARIABLE
C                               THE EQUATION
C       C         REAL          THE CONSTANT C IN     VARIABLE
C                               THE EQUATION
C       SOLVE2    NA                                  SUBROUTINE NAME
C                                                     (3 ARGUMENTS)
C
C       SPECIFICATIONS
C
        IMPLICIT LOGICAL (A-Z)
C
        REAL A,B,C
C
        OPEN(UNIT=5,FILE='INPUT',BLANK='NULL')
        OPEN(UNIT=6,FILE='OUTPUT')
C
        WRITE(6,600)
C
C       WHILE THERE ARE DATA
5          CONTINUE
           WRITE(6,601)
           READ(5,500,END=10)A
           WRITE(6,602)
           READ(5,500,END=10)B
           WRITE(6,603)
           READ(5,500,END=10)C
           IF(A.EQ.0.0)THEN
              WRITE(6,604)
           ELSE
              CALL SOLVE2(A,B,C)
           ENDIF
           GO TO 5
```

```
10       CONTINUE
C    ENDWHILE
C
     WRITE(6,605)
     STOP
C
500   FORMAT(F10.2)
600   FORMAT('1','PROGRAM QUAD2 SOLVES QUADRATIC EQUATIONS.  VERSION OF',
     +' 6NOV83.')
601   FORMAT(' ','GIVE THE VALUE OF THE CONSTANT, A, AS A NUMBER WITH',
     +' A DECIMAL POINT')
602   FORMAT(' ','GIVE THE VALUE OF THE CONSTANT, B, AS A NUMBER WITH',
     +' A DECIMAL POINT')
603   FORMAT(' ','GIVE THE VALUE OF THE CONSTANT, C, AS A NUMBER WITH',
     +' A DECIMAL POINT')
604   FORMAT('0','THE VALUE OF A CANNOT BE ZERO.')
605   FORMAT('0','NORMAL PROGRAM TERMINATION')
     END


     SUBROUTINE SOLVE2(A,B,C)
C
C    PREAMBLE FOR SUBROUTINE SOLVE2
C                                                        2
C    ABSTRACT: SOLVE1 SOLVES THE FORMULA (-B+SQRT(B -4AC))/2A AND THE
C                                2
C              FORMULA (-B-SQRT(B -4AC))/2A FOR X IN A QUADRATIC
C              EQUATION.
C
C    INPUT:    NONE
C
C    OUTPUT:   A MESSAGE REPORTING WHETHER THERE ARE ONE OR TWO ROOTS,
C              WHETHER THE ROOT(S) ARE REAL OR IMAGINARY, AND THE
C              VALUE(S) OF THE ROOT(S).
C
C    ENTRY VALUES: A,B,C
C
C    EXIT VALUES: NONE
C
C    ENTRY AND EXIT VALUES: NONE
C
C    DESIGN HISTORY: HANS LEE, 6NOV83.
C
C    REFERENCE:
C
C    ID DICTIONARY:
C
C    ID       TYPE      MEANING                USE
C
C    A        REAL      THE CONSTANT A IN      ARGUMENT
C                       THE EQUATION
```

```
C      B          REAL       THE CONSTANT B IN    ARGUMENT
C                            THE EQUATION
C      C          REAL       THE CONSTANT C IN    ARGUMENT
C                            THE EQUATION
C      CMPLX      COMPLEX    CONVERT REAL TO      INTRINSIC FUNCTION
C                            COMPLEX
C      CSQRT      COMPLEX    COMPLEX SQUARE ROOT  INTRINSIC FUNCTION
C      CX1        COMPLEX    ONE COMPLEX ROOT     VARIABLE
C      CX2        COMPLEX    THE OTHER COMPLEX    VARIABLE
C                            ROOT
C      SQRT       REAL       SQUARE ROOT          INTRINSIC FUNCTION
C                             2
C      TERM       REAL       B  - 4*A*C           VARIABLE
C      X1         REAL       ONE REAL ROOT OF THE VARIABLE
C                            EQUATION
C      X2         REAL       THE OTHER REAL ROOT  VARIABLE
C                            (IF THERE ARE TWO
C                            ROOTS)
C
C      SPECIFICATIONS
C
       IMPLICIT LOGICAL (A-Z)
C
       REAL A,B,C,TERM,X1,X2
       COMPLEX CX1,CX2
C
       TERM=B*B-4.0*A*C
       IF(TERM.GT.0.0)THEN
          WRITE(6,600)
          X1=(-B-SQRT(TERM))/(2.0*A)
          X2=(-B+SQRT(TERM))/(2.0*A)
          WRITE(6,601)X1,X2
       ENDIF
       IF(TERM.EQ.0.0)THEN
          WRITE(6,602)
          X1=(-B+SQRT(TERM))/(2.0*A)
          WRITE(6,603)X1
       ENDIF
       IF(TERM.LT.0.0)THEN
          WRITE(6,604)
          CX1=(-B-CSQRT(CMPLX(TERM)))/(2.0*A)
          CX2=(-B+CSQRT(CMPLX(TERM)))/(2.0*A)
          WRITE(6,605)CX1,CX2
       ENDIF
       RETURN
C
600    FORMAT('0','THERE ARE TWO REAL ROOTS.')
601    FORMAT(' ','X = ',F10.4,' OR X = ',F10.4)
602    FORMAT('0','THERE IS ONE REAL ROOT.')
603    FORMAT(' ','X = ',F10.4)
```

```
604     FORMAT('0','THERE ARE TWO IMAGINARY ROOTS.')
605     FORMAT(' ','X = ',2F10.4,' OR X = ',2F10.4)
        END
1
4
3
1
2
1
1
2
2
```

```
PROGRAM QUAD2 SOLVES QUADRATIC EQUATIONS.  VERSION OF 6NOV83.
GIVE THE VALUE OF THE CONSTANT, A, AS A NUMBER WITH A DECIMAL POINT
GIVE THE VALUE OF THE CONSTANT, B, AS A NUMBER WITH A DECIMAL POINT
GIVE THE VALUE OF THE CONSTANT, C, AS A NUMBER WITH A DECIMAL POINT

THERE ARE TWO REAL ROOTS.
X =    -3.0000 OR X =     -1.0000
GIVE THE VALUE OF THE CONSTANT, A, AS A NUMBER WITH A DECIMAL POINT
GIVE THE VALUE OF THE CONSTANT, B, AS A NUMBER WITH A DECIMAL POINT
GIVE THE VALUE OF THE CONSTANT, C, AS A NUMBER WITH A DECIMAL POINT

THERE IS ONE REAL ROOT.
X =     -1.0000
GIVE THE VALUE OF THE CONSTANT, A, AS A NUMBER WITH A DECIMAL POINT
GIVE THE VALUE OF THE CONSTANT, B, AS A NUMBER WITH A DECIMAL POINT
GIVE THE VALUE OF THE CONSTANT, C, AS A NUMBER WITH A DECIMAL POINT

THERE ARE TWO IMAGINARY ROOTS.
X =     -1.0000  -1.0000 OR X =     -1.0000    1.0000
GIVE THE VALUE OF THE CONSTANT, A, AS A NUMBER WITH A DECIMAL POINT

NORMAL PROGRAM TERMINATION
```

```
        PROGRAM QUAD3
C
C       PREAMBLE FOR PROGRAM QUAD3
C
C       ABSTRACT: QUAD3 IS AN INTERACTIVE PROGRAM TO SOLVE QUADRATIC
C                 EQUATIONS.
C
C       INPUT:   THE CONSTANTS A, B, AND C.
C
C       OUTPUT:  THE ONE OR TWO VALUES OF X WHICH SOLVE THE QUADRATIC
C                EQUATION, AND A MESSAGE INDICATING WHETHER THERE ARE
C                TWO REAL ROOTS, ONE REAL ROOT, OR TWO IMAGINARY ROOTS.
```

```
C
C       DESIGN HISTORY: HANS LEE, 6NOV83
C
C       REFERENCE:
C
C       ID DICTIONARY:
C
C       ID        TYPE        MEANING                 USE
C
C       A         REAL        THE CONSTANT A IN       VARIABLE
C                             THE EQUATION
C       B̄         REAL        THE CONSTANT B IN       VARIABLE
C                             THE EQUATION
C       C         REAL        THE CONSTANT C IN       VARIABLE
C                             THE EQUATION
C       SELECT    NA                                  SUBROUTINE NAME
C                                                     (3 ARGUMENTS)
C
C       SPECIFICATIONS
C
        IMPLICIT LOGICAL (A-Z)
C
        REAL A,B,C
C
        OPEN(UNIT=5,FILE='INPUT',BLANK='NULL')
        OPEN(UNIT=6,FILE='OUTPUT')
C
        WRITE(6,600)
C
C       WHILE THERE ARE DATA
5           CONTINUE
            WRITE(6,601)
            READ(5,500,END=10)A
            WRITE(6,602)
            READ(5,500,END=10)B
            WRITE(6,603)
            READ(5,500,END=10)C
            IF(A.EQ.0.0)THEN
                WRITE(6,604)
            ELSE
                CALL SELECT(A,B,C)
            ENDIF
            GO TO 5
10          CONTINUE
C       ENDWHILE
C
        WRITE(6,605)
        STOP
C
500     FORMAT(F10.2)
```

```
600   FORMAT('1','PROGRAM QUAD3 SOLVES QUADRATIC EQUATIONS.  VERSION OF',
     +' 6NOV83.')
601   FORMAT(' ','GIVE THE VALUE OF THE CONSTANT, A, AS A NUMBER WITH',
     +' A DECIMAL POINT')
602   FORMAT(' ','GIVE THE VALUE OF THE CONSTANT, B, AS A NUMBER WITH',
     +' A DECIMAL POINT')
603   FORMAT(' ','GIVE THE VALUE OF THE CONSTANT, C, AS A NUMBER WITH',
     +' A DECIMAL POINT')
604   FORMAT('0','THE VALUE OF A CANNOT BE ZERO.')
605   FORMAT('0','NORMAL PROGRAM TERMINATION')
      END



      SUBROUTINE SELECT(A,B,C)
C
C     PREAMBLE FOR SUBROUTINE SELECT
C     ABSTRACT: SELECT DETERMINES WHICH OF THREE SOLUTION CASES FOR THE
C               QUADRATIC EQUATION IS AT HAND
C
C     INPUT:   NONE
C
C     OUTPUT:  NONE
C
C     ENTRY VALUES: A,B,C
C
C     EXIT VALUES: NONE
C
C     ENTRY AND EXIT VALUES: NONE
C
C     DESIGN HISTORY: HANS LEE, 7DEC83.
C
C     REFERENCE:
C
C     ID DICTIONARY:
C
C     ID      TYPE      MEANING            USE
C
C     A       REAL      THE CONSTANT A IN   ARGUMENT
C                       THE EQUATION
C     B       REAL      THE CONSTANT B IN   ARGUMENT
C                       THE EQUATION
C     C       REAL      THE CONSTANT C IN   ARGUMENT
C                       THE EQUATION
C     CMPLXR  NA        THE PROCEDURE WHICH  SUBROUTINE NAME
C                       COMPUTES THE COMPLEX (3 ARGUMENTS)
C                       ROOTS
C     RRONE   NA        THE PROCEDURE WHICH  SUBROUTINE NAME
C                       COMPUTES THE SINGLE  (3 ARGUMENTS)
C                       (I.E., ONE) REAL ROOT
```

```
C      RRTWO      NA          THE PROCEDURE WHICH    SUBROUTINE NAME
C                             COMPUTES THE TWO       (3 ARGUMENTS)
C                             REAL ROOTS
C                                 2
C      TERM       REAL        B  - 4*A*C             VARIABLE
C
C      SPECIFICATIONS
C
       IMPLICIT LOGICAL (A-Z)
C
       REAL A,B,C,TERM
C
       TERM=B*B-4.0*A*C
       IF(TERM.GT.0.0)THEN
          CALL RRTWO(A,B,TERM)
       ENDIF
       IF(TERM.EQ.0.0)THEN
          CALL RRONE(A,B,TERM)
       ENDIF
       IF(TERM.LT.0.0)THEN
          CALL CMPLXR(A,B,TERM)
       ENDIF
       RETURN
C
       END



       SUBROUTINE CMPLXR(A,B,TERM)
C
C      PREAMBLE FOR SUBROUTINE CMPLXR
C
C      ABSTRACT:  CMPLXR OBTAINS THE COMPLEX ROOTS
C
C      INPUT:  NONE
C
C      OUTPUT:  A MESSAGE REPORTING THAT THERE ARE TWO COMPLEX ROOTS
C               TOGETHER WITH THE NUMERIC VALUES OF EACH ROOT.
C
C      ENTRY VALUES: A,B,TERM
C
C      EXIT VALUES: NONE
C
C      ENTRY AND EXIT VALUES: NONE
C
C      DESIGN HISTORY:  HANS LEE, 7DEC83
C
C      REFERENCE:  NONE
C
C      ID DICTIONARY
C
```

```
C      ID        TYPE        MEANING              USE
C
C      A         REAL        THE CONSTANT A IN    ARGUMENT
C                            THE EQUATION
C      B         REAL        THE CONSTANT B IN    ARGUMENT
C                            THE EQUATION
C      CMPLX     COMPLEX     CONVERT REAL TO      INTRINSIC FUNCTION
C                            COMPLEX
C      CSQRT     COMPLEX     COMPLEX SQUARE ROOT  INTRINSIC FUNCTION
C      CX1       COMPLEX     ONE COMPLEX ROOT     VARIABLE
C      CX2       COMPLEX     THE OTHER COMPLEX    VARIABLE
C                            ROOT
C                             2
C      TERM      REAL        B  - 4*A*C           ARGUMENT
C
C      SPECIFICATIONS
C
       IMPLICIT LOGICAL(A-Z)
C
       REAL A,B,TERM
       COMPLEX CX1,CX2
C
       WRITE(6,600)
       CX1=(-B+CSQRT(CMPLX(TERM)))/(2.0*A)
       CX2=(-B-CSQRT(CMPLX(TERM)))/(2.0*A)
       WRITE(6,601)CX1,CX2
       RETURN
C
600    FORMAT('0','THERE ARE TWO IMAGINARY ROOTS.')
601    FORMAT(' ','X = ',2F10.4,' OR X = ',2F10.4)
       END



       SUBROUTINE RRONE(A,B,TERM)
C
C      PREAMBLE FOR SUBROUTINE RRONE
C
C      ABSTRACT:  RRONE OBTAINS THE SINGLE REAL ROOT
C
C      INPUT:  NONE
C
C      OUTPUT:  A MESSAGE REPORTING THAT THERE IS ONE REAL ROOT
C               TOGETHER WITH ITS NUMERIC VALUE.
C
C      ENTRY VALUES: A,B,TERM
C
C      EXIT VALUES: NONE
C
C      ENTRY AND EXIT VALUES: NONE
C
```

```
C      DESIGN HISTORY:  HANS LEE, 7DEC83
C
C      REFERENCE:  NONE
C
C      ID DICTIONARY
C
C      ID        TYPE        MEANING              USE
C
C      A         REAL        THE CONSTANT A IN    ARGUMENT
C                            THE EQUATION
C      B         REAL        THE CONSTANT B IN    ARGUMENT
C                            THE EQUATION
C      SQRT      REAL        SQUARE ROOT          INTRINSIC FUNCTION
C                             2
C      TERM      REAL        B  - 4*A*C           ARGUMENT
C      X1        REAL        THE ONE REAL ROOT    VARIABLE
C
C      SPECIFICATIONS
C
       IMPLICIT LOGICAL(A-Z)
C
       REAL A,B,TERM,X1
C
       WRITE(6,600)
       X1=(-B+SQRT(TERM))/(2*A)
       WRITE(6,601)X1
       RETURN
C
600    FORMAT('0','THERE IS ONE REAL ROOT.')
601    FORMAT(' ','X = ',F10.4)
       END



       SUBROUTINE RRTWO(A,B,TERM)
C
C      PREAMBLE FOR SUBROUTINE RRTWO
C
C      ABSTRACT:  RRTWO OBTAINS THE TWO REAL ROOTS
C
C      INPUT:  NONE
C
C      OUTPUT:  A MESSAGE REPORTING THAT THERE ARE TWO REAL ROOTS
C               TOGETHER WITH THE NUMERIC VALUES OF EACH ROOT.
C
C      ENTRY VALUES: A,B,TERM
C
C      EXIT VALUES: NONE
C
C      ENTRY AND EXIT VALUES: NONE
```

```
C
C      DESIGN HISTORY:  HANS LEE, 7DEC83
C
C      REFERENCE:  NONE
C
C      ID DICTIONARY
C
C      ID        TYPE        MEANING                USE
C
C      A         REAL        THE CONSTANT A IN      ARGUMENT
C                            THE EQUATION
C      B         REAL        THE CONSTANT B IN      ARGUMENT
C                            THE EQUATION
C      SQRT      REAL        SQUARE ROOT            INTRINSIC FUNCTION
C                             2
C      TERM      REAL        B  - 4*A*C             ARGUMENT
C      X1        REAL        ONE REAL ROOT          VARIABLE
C      X2        REAL        THE OTHER REAL ROOT    VARIABLE
C
C      SPECIFICATIONS
C
       IMPLICIT LOGICAL(A-Z)
C
       REAL A,B,TERM,X1,X2
C
       WRITE(6,600)
       X1=(-B+SQRT(TERM))/(2.0*A)
       X2=(-B-SQRT(TERM))/(2.0*A)
       WRITE(6,601)X1,X2
       RETURN
C
600    FORMAT('0','THERE ARE TWO REAL ROOTS.')
601    FORMAT(' ','X = ',F10.4,' OR X = ',F10.4)
       END
1
4
3
1
2
1
1
2
2
```

PROGRAM QUAD3 SOLVES QUADRATIC EQUATIONS. VERSION OF 6NOV83.
GIVE THE VALUE OF THE CONSTANT, A, AS A NUMBER WITH A DECIMAL POINT
GIVE THE VALUE OF THE CONSTANT, B, AS A NUMBER WITH A DECIMAL POINT
GIVE THE VALUE OF THE CONSTANT, C, AS A NUMBER WITH A DECIMAL POINT

```
THERE ARE TWO REAL ROOTS.
X =    -1.0000 OR X =    -3.0000
GIVE THE VALUE OF THE CONSTANT, A, AS A NUMBER WITH A DECIMAL POINT
GIVE THE VALUE OF THE CONSTANT, B, AS A NUMBER WITH A DECIMAL POINT
GIVE THE VALUE OF THE CONSTANT, C, AS A NUMBER WITH A DECIMAL POINT

THERE IS ONE REAL ROOT.
X =    -1.0000
GIVE THE VALUE OF THE CONSTANT, A, AS A NUMBER WITH A DECIMAL POINT
GIVE THE VALUE OF THE CONSTANT, B, AS A NUMBER WITH A DECIMAL POINT
GIVE THE VALUE OF THE CONSTANT, C, AS A NUMBER WITH A DECIMAL POINT

THERE ARE TWO IMAGINARY ROOTS.
X =    -1.0000  -1.0000 OR X =    -1.0000    1.0000
GIVE THE VALUE OF THE CONSTANT, A, AS A NUMBER WITH A DECIMAL POINT

NORMAL PROGRAM TERMINATION
```

Chapter 6 Programs

PROGRAM TWOIN

PROGRAM POWERS
SUBROUTINE CINTOB
SUBROUTINE MATAIB
SUBROUTINE MATMUT
output from POWERS/CINTOB/MATAIB/MATMUT

```
      PROGRAM TWOIN
C
C   ABSTRACT : TWOIN INPUTS THE VALUES OF A TWO DIMENSIONAL ARRAY
C              A FULL ROW AT A TIME.  THEN PRINTS THE ARRAY.
C
C   INPUT :   THE VALUES OF A ( A MATRIX )
C
C   OUTPUT :  THE VALUES OF A.
C
C   DESIGN HISTORY :
C           TRINA LEE, 12MAR85
C
C   CODING HISTORY :
C           CAROL HOFMANN, 20JUL85
C
C   REFERENCE: CLIENT'S PROGRAM REQUEST
C
C   ID DICTIONARY :
C
```

```
C   ID        TYPE        MEANING                    USE
C
C   A         INTEGER     NONE                       MATRIX
C   COL       INTEGER     COLUMN                     VARIABLE
C   NCOLS     INTEGER     NUMBER OF COLUMNS          VARIABLE
C   NROWS     INTEGER     NUMBER OF ROWS             VARIABLE
C   ROW       INTEGER     ROW                        VARIABLE
C
      IMPLICIT LOGICAL (A-Z)
      INTEGER NCOLS, NROWS
      INTEGER COL, ROW, A(10,10)
      COMMON/BUGBLK/ BUG
      OPEN (5, FILE='INPUT' ,BLANK='NULL')
      OPEN (6, FILE='OUTPUT')
C
      BUG = .TRUE.
      WRITE (6,600)
C
C                                    INPUT NUMBER OF ROWS AND COLUMNS
C                                    OF A TWO DIMENSIONAL MATRIX
C
      WRITE(6,610)
      READ(5,500) NROWS
      WRITE(6,620)
      READ(5,500) NCOLS
C
C                                    READ VALUES OF EACH ROW FROM FILE
C                                    INPUT, AND PRINT THE ARRAY.
C
      DO 10 ROW= 1,NROWS
        READ(5,510) (A(ROW,COL),COL=1,NCOLS)
        IF (BUG) THEN
          WRITE(6,630) (A(ROW,COL),COL=1,NCOLS)
        END IF
 10    CONTINUE
C
      WRITE (6,640)
      STOP 'TWOIN'
C
C   FORMATS
C
 500  FORMAT(I2)
 510  FORMAT(10(I2,2X))
 600  FORMAT(' START OF PROGRAM TWOIN')
 610  FORMAT(' GIVE THE NUMBER OF ROWS REQUIRED (AN INTEGER,',
     +        ' LESS THAN 11.)')
 620  FORMAT(' GIVE THE NUMBER OF COLUMNS REQUIRED (AN INTEGER,',
     +        ' LESS THAN 11.)')
 630  FORMAT(' ',11(I5,2X))
 640  FORMAT(' NORMAL PROGRAM TERMINATION')
```

```
C
      END
   4
   6
  17  16  15  14  13  12
  10   9   8   7   6   5
   4   3   2   1   0
  -1  -2  -3  -4  -5  -6



      PROGRAM POWERS
C
C  ABSTRACT : POWERS RAISES A GIVEN MATRIX TO A GIVEN POWER.
C
C  INPUT :    THE MATRIX, AND THE POWER TO WHICH IT IS TO BE RAISED.
C
C  OUTPUT :   ALL POWERS OF THE MATRIX
C
C  DESIGN HISTORY :
C            TRINA LEE, 12MAR85
C
C  PROGRAM HISTORY :
C            CAROL HOFMANN, 30MAR85
C
C  REFERENCES :
C            LINEAR ALGEBRA BY JOHNSON AND REISS
C
C  ID DICTIONARY :
C
C    ID       TYPE      MEANING              USE
C    A        REAL      FIRST MATRIX         VARIABLE ARRAY
C    COL      INTEGER   COLUMN               VARIABLE
C    N        INTEGER   NUMBER OF ROWS       INPUT CONSTANT
C    NPOW     INTEGER   NUMBER OF POWERS     VARIABLE
C    NREPS    INTEGER   NUMBER OF REPITIONS  COUNTER
C    POWER    INTEGER   POWER TO RAISE       INPUT CONSTANT
C    ROW      INTEGER   ROW                  VARIABLE
C
      IMPLICIT LOGICAL (A-Z)
      INTEGER COL, N, NPOW, NREPS, POWER, ROW
      REAL A(10,10), B(10,10), C(10,10)
      COMMON/BUGBLK/BUG
      OPEN (5, FILE='INPUT', BLANK='NULL')
      OPEN (6, FILE='OUTPUT')
C
      IF (BUG) THEN
        WRITE (6,600)
      ENDIF
C
```

```
C                                       INPUT VALUES OF A SQUARE MATRIX
C                                         AND POWER TO WHICH IT
C                                         SHOULD BE RAISED
C
      READ(5,500) N
      READ(5,500) POWER
C
C                                       READ VALUES OF EACH ROW FROM
C                                            FILE INPUT
C
      DO 10 ROW= 1,N
        READ(5,510) (A(ROW,COL),COL=1,N)
 10   CONTINUE
C
      IF (BUG) THEN
        DO 20 ROW= 1,N
          WRITE(6,610)(A(ROW,COL),COL=1,N)
 20     CONTINUE
      ENDIF


C
C                                       RAISE MATRIX TO A POWER
C
      NPOW = POWER-1
      CALL MATAIB(A,B,N)
      CALL MATMUT(A,B,C,N)
      DO 30 ROW = 1,N
        WRITE(6,610)(C(ROW,COL),COL=1,N)
 30   CONTINUE
      DO 40 NREPS = 1,NPOW
        CALL CINTOB(B,C,N)
        CALL MATMUT(A,B,C,N)
        DO 50 ROW = 1,N
          WRITE(6,610)(C(ROW,COL),COL=1,N)
 50     CONTINUE
 40   CONTINUE

      IF (BUG) THEN
        WRITE(6,620)
      ENDIF
C
C   FORMATS
C
 500  FORMAT(I2)
 510  FORMAT(10(F6.2,2X))
 600  FORMAT(' BEGINNING PROGRAM POWER')
 610  FORMAT(' ',10(F8.2,2X))
 820  FORMAT(' NORMAL PROGRAM TERMINATION')
C
      END
```

```
1      SUBROUTINE MATMUT(A,B,C,N)
C
C   ABSTRACT : MATMUT MULTIPLIES MATRIX A BY MATRIX B AND PUTS THE
C              RESULTING MATRIX IN MATRIX C
C
C   INPUT :    NONE
C
C   OUTPUT :   NONE
C
C   ENTRY VALUES : A, B, N
C
C   EXIT VALUES : C
C
C   ENTRY AND EXIT VALUES : NONE
C
C   DESIGN HISTORY :
C            TRINA LEE, 12MAR85
C
C   PROGRAM HISTORY :
C            CAROL HOFMANN, 30MAR85
C
C   REFERENCES :
C            LINEAR ALGEBRA BY JOHNSON AND REISS
C
C   ID DICTIONARY :
C
C     ID      TYPE      MEANING            USE
C     A       REAL      FIRST MATRIX       ARRAY ARGUMENT
C     B       REAL      SECOND MATRIX      ARRAY ARGUMENT
C     C       REAL      RESULTANT MATRIX   ARRAY ARGUMENT
C     COL     INTEGER   COLUMN             VARIABLE
C     K       INTEGER   COLUMN OR ROW      VARIABLE
C     N       INTEGER   NUMBER OF ROWS     CONSTANT ARGUMENT
C     ROW     INTEGER   ROW                VARIABLE
C
       IMPLICIT LOGICAL(A-Z)
       INTEGER COL, K, N, ROW
       REAL A(10,10), B(10,10), C(10,10)
       COMMON/BUGBLK/ BUG
C
       IF (BUG) THEN
         WRITE (6,610)
         WRITE (6,600)A(1,1),B(1,1),N
       ENDIF
C
C                                      SET ALL ELEMENTS OF MATRIX C
C                                               TO ZERO
C
       DO 10 ROW=1,N
         DO 20 COL=1,N
           C(ROW,COL)=0
```

```
  20     CONTINUE
  10     CONTINUE
C
C
C                                          MULTIPLY MATRIX A TIMES MATRIX B
C
       DO 30 ROW=1,N
         DO 40 COL=1,N
           DO 50 K=1,N
             C(ROW,COL)=A(ROW,K)*B(K,COL)+C(ROW,COL)
  50       CONTINUE
  40     CONTINUE
  30   CONTINUE
C
       IF (BUG) THEN
         WRITE (6,600)A(1,1),B(1,1),N
         WRITE (6,620)
       ENDIF
C
       RETURN
C
C   FORMATS
C
 600   FORMAT(' ',F6.2,2X,F6.2,2X,I2)
 610   FORMAT(' ENTERING SUBROUTINE MATMUT')
 620   FORMAT(' LEAVING SUBROUTINE MATMUT')
       END


 1     SUBROUTINE CINTOB (B, C, N)
 C
 C ABSTRACT : CINTOB COPIES MATRIX C INTO MATRIX B
 C
 C INPUT :    NONE
 C
 C OUTPUT :   NONE
 C
 C ENTRY VALUES : C, N
 C
 C EXIT VALUES : B
 C
 C ENTRY AND EXIT VALUES : NONE
 C
 C DESIGN HISTORY :
 C           TRINA LEE, 12MAR85
 C
 C PROGRAM HISTORY :
 C           CAROL HOFMANN, 30MAR85
 C
 C REFERENCES :
 C           LINEAR ALGEBRA, BY JOHNSON AND REISS
 C
```

```
C    ID DICTIONARY :
C
C       ID       TYPE       MEANING              USE
C       B        REAL       MATRIX               ARRAY ARGUMENT
C       C        REAL       MATRIX               ARRAY ARGUMENT
C       COL      INTEGER    COLUMN               VARIABLE
C       N        INTEGER    NUMBER OF ROWS       CONSTANT ARGUMENT
C       ROW      INTEGER    ROW                  VARIABLE
C
      IMPLICIT LOGICAL(A-Z)
      INTEGER COL,ROW,N
      REAL B(10,10),C(10,10)
      COMMON/BUGBLK/ BUG
C
      IF (BUG) THEN
        WRITE (6,610)
        WRITE (6,600)C(1,1),C(1,2),N
      ENDIF
C
C                                         COPY MATRIX C INTO MATRIX B
C
      DO 10 ROW=1,N
        DO 20 COL=1,N
          B(ROW,COL) = C(ROW,COL)
 20     CONTINUE
 10   CONTINUE
C
      IF (BUG) THEN
        WRITE (6,600)C(1,1),B(1,1),N
        WRITE (6,620)
      ENDIF
      RETURN
C
C    FORMATS
C
600   FORMAT(' ',F6.2,2X,F6.2,2X,I2)
610   FORMAT(' ENTERING SUBROUTINE CINTOB')
620   FORMAT(' LEAVING SUBROUTINE CINTOB')
C
      END


1     SUBROUTINE MATAIB(A,B,N)
C
C    ABSTRACT : MATAIB COPIES MATRIX A INTO MATRIX B.
C
C    INPUT :    NONE
C
C    OUTPUT :   NONE
C
```

```
C    ENTRY VALUES : A, N
C
C    EXIT VALUES : B
C
C    ENTRY AND EXIT VALUES : NONE
C
C    DESIGN HISTORY :
C                TRINA LEE, 12MAR85
C
C    PROGRAM HISTORY :
C                CAROL HOFMANN, 30MAR85
C
C    REFERENCES :
C
C    ID DICTIONARY :
C
C    ID       TYPE      MEANING                USE
C    A        REAL      MATRIX                 ARRAY ARGUMENT
C    B        REAL      MATRIX                 ARRAY ARGUMENT
C    COL      INTEGER   COLUMN                 VARIABLE
C    N        INTEGER   NUMBER OF ROWS         CONSTANT ARGUMENT
C    ROW      INTEGER   ROW                    VARIABLE
C
     IMPLICIT LOGICAL (A-Z)
     INTEGER COL, N, ROW
     REAL A(10,10), B(10,10)
     COMMON/BUGBLK/ BUG
C
     IF (BUG) THEN
       WRITE (6,610)
       WRITE (6,600)A(1,1),A(1,2),N
     ENDIF
C
C                                            COPY MATRIX A INTO MATRIX B
C
     DO 10 ROW=1,N
       DO 20 COL=1,N
         B(ROW,COL) = A(ROW,COL)
  20     CONTINUE
  10   CONTINUE
C
     IF (BUG) THEN
       WRITE (6,600)A(1,1),B(1,1),N
       WRITE (6,620)
     ENDIF
C
     RETURN
C
C    FORMATS
C
```

```
600     FORMAT(' ',F6.2,2X,F6.2,2X,I2)
610     FORMAT(' ENTERING SUBROUTINE MATAIB')
620     FORMAT(' LEAVING SUBROUTINE MATAIB')
C
        END
```

```
   4
   3
0.11    0.22    0.33    0.34
0.25    0.10    0.45    0.20
0.33    0.33    0.33    0.01
0.34    0.44    0.12    0.20
```

```
BEGINNING PROGRAM POWER
       .11        .22        .33        .34
       .25        .10        .45        .20
       .33        .33        .33        .01
       .34        .44        .12        .20
ENTERING SUBROUTINE MATAIB
   .11      .22   4
   .11      .11   4
LEAVING SUBROUTINE MATAIB
ENTERING SUBROUTINE MATMUT
   .11      .11   4
   .11      .11   4
LEAVING SUBROUTINE MATMUT
       .29        .30        .29        .15
       .27        .30        .30        .15
       .23        .22        .37        .18
       .26        .25        .37        .24
ENTERING SUBROUTINE CINTOB
   .29      .30   4
   .29      .29   4
LEAVING SUBROUTINE CINTOB
ENTERING SUBROUTINE MATMUT
   .11      .29   4
   .11      .29   4
LEAVING SUBROUTINE MATMUT
       .25        .26        .35        .19
       .25        .25        .34        .18
       .26        .27        .32        .16
       .30        .31        .35        .19
ENTERING SUBROUTINE CINTOB
   .25      .26   4
   .25      .25   4
LEAVING SUBROUTINE CINTOB
ENTERING SUBROUTINE MATMUT
   .11      .25   4
   .11      .25   4
LEAVING SUBROUTINE MATMUT
       .27        .28        .34        .18
       .27        .28        .33        .18
       .26        .26        .34        .18
       .29        .29        .38        .20
NORMAL PROGRAM TERMINATION
```

Chapter 8 Programs

```
          PROGRAM BINOM
          FUNCTION FACT
          output from BINOM/FACT
```

```
          PROGRAM BINOM
C
C     PREAMBLE FOR PROGRAM BINOM
C
C     ABSTRACT: PROGRAM BINOM COMPUTES THE PROBABILITY OF OBTAINING
C               V SUCCESSES IN N TRIALS OF A BINOMIALLY DISTRIBUTED
C               RANDOM VARIABLE.
C
C     INPUT:   N, P, AND V
C
C     OUTPUT:  PROB
C
C     DESIGN HISTORY: HANS LEE, 29AUG85
C
C     REFERENCE:
C
C     ID DICTIONARY:
C
C     ID      TYPE      MEANING            USE
C
C     COMB    REAL      COMBINATORIAL      VARIABLE
C     FACT    INTEGER   FACTORIAL          FUNCTION NAME
C                                          (1 ARGUMENT)
C     N       INTEGER   NUMBER OF TRIALS   VARIABLE
C     P       REAL      PROBABILITY OF     VARIABLE
C                       SUCCESS
C     PROB    REAL      PROBABILITY        VARIABLE
C     Q       REAL      PROBABILITY OF     VARIABLE
C                       FAILURE
C     V       INTEGER   NUMBER OF SUCCESSES VARIABLE
C
C
C     SPECIFICATIONS
C
      IMPLICIT LOGICAL (A-Z)
C
      INTEGER FACT,N,V
      REAL COMB,P,PROB,Q
C
      OPEN(UNIT=5,FILE='INPUT',BLANK='NULL')
      OPEN(UNIT=6,FILE='OUTPUT')
C
C     WHILE THERE ARE DATA
```

```
5          CONTINUE
           WRITE(6,600)
           READ(5,500,END=10)P
           WRITE(6,601)P
           WRITE(6,602)
           READ(5,501,END=10)V
           WRITE(6,603)V
           WRITE(6,604)
           READ(5,501,END=10)N
           WRITE(6,605)N
           Q=1.0-P
           COMB=FACT(N)/(FACT(V)*FACT(N-V))
           PROB=(COMB)*(P**V)*(Q**(N-V))
           WRITE(6,606)PROB
           GO TO 5
10         CONTINUE
C      ENDWHILE
C
       WRITE(6,607)
       STOP
C
500    FORMAT(F8.5)
501    FORMAT(I10)
600    FORMAT('0','GIVE P, THE PROBABILITY OF SUCCESS, AS A REAL VALUE ',
      +'OF THE FORM X.XXXXX')
601    FORMAT(' ','P = ',F8.5)
602    FORMAT('0','GIVE V, THE NUMBER OF SUCCESSES, AS AN INTEGER OF ',
      +'THE FORM III')
603    FORMAT(' ','V = ',I10)
604    FORMAT('0','GIVE N, THE NUMBER OF TRIALS, AS AN INTEGER OF ',
      +'THE FORM III')
605    FORMAT(' ','N = ',I10)
606    FORMAT('0','THE REQUESTED PROBABILITY IS ',F8.5)
607    FORMAT(' ','NORMAL PROGRAM TERMINATION')
       END
       INTEGER FUNCTION FACT(N)
C
C      PREAMBLE FOR INTEGER FUNCTION FACT
C
C      ABSTRACT:  THE FUNCTION, FACT, RETURNS THE FACTORIAL OF THE
C                 VALUE OF ITS ARGUMENT
C
C      INPUT:  NONE
C
C      OUTPUT:  NONE
C
C      ENTRY VALUE: N
C
C      EXIT VALUE: FACT
C
```

```
C      ENTRY AND EXIT VALUES: NONE
C
C      DESIGN HISTORY:  HANS LEE, 28AUG85
C
C      REFERENCE:
C
C      ID DICTIONARY
C
C      ID       TYPE       MEANING              USE
C
C      FACT     INTEGER    FACTORIAL            FUNCTION NAME
C      INDEX    INTEGER    INDEX                VARIABLE
C      N        INTEGER    N                    VARIABLE
C      TEMP     INTEGER    TEMPORARY            VARIABLE
C
C      SPECIFICATIONS
C
       IMPLICIT LOGICAL(A-Z)
C
       INTEGER INDEX,N,TEMP
C
       TEMP=1
       IF(N.LT.0)THEN
          WRITE(6,600)N
          STOP
       ENDIF
       DO 5 INDEX=1,N,1
          TEMP=TEMP*INDEX
5      CONTINUE
       FACT=TEMP
       RETURN
C
600    FORMAT('0','FACTORIAL FUNCTION NOT DEFINED FOR VALUES LESS THAN ',
      +'ZERO.'/' ','ARGUMENT OF N HAD VALUE OF ',I10)
       END
0.5
2
3
0.9
2
3
0.75
6
8
0.75
8
8
0.75
0
8
```

```
0.75
-2
8
```

```
      PROGRAM BINOM2
C
C     PREAMBLE FOR PROGRAM BINOM
C
C     ABSTRACT: PROGRAM BINOM2 COMPUTES THE PROBABILITY OF OBTAINING
C               V SUCCESSES IN N TRIALS OF A BINOMIALLY DISTRIBUTED
C               RANDOM VARIABLE.
C
C     INPUT:   N, P, AND V
C
C     OUTPUT:  PROB
C
C     DESIGN HISTORY: HANS LEE, 29AUG85
C
C     REFERENCE:
C
C     ID DICTIONARY:
C
C     ID       TYPE         MEANING               USE
C
C     COMB     REAL         COMBINATORIAL         VARIABLE
C     FACT     INTEGER      FACTORIAL             FUNCTION NAME
C                                                 (1 ARGUMENT)
C     N        INTEGER      NUMBER OF TRIALS      VARIABLE
C     P        REAL         PROBABILITY OF        VARIABLE
C                           SUCCESS
C     PROB     REAL         PROBABILITY           VARIABLE
C     Q        REAL         PROBABILITY OF        VARIABLE
C                           FAILURE
C     V        INTEGER      NUMBER OF SUCCESSES   VARIABLE
C
C
C     SPECIFICATIONS
C
      IMPLICIT LOGICAL (A-Z)
C
      INTEGER FACT,N,V
      REAL COMB,P,PROB,Q
C
      OPEN(UNIT=5,FILE='INPUT',BLANK='NULL')
      OPEN(UNIT=6,FILE='OUTPUT')
C
C     WHILE THERE ARE DATA
5        CONTINUE
         WRITE(6,600)
```

```
        READ(5,500,END=10)P
        WRITE(6,601)P
        WRITE(6,602)
        READ(5,501,END=10)V
        WRITE(6,603)V
        WRITE(6,604)
        READ(5,501,END=10)N
        WRITE(6,605)N
        Q=1.0-P
        COMB=FACT(N)/(FACT(V)*FACT(N-V))
        PROB=(COMB)*(P**V)*(Q**(N-V))
        WRITE(6,606)PROB
        GO TO 5
10      CONTINUE
C     ENDWHILE
C
      WRITE(6,607)
      STOP
C
500   FORMAT(F8.5)
501   FORMAT(I10)
600   FORMAT('0','GIVE P, THE PROBABILITY OF SUCCESS, AS A REAL VALUE ',
     +'OF THE FORM X.XXXXX')
601   FORMAT(' ','P = ',F8.5)
602   FORMAT('0','GIVE V, THE NUMBER OF SUCCESSES, AS AN INTEGER OF ',
     +'THE FORM III')
603   FORMAT(' ','V = ',I10)
604   FORMAT('0','GIVE N, THE NUMBER OF TRIALS, AS AN INTEGER OF ',
     +'THE FORM III')
605   FORMAT(' ','N = ',I10)
606   FORMAT('0','THE REQUESTED PROBABILITY IS ',F8.5)
607   FORMAT(' ','NORMAL PROGRAM TERMINATION')
      END
      INTEGER FUNCTION FACT(N)
C
C     PREAMBLE FOR INTEGER FUNCTION FACT
C
C     ABSTRACT:  THE FUNCTION, FACT, RETURNS THE FACTORIAL OF THE
C                VALUE OF ITS ARGUMENT.  THIS VERSION ATTEMPTS TO USE
C                RECURSION TO TEST THE RESPONSE OF OUR SYSTEM.
C
C     INPUT:  NONE
C
C     OUTPUT:  NONE
C
C     ENTRY VALUE: N
C
C     EXIT VALUE: FACT
C
C     ENTRY AND EXIT VALUES: NONE
```

```
C
C      DESIGN HISTORY:  HANS LEE, 28AUG85
C
C      REFERENCE:
C
C      ID DICTIONARY
C
C      ID        TYPE         MEANING              USE
C
C      FACT      INTEGER      FACTORIAL            FUNCTION NAME
C      INDEX     INTEGER      INDEX                VARIABLE
C      N         INTEGER      N                    VARIABLE
C      TEMP      INTEGER      TEMPORARY            VARIABLE
C
C      SPECIFICATIONS
C
       IMPLICIT LOGICAL(A-Z)
C
       INTEGER INDEX,N,TEMP
C
       TEMP=1
       IF(N.LT.0)THEN
          WRITE(6,600)N
          STOP
       ENDIF
       IF(N.EQ.0.OR.N.EQ.1)THEN
          TEMP=1
       ELSEIF(N.GT.1)THEN
          TEMP=N*FACT(N-1)
       ENDIF
       FACT=TEMP
       RETURN
C
600    FORMAT('0','FACTORIAL FUNCTION NOT DEFINED FOR VALUES LESS THAN ',
      +'ZERO.'/' ','ARGUMENT OF N HAD VALUE OF ',I10)
       END
0.5
2
3
0.9
2
3
0.75
6
8
0.75
8
8
0.75
0
8
```

```
0.75
−2
8
```

GIVE P, THE PROBABILITY OF SUCCESS, AS A REAL VALUE OF THE FORM X.XXXXX
P =   .50000

GIVE V, THE NUMBER OF SUCCESSES, AS AN INTEGER OF THE FORM III
V =   2

GIVE N, THE NUMBER OF TRIALS, AS AN INTEGER OF THE FORM III
N =   3

THE REQUESTED PROBABILITY IS   .37500

GIVE P, THE PROBABILITY OF SUCCESS, AS A REAL VALUE OF THE FORM X.XXXXX
P =   .90000

GIVE V, THE NUMBER OF SUCCESSES, AS AN INTEGER OF THE FORM III
V =   2

GIVE N, THE NUMBER OF TRIALS, AS AN INTEGER OF THE FORM III
N =   3

THE REQUESTED PROBABILITY IS   .24300

GIVE P, THE PROBABILITY OF SUCCESS, AS A REAL VALUE OF THE FORM X.XXXXX
P =   .75000

GIVE V, THE NUMBER OF SUCCESSES, AS AN INTEGER OF THE FORM III
V =   6

GIVE N, THE NUMBER OF TRIALS, AS AN INTEGER OF THE FORM III
N =   8

THE REQUESTED PROBABILITY IS   .31146

GIVE P, THE PROBABILITY OF SUCCESS, AS A REAL VALUE OF THE FORM X.XXXXX
P =   .75000

GIVE V, THE NUMBER OF SUCCESSES, AS AN INTEGER OF THE FORM III
V =   8

GIVE N, THE NUMBER OF TRIALS, AS AN INTEGER OF THE FORM III
N =   8

THE REQUESTED PROBABILITY IS   .10011

GIVE P, THE PROBABILITY OF SUCCESS, AS A REAL VALUE OF THE FORM X.XXXXX
P =   .75000

GIVE V, THE NUMBER OF SUCCESSES, AS AN INTEGER OF THE FORM III
V =   0

V =   −2

GIVE N, THE NUMBER OF TRIALS, AS AN INTEGER OF THE FORM III
N =   8

```
FACTORIAL FUNCTION NOT DEFINED FOR VALUES LESS THAN ZERO.
ARGUMENT OF N HAD VALUE OF          -2

GIVE N, THE NUMBER OF TRIALS, AS AN INTEGER OF THE FORM III
N =          8

THE REQUESTED PROBABILITY IS    .00002

GIVE P, THE PROBABILITY OF SUCCESS, AS A REAL VALUE OF THE FORM X.XXXXX
P =    .75000

GIVE V, THE NUMBER OF SUCCESSES, AS AN INTEGER OF THE FORM III
```

Chapter 9 Programs

PROGRAM CIRTRI
SUBROUTINE CIRCUM
SUBROUTINE INSCR
SUBROUTINE SOLVE
FUNCTION TRI
output from CIRTRI/CIRCUM/INSCR/SOLVE/TRI

```
      PROGRAM CIRTRI
C
C     ABSTRACT : GIVEN THE LENGTH OF EACH SIDE OF A TRIANGLE, CIRTRI
C                COMPUTES THE AREA OF THE TRIANGLE, THE AREA AND
C                CIRCUMFERENCE OF A CIRCUMSCRIBED CIRCLE AND THE AREA
C                AND CIRCUMFERENCE OF AN INSCRIBED CIRCLE.
C
C     INPUT :    THE LENGTH OF EACH OF THE THREE SIDES OF A TRIANGLE
C
C     OUTPUT :   ECHO OF THE THREE SIDES OF THE TRIANGLE
C
C     DESIGN HISTORY :
C                TRINA LEE, 12MAR85
C
C     CODING HISTORY :
C                CAROL HOFMANN, 20JUL85
C
C     REFERENCES :
C                BURINGTON, RICHARD STEVEN.
C                HANDBOOK OF MATHEMATICAL TABLES AND FORMULAS.
C                SANDUSKY, OHIO: HANDBOOK PUBLISHERS, INC.
C
C     ID DICTIONARY :
C
C     ID      TYPE      MEANING                 USE
C     A       REAL      SIDE A OF TRIANGLE      VARIABLE
C     B       REAL      SIDE B OF TRIANGLE      VARIABLE
C     C       REAL      SIDE C OF TRIANGLE      VARIABLE
C     CIRTRI  NA        CIRCLES AND TRIANGLES   PROGRAM NAME
```

```
C      SOLVE    NA        SOLVE FOR RESULTS      SUBROUTINE NAME
C                                                (3 ARGUMENTS)
C      TRI      LOGICAL   TRIANGLE (RETURNS      FUNCTION NAME
C                         TRUE IF A,B,C ARE      (3 ARGUMENTS)
C                         THE SIDES OF A TRIANGLE)
C
       IMPLICIT LOGICAL(A-Z)
       REAL A,B,C
       COMMON/BUGBLK/BUG
       OPEN(5, FILE='INPUT', BLANK='NULL')
       OPEN(6,FILE='OUTPUT')
C
C
       BUG = .TRUE.
       WRITE (6,600)
C
C                                 READ IN VALUES FOR SIDES OF
C                                 TRIANGLES, IF TRIANGLE IS FORMED
C                                 THEN COMPUTE FUTHER INFORMATION
C
C
C      WHILE THERE ARE DATA
1      CONTINUE
       READ(5,500,END=2)A,B,C
         IF (BUG) THEN
           WRITE (6,610)A,B,C
         ENDIF
         WRITE (6,605)
         IF (TRI(A,B,C)) THEN
           CALL SOLVE (A,B,C)
         ENDIF
       GOTO 1
2      CONTINUE
C      ENDWHILE
C
       WRITE(6,620)
       STOP 'CIRTRI'
C
500    FORMAT( 3 ( F7.2,2X))
600    FORMAT(' START OF PROGRAM CIRTRI')
605    FORMAT(' ')
610    FORMAT(' ',3(F7.2,2X))
620    FORMAT(' NORMAL PROGRAM TERMINATION')
C
       END

1      LOGICAL FUNCTION TRI (A,B,C)
C
C   ABSTRACT : WHEN THE THREE VALUES, A, B, AND C FORM A TRIANGLE, THE
C              FUNCTION RETURNS TRUE.  WHEN THE VALUES DO NOT FIT
C              THE SIDES OF A TRIANGLE, THE FUNCTION RETURNS FALSE.
C
```

```
C   INPUT:     NONE
C
C   OUTPUT:    OUTPUT IS DONE ONLY WHEN THE VALUES DO NOT FORM
C                A TRIANGLE.
C
C   ENTRY VALUES: A, B, C
C
C   EXIT VALUE: TRI
C
C   DESIGN HISTORY: TRINA LEE, 12MAR85
C
C   CODING HISTORY: CAROL HOFMANN, 10AUG85
C
C   REFERENCE: NONE
C
C   ID DICTIONARY
C
C     ID       TYPE      MEANING                    USE
C     A        REAL      SIDE A OF A TRIANGLE       VARIABLE ARGUMENT
C     B        REAL      SIDE B OF A TRIANGLE       VARIABLE ARGUMENT
C     C        REAL      SIDE C OF A TRIANGLE       VARIABLE ARGUMENT
C     TRI      LOGICAL   TRIANGLE                   FUNCTION NAME
C                                                   (3 ARGUMENTS )
C
      IMPLICIT LOGICAL (A-Z)
      REAL A,B,C
      COMMON /BUGBLK/ BUG
C
      IF (BUG) THEN
        WRITE(6,600)
        WRITE(6,610) A,B,C
      ENDIF
C
      TRI = .TRUE.
C
C                                   TEST EACH SET OF SIDES AGAINST
C                                   THE THIRD. IF ANY ARE SHORTER
C                                   THEN IT IS NOT A TRIANGLE.
C
      IF (A .GT. (B+C) ) THEN
        TRI = .FALSE.
        WRITE(6,620)
        WRITE (6,630)'A','B','C'
      ENDIF
      IF (B .GT. (A+C) ) THEN
        TRI = .FALSE.
        WRITE(6,620)
        WRITE(6,630)'B','A','C'
      ENDIF
```

```
      IF (C .GT. (A+B)) THEN
        TRI = .FALSE.
        WRITE(6,620)
        WRITE(6,630)'C','A','B'
      ENDIF
C
      IF (BUG) THEN
        WRITE(6,640)
        WRITE(6,610)A,B,C
      ENDIF
C
      RETURN
C
600   FORMAT(' FUNCTION TRI ENTERED')
610   FORMAT(' A=',F7.2,' B=',F7.2,' C=',F7.2)
620   FORMAT(' THE THREE VALUES DO NOT FORM A TRIANGLE')
630   FORMAT(' ',A1,' IS LARGER THAN ',A1,' + ',A1)
640   FORMAT(' LEAVING FUNCTION TRI')
C
      END
1     SUBROUTINE SOLVE (A,B,C)
C
C    ABSTRACT : SOLVE COMPUTES S, ROOT, CALLS CIRCUM AND INSCR.
C
C    INPUT :     NONE
C
C    OUTPUT :    ROOT, WHICH GIVES THE AREA OF THE TRIANGLE
C
C    ENTRY VALUES : A, B, C
C
C    EXIT VALUES : NONE
C
C    ENTRY AND EXIT VALUES : NONE
C
C    DESIGN HISTORY :
C             TRINA LEE, 12MAR85
C
C    CODING HISTORY :
C             CAROL HOFMANN, 12AUG85
C
C    ID DICTIONARY :
C      ID      TYPE     MEANING                 USE
C      A       REAL     SIDE A OF A TRIANGLE    VARIABLE ARGUMENT
C      B       REAL     SIDE B OF A TRIANGLE    VARIABLE ARGUMENT
C      C       REAL     SIDE C OF A TRIANGLE    VARIABLE ARGUMENT
C      CIRCUM  NA       CIRCUMSCRIBED           SUBROUTINE NAME
C                                               (5 ARGUMENTS)
C      INSR    NS       INSCRIBED A TRIANGLE    SUBROUTINE NAME
C                                               (5 ARGUMENTS)
C
```

```
C     ROOT    REAL      SQUARE ROOT             VARIABLE ARGUMENT
C     S       REAL      S                       VARIABLE
C     SOLVE   NA        SOLVE                   SUBROUTINE NAME
C                                               (3 ARGUMENTS)
      IMPLICIT LOGICAL(A-Z)
      REAL A,B,C,ROOT,S
      COMMON /BUGBLK/ BUG
C
      IF (BUG) THEN
        WRITE (6,600)
        WRITE (6,610) A,B,C
      ENDIF
C
C                                               COMPUTE S AND ROOT, AND INVOKE
C                                               SUBROUTINES FOR COMPUTATION.
C
      S = 0.5*(A+B+C)
      ROOT = S*(S-A)*(S-B)*(S-C)
      WRITE (6,620) ROOT
      CALL CIRCUM (A,B,C,ROOT,S)
      CALL INSCR(A,B,C,ROOT,S)
C
      IF (BUG) THEN
        WRITE (6,630)
        WRITE (6,610) A,B,C
      ENDIF
C
      RETURN
C
600   FORMAT(' SUBROUTINE SOLVE ENTERED')
610   FORMAT(' A=',F7.2,' B=',F7.2,' C=',F7.2)
620   FORMAT(' THE AREA OF THE TRIANGLE IS ',F7.2)
630   FORMAT(' LEAVING SUBROUTINE SOLVE')
C
      END
1     SUBROUTINE CIRCUM(A,B,C,ROOT,S)
C
C   ABSTRACT : CIRCUM OBTAINS THE RADIUS OF A CIRCLE CIRCUMSCRIBED
C              ABOUT A TRIANGLE, THEN OBTAINS THE AREA AND
C              CIRCUMFERENCE OF THE CIRCLE.
C
C   INPUT :    NONE
C
C   OUTPUT :   AREA, CIR
C
C   ENTRY VALUES : A, B, C, ROOT, S
C
C   EXIT VALUES : NONE
C
C   ENTRY AND EXIT VALUES : NONE
```

```
C
C   DESIGN HISTORY :
C                   TRINA LEE, 12MAR85
C
C   CODING HISTORY :
C                   CAROL HOFMANN, 25AUG85
C
C   REFERENCE: CLIENT'S PROGRAM REQUEST
C
C   ID DICTIONARY :
C
C     ID        TYPE        MEANING                   USE
C     A         REAL        SIDE A OF A TRIANGLE    VARIABLE ARGUMENT
C     B         REAL        SIDE B OF A TRIANGLE    VARIABLE ARGUMENT
C     C         REAL        SIDE C OF A TRIANGLE    VARIABLE ARGUMENT
C     CIR       REAL        CIRCUMFERENCE          VARIABLE
C     PI        REAL        PI (3.1415)          CONSTANT
C     R         REAL        RADIUS                 VARIABLE
C     ROOT      REAL        SQUARE ROOT            VARIABLE ARGUMENT
C     S         REAL        S                      VARIABLE ARGUMENT
C
      IMPLICIT LOGICAL (A-Z)
      REAL A,AREA,B,C,CIR,PI,R,ROOT,S
      COMMON /BUGBLK/ BUG
      PARAMETER (PI=3.1415)
C
      IF (BUG) THEN
        WRITE (6,600)
        WRITE (6,610) A,B,C,ROOT,S
      ENDIF
C
C                                    COMPUTE AND OUTPUT AREA AND
C                                    CIRCUMFERENCE OF THE
C                                    CIRCUMSCRIBING CIRCLE.
C
      R = (A*B*C) / (4.0 * ROOT)
      AREA = PI * R * R
      WRITE (6,620) AREA
      CIR = 2.0 * PI * R
      WRITE (6,630) CIR
C
      IF (BUG) THEN
        WRITE (6,640)
        WRITE (6,610) A,B,C,ROOT,S
      ENDIF
C
      RETURN
C
600   FORMAT(' SUBROUTINE CIRCUM ENTERED')
610   FORMAT(' A=',F7.2,' B=',F7.2,' C=',F7.2,' ROOT=',F7.2,' S=',F7.2)
```

```
620   FORMAT(' THE AREA OF THE CIRCLE IS ',F7.2)
630   FORMAT(' THE CIRCUMFERENCE OF THE CIRCLE IS ',F7.2)
640   FORMAT(' LEAVING SUBROUTINE CIRCUM')
C
      END


1     SUBROUTINE INSCR(A,B,C,ROOT,S)
C
C  ABSTRACT : INSCR OBTAINS THE RADIUS OF A CIRCLE INSCRIBED ABOUT
C             A TRIANGLE, THEN OBTAINS THE AREA AND CIRCUMFERENCE OF
C             THE CIRCLE.
C
C  INPUT :    NONE
C
C  OUTPUT :   AREA, CIR
C
C  ENTRY VALUES : A, B, C, ROOT, S
C
C  EXIT VALUES : NONE
C
C  ENTRY AND EXIT VALUES : NONE
C
C  DESIGN HISTORY :
C            TRINA LEE, 12MAR85
C
C  CODING HISTORY :
C            CAROL HOFMANN, 25AUG85
C
C  REFERENCE: CLIENT'S PROGRAM REQUEST
C
C  ID DICTIONARY :
C
C    ID      TYPE      MEANING                   USE
C    A       REAL      SIDE A OF A TRIANGLE      VARIABLE ARGUMENT
C    B       REAL      SIDE B OF A TRIANGLE      VARIABLE ARGUMENT
C    C       REAL      SIDE C OF A TRIANGLE      VARIABLE ARGUMENT
C    CIR     REAL      CIRCUMFERENCE             VARIABLE
C    PI      REAL      PI (3.1415)               CONSTANT
C    R       REAL      RADIUS                    VARIABLE
C    ROOT    REAL      SQUARE ROOT               VARIABLE ARGUMENT
C    S       REAL      S                         VARIABLE ARGUMENT
C
C
      IMPLICIT LOGICAL (A-Z)
      REAL AREA,CIR,PI,R,ROOT,S
      COMMON /BUGBLK/ BUG
      PARAMETER (PI=3.1415)
C
```

```
      IF (BUG) THEN
        WRITE(6,600)
        WRITE(6,610)ROOT,S
      ENDIF
C
C                                          COMPUTE AND OUTPUT AREA AND
C                                          CIRCUMFERENCE OF THE
C                                          INSCRIBING CIRCLE.

      R = ROOT / S
      CIR = 2.0 * PI * R
      WRITE(6,620)CIR
      AREA = PI * R * R
      WRITE(6,630)AREA
  C
      IF (BUG) THEN
        WRITE(6,640)
        WRITE(6,610)ROOT,S
      ENDIF
C
      RETURN
C
600   FORMAT(' SUBROUTINE INSCR ENTERED')
610   FORMAT(' ROOT=',F7.2,' S=',F7.2)
620   FORMAT(' THE CIRCUMFERENCE IS ',F7.2)
630   FORMAT(' THE AREA IS ',F7.2)
640   FORMAT(' LEAVING SUBROUTINE INSCR')
      END
   12.5     15.44    18.6
  102.99  67.4         21
    4.345   5.234    2.657
1START OF PROGRAM CIRTRI

 THE AREA OF THE TRIANGLE IS 9164.12
 THE AREA OF THE CIRCLE IS         .03
 THE CIRCUMFERENCE OF THE CIRCLE IS     .62
 THE CIRCUMFERENCE IS    2474.35
 THE AREA IS   487220.73

 THE THREE VALUES DO NOT FORM A TRIANGLE
 A IS LARGER THAN B + C

 THE AREA OF THE TRIANGLE IS    33.19
 THE AREA OF THE CIRCLE IS         .65
 THE CIRCUMFERENCE OF THE CIRCLE IS     2.86
 THE CIRCUMFERENCE IS       34.08
 THE AREA IS       92.44
 NORMAL PROGRAM TERMINATION
```

Chapter 10 Programs

PROGRAM DRIVERS
SUBROUTINE SORTIT
output from DRIVERS/SORTIT

PROGAM DRIVERB
SUBROUTINE BUBBLE
output from DRIVERB/BUBBLE

```
      PROGRAM DRIVERS
C
C     PREAMBLE FOR PROGRAM DRIVER
C
C     ABSTRACT: PROGRAM DRIVERS READS AN UNSORTED LIST OF POSITIVE
C               INTEGERS INTO THE ARRAY LIST1.  THE VALUES ARE ECHO
C               PRINTED, THEN SENT TO A SORTING SUBROUTINE.  AFTER
C               RETURNING, THE SORTED VALUES ARE PRINTED.
C
C     INPUT:   THE ARRAY LIST1
C
C     OUTPUT:  THE ARRAY LIST1 AS READ, THE SORTED ARRAY LIST2.
C
C     DESIGN HISTORY: M. MISOVICH, 7DEC85
C
C     REFERENCE: NONE
C
C     ID DICTIONARY:
C
C     ID        TYPE        MEANING              USE
C
C     COUNT     INTEGER     COUNT OF ELEMENTS    VARIABLE
C                           IN LIST1 AND LIST2
C     I         INTEGER                          VARIABLE
C     LIST1     INTEGER     UNSORTED LIST        1-DIMENSIONAL ARRAY
C     LIST2     INTEGER     SORTED LIST          1-DIMENSIONAL ARRAY
C     SORTIT    NA          SORT IT              SUBROUTINE NAME
C
C     SPECIFICATIONS
C
      IMPLICIT LOGICAL (A-Z)
C
      INTEGER COUNT,I,LIST1(100),LIST2(100)
C
      OPEN(UNIT=5,FILE='INPUT',BLANK='NULL')
      OPEN(UNIT=6,FILE='OUTPUT')
C
      I=1
      WRITE(6,600)
C
```

```
C       WHILE THERE ARE DATA
5          CONTINUE
           READ(5,501,END=10)LIST1(I)
           WRITE(6,601)LIST1(I)
           I=I+1
           GO TO 5
10         CONTINUE
C       ENDWHILE
C
        COUNT=I-1
        CALL SORTIT(LIST1,COUNT,LIST2)
        WRITE(6,602)
        DO 15 I=1,COUNT
           WRITE(6,601)LIST2(I)
15      CONTINUE
        WRITE(6,603)
        STOP
C
501     FORMAT(I10)
600     FORMAT('1','ECHO PRINT OF UNSORTED LIST')
601     FORMAT(1X,I10)
602     FORMAT('0','SORTED LIST')
603     FORMAT('0','NORMAL PROGRAM TERMINATION')
        END
        SUBROUTINE SORTIT(INLIST,N,SORTED)
C
C       PREAMBLE FOR SUBROUTINE SORTIT
C
C       ABSTRACT: SORTIT SORTS A LIST OF INTEGERS WHICH MUST BE ZERO OR
C                 POSITIVE INTO A NEW LIST IN WHICH THE NUMBERS APPEAR IN
C                 DECREASING VALUE.
C
C       INPUT:  NONE
C
C       OUTPUT: NONE
C
C       ENTRY VALUES: INLIST, N
C
C       EXIT VALUES: SORTED
C
C       ENTRY AND EXIT VALUES: NONE
C
C       DESIGN HISTORY: HANS LEE, 30JUL85
C
C       REFERENCE: NONE
C
C       ID DICTIONARY:
C
C       ID      TYPE      MEANING              USE
C
```

```
C     I          INTEGER                               VARIABLE
C     INDEX      INTEGER      INDEX POINTS TO NEXT     VARIABLE
C                             LOCATION IN SORTED
C     INLIST     INTEGER      INPUTLIST                1-DIMENSIONAL ARRAY
C     LARGE      INTEGER      LARGEST VALUE FOUND      VARIABLE
C                             IN INLIST
C     LOC        INTEGER      LOCATION                 VARIABLE
C                             INLIST (SUBSCRIPT)
C                             WHERE LARGE WAS FOUND
C     N          INTEGER      NUMBER OF ELEMENTS       VARIABLE
C                             ON INLIST
C     SORTED     INTEGER      SORTED LIST              1-DIMENSIONAL ARRAY
C     SORTIT     NA           SORT IT                  SUBROUTINE NAME
C     TEMP       INTEGER      TEMPORARY                VARIABLE
C     USED       INTEGER      INDICATES VALUE          CONSTANT = -99999
C                             MOVED TO SORTED
C
C     SPECIFICATIONS
C
      IMPLICIT LOGICAL (A-Z)
C
      INTEGER USED
      PARAMETER (USED = -99999)
C
      INTEGER I,INDEX,INLIST(100),LARGE,LOC,N,SORTED(100),TEMP
C
C
      INDEX=0
C
C     REPEAT
10        CONTINUE
          TEMP=INLIST(1)
          LOC=1
          DO 5 I=2,N,1
             IF(TEMP.LT.INLIST(I))THEN
                TEMP=INLIST(I)
                LOC=I
             ENDIF
5         CONTINUE
          LARGE=TEMP
          INDEX=INDEX+1
          SORTED(INDEX)=LARGE
          INLIST(LOC)=USED
          IF(.NOT.(INDEX.EQ.N))GO TO 10
C     UNTIL INDEX EQ N
      RETURN
      END
19
3
72
```

```
0
8
31
6
19
95
19
        PROGRAM DRIVERB
C
C       PREAMBLE FOR PROGRAM DRIVERB
C
C       ABSTRACT: PROGRAM DRIVERB READS AN UNSORTED LIST OF POSITIVE
C                 INTEGERS INTO THE ARRAY LIST1.  THE VALUES ARE ECHO
C                 PRINTED, THEN SENT TO A SORTING SUBROUTINE.  AFTER
C                 RETURNING, THE SORTED VALUES ARE PRINTED.
C
C       INPUT:   THE ARRAY LIST1
C
C       OUTPUT:  THE ARRAY LIST1 AS READ, THE SORTED ARRAY LIST2.
C
C       DESIGN HISTORY: M. MISOVICH, 7DEC85
C
C       REFERENCE: NONE
C
C       ID DICTIONARY:
C
C       ID      TYPE         MEANING              USE
C
C       BUBBLE  NA           BUBBLE SORT          SUBROUTINE NAME
C       COUNT   INTEGER      COUNT OF ELEMENTS    VARIABLE
C                            IN LIST1 AND LIST2
C       I       INTEGER                           VARIABLE
C       LIST    INTEGER      LIST TO BE SORTED    1-DIMENSIONAL ARRAY
C
C       SPECIFICATIONS
C
        IMPLICIT LOGICAL (A-Z)
C
        INTEGER COUNT,I,LIST(100)
C
        OPEN(UNIT=5,FILE='INPUT',BLANK='NULL')
        OPEN(UNIT=6,FILE='OUTPUT')
C
        I=1
        WRITE(6,600)
C
C       WHILE THERE ARE DATA
5          CONTINUE
           READ(5,501,END=10)LIST(I)
           WRITE(6,601)LIST(I)
```

```
           I=I+1
           GO TO 5
10         CONTINUE
C      ENDWHILE
C
           COUNT=I-1
           CALL BUBBLE(LIST,COUNT)
           WRITE(6,602)
           DO 15 I=1,COUNT
              WRITE(6,601)LIST(I)
15         CONTINUE
           WRITE(6,603)
           STOP
C
501        FORMAT(I10)
600        FORMAT('1','ECHO PRINT OF UNSORTED LIST')
601        FORMAT(1X,I10)
602        FORMAT('0','SORTED LIST')
603        FORMAT('0','NORMAL PROGRAM TERMINATION')
           END
           SUBROUTINE BUBBLE(LIST,N)
C
C      PREAMBLE FOR SUBROUTINE BUBBLE
C
C      ABSTRACT: BUBBLE SORTS A LIST OF NUMBERS SO THAT THE LIST IS
C                RETURNED WITH THE NUMBERS APPEARING IN THE ORDER OF THEIR
C                DECREASING VALUE.
C
C      INPUT:   NONE
C
C      OUTPUT:  NONE
C
C      ENTRY VALUES: N
C
C      EXIT VALUES: NONE
C
C      ENTRY AND EXIT VALUES: LIST
C
C      DESIGN HISTORY: HANS LEE, 7AUG85
C
C      REFERENCE: NONE
C
C      ID DICTIONARY:
C
C      ID        TYPE       MEANING             USE
C
C      LIST      INTEGER    LIST OF NUMBERS     1-DIMENSIONAL ARRAY
C      N         INTEGER    NUMBER OF ITEMS ON  VARIABLE
C                           THE LIST
C      NPAIRS    INTEGER    NUMBER OF PAIRS     VARIABLE
```

```
C      PAIR     INTEGER     PAIR NUMBER            VARIABLE
C      PASS     INTEGER     PASS NUMBER            VARIABLE
C      TEMP     INTEGER     TEMPORARY              VARIABLE
C
C      SPECIFICATIONS
C
       IMPLICIT LOGICAL (A-Z)
C
       INTEGER LIST(100),N,NPAIRS,PAIR,PASS,TEMP
C
C
       NPAIRS=N-1
       DO 10 PASS=1,N-1,1
          DO 5 PAIR=1,NPAIRS,1
             IF(LIST(PAIR).LT.LIST(PAIR+1))THEN
                TEMP=LIST(PAIR+1)
                LIST(PAIR+1)=LIST(PAIR)
                LIST(PAIR)=TEMP
             ENDIF
5         CONTINUE
          NPAIRS=NPAIRS-1
10     CONTINUE
       RETURN
       END
   19
    3
   72
    0
    8
   31
    6
   19
   95
   19
```

Chapter 13 Programs

PROGRAM GAUSS
SUBROUTINE RDALL
SUBROUTINE RDNZ
SUBROUTINE SEIDEL
output from GAUSS/RDALL/RDNZ/SEIDEL

```
       PROGRAM GAUSS
C
C      PREAMBLE FOR PROGRAM GAUSS
C
C      ABSTRACT: GAUSS USES THE GAUSS-SEIDEL METHOD TO OBTAIN THE
C                SOLUTION TO A SYSTEM OF SIMULTANEOUS LINEAR EQUATIONS
```

```
C              OR REPORTS REACHING A USER SPECIFIED MAXIMUM NUMBER OF
C              ITERATIONS.
C
C     INPUT:   DATAID, HOWRD, MAXIT, MAXRES, AND N
C
C     OUTPUT:  ERROR MESSAGE IF A(I,I) IS ZERO WITH VALUE OF I
C
C     DESIGN HISTORY: H. LEE, 3MAY85
C
C     REFERENCE: NONE
C
C     ID DICTIONARY:
C
C     ID        TYPE        MEANING              USE
C
C     A         REAL        A, THE COEFFICIENTS  ARRAY
C                           AND CONSTANT TERM    (2 DIMENSIONS)
C     DATAID    CHARACTER   DATA IDENTIFICATION  VARIABLE
C     ERRAII    LOGICAL     ERROR IN A(I,I)      VARIABLE
C     HOWRD     CHARACTER   HOW READ             VARIABLE
C     I         INTEGER     ARRAY AND LOOP INDEX VARIABLE
C     MAXIT     INTEGER     MAXIMUM ACCEPTABLE   VARIABLE
C                           NUMBER OF ITERATIONS
C     MAXRES    REAL        MAXIMUM ACCEPTABLE   VARIABLE
C                           RESIDUAL
C     N         INTEGER     NUMBER OF UNKNOWNS   VARIABLE
C     RDALL     NA          READ ALL ELEMENTS    SUBROUTINE
C                           INTO A( , )          (2 ARGUMENTS)
C     RDNZ      NA          READ NONZERO ELEMENTS SUBROUTINE
C                           INTO A( , )          (2 ARGUMENTS)
C     SEIDEL    NA          SEIDEL IS CALLED ONCE SUBROUTINE
C                           FOR EACH DATA SET TO (4 ARGUMENTS)
C                           ITERATE FOR A SOLUTION
C
C     SPECIFICATIONS
C
      IMPLICIT LOGICAL (A-Z)
C
      INTEGER I,MAXIT,N
      REAL A(10,11),MAXRES
      CHARACTER DATAID*80,HOWRD*7
      LOGICAL ERRAII
C
      OPEN(UNIT=5,FILE='INPUT',BLANK='NULL')
      OPEN(UNIT=6,FILE='OUTPUT')
C
      WRITE(6,600)
C     WHILE THERE ARE DATA
1        CONTINUE
         READ(5,501,END=2)DATAID
```

```
            WRITE(6,601)DATAID
            READ(5,502,END=2)HOWRD
            WRITE(6,602)HOWRD
            READ(5,503,END=2)N
            WRITE(6,603)N
            READ(5,504,END=2)MAXIT
            WRITE(6,604)MAXIT
            READ(5,505,END=2)MAXRES
            WRITE(6,605)MAXRES
            IF(HOWRD.EQ.'ALL')THEN
               CALL RDALL(A,N)
            ELSEIF(HOWRD.EQ.'NONZERO')THEN
               CALL RDNZ(A,N)
            ELSE
               WRITE(6,606)
               STOP
            ENDIF
            ERRAII=.FALSE.
            DO 5 I=1,N
               IF(A(I,I).EQ.0.0)THEN
                  WRITE(6,607)I
                  ERRAII=.TRUE.
               ENDIF
5           CONTINUE
            IF(.NOT.ERRAII)THEN
               CALL SEIDEL(A,MAXIT,MAXRES,N)
            ENDIF
            GO TO 1
2           CONTINUE
C     ENDWHILE
      WRITE(6,608)
      STOP
C
501   FORMAT(A80)
502   FORMAT(A7)
503   FORMAT(I2)
504   FORMAT(I5)
505   FORMAT(F10.5)
600   FORMAT('1','PROGRAM GAUSS USES THE GAUSS-SEIDEL METHOD'
     +        /' ','TO SOLVE A SYSTEM OF LINEAR EQUATIONS.'
     +        /' ','PROGRAMMED BY H. LEE, 3MAY85.')
601   FORMAT('0',A80)
602   FORMAT('0','HOWRD = ',A7)
603   FORMAT('0','N     = ',I2)
604   FORMAT('0','MAXIT = ',I5)
605   FORMAT('0','MAXRES= ',F10.5)
606   FORMAT('0','ERROR: HOWRD IS NEITHER ''ALL'' NOR ''NONZERO''')
607   FORMAT('0','A(I,I) IS ZERO FOR I = ',I2)
608   FORMAT('0','NORMAL PROGRAM TERMINATION')
      END
```

```
      SUBROUTINE RDALL(A,N)
C
C     PREAMBLE FOR SUBROUTINE RDALL
C
C     ABSTRACT: RDALL READS ALL (INCLUDING ZERO VALUED) ELEMENTS INTO
C               ARRAY A( , )
C
C     INPUT:   A( , )
C
C     OUTPUT:  NONE
C
C     ENTRY VALUES:  N
C
C     EXIT VALUES:   A( , )
C
C     ENTRY AND EXIT VALUES:  NONE
C
C     DESIGN HISTORY: H. LEE, 3MAY85
C
C     REFERENCE: NONE
C
C     ID DICTIONARY:
C
C     ID        TYPE         MEANING              USE
C
C     A         REAL         A, THE COEFFICIENTS  ARRAY
C                            AND CONSTANT TERM    (2 DIMENSIONS)
C     COL       INTEGER      COLUMN ARRAY         VARIABLE
C                            SUBSCRIPT AND INDEX
C     N         INTEGER      NUMBER OF UNKNOWNS   VARIABLE
C     ROW       INTEGER      ROW ARRAY SUBSCRIPT  VARIABLE
C
C     SPECIFICATIONS
C
      IMPLICIT LOGICAL (A-Z)
C
      INTEGER COL,N,ROW
      REAL A(10,11)
C
      DO 5 ROW=1,N
         READ(5,501)(A(ROW,COL),COL=1,N+1)
5     CONTINUE
      RETURN
C
501   FORMAT(11F5.2)
      END
      SUBROUTINE RDNZ(A,N)
C
C     PREAMBLE FOR SUBROUTINE RDNZ
C
```

```
C        ABSTRACT: RDNZ READS NON-ZERO TERMS INTO A( , )
C
C        INPUT:   A, ROW, COL
C
C        OUTPUT:  NONE
C
C        ENTRY VALUES:  N
C
C        EXIT VALUES:   A( , )
C
C        ENTRY AND EXIT VALUES:  NONE
C
C        DESIGN HISTORY: H. LEE, 3MAY85
C
C        REFERENCE: NONE
C
C        ID DICTIONARY:
C
C        ID      TYPE        MEANING               USE
C
C        A       REAL        A, THE COEFFICIENTS   ARRAY
C                            AND CONSTANT TERM     (2 DIMENSIONS)
C        COL     INTEGER     COLUMN ARRAY          VARIABLE
C                            SUBSCRIPT AND INDEX
C        N       INTEGER     NUMBER OF UNKNOWNS    VARIABLE
C        ROW     INTEGER     ROW ARRAY SUBSCRIPT   VARIABLE
C                            AND INDEX
C        VALID   LOGICAL     VALID ROW AND COLUMN  VARIABLE
C
C        SPECIFICATIONS
C
         IMPLICIT LOGICAL (A-Z)
C
         INTEGER COL,N,ROW
         REAL A(10,11)
         LOGICAL VALID
C
         DO 5 ROW=1,N
            DO 10 COL=1,N+1
               A(ROW,COL)=0.0
10          CONTINUE
5        CONTINUE
C        REPEAT
15          CONTINUE
            READ(5,501)ROW,COL
            VALID=.FALSE.
            IF(ROW.GE.1.AND.ROW.LE.N.AND.COL.GE.1.AND.COL.LE.N+1)THEN
               VALID=.TRUE.
            ENDIF
```

```
          IF(VALID)READ(5,502)A(ROW,COL)
          IF(VALID)GO TO 15
C     UNTIL NOT VALID
      RETURN
C
501   FORMAT(2I2)
502   FORMAT(F5.2)
      END
      SUBROUTINE SEIDEL(A,MAXIT,MAXRES,N)
C
C     PREAMBLE FOR SUBROUTINE SEIDEL
C
C     ABSTRACT: SEIDEL SOLVES A SYSTEM OF LINEAR EQUATIONS BY AN
C               ITERATION METHOD.  ITERATION IS TERMINATED EITHER WHEN
C               A USER SPECIFIED CRITERION, CALLED A RESIDUAL, IS
C               REACHED OR WHEN THE USER SUPPLIED MAXIMUM NUMBER OF
C               ITERATIONS IS REACHED.
C
C     INPUT:   NONE
C
C     OUTPUT:  I, ITER, RESID, X( )
C
C     ENTRY VALUES:  A, MAXIT, MAXRES, N
C
C     EXIT VALUES:   NONE
C
C     ENTRY AND EXIT VALUES:  NONE
C
C     DESIGN HISTORY: H. LEE, 3MAY85
C
C     REFERENCE: NONE
C
C     ID DICTIONARY:
C
C     ID        TYPE       MEANING             USE
C
C     A         REAL       ARRAY OF COEFFICIENTS ARRAY
C                          AND CONSTANTS       (2 DIMENSIONS)
C     ABS       REAL       ABSOLUTE VALUE      INTRINSIC
C                                              FUNCTION
C     DIF       REAL       ABSOLUTE VALUE OF THE VARIABLE
C                          DIFFERENCE BETWEEN
C                          XNEW AND X(I)
C     I         INTEGER    INDEX, ARRAY        VARIABLE
C                          SUBSCRIPT
C     ITER      INTEGER    ITERATION COUNT     VARIABLE
C     J         INTEGER    INDEX, ARRAY        VARIABLE
C                          SUBSCRIPT
C     MAXIT     INTEGER    MAXIMUM NUMBER OF   VARIABLE
C                          ITERATIONS
```

```
C     MAXRES    REAL        MAXIMUM RESIDUAL     VARIABLE
C     N         INTEGER     NUMBER OF EQUATIONS  VARIABLE
C     RESID     REAL        RESIDUAL             VARIABLE
C     SUMONE    REAL        SUM ONE              VARIABLE
C     SUMTWO    REAL        SUM TWO              VARIABLE
C     X         REAL        X, THE UNKNOWNS      ARRAY
C                                                (1 DIMENSIONAL)
C     XNEW      REAL        THE NEW VALUE OF X(I) VARIABLE
C
C     SPECIFICATIONS
C
      IMPLICIT LOGICAL (A-Z)
C
      INTEGER I,ITER,J,MAXIT,N
      REAL A(10,11),DIF,MAXRES,RESID,SUMONE,SUMTWO,X(10),XNEW
C
      ITER=0
      DO 5 I=1,N
         X(I)=0.0
5     CONTINUE
C     REPEAT
8        CONTINUE
         ITER=ITER+1
         RESID=0.0
         DO 10 I=1,N
            SUMONE=0.0
            SUMTWO=0.0
            DO 15 J=1,I-1
               SUMONE=SUMONE+A(I,J)*X(J)
15          CONTINUE
            DO 20 J=I+1,N
               SUMTWO=SUMTWO+A(I,J)*X(J)
20          CONTINUE
            XNEW=(A(I,N+1)-SUMONE-SUMTWO)/A(I,I)
            DIF=ABS(XNEW-X(I))
            IF(DIF.GT.RESID)THEN
               RESID=DIF
            ENDIF
            X(I)=XNEW
10       CONTINUE
         IF(.NOT.(RESID.LE.MAXRES.OR.ITER.EQ.MAXIT))GO TO 8
C     UNTIL RESID LE MAXRES OR ITER EQ MAXIT
      DO 25 I=1,N
         WRITE(6,601)I,X(I)
25    CONTINUE
      WRITE(6,602)ITER,RESID
      RETURN
C
601   FORMAT('0','X(',I2,') = ',F10.5)
```

```
602   FORMAT('0','ITER = ',I5,5X,'RESID = ',F10.5)
      END
SAMPLE DATA SET
ALL
2
100
0.001
1    1    3
1    3    7
```

```
PROGRAM GAUSS USES THE GAUSS-SEIDEL METHOD
TO SOLVE A SYSTEM OF LINEAR EQUATIONS.
PROGRAMMED BY H. LEE, 3MAY85.

SAMPLE DATA SET

HOWRD = ALL

N = 2

MAXIT = 100

MAXRES = .00100

X(1) = 1.00030

X(2) = 1.99990

ITER = 9     RESID = .00061

NORMAL PROGRAM TERMINATION
```

Appendix D

FORTRAN Statements

Used in this Text

NOTATION

a1, a2	argument1, argument2	
fsn	format statement number	
sn	statement number	
[ ]	indicates optional syntax	
. . .	indicates optional continuation of syntax	
⟨limited use⟩	indicates statements which we feel must be limited in application; see notes at end of this list of statements	

CALL subroutine_name [(a1, a2, . . .)]

CHARACTER [*length [,]] name [, name] . . .

⟨limited use⟩ COMMON

COMPLEX variable [, variable] . . .

sn   CONTINUE

DO statement_number initial_value = expression, terminal_value
    [, incremental_value]

DOUBLE PRECISION variable [, variable] . . .

ELSE

ELSEIF

END

ENDIF

fsn   FORMAT (format specifications)

type FUNCTION name ([a1 [, a2] . . .])

⟨limited use⟩ GOTO sn

IF (expression) THEN

⟨limited use⟩ IMPLICIT

INTEGER variable [, variable] . . .

LOGICAL variable [, variable] . . .

OPEN (open list)

PARAMETER (parameter = expression [, parameter = expression] . . .)

⟨limited use⟩ PRINT *, variable [, variable] . . .

PROGRAM name

⟨limited use⟩ READ *, variable [, variable] . . .

READ (unit, fsn, END = sn) variable [, variable] . . .

REAL variable [, variable] . . .

RETURN

STOP [character constant]

SUBROUTINE name [([a1 [, a2] . . .])]

variable = expression

WRITE (unit, fsn) [variable [, variable] . . .]

NOTES on ⟨limited use⟩ statements:

The following are limited in their use as follows:

COMMON is used only in the construction

COMMON/BUGBLK/BUG

GOTO is used only to implement the indeterminate repetitions.

IMPLICIT is used only in the construction

IMPLICIT LOGICAL (A–Z)

PRINT * and READ * are used only until FORMAT statements
have been introduced.

References

American National Standard Programming Language FORTRAN, ANSI X3.9–1978. (1978) New York: American National Standards Institute, Inc.

KNUTH, DONALD E. (1973) *The Art of Computer Programming, Vol. 3, Sorting and Searching.* Reading, Mass.: Addison-Wesley.

LEWIS, HARRY R., and CHRISTOS H. PAPADIMITRIOU. (1981) *Elements of the Theory of Computation.* Englewood Cliffs, N.J.: Prentice Hall.

MCGETTRICK, A. D., and P. D. SMITH. (1983) *Graded Problems in Computer Science.* Reading, Mass.: Addison-Wesley.

NASSI, I., and B. SCHNEIDERMAN, (1973) *ACM SIGPLAN Notices* 8, no. 8 (August, 1973): 12–26.

RICE, JOHN R. (1983) *Numerical Methods, Software, and Analysis.* New York: McGraw-Hill.

Index

Page numbers in *italics* indicate illustrations.

-99999, as special value in programming, 185
//, as character operator for concatenation, 143
= character, as replacement operator, 25
1's complement, of 60-bit word, 222-23
1-alternative selection
    code skeleton for, 266-67, *267*
    in logical function TRI, 168, *169-70*
1-alternative SELECTION, control structure diagram
    for, *43*, *75*
2-alternative selection
    code skeleton for, *267*
    in logical function TRI, 168, *169*
2-alternative SELECTION, control structure diagram
    for, *43*, *75*

A edit specification, 58
Absolute value function, *148*
ABSTRACT, in preamble, 70, 274
Accumulation of truncation errors, 227
Address, of variable, 109
Algebraic notation
    to be converted to program language, 3
    translated to computer language, 76-77
Algorithm
    computation as, 87-89
    concept of, 194
    design of, PROGRAM CHKBAL as example,
      80-90
    development of, 66-67
Algorithms, 50
American Standard Code for Information
    Interchange (ASCII), 141
Angle of deformation, 254
ANSI FORTRAN, 13
Apostrophe, 20
    as delimiter, 33
    in character strings, 136-37
    used in computer language, 77-78
Apostrophe edit descriptor, 138
Argument, 22
Argument lists, 277
Arguments, for communication between program
    units, 149
Arithmetic assignment statement, 24-25
Arithmetic expressions, 134
    translation of in FORTRAN, 213-19
Arithmetic operators, *135*, 137
Array element, 120
Array element name, 120
Arrays
    introduction to, 109-10

334

names of, 123
properties of, 110
size of, 120
specification of, 119
specifying type and dimension information for,
    273
vocabulary, restrictions, and size of, 120
Arrays, one-dimensional
    design segments including, *115*, *116*
    mathematical operations using, 114-16
    notation and vocabulary for, 110-12
    use of two or more, 113-14
Arrays, two-dimensional, 116-17
    compared to matrices, 116-17
    design segments including, *118*
    input and output of, 117-19
ASCII (American Standard Code for Information
    Interchange), 141
Assembly language, for type, 208-12
Assembly-level language, 207
Assignment statements
    character strings in, 139
    name of function in, 150-51
Asterisk, 20
    as indicator to use system-defined unit for
      input, 52
    as part of FORMAT statement, 53
    as place-holder, 52
    as prompt character, 21
    to indicate multiplication, 76-77
Automatic type conversion, in FORTRAN, 213-14,
    216-19

Base, 226
Binary floating point arithmetic, IEEE standards
    for, 220
Binary integers, 221-23
Binary representation, of data, 206-7
Bits (binary digits), 221-23
BLANK = 'NULL' default value, 258
Blank = parameter, 51, 55
BLANK = ZERO, 55
Blank significance property, 258-59
Blanks
    treatment of, 198, 258
    within apostrophes, 33
BN edit specification, 258
Bubble sort
    compared to selection sort, 192-93
    definition of, 189-90
    design for, 190-92, *192*
    illustration of, *190*
Bubble sort. *See also* Sort; Sorting

top-down, 179-80
units in, 158-59
vocabulary for, 78
Design. *See also* Programming
DESIGN HISTORY, in preamble, 70, 275
Determinant repetition, 40
  code skeleton for, *268*
Determinant REPETITION, control structure diagram
    for, *43*, *76*
Dimension bound, 119
Dimension declarator, 119
Divide-and-conquer strategy, 10
Division by zero, 90, 197

Echo, of input, 164
Echoing, as part of error checking, 203
Edit descriptors, 53, 138
  compilation and, 208
  for FORMAT statement, 207-8
  notation used in, 53-55
Elements, of matrix, 121
END of _____ FUNCTION _____, 74
END statement, 6, 16, 17
  assignment statements and, 149-50
  differentiated from RETURN statement, 25
End-of-file, 30
END = construction, 31-32
ENDWHILE, 30
ENPORT-6, 256
ENTRY AND EXIT VALUES, in preamble, 275
Entry arguments, 129
ENTRY VALUES, in preamble, 70, 275
Equality, testing for, 197-98
Error detection, maximizing, 199
Errors, logical, 203, 204
Exceptional cases, treatment of, 198
Exchange sorts, 188-89
EXECUTION, 20
Execution phase, of program, 207
Exit argument, 129
EXIT VALUES, in preamble, 70, 275
Explicit numeric (integer) values, 273
Explicit ordering, 38-39
Explicit type specification statement, 208
Exponent, 226
Exponential function, *148*
Expressions, in FORTRAN, 134-35
External functions, 147-48
  definition of, 149-51
  use of, 148-49

Factorial function, defining, 152, 155
Factorials, computed with external functions, 149
Field, 55-56
Field width, w, 54
File, 30
Files, opening, 271
Fixed-point representation, 223
Flagging, for output messages, 200
Flow-of-control, 2-3, 30
  control structures for, 2
  diagrams for, 42-44, *43*, 78

specifications for, 42
templates for, 72-75
Format specifications list, 53
FORMAT statement, 50
  carriage controls in, 60-61
  character strings in, 60, 137-38
  edit descriptors for, 207-8
  field specification in, 56
  style requirements for, 271, 272
  stylistics for, 62
  used with WRITE statement, 60
  with input and output statements, 207-8
FORTRAN
  assembly-language translations of, 208-12
  automatic type conversion in, 213-14, 216-19
  compiler for, 207
  environment of, 257
  expressions in, 134-36
  Full Language, 258
  history of, 12-13
  indeterminant repetition structures in, 266
  mathematical operations in, 213
  mixed-mode arithmetic in, 213-14, 216-19
  prohibition of recursion in, 155-56
  punched cards in, 15-16
  Subset Language, 258
  type specification in, 19, 208-19
FORTRAN 77
  character set for, 136
  coding for, 15-18
  compiler for, 17-18, 213
  development of, 12, 13
  IEEE standards for binary floating point
      arithmetic in, 220
  portability of programs in, 256-59
  stylistic conventions for, 270-73
  subroutines in, 22, 24
  use of columns in, 16
FORTRAN 77 job, code skeleton of, 261-62, *262*
FORTRAN version 5 processor, 257
FTC, design of, *6*
Full bars, in sketch diagrams, 161
FUNCTION
  compared to SUBROUTINE, 263
  redefinition of, 272
Function reference, 147
  computing, 203-4
FUNCTION unit, 68
  as procedure, 74-75
  as single value, 74
  code skeleton for, *151*, *264*
  design of, 73
  external functions in, 149-51
  unit, template for flow-of-control of, *73*
Functions
  factorial, 152, 155
  recursive, 74
  referencing of, 147
  type associated with, 150
  user defined. *See* External functions
Functions. *See also* External functions; Intrinsic
      functions
Fw.d edit descriptor, 54

Gauss-Seidel method
    as iteration method, 235
    convergence in, 237
    design considerations in, 248, 252-53
    design of program for, 241-48
    design of program for, 241-45, *247*
    first eight iterations in, 235-36
    general form of solution in, 237-38
    iteration count method in, 240
    residual in, 241
    searching for patterns in, 234, 237, 238-40
    solution accuracy in, 240-41
    termination criteria for, 240-41
GOTO statement, 269, 273
Gw.d edit descriptor, 54

ICHAR(a) intrinsic function, 141-42, *141*
ID DICTIONARY, in preamble, 70-72, 276
Imaginary solutions, 93
IMPLICIT LOGICAL (A-Z) specification, 200,
    272-73
Implicit ordering, 38-39
IMPLICIT statement, precedence of, over default
    naming convention, 208
Implicit type specification, 208
Implied naming convention, 208
IMSL (International Mathematics and Statistics
    Library), 256
Indefinite values, 233
Indeterminant posttested REPETITION,
    control structure diagram for, *43*, *76*
Indeterminant pretested REPETITION,
    control structure diagram for, *43*, *76*
Indeterminant repetition, 40-41
INDEX(a1, a2) intrinsic function, *141*, 142
Indicator words and phrases, in sketch diagrams,
    161
Infinite loop, 40
INLIST array, 184
Input, echoing of, 164
INPUT file, 52
INPUT, in preamble, 70, 275
INPUT-TRANSFORMATION-OUTPUT, 87-89, 91
Input-transformation-output analysis, 45
Integer edit specification (Iw), 54
Integer function FACT(N), design of, *154-55*
INTEGERs, 19
Integers
    algorithm for, 50
    representation of, on CYBER computers, 220-25
International Business Machines Corporation, 12
Intrinsic functions
    ANSI-specified, 146
    commonly used, *148*
    definition of, 145
    for character values, 140-41
    for lexical comparison of strings, *140*
    for use with character strings, 141-42
    generic, 146
    specific, 146
    syntax and grammar of, 147
Iolist, 50-51, 53

Iteration method, for solving systems of linear
    equations, 235
Iw (integer edit specification), 54

Keyword CALL, 22
Keyword CHARACTER, 33
Keywords, 17

Left margins, in sketch diagrams, 161
LEN(a), *141*, 142
Line printer, 17
Linear algebra
    addition of matrices in, 122
    basic definitions in, 121
    introduction to, 120-21
    multiplication of matrices in, 122-23
LISP language, 256
List, of variables, 22
Loader, 207
Location
    in computer memory, 20
    of variable, 109
Logical errors, 203, 204
Logical expression, 39
Logical function TRI, design of, 168-73, *168*,
    169, *170-71*
Logical operators, *135*
Logical structures, types of, 38-39

Machine language, conversion to, 206, 207
Machine-language instructions, 50
Main program, 16
Mantissa, 226
MATHEMATICA, 256
Mathematical definitions, in design, 89-90
Mathematical operations, using one-dimensional
    arrays, 114-16
Mathematical subscripts, in matrices, 124-27
Matrices
    addition of, 121
    multiplication of, 121-27, *127*
Matrix, 116-17, 121
    column, 121
    columns in, 121
    compared to two-dimensional array, 116-17
    definition of, 120
    elements of, 121
    mathematical subscripts in, 124-27
    order of, 121
    row, 121
    rows in, 121
    square, 121, 127-29, *128*, 130, *131*
Matrix multiplication
    design considerations for, 123-31
    raising a square matrix to integer powers in,
        130-31
    squaring of square matrix in, 127-29
Maximum array size, specifying, 277
MAXSYMA, 256
MEANING, in preamble, 276
Memory. *See* Computer memory
Message printout, PROGRAM ONE for, 15-18

337

338